Human Dignity and Social Justice

Human Dignity and Social Justice

Pablo Gilabert

Great Clarendon Street, Oxford, ox2 6dp,
United Kingdom

Oxford University Press is a department of the University of Oxford.
It furthers the University's objective of excellence in research, scholarship,
and education by publishing worldwide. Oxford is a registered trade mark of
Oxford University Press in the UK and in certain other countries

© Pablo Gilabert 2023

The moral rights of the author have been asserted

Impression: 1

All rights reserved. No part of this publication may be reproduced, stored in
a retrieval system, or transmitted, in any form or by any means, without the
prior permission in writing of Oxford University Press, or as expressly permitted
by law, by licence or under terms agreed with the appropriate reprographics
rights organization. Enquiries concerning reproduction outside the scope of the
above should be sent to the Rights Department, Oxford University Press, at the
address above

You must not circulate this work in any other form
and you must impose this same condition on any acquirer

Published in the United States of America by Oxford University Press
198 Madison Avenue, New York, NY 10016, United States of America

British Library Cataloguing in Publication Data

Data available

Library of Congress Control Number: 2022945708

ISBN 978-0-19-287115-2

DOI: 10.1093/oso/9780192871152.001.0001

Printed and bound in the UK by
Clays Ltd, Elcograf S.p.A.

Links to third party websites are provided by Oxford in good faith and
for information only. Oxford disclaims any responsibility for the materials
contained in any third party website referenced in this work.

Preface

Human dignity: social movements invoke it, several national constitutions enshrine it, and it features prominently in international human rights documents. But what is it, why is it important, and what is its relationship to human rights and social justice? My research offers a systematic defence of the view that human dignity is the moral heart of justice. In *Human Dignity and Human Rights*,[1] I advanced an account of human dignity for the context of human rights discourse, which covers the most urgent, basic claims of dignity. In this book, I extend the dignitarian approach to more ambitious claims of maximal dignity of the kind encoded in democratic socialist conceptions of social justice. In particular, this book focuses on the just organization of working practices. It recasts in a dignitarian format the critique of capitalist society as involving exploitation, alienation, and domination of workers, and revamps a neglected but inspiring socialist principle. In my dignitarian interpretation, the Abilities/Needs Principle ('From each according to their ability, to each according to their needs!') yields reasonable and feasible requirements on social cooperation geared to empowering each human being to lead a flourishing life. While my previous book offered the first systematic philosophical account of human dignity in human rights discourse, the current book presents the first systematic application of the dignitarian framework to the core ideals of democratic socialism.

Overall, this book has the following key original and distinctive features:

(i) A systematic philosophical account of the content and significance of human dignity as a central idea for social justice.

(ii) A new interpretation of the critiques of capitalism as involving exploitation, alienation, and domination.

(iii) A novel proposal for how to understand the Abilities/Needs Principle.

(iv) A dynamic account of the relation between justice and feasibility and an application of it to the comparison between socialism and capitalism.

[1] Gilabert (2019a).

vi Preface

Let me state these contributions in more detail. The first includes conceptual and substantive dimensions. Regarding the former, this book clarifies the network of concepts associated with dignity. I propose definitions of the concepts of *status-dignity, condition-dignity, the basis of dignity, dignitarian norms, the circumstances of dignity,* and *dignitarian virtue.* These definitions tidy up the often rather confusing discourse of dignity. They also help make it consistent. Take, for example, the first three notions. Status-dignity is a moral status that people have in accordance with which respect and concern are owed to them. The specific forms of concern and respect are specified by the dignitarian norms. Finally, condition-dignity marks states of affairs in which dignitarian norms are fulfilled. Now, it is sometimes said that because they have dignity, people may not be enslaved. It is also said that when they are enslaved, people lack dignity. Some critics use examples like this to charge dignitarian talk of incoherence. But the alleged incoherence dissolves if we use the distinctions I propose. Slaves' status-dignity is independent of whether it is recognized or honoured by any convention or practice. As a moral status it remains all along. It is because of this that slaves are morally entitled to resist oppression, and slave-owners are required to give it up. What slaves lack is condition-dignity, the predicament in which dignitarian norms prohibiting slavery are implemented, which is precisely what the work of social justice must bring about.

This book also explains how human dignity generates core substantive ideals. Thus, according to the *Dignitarian Approach,* we have reason to organize social life in such a way that we respond appropriately to the valuable features of individuals that give rise to their dignity. On this view, what we owe to each other is treatment that enacts respect and concern that fits our moral status as beings with dignity, and this in turn means that we should take seriously the valuable features that give each of us such a status by thinking and acting in ways that respond to these features in appropriately favourable ways.

To articulate the normative requirements flowing from this approach, I explore an ideal of *Solidaristic Empowerment,* according to which we should support individuals in their pursuit of a flourishing life by fulfilling both negative duties not to destroy or block their valuable capacities and positive duties to protect and facilitate their development and exercise of these capacities. People indeed have valuable capacities—for sentience, moral and prudential reasoning, knowledge, creativity, aesthetic appreciation, and so on. Although not all have the same set of valuable capacities, they have dignity whenever they have some of them. People flourish when they unfold these capacities. To respond appropriately to their dignity, we should treat them well by supporting this flourishing. We should avoid destroying or blocking

Preface **vii**

people's capacities, and we should take feasible and reasonable steps to help them succeed as they develop and exercise them. An important job of a conception of social justice is precisely to articulate the content of the negative and positive duties of solidaristic empowerment that we have towards each other, and to identify the practices and institutions that could implement them.

The central notion of status-dignity marks an inherent, non-instrumental, egalitarian, and high-priority moral status of human persons. People have this status in virtue of their valuable capacities rather than as a result of their nationality, race, class, or other conventional or less morally significant features. Basing human rights on status-dignity allows us to explain and defend universalistic demands for various civil, political, and social entitlements. Now, articulating liberal and socialist ideals within a dignitarian framework that also grounds human rights is helpful for underscoring the universalism of social justice and the importance of civil and political liberties within it. We can thus avoid problematic forms of liberalism that take principles of social justice to apply domestically but not globally, and correct views of socialism that neglect the importance of guaranteeing personal privacy, freedom of speech, and a vibrant democratic political process.

This book explains how the Dignitarian Approach helps articulate the content, justification, and feasible implementation of certain specific and contested demands of social justice. I focus, in particular, on exploring institutions and practices of *work*. Although often neglected in contemporary liberal political philosophy, they are of great practical importance. Many people spend about half of their waking hours at work, and working is for most a precondition for subsistence and social respect. Work is also a potential medium of forms of self-determination and self-realization that cannot be achieved to a sufficient extent in other activities. The second and third contributions of this book consist in proposing a new, dignitarian articulation of the critique of certain injustices in the organization of working practices and in formulating a positive framework to identify alternatives that deliver greater fulfilment of what human dignity calls for.

The Dignitarian Approach can be deployed not only to articulate claims of basic justice such as human labour rights, but also more ambitious ideals of social justice regarding work. Human rights include demands of basic dignity, such as that people have access to working activities; work on jobs that are chosen rather than coercively imposed; avoid discrimination based on gender, sexual orientation, or race; receive adequate remuneration; and be entitled to form unions and engage in political activities to defend their interests. But workers can make justified claims to more than basic dignity. They

viii   Preface

can also envision maximal dignity. The socialist critique of capitalism holds that the dignity of workers is also underappreciated when they are pushed into practices that involve *domination, exploitation,* and *alienation,* i.e. when workers are inappropriately subject to the will of others in the shaping of the terms on which they work, when their vulnerability is inappropriately taken advantage of by more powerful employers to get them to give more than they ought to, and when their ability to fashion a positive sense of themselves through activities that feature the expression of talents and skills is stunted rather than unleashed. Full justice for workers requires real opportunities for productive practices in which they access the highest levels of self-determination and self-realization that are feasible and can be secured at reasonable cost for all. To achieve this, social cooperation should be structured so that workers are not only asked to give, but are also entitled to receive in fair ways. As I interpret it, the socialist slogan 'From each according to their abilities, to each according to their needs!' (the *Abilities/Needs Principle*) enjoins schemes of fair cooperation that empower workers to lead flourishing lives in which they develop and exercise the capacities at the basis of their dignity, not only to survive and avoid the most egregious abuses which human rights discourse condemns. Although this principle has been ignored in political philosophy, a dignitarian interpretation of it can illuminate its content and strength as a guideline for solidaristic cooperation.

In sum, the second and third contributions of this book's development of the Dignitarian Approach are to provide socialist political philosophy with sharp foundations for its critique of capitalist domination, exploitation, and alienation, and appealing grounds for the positive vision of a solidaristic society encoded in the Abilities/Needs Principle.

Finally, the fourth contribution of this book is that it offers a novel account of the relation between justice and feasibility and an application of it to the comparison between socialism and capitalism. It is common in political theory and practice to challenge normatively ambitious proposals by saying that their fulfilment is not feasible. But there has been insufficient conceptual exploration of what feasibility is, and not enough substantive inquiry into why and how it matters for thinking about social justice. This book provides a systematic treatment of these issues, and proposes *a dynamic approach to the relation between justice and feasibility* that illuminates the importance of political imagination and dynamic duties to expand agents' power to fulfil ambitious principles of justice. The bold profile of dignitarian justice is thus vindicated, while the specific link between dynamic duties, dynamic power, and dynamic virtue are articulated. A democratic rather than authoritarian framework for political change is defended and deployed to illuminate the comparison between socialism and capitalism.

Although the chapters of this book are composed in such a way that they can be read separately, they form a structured whole, starting with the theoretical framework of dignity in social justice (Chapters 1–4) and proceeding with its deployment to illuminate core themes in the socialist critique of capitalism (Chapters 5–8). Chapter 1 delineates the essential elements of the Dignitarian Approach. Chapter 2 explores two important historical sources inspiring some of its central ideas and their application to social justice. As articulated, Kantian dignity and Marxian socialism turn out to be quite appealing and mutually supportive. Chapter 3 offers a new interpretation of the powerful (but neglected) Abilities/Needs Principle, showing that it can be seen as a fitting articulation of what the dignitarian ideal of Solidaristic Empowerment demands for economic life. Chapter 4 explores the relation between justice and feasibility, proposing a dynamic view of the pursuit of social justice (including socialism) in which the ambitious requirements of a dignitarian perspective can gain practical traction. Chapters 5 through 7 then examine in detail the phenomena of exploitation, alienation, and domination, deploying the Dignitarian Approach to explain what is morally problematic about them. Chapter 8 concludes by suggesting fruitful ways to think about the comparison between socialism and capitalism.

The two main objectives of this book are to extend the Dignitarian Approach I first developed in the context of human rights to the more ambitious domain of social justice and to provide a fresh exploration of central topics in socialist political philosophy, such as the Abilities/Needs Principle and the critiques of exploitation, alienation, and domination of workers. The Dignitarian Approach is systematically articulated in Chapter 1. In later chapters, it is deployed in *media res*, as discussion of the substantive issues addressed proceeds. This, I think, is the most effective way to show its explanatory power. It will also allow me to highlight this book's new conceptual and normative points about important topics in socialist political thought.

I would like to make two general remarks about the nature and limits of this book. The first is that it is a work of philosophy. My focus is on core conceptual and normative structures. I seek to outline the content of the idea of dignity, the connections between justice and feasibility, the central substantive principles of the Dignitarian Approach and of socialist justice, and their relevance for understanding what is wrong with working practices that feature exploitation, alienation, and domination. Although I inevitably rely on

x Preface

empirical claims at various point in my arguments (and do so by drawing on the work of social scientists), they are not the main subject of my inquiry. Similarly, although I mention potential practical implications of the moral ideas I defend, I do not try to offer detailed policy blueprints or specific proposals for political action. As I see it, philosophy can and should work in cooperation with social science and policy, but it has its own distinctive roles.

Second, this book has an exploratory character. For example, my discussion of socialism is avowedly limited. It is primarily concerned with proposing attractive normative ideas to orientate discussion on the contours of a socialist society, while allowing that there could be a diversity of plausible institutional frameworks implementing them, and recognizing that much uncertainty and debate remains about what their best versions would be. Furthermore, some points (such as those regarding the Dignitarian Approach) are more general than others (such as those about Abilities/Needs Principles and the problems of working practices in capitalism). The connections between them are articulated as identifying fruitful explanations rather than as providing the only valid account possible.[2] This reflects my view of philosophical methodology. I see philosophical conceptions as offering illuminating ideas and explanations rather than as unearthing necessary and inescapable conditions. Like John Rawls, I view the defence of philosophical conceptions as a matter of seeking a reflective equilibrium in which they are shown to clarify, systematize, and illuminate our treatment of significant substantive issues.[3] Thus, as the book proceeds, I will regularly signpost when the Dignitarian Approach is used and makes a genuine difference in articulating and defending various socialist ideas. I will also note its independent plausibility and comparative advantages with respect to other approaches. I will argue that it furnishes appealing conceptual and normative resources, without claiming that this amounts to anything like a transcendental or quasi-transcendental argument for it.

Although I do not claim that the Dignitarian Approach is strictly necessary, I do try to show that on the interpretation of it I offer it is sufficient for the relevant jobs. I believe that the arguments in this book, as well as those in *Human Dignity and Human Rights*, provide satisfactory results. My hope is

---

[2] Although I of course find the assemblages of ideas about the topics covered in this book correct, others could be offered. For example, a reader could find much of what I say about the critiques of exploitation, alienation, and domination appealing, and acknowledge that my dignitarian articulation of them is illuminating, but prefer other fundamental normative premises to make similar points. If other accounts can generate the same results, then that is good news. Parallel but different arguments can reach the same conclusion, and if it is a true conclusion, so much the better.

[3] Rawls (2001: sect. 10). On philosophical views as not having to seek necessary and inescapable conditions, see Nozick (1981: Introduction).

that all things considered the proposed account of dignity and its implications for social justice are worth endorsing or that, at the very least, they reveal fruitful possibilities heretofore missed. That said, the Dignitarian Approach is a normative research program, not a closed or finished theoretical system. The search for reflective equilibrium is always open-ended. I share this book in its imperfect form with the expectation that you will pick up where I left and go further. Philosophy, like social justice, is an ongoing and cooperative endeavour.

Acknowledgements

Although the dignitarian approach to socialism presented in the book is new, some of the material used in it has been published before in the form of papers in journals or book chapters. However, a significant amount of the text in the book has not appeared before. And the previous material that is used in this book has been extensively revised. To make clear these links, I state below the list of my publications that are relevant to this project. The relations with this book are as follows. As stated in the Preface, this book completes the discussion started in (i) by extending the dignitarian account to the context of social justice (which is different from that of human rights). Some of the book's chapters reproduce earlier material but with very significant revisions and additions. This is the case with Chapters 2, 3, 4, 5, and 6, with relation to papers (f), (d), (e), (k), and (l). Some parts of sections in the book draw partially, with revisions, on parts of earlier papers. This is the case with (g) and (m) in Chapter 1, (a) and (b) in Chapter 3, (c) and (h) in Chapter 7, and (a) and (j) in Chapter 8. Finally, some parts of the book do not correspond closely to any of the texts in the list. This is the case with Chapter 1, Chapter 7 (the lengthiest chapter of the book), and Chapter 8.

(a) 'Feasibility and Socialism'. *The Journal of Political Philosophy* 19.1 (2011): 52–63.

(b) 'Cohen on Socialism, Equality, and Community'. *Socialist Studies* 8.1 (2012): 101–121.

(c) 'Solidarity, Equality, and Freedom in Pettit's Republicanism'. *Critical Review of International Social and Political Philosophy* 18.6 (2015): 644–651.

(d) 'The Socialist Principle "From Each According To Their Abilities, To Each According To Their Needs"'. *Journal of Social Philosophy* 46.2 (2015): 197–225.

(e) 'Justice and Feasibility: A Dynamic Approach'. *Political Utopias: Contemporary Debates*, ed. M. Weber and K. Vallier (Oxford: Oxford University Press, 2017), 95–126.

(f) 'Kantian Dignity and Marxian Socialism'. *Kantian Review* 22.4 (2017): 553–577.

xiv Acknowledgements

(g) 'Dignity at Work'. *Philosophical Foundations of Labour Law*, ed. H. Collins, G. Lester, and V. Mantouvalou (Oxford: Oxford University Press, 2018), 68–86.

(h) 'A Broad Definition of Agential Power'. *Journal of Political Power* 11 (2018), 79–92

(i) *Human Dignity and Human Rights* (Oxford: Oxford University Press, 2019).

(j) 'Socialism'. (With Martin O'Neill). *Stanford Encyclopedia of Philosophy.* (July 2019).

(k) 'Exploitation, Solidarity, and Dignity'. *Journal of Social Philosophy* 50.4 (2019): 465–494.

(l) 'Alienation, Freedom, and Dignity'. *Philosophical Topics* 48 (2020): 51–80.

(m) 'Defending Human Dignity and Human Rights'. *Journal of Global Ethics* 16 (2020): 326–42.

Besides acknowledging the publishers of these papers, I also thank the editors and referees for their comments.

I am very grateful for the help I have received in the completion of this book. The referees of Oxford University Press provided incisive critical comments and helpful suggestions. My OUP editor, Dominic Byatt, was attentive, supportive, and resourceful. Rachel Addison copy-edited the manuscript for OUP and helped improve it. I thank the many people who helped me with comments on specific chapters and arguments presented in this book, and for conversations on related matters. They include Arash Abizadeh, Samuel Arnold, Christian Barry, Hugh Collins, Peter Dietsch, Eva Erman, Adam Etinson, David Estlund, Rainer Forst, Francisco Garcia Gibson, Roberto Gargarella, Mariano Garreta-Leclerq, Anca Gheaus, Robert Goodin, Carol Gould, Joseph Heath, Lisa Herzog, Adam Hosein, Jakob Huber, Martin Jay, Jan Kandiyali, Robert Kaufman, Cristina Lafont, Ben Laurence, David Leopold, Éliot Litalien, Catherine Lu, Colin Macleod, Steven Macedo, Virginia Mantouvalou, Itzel Mayans, Nadine Medawar, Julio Montero, Emilio Nadra, Martin O'Neill, Tom O'Shea, Serena Olsaretti, Kristi Olson, Matthew Palynchuk, Vida Panitch, Darío Perinetti, Tom Parr, Veronica Ponce, Jahel Queralt, Romina Rekers, Will Roberts, Andrea Sangiovanni, Nicholas Southwood, Lucas Stanczyk, Natalie Stoljar, Christine Sypnowich, Moisés Vaca, Philippe Van Parijs, Laura Valentini, Roberto Veneziani, Nicholas Vrousalis, Daniel Weinstock, David Wiens, Andrew Williams, Erik Wright, and Lea Ypi. Thanks also to the audiences in many conferences and lectures in which I presented ideas that shaped this book. My research was supported by a grant from the Social Sciences and Humanities Research Council of Canada, and by the funding and stimulating environments provided through visiting fellowships at the Recherche en Éthique at the University of Montreal and the Philosophy Department of the University of California-Berkeley. I owe especial thanks to my students at Concordia University, with whom I explored the issues addressed in this book in seminars over the years.

I dedicate this book to Nadine, with deep gratitude and joyful hope.

Contents

I. THEORETICAL FRAMEWORK

1. The Dignitarian Approach — **3**
1. Introduction — 3
2. The Dignitarian Approach — 4
  2.1 An account of dignity — 4
  2.2 Fruitfulness of the Dignitarian Approach — 14
3. From Basic to Maximal Justice. The Case of Justice at Work — 37
  3.1 Labour rights — 38
  3.2 Basic labour rights — 41
  3.3 Towards maximal labour rights — 48
4. The Dignitarian Approach And Social Critique — 53

2. Kantian Dignity and Marxian Socialism — **55**
1. Introduction — 55
2. Kantian Dignity — 57
  2.1 Resources in Kant — 57
  2.2 Difficulties and revisions — 63
3. Marxian Socialism — 74
  3.1 Capitalism and socialism — 74
  3.2 The critique of capitalism — 77
  3.3 The socialist project — 83

3. The Abilities/Needs Principle — **87**
1. Introduction — 87
2. The Marxian Platform — 89
3. Exploring The Abilities/Needs Principle — 90
  3.1 Initial appeal — 90
  3.2 Is the principle trivial, redundant, or manifestly inferior to others? — 92
  3.3 Need to develop an interpretation of the principle — 95
4. Developing The Abilities/Needs Principle — 97
  4.1 ANP is not the only principle socialists should accept — 97
  4.2 ANP and dignity — 97
  4.3 Needs — 98
  4.4 The demands of ANP — 105
  4.5 Implementing ANP — 115
5. Transition — 122
6. Ideological Manipulation and The Duty to Contribute — 131

xviii Contents

4. Justice and Feasibility   137

1. Introduction   137
2. The Nature, Importance, and Role of Feasibiity   138
      2.1 What?   139
      2.2 Why?   142
      2.3 How?   145
3. The Pursuit of Justice: A Dynamic Approach   150
      3.1 Three dimensions of a conception of justice
   and deliberative reflective equilibrium   150
      3.2 Transitional standpoint, political imagination, and dynamic
   duties   157
4. Feasibility and Dignity   168

II. RETHINKING THE SOCIALIST CRITIQUE OF CAPITALISM

5. The Critique of Exploitation   175

1. Introduction   175
2. Exploitation as Contra-Solidaristic use of Power   179
3. Dignity, Solidarity, and the Abilities/Needs Principle   186
      3.1 Dignity and solidaristic empowerment   186
      3.2 The Abilities/Needs Principle and exploitation   190
4. Exploitation as a Multidimensional Social Process   194
      4.1 Contrast with other accounts   194
      4.2 A multidimensional process   200
5. Agency and Structure   203

6. The Critique of Alienation   207

1. Introduction   207
2. Alienation: An Analytical Framework   209
      2.1 Basic definition   209
      2.2 Subjective and objective alienation   209
      2.3 Descriptive and normative accounts of alienation   211
      2.4 Prudential and moral variants of normative accounts   212
      2.5 Dynamic patterns   214
3. Human Flourishing and Freedom   216
      3.1 The normative dimension of alienation   216
      3.2 Human flourishing and the prudential critique of alienation   217
      3.3 Freedom and the moral critique of alienation   220
4. Dignity   224
      4.1 The Dignitarian Approach   224
      4.2 Problematic essentialism?   225
      4.3 Gap between the good and the right?   229
      4.4 Paternalistic imposition?   230
      4.5 The two-level justification objection   232
      4.6 Further issues   234

Contents **xix**

4.7 Dynamic patterns and the critique of alienated
self-determination and self-realization 237
5. On Recent Developments in Capitalist Conditions of Work 242

7. The Critique of Domination 249

1. Introduction 249
2. The Case of the Domination of Workers in Capitalism 250
3. Domination: An Analytical Framework 256
   3.1 Definition of domination 257
   3.2 Structural domination 264
   3.3 Change 270
   3.4 Agential power, self-determination, and non-domination 273
4. The Dignitarian Approach and Domination 278
   4.1 Domination as a limited but important normative factor 278
   4.2 The Dignitarian Approach 283
   4.3 Human dignity and the justification of the critique of
   domination 285
   4.4 The advantages of the Dignitarian Approach to domination 293
5. Appendix I: Analytical Grid of Power 316
6. Appendix II: Domination, Alienation, and Exploitation 318

8. Comparing Socialism and Capitalism 323

Bibliography 341
Index 353

PART I
THEORETICAL FRAMEWORK

1
The Dignitarian Approach

1. Introduction

Human dignity figures prominently in moral and political discourse. But what is it? And why is it important for human rights and social justice? My research programme tries to answer these questions. In this book, I extend the account of dignity I initially developed for human rights (and presented in the book *Human Dignity and Human Rights*)[1] to the more ambitious context of social justice, with a special focus on revamping some socialist ideas. I start in this chapter by outlining the Dignitarian Approach—the view that we have reason to organize social life in such a way that we respond appropriately to the valuable features of individual human beings that give rise to their dignity. The essential aspects of this approach are presented. They include the correlative ideal of Solidaristic Empowerment and the conceptual network of dignity comprising the notions of status-dignity, condition-dignity, dignitarian norms, the basis of dignity, the circumstances of dignity, and dignitarian virtue. The fruitfulness of the Dignitarian Approach for the justification of requirements of social justice is clarified, showing that it helps us vindicate a commitment to universalism and to justify moral humanist rights, foreground the importance of combining self-determination and mutual aid, illuminate the stance of people struggling against social injustice, and explore the arc of humanist justice. The chapter then explains and motivates this book's specific focus on labour rights, showing how the arc going from basic to maximal labour rights can be encompassed, and how the critique of injustices in which those rights are violated can be articulated.

[1] Gilabert (2019a).

Human Dignity and Social Justice. Pablo Gilabert, Oxford University Press.
© Pablo Gilabert (2023). DOI: 10.1093/oso/9780192871152.003.0001

4 Human Dignity and Social Justice

2. The Dignitarian Approach

2.1 An account of dignity

I propose the following substantive normative view:

Dignitarian Approach
We have reason to organize social life in such a way that we respond appropriately
to the valuable features of individuals that give rise to their dignity.

On this view, what we owe to each other is treatment that enacts respect and
concern for our normative status as beings with dignity, and this in turn
means that we should take seriously the valuable features that give each of
us such a status by thinking and acting in ways that respond to these features
in appropriately favourable or fitting ways.

To articulate the normative requirements flowing from this approach, I
explore the following ideal:

Solidaristic Empowerment
We should support individuals in their pursuit of a flourishing life by implementing
both negative duties not to destroy or block their valuable capacities and positive
duties to protect and facilitate their development and exercise of these capacities.

People have valuable capacities—for sentience, moral and prudential reasoning and judgement, knowledge, and so on. Although not everyone has all,
or the same set of valuable capacities, they have dignity whenever they have
some of them. People flourish when they develop and exercise their valuable capacities. To respond appropriately to their dignity, we should treat
them well by supporting this flourishing. If, of two alternative feasible sets
of acts, practices, or institutions, one would be more supportive of people's
flourishing than the other, this would give us strong reason to choose it. We
should avoid destroying people's capacities, and we should take feasible and
reasonable steps to help people succeed as they develop and exercise them.
An important job of a conception of justice is precisely to articulate the content of the negative and positive duties of solidaristic empowerment that we
have towards each other, and to identify the practices and institutions that
could implement them.

A clarification about Solidaristic Empowerment is in order. Why not simply talk about 'solidaristic support' instead? I use the idea of empowerment
to mark the importance that individuals gain the ability to shape their own

The Dignitarian Approach 5

lives and take the initiative in striving for what is right and good for them. But I acknowledge some limitations of this idea. In particular, some people may not have the form of agency that is needed to have moral duties—for example because they lack the cognitive capacities for moral reasoning, even though they have other valuable capacities that deserve support. In these cases, the set of rights-holders regarding solidaristic support is wider than the set of duty-bearers. I do not hold that, to have dignity and be entitled to treatment under the banner of justice, an individual must also be able to give it.[2] I ask the reader to remember the caveat entered in this paragraph as the book proceeds. Although of great importance when present, the absence of more sophisticated forms of agency does not imply the lack of status-dignity, and the accompanying rights, that result from the less sophisticated ones that are present. Justice may have to be given to those who cannot give it.

In this book, I explore the Dignitarian Approach in the context of social and political philosophy, to account for social justice.[3] Although the articulation of this approach is original, it is certainly influenced in many ways by previous contributions in the field. As the book proceeds, it will be evident that the proposed approach continues earlier efforts in the philosophy of human rights, socialism, and feminism, all of which have been particularly attuned to the importance of simultaneously illuminating values of self-determination and mutual aid. On the other hand, adopting the ideal of Solidaristic Empowerment conflicts with accepting other views, such as certain forms of collectivism that neglect the importance of individual freedom in the name of communal harmony, and certain forms of libertarianism that downplay the importance of positive duties to help others and take only negative duties not to harm them as key for social justice.[4]

A full conception of social justice has three dimensions. It includes (DI) an identification of core ideals and principles; (DII) a proposal of social institutions and practices implementing the ideals and principles specified at DI; and (DIII) an illumination of the processes of transformation leading agents and their society from where they currently are to the social arrangements

---

[2] That view is not uncommon. It is for example held by Kant, and I reject it in Chapter 2. Rawls (1999: 446) claims that '[t]hose who can give justice are owed justice'. Although clearly influenced by Kant, Rawls's view is however less stark, as it states sufficient, not necessary, conditions for holding rights of justice.

[3] I believe that it has wider reach. At the level of normative ethics, for example, the Dignitarian Approach can be construed as a deontological view of the kind Shelly Kagan calls '*reflection theory*', which takes moral reasons to be a matter of responding appropriately to (and in this way reflecting) the value of the individuals the acting agent relates to. See Kagan (1998: 298–9).

[4] The first set of views are present in authoritarian or deeply hierarchical versions of communitarianism, of the kind expressed in the politics of fascism and in forms of socialism in which a party elite controls the state and the population. The second is in turn present in some right-wing forms of libertarianism. On this kind of libertarianism, see Nozick (1974) and Narveson (1988). On the significance of positive duties of justice, see Gilabert (2010; 2012a: ch. 3).

6   Human Dignity and Social Justice

specified in DII if these are not already in place.[5] As this book will show, the Dignitarian Approach to justice is a research program with implications for each of these dimensions. In this chapter, I outline the fundamental normative ideas animating this program.

I start by clarifying the idea of *dignity* that informs the statements of the Dignitarian Approach and Solidaristic Empowerment given above (which are, themselves, the most general normative ideas in the program—belonging to dimension DI). I do this by identifying a set of related notions constituting the *conceptual network of dignity*. My account of the components in the network is neither the result of an elucidation that merely reports uses in ordinary language nor a stipulation that imposes them in purely top-down fashion. It is instead a deliberative interpretive proposal.[6] I make contact with some existing uses of the concepts, but develop them in specific ways that are illuminating given the normative purpose of articulating the Dignitarian Approach and the ideal of Solidaristic Empowerment and their roles in our thinking about social justice (which are explored in the later sections of this chapter).

I start with the notions of status-dignity, dignitarian norms, and condition-dignity. *Status-dignity* (together with the companion notion of the basis of dignity discussed below) is the core, anchoring idea in the network. Status-dignity is a moral standing of individuals in accordance with which they are owed certain kinds of treatment that involves respect and concern as a matter of rights. People have a moral claim that this treatment be given to them by agents who can affect them; when these agents do not treat them in this way, they wrong them. This standing is inherent to people. It is not the creature of social conventions. To have dignity in this sense, people do not need to be regarded as having it. This standing is also of intrinsic rather than merely instrumental significance. The treatment that dignity calls for is primarily a favourable treatment which is to be undertaken for the sake of the individual who has it, not as a means for getting something else (such as some benefit or profit for the one giving the favourable treatment). Furthermore, dignity in this sense is a high-priority and an egalitarian status. It is typically wrong to

---

[5] This framework is explained in Chapter 4. For my view of how to understand the category of duties of justice, see Gilabert (2016). On the view defended in that paper, duties of justice are duties to preserve or promote people's access to important conditions or goods to which they are entitled and whose fulfilment is prima facie enforceable. This enforcement is all things considered justifiable if it is necessary for or strongly contributes to securing the required preservation or promotion and can be feasibly introduced without imposing unreasonable costs.

[6] For an explanation of this notion and a more extensive account of the conceptual network of dignity, as well as a response to several criticisms to the use of the idea of dignity in moral and political philosophy, see Gilabert (2019a: chs. 5–6). The present discussion is more explicit about some structural aspects of status-dignity and the basis of dignity as they relate to moral requirements.

The Dignitarian Approach   7

adopt plans of action or institutions that discount it or sacrifice it for self-gain, or which recognize it as present in some people but not in others. *Dignitarian norms* state what the required treatment amounts to in various contexts. Human rights and principles of social justice are important examples. Finally, *condition-dignity* is the state of affairs in which the relevant dignitarian norms are fulfilled, and in which people enjoy the treatment that their status-dignity calls for.

The distinction between status-dignity and condition-dignity is crucial to avoid contradiction. It is sometimes said that, because they have dignity, people may not be enslaved. It is also said that when they are enslaved, people's dignity is destroyed. Some critics use examples like this to charge dignitarian talk of incoherence.[7] But the alleged incoherence (the one that appears in saying that slaves at the same time have and lack dignity) dissolves if we use the distinction between status—and condition-dignity. The dignity that slaves have is status-dignity, which is independent of whether it is recognized or honoured by any convention or practice. As a moral status it remains constant. It is because of that that slaves are morally entitled to resist oppression, and slave-owners are required to give it up. A moral norm against slavery is a dignitarian norm, which is justified as a fitting response to people's status-dignity. Its violation deprives people of treatment that is owed them. What slaves lack is condition-dignity, the situation in which dignitarian norms prohibiting slavery are acknowledged and honoured, which is precisely what the work of justice must bring about. The distinction between status-dignity and condition-dignity not only helps us avoid contradiction, but also to show the explanatory link between the two seemingly incompatible utterances: slaves lack (condition-) dignity because the (status-) dignity that they have is not properly recognized.

The next notion in the network is that of *the basis of dignity*. The basis of dignity is constituted by the set of capacities in virtue of which people have status-dignity. There are several important constraints on my use of this notion, which spring from its functional role as the ground of status-dignity. First, the capacities have to be inherently held and relatively general. Thus, to inform the directed obligations owed to those who have them, they have to be integral to their bearers rather than the result of some act of attribution by others or the result of social conventions. To be present recurrently in the people to whom the dignitarian norms apply despite their diverse personal characteristics, they must also be broad and subject to variegated specification. A capacity for prudential reasoning, for example, would fulfil these

[7] Pinker (2008).

8 Human Dignity and Social Justice

conditions. You have it independently of whether others think you do, and even if you use it in slightly different ways than them. Second, to support the high-priority of status-dignity and the norms responding to it, the capacities must also be intrinsically valuable rather than unimportant or problematic. People may be capable of greed and cruelty, but this is not what gives them status-dignity. A statement of the items in the basis of dignity is not a mere description of what people are like, but a substantive normative view about what aspects of them give rise to moral regard, to obligations of respect and concern.[8] Finally, the capacities should be explanatorily relevant. They should help us articulate the content of the dignitarian norms responding to status-dignity. Since these norms require a treatment of individuals that is favourable, the capacities should be such that their unfolding, as supported by the fulfilment of the norms, would make the life of the individuals targeted by the norms go better. The capacities would thus be relevant for the well-being of the people who have them.

I add three points about how to approach the identification of a list of relevant capacities. First, we should be pluralistic about the basis of dignity. The set of valuable capacities is broad. An initial, hypothetical list, which I find intuitively plausible and will rely on in this book, includes the following capacities:

- Sentience: the capacity to have positive and negative subjective experiences, such as pleasure and pain.
- Self-awareness: the capacity to have a reflective sense of self.
- Technical, prudential, and moral reasoning and choice: the capacities of practical reasoning to identify and choose means to effectively achieve ends, to identify and pursue ends that benefit the agent, and to also appraise and select ends and means from an impartial perspective that favours not only the agent but all other individuals affected.
- Theoretical knowledge: the capacity to inquire and form beliefs about how the world is and functions.
- Empathy and concern: the capacity to grasp what other individuals' lives are like, and to seek to affect them favourably.
- Cooperation: the capacity to engage in joint activities with others for common ends.

---

[8] To avoid misunderstanding, recall that status-dignity is a deontic status, and that the features at the basis of dignity are valuable capacities. Statements of the form 'X's capacities C1 ... Cn are valuable' are not just descriptive reports about what capacities an individual has, but primarily evaluative judgments about their significance. And statements of the form 'If X has capacities C1 ... Cn, then X has status-dignity' are substantive moral judgments, not statements of logical implication. Thus, there is no conflation here of descriptive and normative judgments, or any naturalistic fallacy attempting to derive an 'ought' from an 'is'.

- Aesthetic appreciation: the capacity to appreciate objects in terms of their beauty.
- Creativity and imagination: the capacity to entertain how things might be (as different from how they are).

Each of these features seem good candidates to mark the people who have them as beings with status-dignity. Second, the list can be seen as presenting sufficient conditions for status-dignity and to do so in a disjunctive way. To have dignity, an individual need not have them all.[9] (I will qualify this point below, however.) Finally, the account should allow for the fact that the set of capacities can display internal structures or configurations. The items in it may have different specific contents, relations, and normative weights, and thus combine in various significant ways in different individuals and situations. For example, prudential and moral reasoning may be more or less present in different individuals, and, when present, they may constrain other features, so that the value of supporting other capacities in ways that undermine the self-determination people are capable of through this reasoning would be severely compromised.

As I see things, a substantive account of the basis of dignity is fundamental in terms of the determinative grounds of status-dignity. But it is open to various forms of evidentiary support and epistemic improvement.[10] The characterization of the list of valuable features in the basis of dignity is certainly open to controversy and any proposed list should be tested through an ongoing effort to reach deliberative reflective equilibrium in our thinking about morality and social justice.[11] Thus, we can ask directly whether candidates in a proposed list are intuitively plausible. Less directly, we can explore their significance by considering the practical implications of implementing dignitarian norms requiring their support. This may sometimes lead us to revise our initial hypothesis about what items should belong in the list, or our view of its internal structure.

Thus, for example, imagine that we start with a narrow view of the basis of dignity as only including capacities for sophisticated forms of reasoning but come to see it as faulty when we notice that it does not help us explain duties of health care to limit the suffering of people with severe cognitive disabilities.

---

[9] This point is also made in Nussbaum (2008). I provide a summary of similarities and differences with Nussbaum's approach to dignity in Chapter 3, Section 4.3.

[10] On the distinction between determinative and epistemic justification, see Cullity (2018: 12–4, 24).

[11] For further elaboration on the conceptual, substantive, and methodological issues involved in providing a view of the basis of dignity, see Gilabert (2022) and 'Inclusive Dignity'.

10   Human Dignity and Social Justice

We recognize, for example, that sentience—the capacity for having negative and positive qualitative experiences such as pain and pleasure—must be added as a key item. We may also come to revise our view about the standing of the items of our initial list. It could be that the items in that list are not equally significant, or that some become morally significant only if others are present. For example, a capacity for theoretical knowledge might appear relevant only when associated with a capacity for qualitative experiences or for practical agency or striving, and this may explain why we think that human individuals have rights to support regarding their cognitive processes which computers without sentience or desires lack.[12] I am open to this point, and thus I am prepared to revise the account of the initial list given above so that sentience and some form of basic striving are viewed as necessary for status-dignity. We may also come to see that, when present, the capacities for autonomous judgement and choice have special weight and a constraining role. This may happen as we articulate norms for the organization of important institutions in our societies. We may find that it is crucial that political institutions engage people as rule-makers besides rule-takers, and so acknowledge that political liberty has priority over securing certain economic advantages. We may also think that the economy should include some opportunities for work that involve self-realization, so that people can develop and exercise their capacities for creative and cooperative production, but also that we should shape access to these practices so that people have a choice as to whether they pursue them rather than other options. These are the kinds of considerations that would lead us to sharpen our views about the list of capacities we started with. They are the kinds of considerations that led me to endorse the list of capacities given in the previous paragraph, to acknowledge that some items in it such as sentience and basic striving or agency might be necessary, and to give especial weight to support for self-determined prudential and moral reasoning when people are capable of it.

When do dignitarian norms apply? We answer this question by illuminating the *circumstances of dignity*. These are the circumstances in which dignitarian norms are practically relevant, i.e., in which their fulfilment is necessary—in the sense of morally 'called-for'—and feasible. In these circumstances, there are threats and obstacles to the achievement of condition-dignity, and they can be overcome. Consider, for example, the phenomena of material scarcity and the presence of disvaluable psychological features such as aggressiveness, domineeringness, greed, or callousness. They pose

---

[12] I thank Gwen Bradford and Valéry Giroux for discussion on this point. For arguments that sentience and agency are particularly strong candidates for necessary conditions of moral standing, see Kagan (2019: ch.1).

The Dignitarian Approach **11**

challenges for people's flourishing, which requires material resources to unfold and is stunted when the people pursuing it are attacked or neglected by others. Such challenges can be addressed, however, when people deploy their valuable capacities of empathy and concern, cooperation, and creativity, and act together to increase their technological powers and devise protective institutions. It is important to note that the circumstances, and the dignitarian norms applying in them, can be more or less *abstract* or *specific*. Some conditions are fairly general, while others are quite circumscribed. (To mark the difference, we can use a notion of *situations of dignity* to identify specific instances of the circumstances of dignity.) All human beings, in any historical epoch, are vulnerable to illness and death, and need help from others to cope with them. So, quite general norms of support for people falling ill and managing pain are likely to hold for any society. But particular illnesses and resources to deal with them are quite specific. Palliative care would be required in any society, but requirements regarding the production and fair distribution of certain vaccines would only apply in more circumscribed situations. Reference to the circumstances and situations of dignity is relevant for identifying the content of dignitarian norms because it helps notice how people's valuable capacities can be set back and how they can be supported by agents who can affect them.

Dignitarian norms may be more or less ambitious. To mark their span, we can say that they cover a spectrum between *basic dignity* and *maximal dignity*. Norms concerned with basic dignity require support for people's access to a *decent life*, while norms regarding maximal dignity target people's empowerment to lead a more fully *flourishing life*. Whereas basic condition-dignity involves people's enjoyment of a socially urgent threshold of support for the development and exercise of their valuable capacities, maximal condition-dignity involves the highest level of support that is feasible and reasonable to demand. Although the distinction is intuitive enough, what precisely should count as basic and maximal dignity is of course a matter of substantive debate and argument. We could say, for example, that basic dignity is what conceptions of human rights should focus on, and that maximal dignity is what is covered by more ambitious conceptions of social justice such as liberal egalitarianism and democratic socialism. This will be the view adopted in this book.

A response to status-dignity can thus give raise to diverse *social ideals*, or projects to enact dignitarian treatment. The ideal of Solidaristic Empowerment is a general example. Social ideals can be articulated in more or less detail through dignitarian norms which are more or less specific. There is conceptual space for diverse and even conflicting dignitarian ideals or

12 Human Dignity and Social Justice

specifications of them. A *dignitarian forum* can thus be envisioned in which people embrace core ideas about dignity but debate on how best to articulate and pursue them. It is important that the conceptual network of dignity is presented here in a way that allows for this debate instead of foreclosing it through definitional fiat (a point to which I will return later).

It is also important, I think, to allow for the possibility that dignitarian ideals and norms have a broad *site* of application, so that they may in principle cover both the rules of large institutions and the more personal attitudes and choices of individuals in various situations in their daily life. Think about racism, which is arguably a paradigmatic example of contra-dignitarian treatment. Letting conventional social stereotypes about race shape people's access to social advantages, such as educational opportunities and jobs, is odious. Countering racism may thus include the introduction of formal constraints on institutions, backed by penalties and incentives. But arguably racism must also be countered by shaping our own personal attitudes and choices in anti-racist ways. The formal institutional rules against racism will not be introduced, or maintained, if sufficiently many of us do not embrace them. Furthermore, these rules cannot cover every racist act, and will likely be open to loopholes and specious interpretations. If sufficiently many of us do not develop strong anti-racist attitudes, their implementation will not go very far. And, in any case, countering racism also arguably involves aspects of our personal behaviour and demeanour that either cannot be reliably steered through formal or coercive rules, or which would be wrong to make a target for such rules because doing so would be unduly intrusive or perhaps even backfire.

We have indeed reason to see the site of ideals and principles of justice to be wide, including both institutions and informal interpersonal contexts. There are many reasons for embracing this wide site view. We can summarize them as follows. First, as discussed in the previous paragraph and as G. A. Cohen argued, it gets a better picture of what constitutes the fulfilment of justice.[13] A society in which racism is absent in both institutions and interpersonal rapports is more just than one in which racism is only absent in institutions. Second, the wide view helps to secure the stability of just institutional frameworks: people who enact the relevant ideals and principles in their day-to-day interactions will keep them closer to their hearts and minds and will be more ready to support, vote for, and campaign for institutional policies servicing them, and protest when these are missing. Furthermore, the broad focus helps in the accessibility of just institutions. People experimenting with the fulfilment of certain ideals and principles in their daily lives may come to

---

[13] Cohen (2008: ch. 3).

appreciate their force and seek further implementation of them at the institutional level. Finally, in hostile contexts interpersonal realization may be all that is immediately feasible in terms of enacting the relevant ideals and principles.[14]

Considering attitudes and choices is also relevant for understanding *dignitarian virtue*, which we can characterize as people's dispositions to think, feel, and act in tune with dignitarian norms. Dignitarian virtue is instrumentally important for the members of a society to develop and sustain just institutions, and it is directly constitutive of respectful and concernful relationships between them. The idea of dignitarian virtue also enables us to make a distinction between two kinds of status-dignity, which in turns allows us to dispel what might otherwise seem to be contradictory judgements as well as to illuminate important moral phenomena. In addition to *endowment-based* dignity, which is the central notion of status-dignity clarified at the outset of this discussion, we can identify a different, and not fundamental form of status-dignity, which we may call *achievement-based* dignity. Achievement-based dignity is held by an individual on the basis of specific features of them that have arisen as a result of their choices, or are, more broadly, such that the individual can reasonably be held responsible for them. Consider a politician (let's call him Mr Horn) who campaigns for, and, once in office, implements policies that discriminate against people from certain racial or ethnoreligious groups. There is a sense in which Mr Horn is a morally corrupt politician who lacks dignity. We may indeed lose some respect for him because he has chosen to act in racist or xenophobic ways that run afoul of justified norms of equal consideration, stoking up fear and prejudice for electoral gain. Mr Horn displays a deficit regarding achievement-based dignity. But it is crucial to distinguish this sense of dignity from the more fundamental one tracked by the core notion of status-dignity as endowment-based dignity. Mr Horn retains this more fundamental dignity independently of his attitudes and behaviour, and must be treated accordingly. Even if we lose some respect for

---

[14] Could there be cases in which we must engage in tradeoffs between dignitarian institutions and dignitarian interpersonal treatment? Yes, it could be that institutional and psychological resources are scarce and hard choices have to be made. But before engaging in the tradeoff exercise, we must be sure that it is indeed unavoidable (rather than the result of moral laziness). If it is, we should choose the combination that gives us maximal dignitarian value. This will likely include greater focus on institutions than interactions because of the larger causal impact of the former. But even then, we should recognize the loss of the elements put aside in the tradeoff, and that they leave a remainder. This acknowledgement would appropriately shape our demeanour as we face each other. Furthermore, we should make choices with an eye to enabling changes in the future that diminish the need for the tradeoffs we are forced to make now. The relation between the focus on institutions and interactions is more complex than might initially appear, in that there are positive linkages between them. These linkages must be factored into the description of the options to choose from. Some institutions may be better than others, other things equal, because they are more likely to encourage dignitarian interactions. And some interactions may be preferable, other things equal, because they foster the prospect for dignitarian institutions. I thank Daniel Weinstock for discussion on these issues.

14 Human Dignity and Social Justice

him on account of his deficits regarding achievement-based dignity, we must continue to respect him in some other ways and refrain from responding to his wrongdoing in contra-dignitarian manners. We may publicly criticize and condemn his behaviour, protest energetically against his policies, campaign for another politician to take his job in the next election, and so on, but we may not torture or shoot him. We must not violate his human rights (which Mr Horn retains as bearer of endowment-based status-dignity).

The distinction between endowment-based and achievement-based dignity is indeed quite important for explanatory and practical reasons. Deficits in achievement-based dignity precisely consist in failures to respond appropriately to the endowment-based dignity of others (which is what treatment on the basis of dignitarian norms requires). And the features in the basis of their own status-dignity, such as their valuable capacities for moral judgement and empathy, enable agents to see this deficit and change course— to cultivate new dispositions and choose different and better acts in the future. In this way, the basis of dignity that grounds status-dignity in the endowment-based sense is also a source of practical hope for progressive change. We can pivot away from contempt and indifference towards others and choose instead to cultivate our dignitarian virtue. When we use our dynamic power to change ourselves and our social environment in this way, we display what we can call *dynamic dignity*.[15]

2.2 Fruitfulness of the Dignitarian Approach

The Dignitarian Approach can be used to weave elements in the conceptual network of dignity to articulate substantive moral conceptions. We can vindicate our commitment to universalism and justify moral humanist rights, foreground the importance of combining self-determination with mutual aid, illuminate the stance of those struggling against social injustice, explore the arc of humanist justice, and appreciate the need for both general norms and specific responses to the variety of individuals' predicaments. I do not claim that these commitments could not be illuminated in any other way. But the fact that the Dignitarian Approach does illuminate them well provides epistemic reasons, in reflective equilibrium, to embrace it.[16] In this section,

---

[15] This may also be a case of self-respect, and a matter of duties to respond to our own dignity. My account is open to the possibility that dignitarian norms include self-directed duties.

[16] Justifying the statements of the Dignitarian Approach and Solidaristic Empowerment in reflective equilibrium involves several operations, such as (a) noting their intrinsic intuitive appeal as general statements, (b) discovering their fruitfulness for explaining more specific requirements (such as those regarding just labour practices), (c) confirming them by noticing that they have plausible implications that

The Dignitarian Approach   **15**

I identify how the Dignitarian Approach is fruitful for these important normative tasks. The points are presented in a relatively schematic way. The rest of the book offers elaborations of them.

2.2.1 Articulating universalist humanism and justifying moral humanist rights

Many of us have the moral view that we should see all human individuals as equally being ultimate units of respect and concern. This universalist and egalitarian perspective often animates the critique of the mistreatment that is common in colonialism, imperialism, authoritarianism, racism, the exclusion of women from education and jobs, the discrimination against LGBTQ+ people, and the marginalization of workers without property from the political process that structures their life chances. When we criticize these social phenomena, we assume that there are norms with universal scope that require favourable treatment of every individual as a moral equal. The first important advantage of the Dignitarian Approach is that it helps explain and defend this inclusive moral stance. It proposes that we see universal norms as dignitarian norms. The treatment they require is fitting as a response to people's human dignity.[17] It is what is owed to them given relatively general and important features such as the valuable capacities in the basis of their dignity. Dignitarian treatment of this kind is to be distinguished from, and should constrain, other forms of favourable treatment that is based on more parochial, less important, or conventional features such as nationality, class, or ethnicity.

A central case of the kind of universal norms just mentioned is constituted by what we can call *moral humanist rights*. The Dignitarian Approach helps us articulate and justify them. Let me explain.

In general, rights are justified claims which some individuals (the rightholders) have against certain agents (the duty-bearers) with respect to some objects in some circumstances.[18] There are different kind of rights. Here I focus on rights which are moral and humanist. Moral rights are rights that exist independently of whether they are already recognized by those to whom

---

match our considered judgments regarding the issues addressed by those specific requirements, (d) noting that in cases of conflict with some considered judgments, they offer an overall plausible rationale for their revision, (e) showing that they generate views that compare well with other approaches, and (f) checking that they are consistent and can interact fruitfully with important non-moral truths (offering, for example, insights as to how to combine scientific research and moral and political deliberation). On the philosophical methodology adopted in this book, see also Preface; Chapter 2, Section 2.2 (v); and Chapter 7, Section 4.4.

[17] Notice that in the Dignitarian Approach presented here, the moral status marked with a phrase like 'human dignity' is different from the more contingent and conventional social status sometimes ascribed to particular people occupying high positions in existing economic, political, and cultural hierarchies.

[18] My concern here is with so-called 'claim-rights'. For a comprehensive analysis of rights, see Wenar (2021).

16   Human Dignity and Social Justice

they apply. A moral right to political participation exists, for example, even if an authoritarian regime denies it, and indeed can be invoked to criticize and change that regime. Humanist rights, in turn, are moral rights which people have primarily as human individuals rather than as members of some narrower, and often conventional, group, such as on account of their nationality, class, ethnic group, and so on. A paradigmatic example is human rights, which are held by people as human beings rather than as, say, Americans, males, whites, heterosexuals, or property-owners.

Some points of clarification about moral humanist rights are in order. First, some of them may mention particular groups, but the reference to these groups contributes to the justification of these rights only as a way to specify what other moral humanist rights that do not mention the particular groups require in certain circumstances. They are derived moral humanist rights. Thus, the right to form a union in a certain firm is held by workers in that firm, not by an individual who is not a worker, or who does not work in that firm. But this right specifies a more general right to form unions, which is held by all workers, and that right in turn can be seen as a specification of an even more general right to self-determination in working practices, which is held by any individual if they work. Furthermore, some moral humanist rights are operative only regarding some subset of humanity because of differences between their abilities or other morally relevant properties. Some derived rights to make certain decisions within a certain practice or institution may be operative only for those who have the ability to make them, but everyone has, more generally, the potential right to have this specific right if they had, or could form, that ability in the context. I will say more about unity and diversity in 2.2.5. Second, there may be different kinds of rights within the space of moral humanist rights. For example, some rights which are in principle enforceable (when this is feasible and imposes no unreasonable costs) may be within the narrower remit of a theory of social justice (which is a subset of moral theory). Furthermore, such rights may concern rather basic requirements of justice of the kind typically targeted by human rights doctrine, while others may be more ambitious, as in the case of the principles of liberal egalitarian, or democratic socialist, theories. Humanist rights indeed include, but are potentially wider than, human rights.[19] For example, socialists argue for rights of workers to control productive resources that are more exigent than what human rights doctrine tends to recognize. We return to this point in 2.2.4. Finally, the present focus on human beings does not assume

---

[19] In Gilabert (2019a: ch.11), I argue that the arc of humanist justice spans rights to basic and maximal dignity.

that other animals do not have moral rights. The relevant contrast when justifying moral humanist rights is not between human beings and the rest of nature, but between people viewed (at the fundamental level) as human individuals and people viewed as members of a nation, a social class, and so on. Non-human animals have their valuable capacities (sometimes overlapping with those of human individuals, sometimes not), and they have their own dignity and moral rights (even if they are not humanist rights).[20]

Hereafter, and unless I say otherwise to prevent ambiguity, when I talk about rights, I refer to moral humanist rights. How can these rights be justified? There are in fact two different questions of justification. First, there is the question of what justifies moral humanist rights as a category of rights different from others. Second, there is the question of what justifies particular moral humanist rights (such as certain civil rights, political rights, labour rights, or health care rights). Moral humanist rights can be more or less abstract or specific, and thus their justification may involve more or less detailed reference to specific features of the right-holders, duty-bearers, objects, and circumstances. The Dignitarian Approach can be used to perform these two justificatory tasks.

Concerning the first kind of justification—the one explaining the existence of moral humanist rights as a general normative category—we can draw on the general statements of the Dignitarian Approach and the ideal of Solidaristic Empowerment. I find these statements intuitively compelling, and I hope readers do too. The Dignitarian Approach states a general, deontic relational structure, according to which there are obligations, and correlative claims, regarding how we are to treat each other with respect to the unfolding of our valuable capacities: the value of these capacities must be reflected through appropriate favourable treatment. Solidaristic Empowerment, in turn, states a general duty to be supportive of the flourishing of the persons we can affect. It has, as a correlative, a general right to be treated in

---

[20] For a powerful critique of dignitarian conceptions of human rights built on the assumption of human supremacy, see Kymlicka (2018). Kymlicka's charge is that human supremacism involves not only exclusionary attitudes towards the rights of non-human animals, but also insufficient recognition of the rights of human individuals (in particular children, the elderly, and people with disabilities). This critique does not really apply to the dignitarian approach that I endorse, as it does not rely on the crucial assumption that what grounds the dignity of human individuals (and their basic equality) must be features of them that make them different, and superior, to animals (Ibid: 768). Kymlicka acknowledges that there can be dignitarian views that do not make this assumption (Ibid: 765 768, 770). The critique seems however to be biting against the specific conceptions of dignity that Kymlicka discusses, such as those offered by Jacques Maritain, George Kateb, and Catherine Dupré. It may also be challenging for Waldron's recent idea of 'distinctive equality', according to which human beings are 'one another's equals on a basis that does actually differentiate them from animals' Waldron (2017: 31). Waldron links this idea to human dignity (Ibid: 31, 51-2, 100-2). I discuss Kymlicka's challenge in 'Inclusive Dignity'. For a survey of various emerging questions facing inclusive views of moral status, see Sebo (forthcoming).

18 Human Dignity and Social Justice

such supportive ways by those who can affect us. What, exactly, agents owe it to others to do for their sake, and what they, specifically, have a claim to, lies downstream from these general statements, and should be the focus of normative inquiry identifying various dignitarian norms. It is then plausible to hold that there is indeed a category of moral humanist rights regarding solidaristic empowerment in which the rights differ from other putative rights. These rights are dignitarian norms which articulate appropriate responses to status-dignity, and their fulfilment would constitute condition-dignity. They are distinctive in that they are grounded in the valuable capacities of people at the basis of their dignity. The solidaristic duties correlative to them are focused on supporting people's ability to maintain, develop, and exercise such capacities in various social contexts in which support is needed and feasible to provide.

Recall the points made in the first paragraph of this section regarding the universalist stance we adopt when we criticize violations of certain rights. This stance embraces moral humanist rights. And the Dignitarian Approach vindicates and explains it. To see this, consider why it is implausible to say that we should include owners of means of production (such as land and factories) in the political process but exclude people who are not property-owners. The latter are deeply affected by the laws generated by the process just as much as the former are. And they also have capacities for moral and political judgement. It is fundamentally because of facts like these that we have reason to grant people political rights to shape the institutions under which they live. The political process includes the determination of conventions regarding legal property rights. So, existing legal statuses regarding property may not be invoked as constraints on entry or participation in the process that is to shape them. More fundamental, moral reasons regarding the status-dignity of the people affected— such as their having capacities for moral and political judgement—must be given priority. And it is implausible to say that the political process should welcome some affected people with these capacities but bar other people affected who also have them. Dignitarian considerations have a tendency to shatter, or overflow, exclusionary views of the scope of moral rights.

Let us turn now to the second kind of justification—the one targeting various moral humanist rights. A common strategy for justifying specific rights is to show that their implementation would support important interests of the people affected. This is the 'interest theory' of rights, which I find plausible. A version of it can be stated as follows:

The Dignitarian Approach **19**

General schema for justifying rights

The main idea is that rights require feasible and reasonable support for the morally important interests of the individuals affected.[21] More precisely: In circumstances C, A (a right-holder) has a right to O (an object) against B (a duty-bearer) just in case there are feasible and reasonable demands on B that they support,[22] in some ways to be specified, A's access to O. The specification of what B owes to A regarding O tracks the moral importance of A's interest in O, the feasible ways for B to support A's access to O, and the subset of such feasible forms of support that do not involve morally unacceptable burdens on B or others (given the importance of their own interests) and on A (given the importance of other interests of A besides that concerning access to O). Further normative considerations (such as the significance of responsibility and fairness), and feasibility considerations (such as the possibility of progressive implementation over time as circumstances change) may also be relevant.

We can see in rough outline how this schema can be used to justify specific rights. Consider health care rights. People have an important interest in accessing life-saving medical care. It is reasonable for others to contribute to institutions and practices that provide some of this care. They may be asked to pay taxes to fund public hospitals, for example. But there are limits to how health provision may be organized. Because of other important interests that they have, such as in controlling what happens to their bodies, people typically may not be forced to undergo treatment they explicitly and competently reject, or to provide organs for others against their will. Some forms of treatment might be quite desirable for patients, but infeasible to provide given limits in medical technology, or unduly costly to fund given other competing social priorities which may be weightier in the present circumstances, and as a result this provision might not be the object of a right in the relevant context. This predicament could change over time through the development of new medical technology, which may itself be the target of a dynamic duty for society so that new forms of health care become feasible and reasonable to require in the future.[23]

---

[21] 'A person has a right if, and only if, his interest is sufficient to hold another duty bound to do something on the ground that that action respects or promotes that interest' (Raz 1994: 31; see Raz 1986: ch.7). The schema I propose gives this view more structure by tracking the interests of the various individuals involved in rights and their correlative duties, as well as their circumstances. Raz (1994: 35) acknowledges that these complexities are relevant.

[22] I use 'support' as an umbrella term to range over the possible negative and positive duties in the standard triad (in human rights discourse) referring to duties to respect (not deprive of the relevant object of the right), protect (help in maintaining the object when a third party poses a threat), and fulfil (in the narrow sense of providing access to the object when the right-holder lacks it). The term 'implementation' I use later to state the Schema of Dignitarian Justification is a broad expression meant to refer to the satisfaction of any of these duties.

[23] Regarding responsibility, it could for example be said (controversially) that if resources used to meet some needs are scarce and a beneficiary uses them recklessly, when they come forward asking for further

20 Human Dignity and Social Justice

But what interests matter for the articulation of rights? The Dignitarian Approach helps answer this question, and it thereby allow us to sharpen the foregoing schema in a fruitful way. We can frame the identification of the relevant interests as follows:

Schema of Dignitarian Justification

Rights are justified if, and to the extent that, their implementation (through some institutions, practices, or acts) is either necessary for, or strongly contributes to, the feasible and reasonable support for interests regarding the maintenance, development, and exercise of certain valuable capacities of the relevant individuals—the ones at the basis of their dignity.

What is key, then, in justifying a certain right, is to show, regarding the putative right-holders and duty-bearers in the relevant circumstances, that (i) the object of the right concerns the right-holder's maintenance, development, or exercise of capacities in the basis of dignity—and thus that they have a morally important interest in accessing it; and that (ii) the requirements the right imposes on the duty-bearers are feasible and reasonable (given their abilities and important interests regarding the maintenance, development, and exercise of their own valuable capacities).

The Schema of Dignitarian Justification helps us to address a worry about the relation between interests and rights. On the face of it, to say that someone has an interest in something does not imply that they have a right to it, even if that right is to be seen as holding only pro tanto or presumptively. There seems to be a logical gap in moving from statements about interests to statements about rights. The Dignitarian Approach bridges this gap. The valuable capacities at the basis of dignity give rise both to interests (in their maintenance, development, and exercise) and to rights to their support. When the object of your interest is linked to what gives you standing to be a rights-holder, or to claim rights—the capacities at the basis of your dignity—taking it as giving rise to a right seems appropriate. We can thus accept the following principle:

Bridge Principle

When individuals have dignity, they have the deontic status of being owed (reasonable and feasible) support by every agent who can affect the satisfaction of

---

help their claim might have less weight than that of another who is also requiring help but has not similarly squandered resources in this way. Regarding fairness, a person could complain if they are singled out arbitrarily (for no reason, or for bad reasons, such as their race) to forgo a certain benefit or shoulder certain burdens in social cooperation (when the allocation could have been done impartially, such as by lot or through rotation). As Wallace (2019: 165), puts it, people may have a normative interest in being treated fairly which is flouted in cases like this.

The Dignitarian Approach **21**

their interests in retaining, developing, and exercising the capacities that give rise to that dignity.

The Bridge Principle helps us identify what interests are sufficiently important to give rise to rights. This book will explore the application of this dignitarian account of rights to particular cases, notably those related to working practices. At this point I am only outlining the main contours of this kind of justification. An additional, and important, point to note is that in circumscribing the set of relevant interests (to cover those linked to the maintenance, development, and exercise of the valuable capacities in the basis of dignity), the Dignitarian Approach allows us to give some structure to the difficult question of the normative weight of various putative right-claims. Putative rights supporting valuable capacities at the basis of dignity are best seen as holding pro tanto, or as at least presumptively. This is so because, in practice, such rights could conflict with other rights applying in the same circumstances, so that, in these circumstances, all things considered judgements must be reached about which of these conflicting rights, or what aspects of their implementation, should be prioritized. This weighing exercise is a task faced by any plausible conception of rights. Unfortunately, there is no compelling algorithm that tells us how exactly to proceed in this exercise, as the interests supported by various rights are only imperfectly comparable, and their appropriate interpretation in specific situations is always somewhat indeterminate. Although these difficulties are not eliminated, they are made more tractable if we know what is the ground of the interests and the rights that support them. Here it is indeed helpful to refer to the basis and the circumstances of dignity. To identify the force of a set of pro tanto rights in a certain situation, and reach an all things considered judgement about who owes what to whom, we can look at the challenges faced by the individuals involved, and consider how the feasible responses to these challenges might affect the maintenance, development, and exercise of their valuable capacities. When, in these circumstances, certain forms of support for certain capacities seem more important that other forms of support regarding these or other capacities, then we can grant the rights regarding the former greater weight (for these circumstances).[24]

---

[24] Wenar (2021: sect. 6) outlines a contrast between deontological, status-based theories of rights which 'hold that human beings have attributes that make it fitting to ascribe certain rights to them, and make respect for these rights appropriate', and consequentialist, instrumental theories that 'hold that respect for particular rights is a means for bringing about some optimal distribution of advantages'. 'A status-based justification ... begins with the nature of the rightholder and arrives immediately at the right. The instrumental approach starts with the desired consequences (like maximum utility) and works backward to see which rights-ascriptions will produce these consequences'. The dignitarian view is surely a version of the status-based conception. However, I believe that its complexity allows it to address the problems Wenar identifies for conceptions of this kind. For example, the dignitarian account does not move immediately from status to the flat assertion of specific rights. It requires that we inquire about how the interests linked

22 Human Dignity and Social Justice

One way to give even more structure to this exercise is to use a contractualist framework of reasoning. According to moral contractualism (quite roughly), everyone should follow the norms that no one could reasonably reject, or which everyone could rationally accept.[25] We can test the correctness and weight of various competing rights norms by considering what reasons those affected by their general implementation might have to accept or reject such implementation, and articulate judgements about the best specific application of the rights that reflect the strength of those reasons. References to the relative importance of the capacities affected would be a key input for the articulation of these reasons. Thus, for example, the capacities to make moral and political judgements have great weight in defending a right to political participation in which people can use them, and reasons invoking them may outweigh other reasons tracking the hedonistic enjoyment of those living under the relevant political decisions.

It might be objected that human dignity plays no crucial role in the justification of moral humanist rights. Once we identify the important interests in unfolding certain capacities, we can simply refer to them and drop reference to dignity. The idea of human dignity merely passes the buck to other ideas.[26] But human dignity does have a distinctive, structural contribution in this process. It helps organize our moral thinking so that it focuses on the claims that individuals have in social life given certain valuable features of them that give them the status of rights-bearers, and the challenges they face to unfold them. Either the buck is not fully passed, or we learn where and how it is to be passed—to discussion of individuals' morally important features, not conventional features like their nationality, class, race, etc. or to features which are morally indifferent like the colour of their eyes, bad like their cruelty, or

---

to the unfolding of the capacities at the basis of the status might be affected in the relevant circumstances and that we consider a plurality of those interests so that the possibility of a variety of pro tanto specific rights that might conflict is taken into account.

[25] For detailed articulation of moral contractualism, see Scanlon (1998) and Parfit (2011: ch.15). Notice that I do not take the contractualist framework as moral bedrock. Its role, as I see it, is to help operationalize the Dignitarian Approach. That we owe to each other a treatment that is mutually justifiable, and what reasons justify it in each case, depend on deeper dignitarian considerations. For more on my take on contractualism, see Gilabert (2012a; ch.2, ch.8; 2019a: ch.8).

[26] Consider the relations between the following points:

   (i) X has a moral humanist right to O.
  (ii) X has moral humanist rights.
 (iii) X has an interest in accessing O.
 (iv) X has capacities C1... Cn.
  (v) Capacities C1 ... Cn are valuable.
 (vi) Having access to O supports X's maintenance, development, or exercise of C1 ... Cn.
(vii) X has status-dignity.
(viii) C1 ... Cn are at the basis of X's dignity.

The objection I am addressing is that (vii) and (viii) do not add anything crucial to (i)–(vi).

not as important as to give rise to the standing of a rights-bearer. We can say that human dignity is a high-level moral property that we can refer to in order to articulate a certain form of deontological conception. This is a reflective theory of justice according to which humanist moral rights are appropriate responses to the valuable features of individual human beings. Dignity is a high-level consideration gathering or subsuming, and framing, reference to other, lower-level ones (such as the items in the basis of dignity in the relevant circumstances, the specific configurations of them in various individuals, and the nexus of norms stating appropriate responses they owe to each other). As such, dignity imposes several functional conditions on the evaluative basis and types of responses to individuals that are fitting.[27]

Dignity does not really drop out of the process of normative justification. It is not enough to say that (a) X has a moral humanist right to O because (b) X has an interest in accessing O, or accessing O contributes to the unfolding of a valuable capacity of X. We need also to note that (c) the interest and the capacity raise to the level of calling for morally obligatory responses. Reference to dignity, such as by saying that (d) X has status-dignity on the basis of the set of capacities C1, C2, ... Cn, helps articulate (c) and thus to screen relevant instances of (b) so that they succeed in the job of justifying (a). Therefore, reference to dignity is not normatively inert but does important work in our moral reasoning. In sum, and as this section has argued, reference to status-dignity and the basis of dignity helps us to identify a certain type of rights (moral humanist rights) and to determine the content and justification of various rights of this kind. If we didn't already have an idea like dignity to perform these roles, we would have to invent it.

2.2.2 Solidarity and the combination of positive and negative duties

As mentioned above, Solidaristic Empowerment involves both negative and positive duties. Status-dignity gives rise to both. It would be counterintuitive to say that the valuable features at the basis of dignity are appropriately responded to through omission of harm but never also through commission of aid. It would also be problematic to say that aid never raises to the level of obligations of justice. It is an advantage of the Dignitarian Approach that it sharply enables us to make these points clearly.

---

[27] Status-dignity is thus a structuring value property. Recall that it is inherent rather than conventional, pulls non-instrumental regard, is individualistic rather than collectivist, has high priority, and involves deontic constraints rather than mere aspirations or preferences. It thus marks the presence of a certain type of normative considerations, a moral relational normative nexus including directed obligations, correlative claims, and potential normative injuries among individuals with equal and final standing in so far as they can affect each other. On the idea of a relational normative nexus and its instantiation in interpersonal morality, see Wallace (2019).

24   Human Dignity and Social Justice

The idea of solidarity used here is a substantive proposal, not an analysis of the term 'solidarity'. There are in fact many uses of this term, not all of them compatible.[28] As I characterize it here, solidarity includes at least three important components. The first is the avoidance of harmful deprivation. I fail to be solidaristic towards you if I destroy, or block, the development and exercise of your valuable capacities—unless I have strong reasons to do that (the burden of proof is on me). Second, solidarity links up with cooperative mutual provision. When you and I cooperate in the production of some goods, we are ready to support each other's flourishing. But this readiness is not unconditional. I fail to be solidaristic if I benefit from your efforts without putting forward my own when I can do so. If I can but do not reciprocate, I fail to take seriously the significance of your own flourishing, and focus only on my own. This reciprocation need not be one of strict equivalence of output exchanged. What is important is fair reciprocity, that we exert similar levels of effort given what we can achieve. There is an element of altruism in this form of reciprocation. Consider the *Construction Site* case.[29] You and I are building a house, and we need to carry stones to the construction site. I am stronger than you, and thus it is easy for me to carry bigger stones. It would be obnoxious of me to say that we should schedule the transportation of stones so that we carry the same kind of stones when that would involve great hardship for you. We should give and take, but there is no problem in giving more than one takes if everybody is making appropriate efforts given their abilities.

There is a third component of solidarity (as I see it), which includes basic positive duties to help others facing grave deprivation, even if there is no exchange involved (and thus no expected reciprocation of any kind—even at a lower level of output). Consider the Sleepwalking Anna case. Anna is sleepwalking. She is heading down the corridor towards an open window. If she is not stopped by someone else, she will fall and die. She will not wake up even if screamed at, she can only be stopped by blocking her path. You are too far away to stop her in time. But I can do it. Do I have a duty to do so? Is this duty justifiably enforceable—say, may you push me against my will to make me fall in a way that blocks Anna's path even if that would injure my arm? Or, may you threaten me with breaking my arm unless I save Anna? It seems pretty clear that in this scenario I have a positive duty to help Anna. It would not do for me to tell you that I have a negative duty not to kill her—by, say, throwing her out the window—but not a positive duty to save her life—by blocking her path. It also seems true that if I do not save Anna in the feasible

---

[28] I survey some uses in Gilabert (2019a: 175–81).
[29] I develop this case from an example in Carens (2003: 155). For empirical research on cooperation and altruism, see Bowles and Gintis (2011).

The Dignitarian Approach   25

and not unreasonably costly way available to me, you are permitted to coerce me into saving her, even if you impose some costs on me. Again, it would not do to say that costs may only be imposed to enforce negative duties. Imagine that I said that even if I do have a positive duty to save Anna, I also have a liberty right to oppose the enforcement of such a duty by some external agent like you. I should surely be a decent person and help Anna, but I retain the right to resist your commandeering of my assistance if I choose to not give it. This kind of move is sometimes invoked to qualify rights stemming from necessity—if you are starving you have a moral right to try to take some of my abundant bread to eat, but I may legitimately resist. But it seems implausible at least in some cases. In the Sleepwalking Anna case, I do not have a liberty right to resist your incursion on me when I fail to help her as I should.

The foregoing are simply statements of my intuitions. However, my experience is that others agree (even if there is legitimate room of discussion, especially about what are justifiable and proportionate forms of coercion in this case). How can we explain these intuitions? The dignitarian framework provides useful resources. The basic general idea is this. If some features of an individual give rise to that individual's dignity, then any agent who can affect that individual must do so in appropriate ways that involve respect and concern for them. These appropriate ways of treating the individual include negative duties not to destroy or block what is valuable in the individual, such as the features forming the basis of their dignity. One cannot plausibly say that those features are so valuable as to give rise to dignity and yet generate no reason to not be harmful towards them. But if these features are valuable enough to generate negative duties, they are also likely to be valuable enough to generate some positive duties. This is the key claim. The valuable capacities in the basis of dignity that ground negative duties also ground positive duties. If the fact that an individual is capable of self-determination gives you reason not to dominate them, doesn't it also give you reason to protect them when others try to dominate them? If an individual's capacities to pursue a life including love, friendship, knowledge, or productive work gives you reason not to block their pursuit of those goods, don't they also give you reason to help make such pursuit more likely to succeed? What is valuable enough to give rise to dignity must be treated in helpful ways, not only in non-harmful ones. It is callous to believe that one has no positive duty to protect, or foster the development of, the valuable features that give rise to the dignity of people even when we are prepared to recognize that those features can be referred to in order to justify negative duties.

To avoid misunderstanding, notice that I am not saying that the positive duties mentioned are as weighty as the negative ones. What I say is compatible with holding that sometimes causing a harm is worse than not preventing it. The key point is to recognize that there are positive duties. Their specific content, weight, and role within our overall reasons for action is a further—and no doubt important—issue. Notice, also, that I distinguish the third category of duties of solidarity from the second. These basic positive duties involving no element of expected reciprocation are focused on situations that are extremely grievous. Finally, I do not say that solidarity prohibits every path of action that is not maximally beneficial to others (or to everyone considered from an impersonal point of view). I acknowledge that we have a personal prerogative to give some priority to ourselves.

The straightforward affirmation of positive in addition to negative duties allows us to distinguish the ideal of Solidaristic Empowerment from the common ideal of independence understood as self-reliance. Construed as self-reliance, independence is both infeasible and undesirable. The circumstances of dignity are such that people are typically unable to flourish, or even subsist, on their own. They are multiply vulnerable to harm and needy of assistance. They will not develop and exercise their valuable capacities if others do not support them. This is evident when we consider our situation when we are children, very ill, or when we approach the end of our lives. But it is in fact a pervasive feature of our biological and social predicament. Instead of promoting a moral culture that generates shame for those being helped, and guilt amongst those who aid them, we have reason to organize our social life so that we regularly help each other. Condition-dignity should be envisioned as a social state of respectful interdependence. Another idea sometimes associated with independence—the idea of self-determination—retains its significance, however. To be respectful, interdependence should proceed on certain terms: every individual involved should have a recognized right to shape the rules of mutual support, and these rules should give each appropriate levels of control of their own personal pursuits. Thus, it is problematic when a subset of the population makes all the crucial decisions about how to organize an economy, while the rest must simply follow them. In this economy, interdependence is shaped through domination. It is also problematic when some individuals are pushed by others to take up careers and lifestyles they hate when pursuing those they prefer would not involve violating the rights of others. In this society, interdependence is shaped through oppression and denial of personal freedom. Independence as self-reliance is infeasible and undesirable. But independence as self-determination—as the power to participate with others in selecting the general rules that organize our social life, and as the power to decide on our own how our personal life proceeds within it—is a crucial aspect of condition-dignity. The reason is that the capacities for prudential and moral judgement, when present, have a structuring role in shaping an individual's life. It is by unfolding them that an individual can thrive as an agent, with initiative and understanding. It is also by deploying these capacities that individuals can figure out whether they are living on terms that fit their own worth. Solidaristic Empowerment should be interpreted as yielding negative duties to refrain from suppressing self-determination, and positive duties to facilitate it.

2.2.3 Standing up (dignity and self-emancipation)

Dignitarian language can be fruitfully used to characterize the ways in which people react to social injustice. Dignity is particularly significant for understanding protest, activism, and anti-paternalistic politics. For example, a leader of the 'neo-Zapatista' movement in Mexico, Marcos, portrayed their uprising in 1996 to defend the rights of indigenous people in terms of 'insurrectional dignity' and 'rebel dignity'.[30] It is a common phenomenon for people to gain a sense of dignity when they stand up for their rights, and a sense of indignity when they are servile and submit to unjust treatment.

In agreement with Amartya Sen, I think that when we judge social processes we should not only assess their final results (their 'culmination outcome') but must also appraise the internal features of the process that leads to them. We should, in Sen's terms, illuminate 'comprehensive outcomes'.[31] Appraising whether certain actions 'make the world a better place' (as the common phrase goes) should include considering the internal features of the actions themselves. So, for example, of two political processes that lead to equivalent final results in terms of condition-dignity, if one of them reaches those results while engaging the self-determining agency of those affected while the other does not, we should prefer the former, as it is more responsive to the dignity of the people affected (to their capacities to reason and make choices about what is good and right). Thus, an act of 'rebel dignity' is intrinsically significant because it features agents enacting self-respect and self-esteem in the process of rebuilding their society. The rebels signal to themselves, and to others, that they are not available for abuse. It also gives those who mistreat them, and the bystanders laying around, an opportunity to do better. It may thus trigger a process in which people develop dignitarian virtue.

---

[30] The Spanish expressions are '*la dignidad insurrecta*' and '*la dignidad rebelde*'. See http://enlacezapatista.ezln.org.mx/1996/01/01/cuarta-declaracion-de-la-selva-lacandona/
[31] Sen (2009: 215–7).

28 Human Dignity and Social Justice

However, as Michael Blake has suggested in a paper about my earlier work on this topic, things do not always proceed so neatly.[32] Acts of rebellion in the face of injustice can sometimes prompt backlash and brutal responses, so that after they are undertaken there is more abuse overall. Importantly, that abuse may be visited not just upon the rebels, but upon other victims as well. Is rebel action with these prospective results (or the risk of them) still all things considered justifiable? We should hesitate to say that it always is. Also, like Blake, I think that we should avoid being unduly judgemental and sanctimonious towards individuals making decisions in horrendous circumstances, such as when they ponder whether to defy acts of daily humiliation and harm in concentration camps (as explored in Blake's poignant discussion drawing on texts by Primo Levi and Jean Améry on Nazi concentration camps). These individuals face very hard and tragic choices. I am inclined to cut them a lot of slack. My primary moral reaction is above all one of sorrow about their plight and of anger and condemnation towards the choices made by the more powerful people who put them in the binds they face, and who would respond to their defiance by making things even worse for them and for others. Still, none of this eliminates the important questions about the normative structure of ethically responsible action in response to injustice. These questions are often encountered, in more or less dramatic or tragic forms, by people trying to figure out how to act in non-ideal circumstances. My intuition, like Sen's, is that neither considerations focused on minimizing the badness of final results nor considerations focused on the internal features of the actions responding to injustice suffice on their own. Dignitarian virtue would require attention to both because they both are relevant responses to track the status-dignity of the people affected by the choices. How, more specifically, all things considered judgement should proceed, is a subject that deserves careful reflection.

2.2.4 The arc of humanist justice

Human dignity features prominently in human rights discourse. This is clearly the case in the central human rights documents. The first sentence of the Preamble of the Universal Declaration of Human Rights refers to the 'inherent dignity ... of all the members of the human family'. The fifth sentence expresses 'faith ... in the dignity and worth of the human person'. Article 1 states that '[a]ll human beings are born free and equal in dignity and rights' and that they 'are endowed with reason and conscience and should act

---

[32] Blake (2020: 320–2). I draw here on my response to Blake in Gilabert (2020: 339–40).

The Dignitarian Approach   29

towards one another in a spirit of brotherhood'. Before the Universal Declaration, the United Nations Charter expressed a commitment to 'reaffirm faith in fundamental human rights, in the dignity and worth of the human person, in the equal rights of men and women and of nations large and small'. Important documents following the Universal Declaration invoke human dignity as a grounding idea. The Preambles of the International Covenant on Civil and Political Rights and the International Covenant on Economic, Social, and Cultural Rights state that human rights 'derive from the inherent dignity of the human person'. Human rights documents also present specific rights in dignitarian terms. For example, the Universal Declaration construes 'economic, social and cultural rights as indispensable for [people's] dignity and the free development of [their] personality' (Art. 22).

Human rights discourse provided the context of my earlier work on the Dignitarian Approach. I first outlined the conceptual network of dignity and the central idea of status-dignity as a universal and non-conventional normative standing precisely in order to make sense of how this discourse presented humanist moral rights. But dignitarian justice can be more ambitious, and, in this book, I will explore the extension of the conceptual network and the substantive perspective of Solidaristic Empowerment to articulate claims of social justice that go beyond human rights.

The Dignitarian Approach can thus be used to cover the *arc of humanist justice*. It can serve not only to articulate claims of basic justice such as human rights, but also more encompassing ideals of social justice of the kind that liberal egalitarians and democratic socialists propose. The distinction between the two registers of humanist justice is hard to pin down. But it is intuitive.[33] Consider the rights of workers. Human rights include demands of basic dignity, such as that people have access to working activities; that this access be based on their choice rather than on coercive imposition; that working practices be devoid of discrimination on irrelevant considerations of gender, sexual orientation, or race; that conditions at work include adequate remuneration and proceed in healthy and secure environments; and that workers

---

[33] The distinction concerns the degree of relative urgency of the requirements invoked (which is a function of their relative moral importance, the feasibility of their implementation, and the costs they impose on duty-bearers). It is also dynamic, as its contents may change over time. In Gilabert (2019a: ch.11) I proposed a view, which I labelled a *'two-tiered dynamic humanism'*, according to which we should see humanist, dignitarian justice as having two parts. Human rights are the part ranging over the most urgent dignitarian requirements. These requirements are more than minimal requirements regarding subsistence and the avoidance of extreme oppression. They include, for example, rather ambitious labour rights and strong democratic political rights. But they stop short of democratic socialism or liberal egalitarianism. This is not because the principles of liberal egalitarianism and democratic socialism cannot be seen as humanist, dignitarian justice. In fact, I argue—briefly in that book but more extensively in this one—that humanist and dignitarian justice does generate such principles. They constitute the second part of the two-tiered view.

30 Human Dignity and Social Justice

be entitled to form unions and engage in political activities to defend their interests. But arguably workers can make justified claims to more than basic dignity and justice. They can envision maximal dignity. According to socialists, for example, the dignity of workers is also affronted when society cajoles them into activities that are alienating, and in which their employers exploit or dominate them. Full justice for workers should include real opportunities for productive activity that features the highest levels of self-realization and self-determination that are feasible and can be secured at reasonable cost for all. The economic process of social cooperation should be structured so that workers are not only asked to give, but are also entitled to receive, in fair ways. As I interpret it, the socialist slogan 'From each according to their abilities, to each according to their needs!' (the Abilities/Needs Principle) calls for forms of fair cooperation that empower workers to lead flourishing lives, not merely to survive and avoid the most egregious abuses which human rights discourse condemns. Socialists recommend an organization of the economy (a shaping of its relations of production and its social ethos) in which each contributes and benefits solidaristically, so that all equally can thrive.

As we will see in this book, the Dignitarian Approach is well-suited for extending the framework of dignity from the human rights context to more demanding forms of social justice. An important point about this extension is that, although there is indeed a difference between basic and maximal dignity and justice, there is also continuity between them. Noticing this has theoretical advantages, as we can use the conceptual and normative apparatus used for human rights to explain and defend requirements of liberal egalitarian and democratic socialist justice—showing that humanist moral rights do not only include individuals' access to a decent life but also their access to the most extensive flourishing life that is feasible and reasonable to support. There are also moral and political advantages. Construing left liberal and socialist ideals within a dignitarian framework that also grounds human rights is helpful for underscoring the universalism of social justice and the importance of civil and political liberties within it. We can thus guard against certain historical mistakes, such as those exhibited by versions of liberalism that took principles of social justice to apply domestically but not globally, and by some versions of socialism that neglected the importance of personal privacy, freedom of speech, and a democratic political process that is open to diverse and conflicting views.[34]

---

[34] So, on the dignitarian framework proposed here, we do not need to think of human rights as the last utopia, or take them to be enough. For these worries, see Moyn (2010; 2019). Instead of being seen as a substitute for relinquished ambitious aspirations of justice, human rights can be seen as an aspect of their reconfiguration. Something like this has arguably been at work in some actual political contexts, such as

2.2.5 Capturing the dialectic of generality and specificity

A final fruitful aspect of the Dignitarian Approach that I want to highlight is that it is both appropriately unifying and diversifying. It can help us track common concerns while also responding to specific dignitarian configurations without forcing Procrustean homogeneity across individuals.

When determining whether a certain principle or norm is correct, we can consider the various circumstances in which it would apply, and figure out whether the people affected by its fulfilment would have reason to accept or reject it. One possible approach to fleshing this out would be to say that the acceptance or rejection of a principle, to be reasonable rather than simply self-serving, must be based on shareable grounds—considerations that are compelling for everyone who would be affected by the implementation of the principle. These are reasons (and interests related to them) that everyone would have if placed in some position in which the principle under examination affected them.

But people may be affected by a principle in different ways. How can this be accounted for while still identifying shared reasons? A promising proposal to capture the complexity involved in considering various standpoints of different individuals has been provided by Scanlon by referring to 'generic reasons'.[35] In Scanlon's words, '[g]eneric reasons are reasons that we can see that people have in virtue of their situation, characterized in general terms, and such things as their aims and capabilities and the conditions in which they are placed'.[36] Thus, for example:

> We commonly take it that people have strong reasons to want to avoid bodily injury, to be able to rely on assurances they are given, and to have control over what happens to their own bodies. We therefore think it reasonable to reject principles that would leave other agents free to act against these important interests. Similarly, as agents we typically have reason to want to give special attention to our own projects, friends, family, and thus have reason to object to principles that would constrain us in ways that would make these concerns impossible.[37]

---

in the reconstruction of the Left in Latin America at the turn of the millennium. On the case of Argentina, see, e.g., Verbitsky (2019: ch.8).

[35] Scanlon (1998: 204–6). Scanlon uses the notion of 'interest' to track the generic personal reasons of the people affected by principles. Another, similar, proposal is to rely on 'generalizable interests' (to be discovered in argumentative dialogue). See Habermas (1975; 1992). Habermas's notion of an 'interest' is not fully developed, and at times seems to be narrower than Scanlon's (focusing only on conditions of well-being, or what would be good for the relevant persons).

[36] Scanlon (1998: 204).

[37] Ibid: 204.

32 Human Dignity and Social Justice

Take a schematic principle P, which says that in circumstances F people A should do X to people B. Instances of this scheme would be, for example, that people should do for others what they promised to them to do, that every citizen should pay their share of taxes to fund health care for citizens who need it, that you should rescue someone facing a life-threatening ordeal if you can do it at moderate cost, and so on. The As and the Bs can be coextensive or disjointed. What is key is that all of them must be able to recognize that there is sufficient reason to accept P. If some reasons against P flowing from the standpoint of the As conflict with those in favour of P that flow from the standpoint of the Bs, for example, all of them should be able to recognize that the latter reasons are stronger. The promisors see that the inconvenience of having to do what they promised is less weighty that the insecurity of not being able to count on others keeping their word, and so on. (We should also compare P to alternative principles that could apply instead, but I will here set aside this issue to simplify the discussion.)

This approach seems more sensitive than one focused on strictly identical reasons, as the appraiser of a principle is asked to take into account the specificities of the standpoint of other people, which may not be the same as their own. Generic reasons are not uniform across individuals in that they are not independent of their 'aims and capabilities and the conditions they are placed in'. The appraiser is asked to identify reasons that are generic for individuals *as shaped by such features of their standpoints.* These reasons are not, in this way, strictly universal or shared by all individuals from their specific perspectives. Still, every reasoner could recognize their significance when engaging in impartial, reasonable moral reasoning. Thus, a shared view across all reasoners that a generic reason does justify accepting or rejecting a principle is possible.

Now a difficulty arises. What if the relevant individuals affected by P in the same position (the As and the Bs, say) are significantly different in such a way that they have different important bundles of reasons and interests? For example, not all might have the same valuable capacities. Some might have capacities of reasoning which others with cognitive disabilities do not have. If we insist in only focusing on generic reasons picking out shared reasons and interests, we could fail to find any, or we could miss important clusters of reasons and interests of subsets of persons who would be significantly affected by P. Two sufficiently different individuals, even if they were to be in the same position in which they are affected by some principle, might have different reasons to accept it or reject it.

It might be said that this difficulty is avoided by saying that when an individual considers whether they have reason to reject a principle if they were

The Dignitarian Approach   **33**

to adopt the standpoint of someone affected by it in a certain situation, and that someone turned out to be *someone else*, then the former is to proceed on the basis of all that is specific to the latter, including not just the external circumstances but also the particularities of the latter's 'internal' configuration of capacities (which may be different from those of the former). But then it would not be guaranteed that the reasons unearthed are shareable in the sense of uniform across different individuals. We might have a heap of particular reasons for different individuals. At the very least, we need more clarity about how the counterfactual regarding what 'one would have reason to object to a principle if placed in a certain position in which one would be affected by its implementation' would be built on. What is to be held as constant and what as variable in this exercise?

A sensible approach, at least in theory, would be to concentrate on responding appropriately to the configurations of valuable capacities of those that might be affected by the principle in the relevant circumstances, and to identify the reasons and interests linked to them, even when such reasons and interests are not uniform (and are thus not shared in a strict sense). What is key on this view is to avoid egotistic reasoning and to be truly responsive to others given their dignity (and thus the valuable capacities at the basis of *their* dignity).

Now, we could still identify some very abstract generic reasons and interests which seem strictly shareable, such as to be able to develop and exercise one's valuable capacities, whichever they are. This is a very general consideration that would be shared by people with different sets of capacities. But, although correct and important, such abstract statements will have to be given more specific renderings in order to articulate and assess principles in various circumstances so as to have enough content to orientate behaviour.

At this point, we find ourselves caught in a dialectic of abstraction and specification, sometimes wanting to go for greater abstraction to identify a unified perspective that includes all the individuals affected, sometimes wanting to go for greater specificity to capture what is important for the individuals involved on account of their diversity.[38] This dialectic is in fact fruitful, and both abstraction and specification are valuable so long as we keep in mind the roles they are to play in the normative exercise (which are, respectively, the inclusion of all individuals affected and sensitivity to significant differences between them). Most satisfactory normative exercises

---

[38] Scanlon recognizes this point, saying that we may sometimes want to make the relevant principles more fine-grained to capture more specific positions and standpoints of people affected by them. See Scanlon (1998: 205). Thus, my discussion is not meant as a criticism of Scanlon's proposal, but as a further elaboration of it.

34 Human Dignity and Social Justice

will indeed need both.[39] The reference to the more abstract statements would be useful to show that the principles argued for do not unfairly, or arbitrarily, favour some individuals rather than others. And the specifications would spell out what the appropriate, diverse implications for different individuals would consist of. We can thus explain how the different specific requirements track morally significant differences between the individuals under consideration (their different configurations of valuable capacities as engaged in the circumstances).[40]

Thus, very roughly and schematically, we could identify structures like following. We could state quite general principles and generic reasons like these: P1: 'We should, to the extent that we reasonably can, support every individual in the unfolding of their valuable capacities'; G1: 'Implementing P would help people develop and exercise their valuable capacities—and the interest they have in this'. Elaborating on these considerations, we could generate more specific principles such as P2: 'We should support people A in the unfolding of their capacities C1 and C2 and support people B in the unfolding of their capacities C3 and C4'. We can move from P1 to P2 by making the normative claim N: 'C1, C2, C3, and C4 are valuable capacities at the basis of dignity', and the empirical claim E: 'The people in set A have C1 and C2 and the people in set B have C3 and C4' (plus other relevant considerations about the support called for in P2 being feasible and not undercut or outweighed by other normative considerations).

I want to insist on the importance of the point about capturing diversity. For the Dignitarian Approach this is important, as it has, at the fundamental level, an *individual-centred focus*. If an individual has a specific configuration of valuable capacities that is different from that present in ten other individuals, and a principle P potentially affecting these eleven persons must be assessed, it would be wrong to focus only on what is shared by all, or most of them. The first individual might have valid reasons and interests leading them

---

[39] Another theoretical device could be to conditionalize the statements of reasons and interests, following a schema like 'If individual I has capacity C and thus an interest in its development and exercise, then I has an interest in fostering that capacity, and reason to favour principles that support this fostering'. These statements could be universal, and would not be false but simply not applicable to individuals without the capacities and interests stated. But there is a danger that these statements would be trivially true when the antecedent is false. Furthermore, we have to consider the holistic nature of reasons and interests, as their content and weight partly depend on the fact that the configurations of capacities in the circumstances involve various interactions. Perhaps the conditionalization can be formulated so as to capture these complexities. I will not pursue this possibility further here.

[40] We can thus honour the intuition regarding fairness requiring that we avoid making morally arbitrary distinctions between people when assessing principles that might benefit some more than others. On this intuition, see Scanlon (1998: 209–13). The reference to the affected individuals' configurations of capacities in their circumstances provides a substantive moral rationale which is not arbitrarily self-serving. Hence, some requirements which are not completely general (by, e.g., focusing on how to benefit a specific set of people with certain health care needs) need not be for that reason unfair.

The Dignitarian Approach **35**

to reasonably reject P if its fulfilment curtails the development and exercise of the valuable capacities of this individual but not those of others, while some other principle that can be applied in the circumstances would cater for the whole spectrum of diverse capacities (and thus for the individuals who have them).

This account can be used to respond to worries about that the dignitarian perspective is unduly exclusionary when it comes to people with diverse abilities. In a recent paper on my book *Human Dignity and Human Rights*, Michael Blake offers a powerful exploration of what he calls the 'hermeneutics of dignity'. 'We must', he argues, 'in explaining whether or not a particular life is lived in the conditions of dignity, pay attention to the *meaning* ascribed to particular parts of that life; how such meaning is ascribed makes a difference, quite often, between the presence of a dignified form of life and its absence'.[41] My book did not offer any sustained discussion of this dimension of condition-dignity, and Blake is right that doing so would be important. As his own lively discussion shows, addressing the hermeneutic dimension— the stories people tell about themselves and others to characterize their predicament—would help illuminate significant specific practical challenges. Extending the Dignitarian Approach to cover hermeneutic issues is indeed a worthy project. I briefly want to make two points about how the approach could help in considering these issues.

The first point concerns the issue of how general or specific should the stories about people's predicament be. It is important, I think, to note that here we face desiderata pushing in opposite directions. On the one hand, when we develop views about human rights and social justice, we should want to be able to make generalizations that permit us to address the injustices faced by large groups of people, within a society and across borders. For example, to identify and defend labour rights (to access safe and healthy working conditions, to form unions and strike, and so on), we should be able to talk about recurrent threats faced by workers in a sweatshop in Dhaka just as much as in an Amazon warehouse in New York. This pushes us in the direction of making quite general claims. But, on the other hand, we should also want to illuminate the more specific concerns of people facing particular challenges which are not shared by most, or even many, other people. The situation of people with disabilities, addressed by Blake, is a case in point. Just as the discourse of human rights and social justice makes quite general statements about human rights like the Universal Declaration, it increasingly puts forward more specialized statements, like the Convention on the Rights

---

[41] Blake (2020: 317). I draw here on Gilabert (2020: 338–9).

of Persons with Disabilities. Now, I think that the Dignitarian Approach can justify both desiderata, and orientate us in their fulfilment. What is fundamentally important for this approach is to recognize that we have reason to respond with solidarity (in feasible and reasonable ways) to the challenges faced by each *individual* regarding the maintenance, development, and exercise of the valuable capacities at the basis of *their* dignity. We should, as we might say, scope for status-dignity wherever it lies, and in whatever form it takes. The bundles of valuable capacities of various people may overlap in many respects, but also be disjoint in others. They may also be combined in diverse configurations. To fully respond appropriately to their status-dignity, and to further condition-dignity for them, would require that both respects and their combination be attended to. Dignitarian norms, and their application to cases, can correspondingly be quite plural, and have the content needed to track the interests and challenges that the people to whom they apply face (some more common, some less so, depending on their bundles of capacities and the contours of their material and social circumstances). There is no need for the dignitarian perspective to ignore the differences between people's valuable capacities and between the challenges they face as they seek to flourish with them. Quite the contrary. Attunement to difference is an ingredient of the solidaristic stance to human rights and justice recommended by the Dignitarian Approach.

To discover what is relevant to articulate dignitarian norms, and to motivate compliance with them, it is indeed worth paying attention to stories about people's various common and different predicaments. I think, and this is my second point, that the Dignitarian Approach can help us illuminate the question (foregrounded by Blake), of *whose* stories should matter. There is a sense in which everyone's stories matter, and another sense in which some people's stories are especially important. Everyone's hermeneutic engagement with the issue of what dignitarian norms should be recognized and honoured matters for various reasons. Since the norms should be binding on every agent, it is important that they can all have their say as to whether any proposed norm ought to be followed by them. This is so, first, because self-determination is an important dignitarian consideration. Other things equal, to circumvent it is an affront to people who can make prudential and moral judgements, a treatment of them as norm-followers and decision-takers who may not also be norm-assessors and decision-makers. Their judgements about the relevant matters, which includes their hermeneutical engagement with them, must be given a hearing. Second, nobody has an epistemic crystal ball. Every story is likely to include mistakes and blind spots, which could be revealed if others also voice their views and stories in a respectful dialogue which is at the same time critical and constructive.

The Dignitarian Approach   37

In another sense, however, the stories of the people who are most affected by the issues under discussion should have special (albeit defeasible) weight. As Blake's contribution reveals with its discussion of autism, it may be hard to understand and appreciate the significance of the challenges some people undergo unless we pay attention to their lived experience of those challenges and their insights about how best to overcome them. Judging the predicament faced by an autistic person by simply trying to figure out how close their life can be made to be that of a 'normal' person would miss what exactly the configuration of their valuable capacities calls for in their circumstances, which may be qualitatively different, and not for that reason worse, than what the majority of other people need. Having said this, I would warn against a blanket deference to the stories people tell about themselves. Some such stories may be deeply problematic. Consider a situation in which a privileged individual reacts negatively to demands that they treat underprivileged people as equals rather than, condescendingly, as mere minions to be ordered around or as disposable objects to be completely ignored when they are no longer useful, and says that it would be 'undignified' for them to change their ways, given that their sense of self is hermeneutically bound up with membership in a ruling class with certain special prerogatives that allow them to do these things. We should not have to defer to this individual's narrative, but should instead feel free to recommend that it be revised (together with the social structures that underpin it). Here again the Dignitarian Approach is helpful. Since it takes status-dignity to be an inherent, non-conventional normative status that is independent from subjective attitudes towards it, it provides objective grounds to challenge attitudes (and stories) that fail to give that status the responses that it deserves. Some stories are just bad, not because of who tells them, but because their content is unresponsive to rights people have in virtue of their status-dignity (rather than in virtue of their conventional or customary social standing), which may not be ignored.[42]

3. From Basic to Maximal Justice. The Case of Justice at Work

To show how the Dignitarian Approach helps us cover the arc of humanist justice, in this book I will concentrate on the just structuration of working

---

[42] An interesting issue here is whether the dignitarian perspective can illuminate the normative critique of alienation. A valuable capacity that many people have is the capacity to develop a rich and positive sense of self. Opportunities for and states of successful self-identification would be important for them to enjoy condition-dignity. But such self-identification, to have normative weight, must be appropriate (i.e. track the various prudential and moral reasons that bear on it). I explore this topic in Chapter 5.

38 Human Dignity and Social Justice

practices. Human dignity is widely considered to be central to human rights and labour law, and is regularly invoked by social movements and organizations with liberal or socialist orientations. Surprisingly, however, the content of the idea of human dignity and its precise implications for labour rights remain unclear and underexplored. This book aims to fill these gaps.

3.1 Labour rights

Labour rights, such as rights to freely chosen rather than forced employment, to safe and rewarding working conditions, and to form and join unions, are gaining traction in debates about human rights and social justice. These debates arise partly in response to the increasingly fragile predicament of workers in contemporary capitalist societies (rich and poor alike). Global neoliberal capitalism has fostered policies that weaken the protection of labour rights by reducing governmental regulations of the labour market, by hampering unions and other forms of workers' associational power, and by sustaining forms of production that are intensely harmful to workers. A dramatic showcase of these phenomena occurred in 2013 in Dakar, Bangladesh, when a building containing garment factories collapsed, killing over 1100 workers. Management knew that the building was unsafe, but cajoled workers to enter it through various threats. Significantly, garment workers' ability to unionize was restricted at the time, and governmental protections were insufficient.[43] Sweatshop production in these factories was integrated to a global supply chain linking these workers with brands, retailers, and consumers around the world.

Working conditions are also hard in countries of the Global North. The case of Amazon is emblematic. Its founding CEO, Jeff Bezos, was at one point the world's richest man. But blue-collar workers in the warehouses face gruelling schedules, recurrent workplace injuries, and are forced to pee into bottles.[44]

---

[43] See Lu, 'Worker Rights, Structured Vulnerabilities and Global Labor Justice'. Two years after these events, workers' rights were reported to be routinely violated. An investigation says that '[w]orkers report violations including physical assault, verbal abuse—sometimes of a sexual nature—forced overtime, denial of paid maternity leave, and failure to pay wages and bonuses on time or in full. Despite recent labor law reforms, many workers who try to form unions to address such abuses face threats, intimidation, dismissal, and sometimes physical assault at the hands of factory management or hired third parties'. Mitu Datta, a garment factory worker in Chittagong describes an attack on his wife and him outside the factory as follows: 'Four people were holding me and beating me on the legs with bars and two people were beating her with iron bars. She was beaten on her head and on her back. Her arms were severely injured and bleeding. Bones of one of her fingers were broken. She had to get 14 stitches on her head. When they were beating up Mira, they were saying "You want to do unions activities? Then we will shower you with blood"'. Human Rights Watch (2015).

[44] Bloodworth (2018); Pollard (2018): Sainato (2020); Thompson (2013). See further Anderson (2017: 128–9).

The Dignitarian Approach **39**

The right to unionization is sometimes curtailed.[45] White-collar workers are encouraged to scheme against each other, using an 'Anytime Feedback Tool' widget to report to management on other workers' failures as they try to emerge on top at the end of each year's round of performance evaluations and layoffs.[46] In the more specific context of the coronavirus pandemic in 2020, Amazon in the US, after paying 'almost no taxes' the previous year, offered '*unpaid* time off for workers who are sick and just two weeks paid leave for workers who test positive for the virus. Meanwhile, it demands its employees put in mandatory overtime'.[47] A worker leading protests against the sanitary conditions at Amazon was fired.[48] A vice-president of Amazon resigned after three whistle-blowers complaining about the conditions of safety for Amazon's workers were laid off.[49] A month earlier, Bezos 'saved himself from larger losses by selling a big chunk of his Amazon shares ... before the worldwide scale of the coronavirus crisis was fully acknowledged and before the stock market collapsed'.[50] A few months into the pandemic, his wealth increased dramatically as online purchases through Amazon skyrocketed.[51]

In *Human Dignity and Human Rights*, I offered a philosophical exploration of the nature and grounds of basic labour rights of the kind patently violated in Dakar's garment factories and the Amazon warehouses. In this book, I continue the exploration to include workers' more expansive (or maximal) rights to have real options to engage in work that avoids or minimizes alienation, exploitation, and domination. Assuming the importance of the basic rights that are relevant for having a decent life, I will mostly concentrate on rights to access the conditions for a more fully flourishing life. So, my exploration goes beyond what are often regarded as human rights.

What are labour rights? It is not easy to give a canonical statement of them. There are several reasons for this. First, labour rights can be moral, legal, and/or political. We should not assume, for example, that the best way to articulate them is always through legal codes. Although legal implementation

---

[45] *The Economist* (2020).
[46] Kanto and Streitfeld (2015).
[47] Reich (2020).
[48] Evelyn (2020).
[49] "'They're always talking about customer obsession, and they really mean it," [Tim Bray] said. "We all love the speed and convenience of what Amazon offers." The problem, he says, is that there is nothing in place to stop them from taking advantage of low-level employees to turn a profit. "Our whole economy is focused on growth and efficiency, and the stress and strain on the people at the bottom of the pyramid just doesn't bear enough weight in that equation," he said' Peterson and Mesley (2020).
[50] 'There is no suggestion that Bezos acted improperly by selling the shares or that he was acting on non-public information about the impact of the pandemic. But his timing was near-perfect' Neate (2020a).
[51] Neate (2020b).

40 Human Dignity and Social Justice

is often crucial,[52] sometimes it is infeasible or undesirable.[53] Second, rights can be stated at different levels of abstraction. It is helpful to distinguish between more general and core normative ideas and more specific requirements that implement those ideas in particular social and historical contexts. The boundaries here are not precise. For example, should the normative ideas presuppose the existence of a modern industrialized economy, and, if so, should we assume that it is a capitalist one? Even within capitalism, there are important differences between the organization of production that existed around the middle of the twentieth century and the forms that capitalism displays today (with, for example, intense financialization and globalization, growing inequality of income and wealth, labour contracts and jobs that are becoming increasingly precarious, and decision-making structures and career paths within firms that are more complex and flexible).[54] Finally, a third complication concerns the ambitiousness of the normative ideals about how to arrange labour conditions. For example, we could focus on human rights understood as the most urgent and basic requirements of decent labour, or we could focus on more ambitious requirements of social justice about opportunities for flourishing at work.

My concern in this book is with philosophical issues about the normativity of labour rights (although I will also be sensitive to some relevant scientific and policy considerations). The main philosophical goal is to provide a defence of claims of justice at work based on the idea of human dignity. I understand labour rights as moral humanist rights, which are primarily moral requirements that hold independently of their effective legal or political recognition and implementation, but acknowledge that such a recognition and implementation is often, in modern contexts, a key part of what their fulfilment requires. To further narrow the scope of my discussion, I will concentrate on formulations of rights that are either relevant within a contemporary capitalist economy or can be seen as prompting discussion about social change pointing beyond capitalism. Finally, I will primarily focus on

---

[52] One reason for this is that corporations are unlikely to comply with self-imposed, non-legally binding regulations protecting workers. Locke (2013). Alston (2005: 22) reports that the International Organization of Employers has opposed moving beyond voluntary codes of conduct or introducing independent monitoring of labour standards. See further Deakin (2011).

[53] On these difficulties and on the significance of mechanisms different from legal codes, see Davidov and Langille (2011: chs.15–18). On the historical and geographical diversity of labour law, see Arthurs (2011) and Supiot (2011).

[54] On the distinction between abstract and specific rights, see Gilabert (2011b). Another debatable issue concerns the very definition of work. I use here a fairly ecumenical definition according to which work is an intentional activity of production of goods or services that can satisfy needs or desires. I defend this definition and explore in more detail the issue of the relation between more abstract and more specific labour human rights in Gilabert (2019a: ch.9). For difficulties regarding the specificity of these rights see Collins (2011:143–4).

The Dignitarian Approach **41**

non-basic or maximal labour rights. In the remainder of his section, I summarize the argument for basic labour rights (developed more extensively in my previous work), and present in outline the project regarding maximal rights, which will be developed in this book.

3.2 Basic labour rights

Basic labour rights target support for decent work. Important examples are the rights enshrined in Articles 23–24 of the Universal Declaration of Human Rights and in Articles 6–9 of the International Covenant on Economic, Social and Cultural Rights. Three types of such rights are the following:

(a) Rights regarding access to work (including, for example, opportunities for employment, free choice of employment, non-discrimination in hiring, and some security in holding jobs).

(b) Rights regarding decent conditions at work (such as adequate remuneration, equal pay for equal work, safe and healthy conditions, and rest and holidays).

(c) Rights to form and join unions, and to strike.

These rights are practically salient around the world. The catastrophe in Dakar mentioned above contains problems regarding all three. High unemployment in Europe and worldwide human trafficking for sexual exploitation engage (a). Recent campaigns in the USA and Canada to increase the minimum wage link up to (b). And, everywhere, labour activists are trying to explore new ways to organize workers in precarious and flexible positions as well as maintain, regain, or expand their base in large corporations.

Labour rights can be given a first defence by showing that their fulfilment supports people in the satisfaction of important interests. We can deploy this justificatory strategy by addressing three questions. The first is 'Why is work valuable?' Answering this question helps us defend rights of type (a). The significance of access to work is revealed once we identify important interests in certain goods which work can deliver. The following seems to me a plausible list:[55]

---

[55] Gilabert (2019a: 239–43) (including references). See also Mantouvalou (2015). The Supreme Court of Canada affirmed that employment gives workers 'a means of financial support and, as importantly, a contributory role in society', as well as a sense of 'identity, self-worth, and emotional well-being' *Reference Re Public Service Employee Relations Act (Alta)*, [1987] 1 SCR 313 at para 91, Dickson CJC dissenting; affirmed *Health Services and Support—Facilities Subsector Bargaining Assn v British Columbia*, 2007 SCC 27, [2007] 2 SCR 39. Arthurs (2011: 20).

I1 *Consumption goods*: Consumption goods and services securing (at least) subsistence.

I2 *Self-development*: Unfolding of productive abilities.

I3 *Socializing*: Creating social bonds with other people in shared activities.

I4 *Contribution*: Furthering the well-being of others by helping produce goods and services that satisfy their needs or desires.

I5 *Self-esteem and self-respect*: Sustaining the sense of one's own worth.

The goods tracked by I1 are obviously crucial. Without access to subsistence goods we cannot survive, and carrying out most of our plans involves using consumption goods of various sorts. The goods tracked by I5 are also crucial, as we can hardly pursue any project if we do not take ourselves to be worthy of the well-being it might bring about. I5 relates to the other interests in complex ways. Its satisfaction is partly a function of the satisfaction of the other interests, as we often develop a sense of self-esteem and self-respect as a result of succeeding in tasks delivering the goods tracked by I1–I4, and, in reverse, when we have self-esteem and self-respect, we muster greater willpower to engage in the activities and relationships that cater for those interests.

Interests I2–I4 also strike me as quite important. Part of their importance consists in their instrumental significance for achieving I5. But they have independent significance as well. We can affect our surrounding environment through productive activities that engage our imagination, creativity, knowledge, and other valuable physical, emotional, and intellectual capacities. Developing and exercising such capacities involves achievements that are often important sources of satisfaction for us. We are also social creatures for whom relationships with others are central to our well-being. One reason some jobs are undesirable is that they involve intense isolation, or toxic interpersonal relationships (including harassment, cut-throat competition, backbiting, and so on).[56] Finally, concern for others also surfaces if we consider the importance of the fact that our productive activities generate goods that meet their needs or desires. Sometimes we choose a job precisely because it offers a significant opportunity to deploy our abilities to increase the well-being of others besides our own. Doctors in public health care facilities provide a telling example.[57]

---

[56] On the predicament of workers in precarious jobs, see Thompson (2013). On the harsh conditions for workers in large factories in China, see Duhigg and Barboza (2012). Psychological harm is experienced not only by blue-collar workers in sweatshops, but also by white-collar workers in organizations imposing a toxic social environment. Recall the example of Amazon's 'Anytime Feedback Tool'.

[57] Dr. Mastracci, who left a top US hospital to work in a public hospital in the UK, explains her motives as follows. 'I wanted to work in the NHS because it is a publicly funded and provided healthcare system. To me, access to health care is a fundamental human right. Everyone in the world should have access to it

The second question is 'What are the features that work should have if it is to be valuable in the ways mentioned?' By answering this question, we provide an account of the importance of rights of type (b). They support access to work that delivers on interests I1–I5. Decent work would thus provide adequate remuneration, be devoid of harassment, furnish opportunities for advancement and development of skills, etc. Some interest other than I1–I5 will also be relevant. Thus, to justify limitations on working hours and vacations (with pay if needed to afford them), we can also invoke important interests to be able to participate in the political and cultural life of one's society, and to cultivate personal relationships such as family and friendship.[59]

It could be objected that work is not necessary for satisfying I1–I5. But in most contemporary societies not enough of the attributes tracked by I1–I5 is likely to be accessible for most people independently of work. Even after ambitious reforms, such as the introduction of a universal basic income, work catering for these interests would still occur. This would happen through formal employment that gives workers better conditions (including greater satisfaction of I1–I5 than is currently available) or through care work at home or in the community (or other working activities falling outside the standard labour market). Work plays a crucial role in accessing the five sets of goods mentioned, and cannot be fully substituted by other mechanisms at reasonable cost for most people in (at least) contemporary circumstances.[58]

The third question is 'What do workers need to ensure that their labour conditions will indeed be decent?' Answering this question helps us defend labour rights of type (c). Social science and historical experience support the claim that workers are far less secure in the enjoyment of their rights of type (a) and (b) if they do not boost their bargaining power in their negotiations with employers and their ability to affect the broader political process of society. Unionization rights, and other associational and political rights, increase workers' clout. This is an extremely important instrumental argument to accept rights of type (c). Unless they have rare and highly demanded skills, isolated individual workers are very vulnerable in the labour market, and have much less power than capitalists to influence the political processes

---

... I have a great deal of respect for the NHS and the way it delivers care to every member of society—all walks of life ... [H]ere I have treated everyone from homeless people to celebrities. I like the fact that the NHS has guiding principles and values—almost a moral compass—and is a fair system, where treatment is on the basis of need, not ability to pay'. 'I love this system because there is a general feeling of caring. Other places may have nicely appointed rooms and a great deal of resources, but here that kind of compassion is integral to the success of health care' Mastracci (2016).

[58] Gilabert (2019a: 248–51).

[59] We should also acknowledge the good of free, discretionary time—which could be invested in or out of work. See Rose (2016).

44 Human Dignity and Social Justice

leading to economic legislation that affects them. In addition, it is intrinsically important that workers be able to shape the social process structuring their working conditions as active agents who are protagonists in their own life stories rather than mere recipients of more powerful agents' designs (however benevolent they turn out to be).

Workers need to be able to act collectively. Some workers might complain that they should not be obliged to join a union, or pay fees to support it. An issue here is whether the liberty of these workers is unduly limited by these regulations. One response is that there is no limitation because there is no liberty claim to choose whether to support a union. Another response is that there is a limitation, but that the liberty limited is not significant. Yet another response is that although a significant liberty is limited, the limitation is all things considered justified because it is necessary for, or strongly contributory to, the protection of workers' rights (including other liberties, or their freedom overall). It is worth exploring each of these possible responses. I find the last to be the most promising. Normative considerations often make conflicting demands in practice. In contemporary societies, honouring an individual liberty not to associate is in tension with the fulfilment of workers' right to access just working conditions. Given deep structural inequalities with capitalists and standard collective action problems and free-riding, workers' rights can realistically be enjoyed in a reliable way only if collective agents like unions are set up and sustained to defend them.[60]

Although revealing and consequential, the foregoing reference to interests is not enough for defending labour rights. We need additional considerations to show that the agents who can affect workers' access to the goods catering for those interests owe them support in gaining and maintaining this access. There is a logical gap between interests and rights. To traverse it, we need to deploy an idea that has a foot on both ends of it. This idea must have both evaluative and deontic dimensions; it should both help us think about what people have reason to do to increase their well-being and what they owe to each other.

As pointed out above (in 2.2.1), one of the advantages of the Dignitarian Approach is that it provides a bridging principle to accomplish this.[61] By deploying the Bridge Principle and the Schema of Dignitarian Justification we can provide the additional argument needed for a robust case for labour

---

[60] The rights to strike and collective negotiation can be seen as 'individual rights whose exercise is collective' Supiot (2011: 82–3, 95)—my translation. Importantly, workers also need to defend their rights vis-à-vis the state (either as an employer or when it fails to regulate the economy in supportive ways). I thank Christian Barry for discussion on this.

[61] See further Gilabert (2019a: 204–9).

rights. We can do so by linking interests I1–I5 (and other relevant interests) to the important capacities that ground people's status-dignity. Specifically, the robust defence of labour rights would identify the institutions and practices, the interests, and the capacities targeted in this schema as they concern the life of workers. It involves showing that labour rights are indeed dignitarian norms, i.e. that their fulfilment is either necessary for, or strongly contributory to, the feasible and reasonable support for important interests linked to the valuable capacities of workers.

It is beyond the scope of this chapter to provide a detailed demonstration of how each putative labour right is justified. But I do want to give the reader a sense of why the proposed explanatory strategy is worthwhile. The appeals to human dignity and Solidaristic Empowerment are fruitful for the defence of labour rights (as well as other rights) in at least four important ways. The first concerns the deontic strengthening of the justification of rights in terms of human interests. By drawing on dignity, we can more easily move from interests to rights, from the good to the obligatory. The key idea is that since the interests I1–I5 are linked to valuable capacities that give rise to status-dignity, responding to status-dignity as Solidaristic Empowerment requires would call for taking steps to support the interests people have regarding the maintenance, development, and exercise of their valuable capacities. The satisfaction of I1 is evidently linked to all the capacity-related interests, as subsistence and access to consumption goods is a precondition for engaging in most projects that fulfil those interests. Significantly, the dignitarian strategy would boost the case for rights supporting I2–I4. Amongst the most important human capacities are the capacities for creative production, social cooperation, and to act to further the well-being of other people. Arranging work in ways that cater for I2–I4 would support people's interests in developing and exercising such capacities. I5, in turn, is dependent in part on people's capacity for self-appraisal on prudential and moral grounds. Since some of these appraisals target people's working activities, when labour rights are fulfilled, people's capacity for self-appraisal is to that extent positively engaged. These points boost the case for rights of type (a) and (b).

The dignitarian perspective also helps strengthen the case for rights of type (c)—the rights to unionization and other forms of associational power for workers. Understood as requiring solidaristic empowerment, dignity clearly links to the importance to workers of being able to stand tall in their negotiations with various agents that might significantly affect their labour conditions. When they are given chances to be protagonists in the shaping of their working conditions, workers' capacities for practical judgement are given proper recognition. Furthermore, their ability to defend their rights

46 Human Dignity and Social Justice

in an inegalitarian economy are enhanced. There seems to be a correlation between unionization and reduction of income inequality. Both have been in decline in many countries after the aggressive anti-union policies imposed by the neoliberal push that began in the 1980s. An ideological view gained traction according to which 'corporations are a natural feature of market economies, while unions are an alien intrusion'.[62] But both are social constructions. They can and should be shaped on the basis of sound normative considerations that track workers' empowerment. We should counter anti-union policies and the legal rules that shape corporations in ways that unjustly disadvantage workers. Other forms of political empowerment of workers in the larger political process would also be appropriate. If that process is domesticated by corporations funding politicians' campaigns, offering them jobs before and after they are in office, and threatening to leave the country (and stop paying taxes and creating jobs) if governments impose regulations that limit their power and profits, then workers' enjoyment of their basic labour rights will not be secure.

Of course, much more should be said to articulate the palette of specific labour rights in particular social contexts. But these remarks should be enough to give the reader a sense of how the deontic boosting of the interests-based arguments would proceed. If we do not support the satisfaction of certain important human interests when we can do so at reasonable cost it is not just those interests that are set back. In addition, we are failing to give the people who have those interests the treatment that is owed to them. The object of the interests precisely concerns the development and exercise of capacities that ground their standing to claim rights and that imposes on us obligations to enact respect and concern for them. If we neglect the interests, we also fail to give them the respect and concern we owe to them.

Second, human dignity helps us to account for the universality of some rights. This is so because human dignity is a universal status that all human beings possess independently of their position within any conventional social framework. When we construe labour rights in terms of the support for important capacities, we avoid a parochial focus limited to the 'near and dear'. Every human being who works or can work becomes salient and deserves our moral attention. In the current context of economic globalization, the Dignitarian Approach helps us to adopt an appropriately universalist perspective.[63] We can thus illuminate our duties towards all vulnerable workers, including

---

[62] Quiggin (2016). Corporations (and their power structures) are social and legal constructs that impose conditions on the bargaining between workers and employers at the point of the labour contract (Anderson 2015).

[63] I would add this dignitarian dimension to the account of global justice given in Gilabert (2012a).

The Dignitarian Approach   **47**

sweatshop workers in distant lands and migrant workers on our shores (who are often deprived of many standard protections granted to native workers).

Third, the Dignitarian Approach helps us to further develop our defence of certain specific rights. Thus, when we see how significant self-determination is for condition-dignity, we also see why it is so important that work be freely chosen rather than forced. Similarly, we understand more clearly why unionization and other associational rights are important. If workers are to be dynamic agents rather than mere beneficiaries of the largesse of their employers or the diligence of government officials, they need to be able to participate as active shapers in the social process leading to more just labour conditions for them. Finally, the fact that human dignity is a status that is equally held by all human individuals also helps criticize discrimination. Common demands such as equal pay for equal work can thus gain further support.

By appealing to a rather fundamental idea like dignity, we increase the depth and range of our reasoning about labour rights. This generates a fourth benefit of the dignitarian strategy, which is that it can help us to overcome a perceived crisis of labour law as too narrowly focused on conditions of bargaining between employers and employees in hierarchically organized and integrated large firms. Dignity underpins the territory of social justice much more widely. It allows us to understand the normativity of labour rights, further articulate the duties correlative to them, and see how they relate to other rights. Thus, human work, and the dignity-relevant capacities and interests involved in it, should be treated in their full range of incarnations. We can render visible and address normatively, and legally when appropriate, not only power relations within standard capitalist firms, but also in the household where care work that secures social reproduction is performed, and in the more diffuse and flexible arrangements that proliferate in the current economic landscape (including occasional and precarious jobs, subcontracting, and so on). Furthermore, the focus on solidaristic empowerment allows us to address the full panoply of protections that a right deserves, often through linkage with other rights. Thus, associational rights boosting workers' bargaining power to secure better working conditions should include more than the traditional rights to unionization and strike (although these certainly remain crucial). They also include broader political rights to partake in political parties, local and regional governance entities, and various national and international social movements and institutions that address intersectional concerns regarding class, gender, race, ethnicity, and nationality. Besides the shaping of contractual terms, support for workers might require structural changes of property relations and cultural perceptions of what counts as work (so as to valorize care work, for example). We can also explore personal

48 Human Dignity and Social Justice

empowerment supporting workers' capacities to engage in meaningful productive activities, and more generally to live a decent or flourishing life. An example of this would be a renewed attention to education, and a view of its contents as preparing people to develop their multifarious capacities.[64]

3.3 Towards maximal labour rights

Contributing to the well-being of others through work is something people find important. '[S]urveys on "happiness" seem to suggest that absence of opportunities to make oneself useful correlates strongly with a strong feeling of unhappiness.'[65] But the endorsement of the idea of social contribution can unfortunately be used ideologically, to manipulate people into accepting jobs which do not fulfil their labour rights. 'Not every kind of work is better than being idle, and not every kind of work dignifies the worker.'[66] To properly enact respect and concern towards workers' dignity, work has to be at least decent. But, arguably, conditions of flourishing at work are also worth construing as rights, even if they are less urgent than the basic labour rights normally seen as parts of human rights doctrine (which I discussed briefly above). It would also be a form of ideology to brush aside calls for more than basic rights by saying that decent labour conditions are 'enough'.

Let us make a distinction between basic and maximal labour rights. Whereas the former focus on workers' access to a decent life, the latter go further by tracking workers' access to a fully flourishing life. Both rights can be articulated in terms of human dignity and solidaristic empowerment. The humanist 'spirit of brotherhood', and the rights 'indispensable to [people's] dignity and the free development of [their] personality' mentioned in Articles 1 and 22 of the Universal Declaration of Human Rights can embrace both. Whereas basic labour rights require meeting thresholds of support for the human capacities of workers which are appropriately deemed part of the most

---

[64] The idea of human dignity can (if properly developed) provide the deeper and more fruitful form of normativity that some labour lawyers (like Langille 2011) see as necessary to face changing conditions of labour in our contemporary world. The perceived crisis concerns the weakening of the 'basic pillars that supported labour law and enabled it to flourish after the Second World War—the nation state, the vertically integrated firm, the standard employment relationship, the male breadwinner and female housewife gender contract, industrial unions, and social democracy' Fudge (2011: 120). If we adopt the deep and broad dignitarian perspective, we can illuminate what is normatively significant in work that, e.g., proceeds in a globalized economy, is not framed by a contract of employment, is affected by institutional background conditions outside contract-setting, can be politically supported by novel organizations and movements, and might even flourish within new social structures that are not capitalist.

[65] Offe (2009: 63).

[66] Mundlak (2007: 351). We should be vigilant against manipulation of reference to goods related to interests I1–I5 to discipline people into accepting undignified work.

The Dignitarian Approach   **49**

urgent entitlements every society must grant its members, maximal labour rights call for more comprehensive responses to their dignity that support full human development at work.

The distinction between basic and maximal rights requires more discussion than I offer here.[67] I have suggested elsewhere that we can state it as follows.[68] Basic rights, which human rights affirm with global standing, demand reasonable and feasible support for people's access to conditions in which they lead decent lives, and these include, importantly, access to effective power (and an equal formal—legal—entitlement to it) to shape the terms on which their social life is structured. When they have a decent social life, people enjoy certain central certain civil, social, and political rights—to pursue their conception of a good life, to have necessary material resources to effectively do so, and to participate in politics as law-makers besides mere law-takers. 'Decency' is here a placeholder for the level of support for human capacities that constitutes the forms of condition-dignity that are most urgent. We could also say that basic justice tracks the conditions that must be in place for a social order to be legitimate. When those conditions are met, the members have content-independent reason to comply with the order's rules (although they may of course also campaign for changing them). But decency is not enough. Whereas basic justice supports certain thresholds of development and exercise of valuable human capacities, maximal justice targets the highest levels of development and exercise that are reasonably attainable in the relevant social contexts. Thus, basic justice would require that workers have access to freely chosen jobs that allow them to contribute to society, socialize in ways that are not humiliating, and meet their subsistence needs, while also having political rights to unionize, strike, and participate as active citizens in the broader political process. But they could also justifiably ask that society be structured so that they can flourish at work.

In this book, I will explore how the Dignitarian Approach covers the territory of maximal justice regarding labour conditions. Dignity is a resonant moral and political idea in the context of discussions about work. For example, it was recently invoked in the 'Manifeste Travail' calling for a revalorization of the contribution of workers in the face of the global COVID-19 pandemic.[69] Dignity is also recognized as one of three core ideas behind labour law. The other two ideas are that the inequality in bargaining power between workers and their employers should be compensated for and that

---

[67] White (2021).
[68] Gilabert (2019a: 301–2).
[69] Ferreras et al (2020: 29, 32, 33, 35).

50   Human Dignity and Social Justice

labour is not a mere commodity.[70] Interestingly, when developed through the substantive ideal of Solidaristic Empowerment, the Dignitarian Approach can both capture the content and explain the force of these additional ideas. It is because they have status-dignity and require condition-dignity that workers should have stronger bargaining power and their capacities and activities should not be regarded in exclusively instrumental ways. But human dignity, and the two additional ideas, in fact calls for more than decent labour conditions, as such conditions do not dissolve capitalist relations of production which typically generate unequal bargaining power and commodification of labour. We need to explore maximal labour rights that give workers real opportunities to more fully develop and exercise the capacities that give rise to their dignity.

Injustices regarding work that involve avoidable deficiencies in the implementation of the ideal of Solidaristic Empowerment (and thus failure to enact proper respect and concern for workers' dignity) include domination, alienation, and exploitation, which constitute the familiar triad in socialist critiques of the predicament of workers in capitalist societies. We can briefly state these putatively unjust conditions as follows:

> *Unjust domination*: When workers are inappropriately subject to the will of others in the shaping of the terms on which they work (at the spheres of exchange, production, or in the broader political process).
> *Unjust alienation*: When workers' ability to fashion a positive sense of themselves through activities that feature self-determination and self-realization at work is unduly stunted rather than unleashed.
> *Unjust exploitation*: When the relative vulnerability of workers is inappropriately taken advantage of by more powerful agents to get them to benefit them more than they ought to.

Although basic labour rights call for the elimination of the most egregious injustices regarding domination, alienation, and exploitation, maximal labour rights are meant to offer workers opportunities to avoid these conditions altogether, or at least to avoid them as much as it is reasonably feasible. Domination is overcome to the extent that workers are able to shape the terms on which they work. The greater achievements of social justice envisioned here turn on the extent to which workers are empowered in the three spheres of exchange, production, and broader politics. The issue of domination is mostly procedural, concerning how decision-making occurs in the organization of work. The issue of alienation, in turn,

---

[70] Langille (2011: 104–7).

The Dignitarian Approach **51**

concerns the meaningfulness of work. Meaningful work may itself include procedural dimensions as well (as non-domination is arguably part of non-alienation), but goes further to capture the extent to which people's capacities for creative production, cooperation, and social contribution are unfolded in working activities. The more workers can develop and exercise these capacities, the more they can avoid alienation at work. Finally, the issue of exploitation combines procedural and outcome-orientated considerations about how asymmetrical power is generated and deployed in economic processes. Exploitation is a use of asymmetric power in which the exploiting agents extract benefits from the less powerful exploited agents in wrongful ways.

Dignity at work involves the treatment of people in accordance with the ideal of Solidaristic Empowerment as it pertains to their life as workers. This ideal requires that we create feasible and reasonable social schemes in which we support each other as we pursue the development and exercise of our valuable capacities to produce in personally and socially beneficial ways. The spectrum of dignitarian justice goes from basic rights to decent working conditions to maximal rights to flourish in working practices that are free from domination, alienation, and exploitation. This book will explore the latter end of this spectrum.

It could be objected that a demanding view of labour rights of the kind pursued in this book, calling as it does for the accessibility of work without domination, alienation, or exploitation flouts the liberal requirement of neutrality with respect to conceptions of the good.[71] Six points are worth making in response.

First, some labour rights can partly be defended by saying that their implementation is either necessary for or (more plausibly) strongly contributory to a robust development of the autonomous moral or/and political agency which liberals praise.[72] Two typical linkage arguments are these. First, economic practices have a formative effect on people's political practices, so that

---

[71] An important line of argument from John Rawls is that a theory of justice should not be based on a 'thick' theory of the good featuring a detailed account of what life plans individuals should adopt. See Rawls (1999: sect. 68). An agreement on such a theory seems unlikely, is unnecessary, and should not be pursued. It is unlikely because of the great diversity in individuals' circumstances, abilities, and interests. It is unnecessary because principles of justice can use a 'thin' theory of the good which identifies some goods that are fairly general and abstract and necessary for pursuing more specific and diverse goods. Building a reasonable agreement on these goods seems feasible. Finally, we should not make justice depend on a thick conception of the good that applies to everyone because we would in fact benefit (through division of labour) from situations in which people pursue different plans of life and because we should respect people's freedom to choose their specific plans of life. So long as these pursuits do not involve conflict with the principles of justice (which rely on the thin, not the thick theory of the good), justice is not undermined.

[72] Hsieh (2008); Arnold (2012). These philosophers develop liberal egalitarian approaches to justice in production that eschew perfectionism. They also provide important discussions of the limits of Rawls's views on the topic, while also developing certain Rawlsian insights (e.g. Arnold argues that access to work

52　Human Dignity and Social Justice

domination in the former fosters dispositions that are at odds with autonomy in the latter. Second, concentration of power in the economy allows some individuals to use their greater economic power to tilt the political process in their favour (for example by funding lobbying agencies, by spending money on the campaigns of politicians that favour their interests, by promising jobs to officials when they leave office, and by signalling that they will disinvest in the country if governments make decisions they dislike). It is also important to note that the neutrality requirement has the normative force it has partly because it reflects a substantive moral commitment to freedom, and explores what it requires in circumstances of great diversity of views about the good life. No normative position can be morally neutral all the way down.

Second, I articulate the more ambitious and controversial requirements regarding non-alienating, non-exploited, and non-dominated work in terms of the generation of real options to engage in those kinds of work, not in terms of making work of that kind mandatory.

Third, no moral or political conception can be articulated in sufficient detail (i.e. make clear and determinate demands) without some potentially controversial commitments about the good. The liberties a principle of liberty would protect, or the opportunities a principle of equality of opportunity would foster, for example, cannot be identified or assessed without some sense of what goods would and should be rendered accessible through them.[73]

Fourth, since the controversy about maximal labour rights will persist no matter what framework is introduced (the status quo also being controversial, of course), we need a fair, and ongoing, way to process it. Now, as I see it, the social implementations of labour rights would be authorized and monitored through a democratic political system that gives everyone real opportunities to participate in its evaluation and improvement over time. To this recognition we can add advocacy for a moral and political ethos of fallibilism, humility, and tolerance.

Fifth, work is rather special, in that any society that is not fully automated will to some extent and in some ways push its people to work. It is important that this pressure is accompanied with a real effort to make available forms of

---

involving authority, responsibility, and complexity is a social primary good falling under Rawls's difference principle). See further Chapter 3, note 10.

[73] Hsieh (2012: 759) mentions that 'neutrality-based arguments' require that 'citizens have a meaningful range of options from which to choose'. But how can we discern what subset of the set of all the feasible arrangements of options counts as 'meaningful'? It is hard to do this if our normative framework imposes on itself complete evaluative lobotomy. It is better, I suggest, to be upfront about the evaluative importance of some candidates, while finding a way to introduce them as options rather than as unavoidable outcomes (and so reflecting as well reasonable concerns about personal and political liberty and pluralism).

The Dignitarian Approach **53**

work that are justifiable to the people pushed to work. In such a justification, interests of the kind I explore in this book seem relevant.

Finally, and interestingly, by linking talk of human interests to talk of human dignity we can underwrite and strengthen the points made above. The Bridge Principle discussed in Section 2.2 allows us to link workers' interests in accessing the object of their labour rights with capacities that give rise to their deontic status-dignity. The liberal concerns themselves reflect appreciation of agential capacities for autonomous judgement that are paramount in the basis of dignity. These capacities have great value, and their exercise is crucial for the epistemic and legitimating process which, through political discourse and choice, should set the terms of labour practices. We can in fact identify a hierarchy within the normative space of dignity, with certain civil and political freedoms having priority over specific views of meaningful work.

4. The Dignitarian Approach And Social Critique

The deployment of the Dignitarian Approach when thinking about working practices in capitalist societies will have to involve efforts in social critique. People are called to work in these societies, but the conditions they encounter as they respond to the call involve exploitation, alienation, and domination. Chapters 5–7 of this book will analyse these conditions to explain why they display failures to give people's dignity its due. Social critique consists in part in diagnosing existing injustices like these.

As I see it, a plausible critical theory of social justice should also help in articulating a positive view of what better social arrangements that overcome the injustices criticized might look like. I will not offer blueprints for those arrangements. My task is the more limited—and philosophical—one, of proposing some conceptual and normative ideas to help structure our inquiry and practical experimentation regarding such arrangements. In particular, in Chapters 1–3 I outline the Dignitarian Approach and offer a reinterpretation of the socialist Abilities/Needs Principle. These ideas, I think, are fruitful when explaining our moral worries about exploitation, alienation, and domination, and can orientate proposals for alternative economic institutions and practices through which workers can emancipate themselves from these injustices and achieve greater opportunities for human flourishing.

In addition to criticizing the injustices of capitalism, and exploring the potential increases in justice offered by emancipatory ideals such as the socialist one, I think that social critique has a third role, which involves a

54   Human Dignity and Social Justice

reflexive alertness to the potential problems arising in the political processes through which we try to achieve greater social justice. Chapter 4 of this book, centred on the relation between justice and feasibility, will explore in detail some of the relevant issues about the attempt to move 'from here to there'. But, at other points in the book, I will also address potential misuses of the normative ideals I propose. Thus, consider the ideal of Solidaristic Empowerment, which identifies both negative and positive duties. There could be pernicious interpretations of these duties. For example, there could be *ideologies of independence or security* that point out the importance of negative duties not to subject people to the will of others but go on to problematically neglect that we also have duties to reach out and support them in their pursuits of a better life. Social justice is not only a matter of getting others off our back when they tamper with our self-determination. It is also a matter of extending a helping hand to facilitate the flourishing they seek. On the other hand, there could be pernicious interpretations of the affirmation of positive duties. As pointed out in 3.3, we should beware of manipulative uses of people's interests regarding work to corner them into accepting jobs that do not really allow them to flourish. There could be *ideologies of contribution* that mishandle the appeal to positive duties to engage in production by neglecting that the activities of contribution must come with rights to enjoy self-determination and self-realization in them. These problematic engagements with otherwise justifiable negative and positive duties are not only pernicious in that they operate to the detriment of the condition-dignity of workers, but also in that, foreseeably, they benefit other, more privileged people, unduly. They can also be ideological in presenting this unbalanced allocation of burdens and benefits as unavoidable. The dynamic view of feasibility offered in this book is in part orientated to challenging the presentation of certain historically contingent social circumstances, such as a capitalist organization of the economy, as unsurpassable parameters that we simply have to accept rather than as practical configurations we can overcome. The final Chapter 8 extends this dynamic perspective by offering some suggestions about how to compare capitalism with socialism.

2
Kantian Dignity and Marxian Socialism

1. Introduction

An endeavour to discuss Kant and Marx simultaneously may initially appear rather puzzling. Kant and Marx seem to operate in quite different registers: one was a moralist, the other was hostile to moral talk; one was a critic of feudalism, the other a foe of capitalism; one challenged despotism and proposed a state with a republican structure, the other called for the dissolution of the state; one praised obedience, the other revolution; one entertained a dualist picture of human beings as partly natural and partly non-natural entities, the other rejected any such dualism. One the other hand, there are significant similarities between these important thinkers: both had a progressive view of history as the expansion of human freedom; both praised self-determination and abhorred paternalism; both called for interpersonal and institutional arrangements in which people treated each other as ends and not merely as means; and both had a cosmopolitan view of the scope of the project of human emancipation.

In this chapter, I identify a fresh and fruitful way to develop insights from both philosophers. I argue that we can articulate a Kantian conception of human dignity that helps to justify typically Marxian criticisms of capitalism as involving exploitation, domination, and alienation, and to develop the Marxian view of socialism as involving a combination of freedom and solidarity. Marx's own criticisms of capitalism and his occasional remarks on socialism are in need of normative structuring, which a Kantian conception of human dignity readily provides. That conception has great intuitive appeal, and it gains further support from noticing its explanatory power regarding the critique of capitalism and the defence of socialism. Kant's own account of dignity, on the other hand, should be modified to avoid an unnecessarily narrow view of the basis of human dignity only focused on rational freedom and an insufficient appreciation of some material and social aspects of human flourishing. Thus, my discussion of Kantian dignity and Marxian socialism will simultaneously feature revisions and criticisms of Kant's and

Human Dignity and Social Justice. Pablo Gilabert, Oxford University Press. © Pablo Gilabert (2023).
DOI: 10.1093/oso/9780192871152.003.0002

56 Human Dignity and Social Justice

Marx's contributions besides a discovery of important ways in which they can be used to support each other and to develop our own views.

Although a valuable exercise in itself, the detailed comparison of Kant's and Marx's views is not exactly the task of this chapter. My focus is on developing certain *Kantian* and *Marxian* (or Kant-inspired and Marx-inspired) arguments with the constructive aim of articulating a substantive ethical and political view: dignitarian socialism. This will of course involve drawing on the similarities and disagreements mentioned above. The aim, however, is not to establish a complete interpretive catalogue, but to identify and defend some important components of dignitarian socialism.

This chapter develops aspects of Kant's and Marx's work as powerful resources for a distinctive and appealing normative project, which I call dignitarian socialism. Kantian and Marxian insights help articulate two central ideas of dignitarian socialism. Let me here state these ideas briefly—I will develop them as this chapter proceeds.

The first idea is that of the *Dignitarian Approach*, which holds that we have reason to organize social life in such a way that we respond appropriately to the valuable features of individuals that give rise to their dignity. To articulate a Dignitarian Approach, we need to provide an account of the following dimensions of it (the contours of which were identified in more detail in Chapter 1).

- Status-dignity; dignitarian norms; condition-dignity: *Status-dignity* is a normative standing of some entities such that agents who could affect them ought to treat them with appropriate respect and concern. I focus here on the treatment of human individuals by human agents, although the scope of dignitarian treatment can be wider. How exactly this respect and concern should be enacted is what *dignitarian norms* specify. Such norms sate various negative and positive duties. When these duties are fulfilled, human beings enjoy *condition-dignity*. The distinction between condition-dignity and status-dignity is crucial to avoid incoherent uses of the notion of dignity—as when some people are said to lack dignity because they are treated unjustly *and* to be entitled to a different, better treatment because of their dignity.[1]
- Basis of dignity: Human individuals have status-dignity in virtue of some valuable features of them. An account of these features—the constituents of the *basis of dignity*—informs the articulation of dignitarian norms, as the content of those norms precisely tracks the appropriate responses to those features in various circumstances.

---

[1] In the text, unless disambiguation is necessary, I use 'dignity' to mean *status-dignity*.

Kantian Dignity and Marxian Socialism   57

- Circumstances of dignity: The content of the dignitarian norms also depends on the problems they address. We can identify *circumstances of dignity* in which the dignitarian norms apply. These circumstances can be more or less general (and the same goes for the norms addressing them), and they include problems warranting feasible and desirable responses in which dignitarian treatment is enacted.
- Social ideals, or projects, enacting dignitarian treatment: Dignitarian norms can orientate agents acting in the real world by constituting a *dignitarian social ideal or project*. Agents can, and should, act in such a way that they generate and sustain personal and institutional frameworks in which dignitarian treatment is enacted.

These dimensions of a Dignitarian Approach could of course be articulated in many ways, yielding different substantive dignitarian conceptions. I am particularly interested in a conception that develops the ideal of *Solidaristic Empowerment*, according to which we should support everyone's autonomous pursuit of a flourishing life by affirming both negative duties not to destroy or block their valuable capacities and positive duties to protect and enable their development and exercise. This second idea is at the moral core of dignitarian socialism.

2. Kantian Dignity

2.1 Resources in Kant

Kant's work provides powerful resources for articulating the dignitarian perspective. Kant helps us understand that there is a form of dignity that operates as a deontic status, is inherent to human beings and has universal scope, is fundamentally egalitarian, has very strong justificatory force, and grounds norms that apply in various institutional and personal contexts.

(i) *Dignity as a deontic status.* Dignity is a normative property of human beings, which consists in their being entitled to certain types of respectful and helpful treatment. Kant's *Formula of Humanity* expresses the core moral idea. It enjoins you to '*act so that you use humanity, whether in your own person or in the person of any other, always at the same time as an end, never merely as a means*' (G 4:429).[2] This moral idea of positive telic and not merely

---

[2] Kant's works are referenced as follows. AW = 'An Answer to the Question, "What is Enlightenment?"' G = *Groundwork of the Metaphysics of Morals*. KpV=*Critique of Practical Reason*. TP = 'On the common saying: That May Be Correct in Theory, But It Is of no Use in Practice'. R = *Religion within the Boundaries of Mere Reason*. EF = 'Toward Perpetual Peace'. MS = *The Metaphysics of Morals*. All these texts are in Kant

58 Human Dignity and Social Justice

instrumental treatment is the core of all duties, be they ethical or juridical.[3] We should shape our personal and social projects so that we do not approach people with malice, indifference, or by taking them as mere tools.[4]

Importantly, this notion of dignity differs from other, convention-based status ones. It does not designate the fact of being seen as having certain claims within certain cultural or legal codes. Kant's distinction between natural and positive right helps to see this point. There are various innate and acquired rights that people may have even if there are no legal statutes stating them. In fact, as Kant argues,[5] it may be a requirement of natural right itself that some such statutes (domestic, international, or cosmopolitan) be created in order to render the various first-order natural rights more determinate and their enjoyment more secure.[6] The dignitarian status is deeper and provides critical leverage to assess those codes.

(ii) *Inherence and universal scope.* Kant introduces an idea of *human* dignity. Dignity is an inherent property of human beings, an 'inner worth' which is unlike a 'price'—a 'relative' significance such that its carrier could unproblematically be substituted by some other with equivalent use.[7] Furthermore, the basis of human dignity is constituted by features that pertain to human persons 'as such'; it is not dependent on features that people may acquire when they perform certain acts or occupy certain social positions.[8] In Kant's account, dignity is based in persons' capacities for practical reasoning,

---

(1996a) except for R, which is in Kant (1996b). Citations indicate volume and page from the *Akademie-Ausgabe*.

[3] A juridical expression is the *duty of 'rightful honor'*: 'Do not make yourself a mere means for others but be at the same time an end for them.' This 'internal duty' has as a counterpart an 'external duty' to avoid wronging others (MS 6:236-7).

[4] When Kant says that humanity is an end in itself, he understands the notion of an end in its broadest sense, as 'something *for the sake of which* we act' (rather than in the narrower sense of something that is to be intentionally produced or brought about) Wood (2008: 85). Kant clearly identifies dignity as a deontic status when he presents it as 'consisting in' the normative fact that human beings ought to be treated as ends, and never merely as means (MS 6:462). I agree with Parfit (2011: sect. 35) that Kant introduces with dignity a distinctive sense of 'value'. This sense, as a certain kind of 'standing', is not reducible to the traditional sense of 'being good'.

[5] EF 8:355-6, 378; MS 6:305-8, 311-2, 354-6.

[6] Kant distinguishes between natural and positive rights, claiming that the actual juridical statutes stating the latter must track the moral claims involved in the former (MS 6:224, 229, 237; see also 291). The further divisions in the Doctrine of Right identify the aspects of natural rights. Thus, the division between innate and acquired right (MS 6:237) concerns unconditional natural rights people have in their own person (e.g. to control their body, avoid injury, speak) and their conditional claims to external objects of choice (through property, contracts, and status relationships, all of which require previous acts of—omnilaterally rather than unilaterally authorized—acquisition). The distinction between private and public right (MS 6:242) concerns the natural rights of persons interacting with each other and the rights regarding the relation between citizens of a republic and their state (with its international or cosmopolitan extensions). Public right renders determinate and secure the rights which hold provisionally in a social, but not yet fully institutionally structured state of nature (MS 6:255-7, 264, 267; see also 312-3 and TP 8:289).

[7] G 4: 434; see also G 4:439 and MS 6:462, 483.

[8] Kant presents vices involving violations of duties to self as the 'adoption of principles' that are contrary to the agent's character as a moral being, and thus to 'the innate dignity of a human being' (MS 6:420).

Kantian Dignity and Marxian Socialism 59

including their technical, prudential, and moral deliberation and choice. It is not a matter of their praiseworthy acts, their social class, or their nationality. As a result, human dignity is a robust generator of the idea that there are universal *human rights*—entitlements people have against anyone who can affect them, whoever they are and wherever they are situated in social space.[9]

(iii) *Fundamental moral equality.* Human dignity is an egalitarian status. It is equally held by human individuals in virtue of general features of them, and not due to any specific rank or position within existing social structures. This passage is clear on the egalitarian nature of dignity (and also supports the two previous points):

> [A] human being regarded as a *person*, that is, as the subject of a morally practical reason, is exalted above all price; for as a person (*homo noumenon*) he is not to be valued merely as a means to the ends of others or even to his own ends, but as an end in itself, that is, he possesses a *dignity* (an absolute inner worth) by which he exacts *respect* for himself from all other rational beings in the world. He can measure himself on a footing of equality with them. (MS 6:434–5)[10]

(iv) *Normative force.* Dignity is an 'unconditional, incomparable worth' (G 4:436). Human dignity gives rise to rights and duties that have priority over competing considerations. Thus, considerations that are merely prudential, tradition-based, or positive—in the legal sense—cannot outweigh the requirements that flow from it. Human dignity is 'above any price'.[11] What is owed to individuals in accordance with their dignity need not accommodate agents' existing desires, their cultural or legal conventions, or what flows from their juridical roles. Trampling on the rights of human beings is unacceptable, even if it is convenient to some, and even if it is legally sanctioned.

---

[9] See, e.g., MS 6:463–4 where, after introducing the idea of dignity, Kant talks about some forms of respect that cannot be denied any human person ('even a vicious man') 'as a human being'. In his discussion on cosmopolitan right, Kant introduces the idea of rights that all human beings have as such, and contrasts these with specific prerogatives that people may acquire and lose as they enter or exit certain social positions (see, e.g., EF 8:349–51). Kant uses 'humanity' in two ways, as (a) narrowly comprising the capacity to set oneself ends and (b) more broadly including also the capacity to morally assess one's actions and attitudes. Kant uses (a) when he distinguishes 'humanity' from 'personality' in R 6:26–8. An example of (b) occurs in MS 6:386–7. In the present discussion, I focus on this broader use. 'Humanity' and 'personality' are both constitutive human predispositions. He also mentions a third predisposition, (c) 'animality', which is involved in people's pursuit of survival, procreation, and sociality (R 6:26–7). Satisfaction of (permissible) expressions of this predisposition is obviously normatively relevant, as it constitutes a causal precondition for any autonomous human functioning of people in the real world.

[10] By seeing dignity as equally held by all human beings, Kant departs from the traditional view of it as a social status enjoyed only by people who occupy high positions in social hierarchies Wood (2008: 94). For Kant's separate discussion of contingent 'dignities' attached to offices and positions, see MS 6:315, 328. The specific claims of merit or social rank are different from the rights of humanity in every person (EF 8:350–1).

[11] G 4:434–6; MS 6:434–6, 6:462, 483.

60   Human Dignity and Social Justice

Importantly, Kant claims that morality ought to frame and guide law and politics (EF 8:370–80). If the former requires appropriate responses to human dignity, the latter must follow suit. Morality generates principles of 'natural right', which a 'moral politician' must take as a 'model' to orientate political and legal reform (EF 8:372). In cases of alleged conflict between politics and morals, 'morals cuts the knot', '[t]he right of human beings must be held sacred, however great a sacrifice this may cost the ruling power', and 'all politics must bend its knee before right' (EF 8:380).

(v) *Wide view of site of application of dignitarian norms.* Appropriate treatment responding to persons' dignity is specified through various dignitarian norms. These norms state various forms of respect and concern owed to human beings, and they apply in various sites. Some focus on outer behaviour, others on internal attitudes; some focus on coercively enforceable acts, others on behaviour that cannot or should not be enforced externally; some specify duties attached to roles within certain institutions, others hold independently of such institutions. Dignitarian treatment can, and should, be articulated in various ways to shape the different aspects of social life.

In the systematic account of the *Metaphysics of Morals*, Kant distinguishes between fundamental principles and principles of application (MS 6: 216–7, 411). The fundamental requirement is to preserve and promote human beings' rational freedom (the basis of their dignity). The Doctrine of Right articulates that requirement as it applies to agents' external actions that are appropriately subject to coercion (MS 6:230–1, 237). This doctrine deploys a Principle of Right and a Social Contract Standard to justify laws and policies. The *Principle of Right* states that persons may only act in ways that are compatible with others being permitted to act in the same way (MS 6:230) and the *Social Contract Standard* requires lawgivers to only impose rules which all those subject to them could rationally accept (TP 8:297; EF 8:350–1; MS 6:313–5). In the case of the Doctrine of Virtue, the fundamental requirement is articulated as the categorical imperative, or the supreme obligation of virtue (MS 6:395). This obligation is further specified through various obligatory ends shaping agents' maxims (MS 6:395, 468–9).[12]

(vi) *Exploration of feasible application of dignitarian norms.* We must distinguish between the most general and fundamental dignitarian principles and their application as specific requirements for institutions, maxims, and

---

[12] The very existence of a framework of coercive law, and its specific requirements, must be defended with moral arguments Guyer (2014: 277, 285). Interpreters disagree about the relation between *Ethik* and *Recht* in Kant. Some see the relation as radically discontinuous, some not. Like Guyer (2014: 276–86), I emphasize continuity. Ethics and right (*Ethik* and *Recht*) are two branches of morality (*Moralität*, *Sitten*) (MS 6:214; EF 8:385–6), and articulate the same core dignitarian concerns for different sites of application. For an interpretation emphasizing discontinuity, see Wood (2002).

Kantian Dignity and Marxian Socialism **61**

choices. The latter address the circumstances of dignity, taking into account relevant empirical considerations about human beings' nature and social condition in more or less historically specific contexts.[13]

Besides identifying occasions for their application, empirical considerations help show that dignitarian principles are feasible. According to Kant, we are entitled to believe that we *can* act in the ways we ought to act. But we could also ask whether we are more or less likely to succeed in actually acting in those ways if we endeavour to do so. Various psychological and social mechanisms may affect our eventual paths. A responsible pursuit of moral dignitarian projects that is normatively ambitious but not naïve should take empirical inquiry into these mechanisms very seriously.[14]

(vii) *Importance of freedom.* Respect for freedom is central to dignitarian treatment. Support for people's well-being must proceed in such a way that the capacities for (prudential and moral) self-governance are engaged rather than circumvented or belittled.

Respect for agents' freedom is significant both for personal and institutional contexts. If we help others, we should contribute to their pursuit of happiness as they see it, not as we see it (so long as their plans are not immoral).[15] A government should not be paternalistic towards its subjects.[16] Of particular salience in Kant's moral philosophy is the connection between non-instrumental and telic treatment, dignity, and autonomy as the capacity for moral self-determination. Thus, Kant praises 'the idea of the *dignity* of a rational being, who obeys no law other than that which he himself at the same times gives'.[17] This leads us to the next point.

(viii) *Importance of capacity for moral reasoning:* Kantians sharply distinguish human beings' capacities for moral, prudential, and technical reasoning, and take the first to constrain the others. Moral reasoners have a distinctive dignity.[18] They can engage in activities of introspective and intersubjective

---

[13] Thus, in the Doctrine of Right, specific property rights and international rights assume the fact that human beings live in a finite space (the earth) in which they are bound to affect each other. In the Doctrine of Virtue, the duties to oneself regarding the preservation and development of one's intellectual and moral powers assume that one is tempted to pursue immediate or short-term gratification and let them rust Guyer (2014: 44, 288–9, 293, 314–6).

[14] 'Perpetual Peace' is an exemplar of this morally exigent yet realistic approach. It combines ambitious global norms with shrewd remarks on how people might join peaceful international cooperation out of self-interested motives of fear and commercial gain. Kant is not naïve about human nature. He understands that people often display problematic tendencies to assert their interests at the expense of others and explores their impact in social history. See Wood (2005: 117–8, 132–4).

[15] MS 6:454. See 6:388, 450.

[16] TP 8:290–1, 298; MS 6:318.

[17] G 4:434.

[18] Kant speaks of the 'dignity of humanity as rational nature' (G 4:434), and characterizes agents' rational nature as their capacity to set themselves ends. But Kant also says, more narrowly and strongly, that

62 Human Dignity and Social Justice

deliberation and decision-making that track impartially the good of all. This is not something that merely prudential and technical reasoners focused on their own well-being and the effective means to achieve it can do in good faith—that is, in a way that is not merely strategic.

Autonomy as the capacity for moral reasoning is the ground for the positive telic treatment required by the Formula of Humanity. '[T]he will of a rational being must always be regarded as at the same time lawgiving, since otherwise it could not be thought as an *end in itself*'.[19] Furthermore, discovering on what terms others could rationally will us to treat them in certain circumstances would give us crucial information to figure out how we should treat them in those circumstances. We do not treat others *merely* as means if they could rationally endorse the terms on which we treat them.

The relation between appropriate treatment and autonomy is also envisioned in the *Formula of the Realm of Ends* of the moral law, which presents an ideal social world as 'a systematic union of rational beings through common objective laws, that is, a realm [*Reich*], which can be called a realm of ends (admittedly only an ideal) because what these laws have as their purpose is just the relation of these beings to one another as ends and means' (G 4:434; translation amended). This formula presents an intersubjective rendering of the *Formula of Autonomy* based on 'the idea *of the will of every rational being as a will giving universal law*' (G 4:431).

The link between appropriate treatment and autonomy has its political articulation in Kant's use of the Social Contract Standard to appraise and guide the choices made by legislators in a republic. Kant invokes an 'original contract', '*an idea of reason*, which, however, has its undoubted practical reality, namely to bind every legislator to give his laws in such a way that they *could* have arisen from the united will of a whole people and to regard each subject, insofar as he wants to be a citizen, as if he has joined in voting for such a will. For this is the touchstone of any public law's conformity with right' (TP 8:297).

Because of the supreme importance of moral reasoning, we can give a sharp defence of rights to participate in political decision-making, and to *actually* shape that process in a deliberative way. We can also explain more clearly why,

---

'morality is the condition under which alone a rational being can be an end in itself, since only through this is it possible to be a law-giving member of the kingdom of ends', and, '[h]ence, [that] morality, and humanity insofar as it is capable of morality, is that which alone has dignity' (G 4:435). The capacity for moral reasoning is prominent at the basis of dignity. Most references to dignity in the *Groundwork* occur during Kant's development of the Autonomy and the Realm of Ends formulas of the categorical imperative, which feature human persons as able to regulate themselves on the basis of moral norms which they each can recognize as springing from the will of every rational agent. Thus, Kant says that '[a]utonomy is ... the ground of the dignity of human nature and of every rational nature', and that 'the dignity of humanity consists just in this capacity to give universal law' (G4:436, 440).

[19] G 4:434.

Kantian Dignity and Marxian Socialism   **63**

when identifying the conditions and goods people have a right to access, we should include those supporting agents' autonomy besides their happiness.[20]

2.2 Difficulties and revisions

Kant's views on dignity are not without problems, however, and this section will discuss some important ones. I will also suggest some revisions. The revisions develop the idea of dignity, which is at the core of Kantian moral theory. Although that core is itself partly revised, since the resulting view preserves the main points outlined in Section 2.1, I would still characterize it as a Kantian one.

(i) *Narrow view of the basis of dignity*. Kant's view of the basis of dignity fails to capture all that is intrinsically valuable in human beings and makes them worthy of treatment that is respectful and helpful. According to Kant, the ground of dignity is rational agency, including the capacity to set ends and, especially, the capacity for autonomous reasoning about what is morally right.[21] But we should be more sensitive and recognize that the basis of dignity includes more than moral agency. It is implausible to uniformly lump together every entity that is not a 'person' with moral agency into the ontological heap of 'things'. Certain capacities for practical reasoning falling short of moral reasoning (such as prudential reasoning) may be significant in their own right. And the same might be the case with sentience, the capacity for positive and negative qualitative experiences such as pleasure and pain. We reasonably pay direct attention to these capacities, for example, when we think about what treatments health care practitioners should offer patients with various mental and physical ailments. As I explore further below, Kant has trouble accounting for the significance of supporting people's happiness. This may be partly due to his narrow view of the basis of dignity. Dignity involves worthiness of appropriate, telic, and not merely instrumental treatment, but that treatment must be informed by the value it responds to, which is the basis of dignity. If capacities other than moral agency are not recognized in the basis of dignity, there will be insufficient information to figure out what to do to treat others as ends. To figure out what dignitarian norms

---

[20] These points regarding the special significance of moral reasoning are not well captured by the otherwise congenial accounts of dignity proposed by Nussbaum (2011) and Griffin (2008). The distinctiveness and centrality of moral autonomy is on the other hand recognized by Rawls (1999) in his account of the basis of equality, although Rawls does not develop a theory of dignity. The intersubjective dimension of autonomy and the importance of actual practices of discursive deliberation are emphasized by Kantians in the Frankfurt School. See Habermas (1996) and Forst (2014a).
[21] G 4:428–9, 434–6, KpV 5:87–8, MS 6:434–5, 442–4.

64 Human Dignity and Social Justice

to accept, it is helpful to notice that prudential reasoning, and other capacities (such as for sentience, theoretical knowledge, aesthetic appreciation, or social cooperation), are at the basis of the dignity of human beings. The dignitarian norms will require respecting and furthering people's development and exercise of those capacities as well, as Solidaristic Empowerment would suggest.

(ii) *Narrow view of the scope of dignitarian duties*. Given the narrow view of the basis of dignity, the direct (rather than indirect) rights and duties concerning the treatment of non-human animals and human beings with very low levels of rational agency is missed.

As I argue elsewhere, an account of the basis of dignity which, like Kant's, only features rational agency is insufficient.[22] A more inclusive view is intuitively more plausible because it would help recognize the dignity of non-human animals, and also of human beings with severe cognitive impairments. An appropriate medical treatment of the latter could not go very far in terms of recruiting their rational endorsement, but should still respond to any level of agency that is present and be directly concerned with limiting their misery and facilitating pleasant experiences.

(iii) *Insufficient recognition of the importance of well-being in ethical and political argument*. As Kant says, we must respect agents' freedom. But agents' well-being is significant in its own right. Norms articulating concern for human persons by fostering their well-being are important as well, even if they must be constrained by (or at least weighted against) the norms articulating respect for, and preservation of, people's freedom. Kant's use of the phrase 'dignity' is however tied to duties of respect for autonomy, and not explicitly linked to concern regarding well-being.

Now, duties of concern regarding people's well-being can (and I think should) be seen as part of what dignitarian norms include. Arguably, a direct concern for well-being is already involved in Kant's recognition of the positive dimension of the Formula of Humanity[23] and in his defence of duties of beneficence, which precisely focus on furthering other agents' happiness.[24]

---

[22] Gilabert (2015b; 2022) and 'Inclusive Dignity'. The dignity of human beings need not only include what makes them different from other animals. The key point is to identify a status that individual human beings have independently of their membership of a nation, class, and other contingent social groups that make them harm or ignore each other's freedom and well-being.

[23] '[H]umanity might indeed subsist if no one contributed to the happiness of others but yet did not intentionally withdraw anything from it. But there is still only a negative and not a positive agreement with *humanity as an end in itself* unless everyone also tries, as far as he can, to further the ends of others. For the ends of a subject who is an end itself must as far as possible be also *my* ends, if that representation is to have its *full* effect in me' (G 4:430; see also MS 6:395). For a systematic exploration of positive duties in Kant's practical philosophy, see Gilabert (2010).

[24] MS 6:385, 393–4, 452ff.

Kantian Dignity and Marxian Socialism   65

Additionally, Kant's conception of the 'highest good', the ultimate object of morality, includes both happiness and virtue. This conception may be interpreted as saying that (a) well-being is significant as an ethical aim even though (b) it is constrained by another significant aim that has strict priority—achieving moral virtue.[25]

Even if we accept Kant's critique of paternalism in politics, we do not thereby have to dismiss the importance of happiness for political choice. When we make an autonomous collective choice, we must ask ourselves which amongst the available set of options is best. A natural way to proceed—I do not say the only one—is to choose the set that will make us happier—insofar as no injustice is thereby generated. Regarding persons as ends in themselves can be taken to include taking their happiness as significant.[26]

Should we really correct Kant's views of the relation between happiness and morality? Paul Guyer suggests an interesting way to simultaneously understand Kant's reference to happiness as a component of morality's aims and his reluctance to take it as a basic ground. The ground of morality is the duty to take humanity as an end in itself. This means acknowledging negative obligations not to destroy, and positive obligations to support, the existence and development of persons' capacity to set themselves ends, their freedom of choice. Now, beneficence supports people's achievement of their life plans, and thus their happiness. But what is morally significant in beneficence is not the happiness it fosters, but how it supports freedom of choice. Freedom of choice is extended when more plans are realizable. When we help each other to achieve various ends, we end up having more freedom of choice, as we each have more to rationally choose from (and it is irrational to choose what cannot be achieved).[27]

This is a plausible argument that captures some elements in Kant's texts (See, e.g., MS 6:444–6). But I do not think it presents a satisfactory account of the significance of happiness. When we help others, we do not only care about their greater freedom, we care directly about their well-being, or happiness. Often, the value of freedom constrains the value of well-being, so that it would be wrong to paternalistically impose ways of life on others against

---

[25] KpV 5:109–10. See Parfit (2011: ch. 10).

[26] See KpV 5:110. Kant's views on the significance of happiness are complex and I am only scratching the surface here. As pointed out, Kant claims that happiness cannot be the ground of determination of state's action because such action would involve paternalistic disrespect for citizens and their freedom. But he also worries that such a ground is too indeterminate (as different accounts of what it consists in are inevitable) (TP 8:290–1, 298; MS 6:318). Kant also thinks that focus on the pursuit of happiness may lead to moral corruption, to rationalizing attitudes that go against morality's strict and pure laws (G 4:405, 442). These are important risks, but they can in principle be addressed through lucid individual and political deliberation that is attuned to them.

[27] Guyer (2014: 230–3, 281, 300, 408–9, 454n.2).

66 Human Dignity and Social Justice

their will even if this would result in their being happier. But happiness still matters independently. To see this, consider what expansions of freedom of choice we have reason to foster (both for ourselves and for others). We do not only care about increasing the *number* of options. We also care about their *quality*. Two choice situations may be equal in number of options but not equally significant. Their assessment may turn on the value of the options open, which may track well-being. Some expansions of freedom of choice may be better than others because they include options that are more likely to lead to agents' happiness. Guyer recognizes that happiness may help break ties between option sets.[28] But notice that happiness could not play this role unless it is a significant consideration in its own right. Furthermore, expansion of choice and expansion of happiness need not coincide, and the former need not *always* be preferred if it comes at the cost of the latter. Some people may be less happy when their options are increased—the new options would distract them, or carry anxiety-inducing risks, for example. If the additional options are not independently important, the cost on well-being could be unreasonable. Furthermore, using the options acquired in order to 'enjoy life' is part of what taking oneself as an end calls for. This is why Kant rightly criticizes 'miserly avarice', the maxim of amassing resources (and with them options) without using them to bring about enjoyment (MS 6:432–3).

In these remarks, I have used 'happiness' and 'well-being' as equivalent. Kant does so too (for example in MS 6 6:452). Kant sometimes endorses a hedonistic view in which happiness and well-being involve contentment with one's life (KpV 5:22, 5:60–1; MS 6:452, 480). Other times he construes happiness along a desire satisfaction view, as 'the satisfaction' of a 'system' of 'inclinations' (KpV 5:73; 5:124). In other occasions Kant combines these views.[29] Kant seemingly was not aware of the difference between these (and other) conceptions of prudential value, which are familiar to us in contemporary debates in ethics.[30]

In general, and from a contemporary perspective, Kant's views on morality and well-being can be criticized on two scores. First, Kant has a tendency to confuse (a) a view of morality as concerned with happiness with (b) the reduction of morality to self-centred prudence (itself understood as seeking happiness construed as self-centred maximal contentment or satisfaction of actual desires) (see, e.g., G 4:405, 442). The problem is that (a) does not imply (b), as a moral principle requiring the fostering of happiness for all can

---

[28] Ibid: 229–32.
[29] See Hill (2002: 168–9, 194–5).
[30] For the view that Kant does not develop a systematic substantive account of non-moral goodness, see Parfit (2011: vol.1, 243; vol. 2, 675–7); and Wood (1999: 67, 365n.11).

Kantian Dignity and Marxian Socialism **67**

be identified which is impartial rather than self-centred, and would thus not exactly be a requirement of prudence as Kant understands it.[31] Second, Kant fails to appreciate that well-being can be construed as a matter of access to objective goods which are not reducible to the satisfaction of agents' present desires, or to the enjoyment that might result from that satisfaction.[32] Objective goods could support universal principles regarding well-being of the kind Kant requires (in KpV 5:36). Because of these reasons, Kant has difficulty understanding how concern for well-being can feature as central in a moral reasoning that is impartial rather than self-centred, and which relies, at the most fundamental level, on categorical rather than desire-based reasons.

Let us return to the main thread of our argument. Why should well-being matter within a dignitarian framework? My hypothesis is that well-being (at least in part) coincides with the development and exercise of the capacities that give rise to human dignity. Whether we adopt an objectivist, desire-satisfaction, or hedonistic view of well-being (or some combination thereof), states of well-being are likely to feature in the conditions protected and promoted by the fulfilment of dignitarian norms. On an objectivist account (which I favour), well-being involves access to intrinsic goods, which could include the development and exercise of various valuable human capacities. Success in this development and exercise could involve the satisfaction of informed desires of the kind desire-satisfaction theories centre on. And, finally, the enjoyment that often comes with these developments and exercises of capacities are of the kind a hedonistic theory might praise (and might, additionally, be highlighted by an objectivist theory that takes pleasure as one of the items in list of goods—perhaps because of the value of the capacity of sentience or because enjoyment is constitutive of what it is to develop and exercise capacities well).

So, by adding a more explicit and positive focus on supporting people's pursuit of their well-being to the respect and promotion of their freedom we do not only complement what Kant explicitly says about the targets of moral action and institutions. We also develop the dignitarian framework by

---

[31] At one point Kant appears to acknowledge this possibility, but dismisses it on grounds that I think could be addressed through the second point I go on to make. Thus, Kant recognizes that happiness can, as a purpose, 'be presupposed surely and a priori in the case of every human being, because it belongs to his essence' (G 4:415–6), but he points out that we can form no determinate picture of what happiness involves that holds necessarily for all agents in all contexts (G 4:418–9). Even if we were to find views of happiness that are in fact unanimously accepted by all—which does not seem likely—'this unanimity itself would still be only contingent', as '[t]he determining ground would still be only subjectively valid and merely empirical and would not have the necessity which is thought in every law, namely objective necessity from a priori grounds' (KpV 5:26). See also KpV 5:36, where it is said that a principle of universal happiness might 'give *general* rules but never *universal* rules'.
[32] For a proposal of a Kantian approach on perfectionist lines, see Brink (2019).

68 Human Dignity and Social Justice

showing how it generates concern for well-being as a dimension of our appropriate responses to status-dignity. Well-being is part and parcel of dignitarian morality, not a concession it grudgingly makes to objectors to it. An important corollary for a theory of rights is that there is no insurmountable gap in moving from interests in well-being to rights to access it when the former concern the development and exercise of the capacities in the basis of dignity which ground the deontic space of rights itself. The capacities at the basis of dignity bridge the gap by simultaneously grounding interests in, and rights to, their development and exercise. We can use the Bridge Principle stated in Chapter 1 (Section 2.2.1) to generate moral rights to support for the interests linked to well-being.

Now, if we accept this broader dignitarian outlook, we must see social, legal, and political philosophy as asking not only what, if anything, might justify the coercive imposition of constraints on people's choices regarding external action, but also how people's well-being might justifiably be fostered. A theory of justice can, pace one of Kant's observations, focus on needs besides choices (MS 6:230). Thus, I suggest that we interpret the Social Contract Standard as allowing us to draw on shareable reasons regarding well-being when assessing alternative social institutions, laws, and policies. We do not need to rely only on the normative idea of being one's own master and avoiding submission to the will of others (MS 6:238). In fact, we have to appeal to something else if we are to figure out what to choose (together) as the appropriate terms of our social life.[33] And notions of well-being linked to the development and exercise of capacities that give rise to human dignity fit the bill quite nicely.[34] Kant already draws on considerations of this kind in his

---

[33] An application of the Social Contract Standard based on considerations of well-being, or on the real freedoms or capabilities to achieve various forms of well-being, might pit that standard against the Principle of Right. Although this conflict is not necessary, when it arises (i.e., when some types of act that could be consistently available to all are prohibited) we might conclude that, all things considered, some deliverances of the formal test of the Principle of Right can be overridden. Another option is to constrain that test so that it kicks in only after the range of important liberties is determined (perhaps drawing, in part, on considerations about well-being to identify them). On the possible conflict between the standards, see Gilabert (2010: sect. V).

[34] I side with Rawls in the contrast between his and Kant's approaches to justice as depicted by Ripstein (2009: 3–6). Ripstein says that Kant, unlike Rawls, does not focus on how to fairly distribute the burdens and benefits of social cooperation because he is concerned with the different, formal issue of justifying social frameworks that do not violate people's right to be their own master—their right not to be subordinated to others' choices. If appropriately responding to people's dignity requires fostering their well-being (in autonomy-respecting manners), then how much and in what ways each of us should contribute to this fostering is a crucial question indeed. One reason why we should accept (impartially selected and implemented) constraints on some of our economic choices would be, precisely, that such constraints might foster people's well-being. As Rawls realizes, we need to choose between different possible but incompatible bundles of liberties, and not every conceivable liberty should be enshrined in principles of justice (even if they could be simultaneously available to all). A substantive argument is needed to identify what liberties should be defended, and the conditions for their effective exercise should be identified as well. Thus, some economic liberties to engage in capitalist relations of production do not have the moral importance

Kantian Dignity and Marxian Socialism   69

ethical doctrine. Saving the differences, it could also be done at the level of the doctrine of right. Or so a full development of the Dignitarian Approach that includes the ideal of Solidaristic Empowerment would, in my opinion, require.

(iv) *Limits of independence.* We should not have to approach social life in such a way that helping others is humiliating to them and a source of guilt for us. An extreme ideal of independence as self-reliance (to be distinguished from independence as autonomy) seems both infeasible and undesirable. As socialists and feminists have argued after Kant, human beings are inescapably interdependent. To manage that interdependence properly, they should recognize solidarity as essential for achieving just social relations. The Kantian ideal of a realm of ends should be seen as supporting such a combination of autonomy and solidarity in both interpersonal and institutional settings.

Kant affirms an idea of independence. He often construes it as self-determination, championing agents' ability to determine themselves to act on the basis of what their own prudential and moral reasoning recommends rather than on the basis of unchecked inclinations,[35] or the opinions and instructions of others.[36] The political expression is active citizenship[37] and the rejection of paternalistic despotism.[38] In other cases, Kant links independence to the idea of self-reliance, of not depending on others for the satisfaction of one's needs (except as a member of a state).[39] This leads Kant to a qualified characterization of beneficence. The worry is that beneficence may be 'humiliating' to the people helped.[40] It is preferable that the rich help the poor anonymously, without humbling them or making them feel that they are put under obligation. Sometimes people fail to show gratitude because they fear this would signal their dependence on those who help them, and thus their inequality and perhaps lack of dignity.[41]

Kant is right to praise independence as self-determination. In recognizing this kind of independence, we can indeed 'feel [our] own dignity'.[42] Kant

---

of freedom of speech, religion, and political activity, and could justifiably be restricted to secure the fair value of the latter liberties and to service other concerns such as fair equality of opportunity to participate in economic activity and the requirement that every participant (especially the worst-off) benefit from it. See Rawls (2001: sect. 32). (Rawls himself focuses on rather general social primary goods rather than on a full picture of well-being. But these goods are still meant to be part of what people need as they pursue their more specific, personal conceptions of the good.)

[35] KpV 5:117–9, 152, 269.
[36] AW 8:35; MS 6:237–8.
[37] EF 8:350. '[T]reatment of the human being' as free is 'in keeping with his dignity' (WA 8:42).
[38] TP 8:290–15. Recall that, even in ethical duties of beneficence, helpers must refrain from imposing their own view of happiness (MS 6:454).
[39] G 4:434; TP 8:294–6; MS 6:237–8, 314–5.
[40] MS 6:448-9, 453.
[41] MS 6:459.
[42] KpV 5:152.

70 Human Dignity and Social Justice

is also correct to address the problem of paternalism, and to spot the significant interaction between conditions of economic dependence and lack of active self-determination. I am less sure that we should accept his tendency to affirm independence as self-reliance. Self-reliance seems infeasible given our causal dependency on others to achieve most of what we value. And it seems undesirable to construe help as giving rise to humiliation, both because this would deter people from helping each other and thus from getting benefits they need, and because the practices of help could be in themselves valuable instances of telic treatment of persons.

Perhaps these points can be reconciled through Kant's caveat that economic reliance on others is not a problem if the relation is under the framework of equal citizenship (for example, if the poor are helped as citizens through public services based on general taxation by the government rather than as private persons assisted by other private persons). But even at the political level, citizens will have different amounts of actual power to affect governmental decision-making (some may be more charismatic, or more intelligent, or more knowledgeable, or be part of a majority rather than a minority, etc.). Although we should aim at equal empowerment in politics, factual inequalities will likely remain. An ethics of solidaristic use of unequal power seems necessary.[43]

A further point cuts deeper to show the limits of Kant's idea of independence as self-determination. If we only see the contours of a just society as constituted by the constraint that it should prevent dependence as the subjection to the choice of others, then we will not be fully able to respond to the value of people's capacities giving rise to their status-dignity. Two societies might be constructible in which nobody subjects others to their will. But one may feature many more opportunities, equally distributed, for all to achieve higher levels of development and exercise of their valuable capacities. A narrow focus on independence cannot help us explain why it is preferable. A wider notion of empowerment is needed to do that. This idea focuses on abilities to flourish in various ways, and is a fitting target for solidaristic action and institutions. This is the kind of thought that socialists have come to add since the nineteenth century to the liberal concern with non-domination and formal equality of opportunity.[44] A dignitarian framework can capture this move, but at the (reasonable) cost of abandoning the narrow construal of

---

[43] To be fair to Kant, he recognizes that benevolence and gratitude may be appropriate even after extensive duties of right have been established, and he worries about the rejection of those relations of assistance that is based on wounded 'pride' (MS 6:458).

[44] The problems with independence seem to me to affect Ripstein's (2009) construction of a political conception singly based in it. It also arises in the recent theory of republicanism proposed by Pettit (2012). I address this worry in Chapter 7.

Kantian Dignity and Marxian Socialism   **71**

freedom as independence. This point works in cooperation with the call for more attention to the importance of well-being made above. And it can mobilize other resources in Kant's work, such as his postulate concerning property rights—stating that access to material resources is necessary for effective freedom (MS 6:230)—as a step in an argument calling for greater empowerment to develop and exercise one's valuable human capacities. We are already in socialist territory. But before turning to Marxian socialism, let me address a final issue regarding Kant.

(v) *Method of justification.* As I see it, the Dignitarian Approach has important similarities with Kant's account of determinative justification. So, first, like the Kantian approach, I think that a moral conception includes, at the fundamental level, a set of correlated intrinsic values and core principles. In Kant, the value involved is that of rational nature and the core principle is the moral law. In my account, the core statement of the Dignitarian Approach commands responsiveness to the valuable capacities of individuals, while Solidaristic Empowerment provides a general normative ideal to orientate actions that enact such responsiveness. Like Kant's, my approach is deontological, not consequentialist. Morality is primarily a matter of responding appropriately to individuals on account of their dignity, by supporting them in their development and exercise of their valuable capacities, not about promoting intrinsic value by bringing about optimific states of affairs which display as much of that value as possible in the aggregate. The core duties are directed to individuals who have status-dignity, not to impersonal states of affairs.

I also agree with Kant's view of moral theory as including different levels. In Kant's moral theory, there are three levels, including the moral law and the value of rational nature; the core duties and rights constituting the metaphysics of morals; and, finally, various specific judgments about particular situations. As Allen Wood argues, the relation between these levels is not one of straightforward deduction, but one of interpretive specification.[45] I also think of the Dignitarian Approach as generating sequences of norms at different levels, with more specific requirements interpreting what more general requirements would call for in view of more determinate circumstances and problems.

On the other hand, when it comes to epistemic rather than determinative justification, I prefer a methodology that differs from some Kantian accounts. In particular, I endorse a reflective equilibrium approach according to which we should seek coherence among our judgments at all levels of abstraction,

---

[45] Wood (2008: 54–65).

72 Human Dignity and Social Justice

allowing judgments at any level to perform confirmatory and challenging roles. I am sceptical of transcendental arguments of the kind favoured by some Kantians. I do not think that the Dignitarian Approach, or Kant's own principles, can be shown to be strictly necessary presuppositions of moral reasoning or choice.[46]

Kant thinks that principles have normative authority only if they are valid for every rational being as such. This constraint of justifiability as validity for every rational being as such can be interpreted in different ways. Consider two. The first, more austere way, and the one that often Kant and Kantians prefer, views the constraint as requiring that the justification of a principle show that denying it would be inconsistent with a conception of oneself as a rational agent.[47] Although quite thin, this strategy is not fruitless. It relies on the powerful idea that when we reason about what principles are correct, we must take reason itself as being of crucial importance, so that we must at least accept those principles that require a treatment of rational beings that respects and furthers the existence and development of their rational nature. Fundamental principles stating this general duty of respect and concern (like Kant's Formula of Humanity) and their implications (such as the critique of social arrangements involving domination and paternalism, in which some people circumvent other people's own reasoning about how to live their lives), can in this way be derived. If we must presuppose the value of rational nature as we engage in moral reasoning, we must accept principles that require supportive responses to it.

A second, more substantive strategy consists in trying to show that the principle we are trying to justify is valid for every rational being in the sense that every rational being has reason to endorse it. It is not logically impossible that we see ourselves as rational beings and deny a correct principle. Coherent wrongdoers are possible. Because of this, the previous strategy seems too thin. At least sometimes, the issue is not whether we could consistently reject a principle, but whether in doing so we would fail to respond to reasons that we have. This strategy does not restrict itself to the identification of the necessary presuppositions of normative reasoning in general, but calls instead for discovering substantive reasons. Now, the content of these reasons need not only be focused on what can be gleaned from the bare idea of a rational being. These can instead be the reasons that a rational being considering the

---

[46] See the various methodological options outlined in Guyer (2014: 216–9). The third option mentioned by Guyer is promising, and is akin to the reflective equilibrium one.

[47] Kant says that 'just because moral laws are to hold for every rational being as such, [... we should] derive them from the universal concept of a rational being as such' (G 4:412). Morality must be 'connected (completely a priori) with the concept of the will of a rational being as such' (G 4:426). See also G 4:408, 413, KpV 5:25–6.

Kantian Dignity and Marxian Socialism **73**

relevant issues covered by a principle has. They include, but can go beyond, the importance of preserving, developing, and exercising a rational being's capacities for reasoning.[48] The rational being may have other intrinsically valuable capacities worth taking into consideration for their own sake, and this being may have to consider how to treat other beings who are not similarly rational but have some of those additional capacities (as would be the case with some people with severe cognitive disabilities). We can in this way cater more fully to the fundamental moral equality of each individual.

I should say, however, that this strategy is still compatible with Kant's main requirement that fundamental moral reasons be 'categorical', because the substantive reasons this strategy asks us to consider are objective reasons, not desire-dependent considerations. Furthermore, taking some of these reasons to track the intrinsic significance of certain capacities other than those of rational nature is consistent with seeing that significance as constrained by reasons to support rational self-determination when the capacities for it are present. So Kant's idea of a morally good will as having unconditional value and other goods of nature or fortune as having conditional value (G 4:393) can be accommodated—as there is a difference between a value being intrinsic and the favourable response to it being unconstrained.

These remarks allow us to counter a challenge to dignitarian justifications of fundamental moral equality. Andrea Sangiovanni offers a justification of moral equality which is, he says, a superior alternative to the common, dignitarian one. Instead of trying to ground moral equality in features of human beings giving rise to their dignity, he grounds it in an exploration of the wrongness of treating other people as inferiors. He has good challenges to some aristocratic, catholic, and some Kantian conceptions of dignity (as failing to both deliver a rationale for dignity and an egalitarian approach). But I think that the alternative proposal he offers does not succeed. The main problem is that, as it is developed, it ends up invoking the kinds of considerations that the dignitarian approaches themselves focus on. So, for example, Sangiovanni says that what is at the centre of our rejection of the treatment of others as inferiors is our rejection of 'social cruelty'. He defines social cruelty as 'the *unauthorized, harmful, and wrongful use of other's vulnerability to attack or obliterate their capacity to develop and maintain an integral sense of self*'.[49] Clearly, the ground for the commitment to moral equality is here a commitment to respond appropriately to people's capacity

---

[48] For the view that Kant could accept this account, see Parfit (2011: sect. 41). For the view that a position like this involves a (justifiable) departure from Kant, see Scanlon (2011).
[49] Sangiovanni (2017: 76). See also similar claims regarding sentience as the ground for basic moral status (Ibid: 67ff). I discuss the issue whether moral status is scalar or graded in 'Inclusive Dignity'.

74 Human Dignity and Social Justice

to develop and maintain an integral sense of self. What makes social cruelty wrongful is precisely the failure to so respond. The treatment of others as inferiors, and social cruelty, are not the central notion, but instead track the more fundamental commitment to respond appropriately to certain valuable features of people, which is precisely the kind of thought underlying some dignitarian approaches to the justification of moral equality. The same holds for Sangiovanni's reference to the importance of vulnerability. We must always ask: 'Vulnerability to what?' and 'Vulnerability of what?' Cruel treatment is wrongful, at least in part, because it targets vulnerability regarding the development of valuable capacities, not just any random capacities. Vulnerability is indeed a general human condition, a part of the circumstances of dignity. But the vulnerability of morally unimportant or even morally problematic capacities does not exercise our critical appraisal in the way that the setting back of valuable capacities (like the one concerning an integral sense of self) does. When developed and justified, the norm against social cruelty turns out to be derivative. Sangiovanni's account throws the ball right back into the dignitarian quarter he was trying to avoid.

It is important to note that Sangiovanni does not consider all the variants of dignitarianism. My own account, for example, is different from the ones he discusses. It has similarities with the Kantian model, but is not an instance of what he calls the Regress or Address views (which are instances of the more austere strategy I mentioned above and are aptly criticized by Sangiovanni as being too thin). As I see it, the Kantian approach could instead be seen as a kind of *Response or Reflection Model*. Our practical reasoning should track— reflect, respond to—the value of the entities the reasoning agent is relating to, or can affect. Part of Kant's arguments fall into this schema. My view of the basis of dignity is, however, broader than Kant's (including more than rational agency—for example, mere sentience is relevant too).[50]

3. Marxian Socialism

3.1 Capitalism and socialism

We can go beyond Kant in identifying the radical social consequences of equal dignity. Besides criticizing feudalism and absolutism, we can challenge capitalism.

---

[50] It is also not obvious that the rejection of social cruelty must be correlated with embracing moral equality. Hierarchical social structures could be endorsed while also challenging some abuses within them as socially cruel. Only a view of the wrongness of social cruelty that already encodes a commitment to the equal standing of others will really correlate fully. But then the reactive attitudes regarding social cruelty are heuristically relevant to discover commitments to moral equality, not a determinative justification for them; they would be tracking equality rather grounding it.

Kantian Dignity and Marxian Socialism **75**

Although the idea of human dignity is the heart of his moral outlook, and he claimed that every human being has equal dignity, Kant did not identify all the radical implications of this idea for the shaping of social institutions and practices.[51] For example, although Kant claimed that in a just society people would have equal formal opportunities to compete for economic advantages instead of being inescapably destined to certain positions such as those of lords or serfs, or masters and slaves, he also took this society to allow for great inequalities regarding income, wealth, and other economic advantages. We can go further and consider whether egalitarianism about status-dignity generates egalitarianism about access to economic advantage. A key task for a dignitarian perspective is to explore how equality regarding status-dignity should translate into various forms of condition-dignity—bundles of equal civil, political, and social rights that people should enjoy.

In this exploration, Marx's work provides important insights. With these insights, we can develop the dignitarian account to include a more direct normative focus on well-being besides autonomy, a greater awareness of the social and historical conditions for the fulfilment of dignitarian norms, a fuller understanding of why and how economic life is a crucial site for dignitarian analysis, a greater recognition of the importance of positive duties of solidarity, and a discovery of the phenomenon of ideology. This section discusses these insights by addressing two key Marxian themes: the critique of capitalism and the delineation of an alternative, socialist project. The Kantian Dignitarian Approach outlined in the previous section helps articulate these Marxian themes in original ways by providing an explicit normative structure which is not readily apparent in Marx's texts.

In the interpretive debates about the normative underpinnings of Marx's critique of capitalism and his advocacy for socialism, some have argued that Marx did, and others that he did not, have views about justice. I agree with Norman Geras that Marx did hold quite strong views about justice even though he was not fully aware that he did so. I also agree with Geras that much of Marx's hostility to justice talk has to do with a specific (and in fact normatively fruitful) misgiving about proposals of social change that do not pay attention to feasibility considerations.[52] Marx's work can help us explore the material and social conditions for the feasibility, and thus in part for the successful pursuit of a dignitarian project. The degree to which people succeed at becoming virtuous and happy partly depends on the social and material circumstances in which they act, and on what they do in response to them (including changing them over time). Much of our normative thinking should thus be focused on figuring out how to frame our reaction to our social

---

[51] Wood (2008: 194–5, 323–4n.5).
[52] Geras (1989). For the historical debates about Marxian socialism and Kant's morality, see Love (2017).

76 Human Dignity and Social Justice

and material circumstances. Interestingly, Kant's own work on politics, law, and history did not ignore them. Marxists can take this exploration further (provided that they also overcome a self-contradictory wholesale rejection of normative inquiry).

Amongst those who find normative views in Marx's works, it is common to distinguish between three strands, which are roughly aligned with utilitarianism, Aristotelian value theory, and Kantian deontology.[53] I think that they can be interpreted so that they form an integrated view rather than be the disjointed fragments of a collapsing rag. The dignitarian framework will precisely help to show how these strands in Marx's normative perspective can be weaved harmoniously into a powerful approach.

In general, dignitarianism says that we ought to treat entities, including human beings, in ways that enact appropriate responses to their valuable features. This general principle is a deontic constraint, and can (and should) be specified by identifying various norms that state the kinds of respect and concern owed to various entities in various contexts. Although dignitarianism is fundamentally a deontological view, it can integrate insights from other approaches. Evaluative judgments of an Aristotelian flavour may come in as we identify what renders various features of the relevant entities valuable, and when we figure out what goods and conditions they should be supported in accessing. A theory of virtues as the dispositions to feel, think, and act in ways that are responsive to the valuable features of people and other entities agents affect would also be part of the dignitarian framework. Finally, the selection of norms and their specific implementation would engage aspects of consequentialist reasoning, by including a future-orientated concern with well-being promotion. Utilitarians' concern for pleasure would also have room within dignitarianism, as the capacity to feel pain and pleasure would be amongst the features of various entities, including human beings, which give rise to their status-dignity.

The foregoing points about dignitarianism can be developed in the more circumscribed case of dignitarian socialism. Before we proceed, we should have working definitions of capitalism and socialism, the two social systems on whose contrast Marx and socialists concentrate. It comprises three key points (I state them starkly, but each involves a possible continuum between more or less capitalist or socialist societies and various combinations):

1. In capitalism, the bulk of the means of production—the natural and technological resources workers use to produce—are privately owned

---

[53] See overviews in Elster (1985) and Lukes (1985).

and controlled. In socialism, the means of production are socially owned and controlled.

2. In capitalism, production is predominantly orientated toward profit, while in socialism it is primarily orientated toward the satisfaction of needs.

3. In capitalism, a class division develops between capitalists and workers. Capitalists own means of production and most workers do not. To survive, workers must sell their labour power (which they fully own in capitalism as well as in socialism, unlike in slave or feudal societies) to capitalists, and work under their direction for a wage. Socialism dissolves this class division.[54]

3.2 The critique of capitalism

Kant does not have much to say about the relationship between capitalist employers and wage workers. He does, however, critically discuss slavery and serfdom, saying that they could not rightfully emerge contractually. A contract of slavery would be self-contradictory, as someone who becomes a slave has lost all freedom and with it any duty to keep a contract. A contract of serfdom would also be problematic, as it would generate a relationship in which there are no determinate constrains on how much the lord can get out of the serf, so that the lord could use the serf up without their consent (MS 6:283, 330). Kant also explicitly mentions the importance of securing formal equality of opportunity by eliminating hereditary prerogatives (TP 8:292). He recognizes that this is compatible with significant economic inequalities of economic advantage, including that between employers and employees, and in fact finds such inequalities unproblematic so long as they reflect the talents and industry of those involved (TP 8:292–3). He even claims that those not holding property (including property-less workers) may be denied the right to vote because holding property is a precondition for being one's own master (TP 8:295, MS 6:313–5). So, Kant is far from offering a socialist analysis of economic inequality.[55] On the other hand, Kant tempers this meritocratic acceptance of inequality of condition by also allowing for provisions

---

[54] For a fuller discussion of the contrast between socialism and capitalism, see Chapter 8.

[55] Even if it were true that to be one's own master one must have property (or, more plausibly, that having property increases the likelihood of successful self-determination), the theorem of a Kantian philosophy of freedom (which affirms the 'innate equality' of all human beings as entitled to be their own masters— MS 6:237–8) should be to require widespread extension, or even socialist control, of productive assets so that *every* human being who could determine themselves *does* effectively come to enjoy such condition. Kant was clearly troubled by this issue: 'It is, I admit, somewhat difficult to determine what is required in order to be able to claim the rank of a human being who is his own master' (TP 8:295).

78 Human Dignity and Social Justice

of governmental assistance for poor people (MS 6:325–7). And, quite importantly, Kant recognizes, like Marx, that many problems are to be addressed first as a matter of how the structure of a society is organized rather than as a matter of the adoption of good attitudes by isolated individuals. The following remark on beneficence is one many socialists would endorse:

> Having the resources to practice such beneficence as depends on the goods of fortune is, for the most part, a result of certain beings being favored through the injustice of the government, which introduces an inequality of wealth that makes others need their beneficence. Under such circumstances, does a rich man's help to the needy, on which he so readily prides himself as something meritorious, really deserve to be called beneficence at all? (MS 6:454; see KpV 5:155n.)

It is not that *interpersonal* instances of instrumental or telic treatment are not important. It is, rather, that there are *structural* instances of those kinds of treatment, and the forms of social relations they involve should be given pride of place in social critique and change because of their enormous symbolic and causal significance. Let me elaborate by considering the three main socialist charges against capitalism, which concern exploitation, domination, and alienation.[56]

(i) *Exploitation.* In the technical Marxian sense, the exploitation of workers consists in the extraction of their surplus labour (the part of their work that goes beyond securing their own reproduction as workers). Class societies involve exploitation. The immediate producers, the workers, engage in both necessary and surplus labour. The latter (or its product) is appropriated by the members of the dominant classes. Masters exploit slaves, lords exploit serfs, and capitalists exploit waged workers.[57] Now, in ordinary language, 'exploitation' has a normative connotation. One common rendering is to say that it consists in taking unfair advantage of others. The exploitation of workers involves a morally problematic transfer of valuable resources (such as the product of surplus labour) from them to their exploiters. But

---

[56] I develop each of these points in detail (and in ways that go beyond Marx) in later chapters.
[57] The source of capitalist profit is the exploitation of labour. Labour power is a peculiar commodity: it can create more value than it costs. Its deployment can involve *surplus labour* besides *necessary labour*. The exchange value of labour power (expressed in a wage) is the amount of labour that is socially necessary to produce and reproduce it over time. But workers normally work more than is necessary to produce what they consume with their wages. Besides the time spent in necessary labour, they spend time in surplus labour, the results of which are appropriated by the capitalists, who employ them and control the product of their work. Profit is based on surplus value (i.e., on the difference between the value created by the use of labour power and the value of that labour power itself—as well as other costs of production). See Marx (1990: 270–80, 293–306). These points can be stated without relying on Marx's controversial theory of value, by saying that workers create what has value rather than value itself. See Cohen (1988: ch.11). It is not fully clear whether Marx thinks that exploitation is unjust. For exhaustive discussion of negative and positive textual clues see Geras (1989).

Kantian Dignity and Marxian Socialism   79

what renders the transfer morally problematic? On the account that I favour, exploitation is a form of wrongful use of superior power.[58] It involves taking advantage of others who are weaker by getting them to give you more than they should.

Capitalists exploit workers by using their superior bargaining power (resulting from their private control of the means of production) to extract from them more than they might (and ought to) give if they were not so vulnerable. The Kantian dignitarian account explains what's wrong with this. One of the most evident ways in which capitalism is an affront to dignitarian ideals is that it enshrines instrumental treatment of others as a typical aspect of production and exchange. As the competitive economic agents that they are, capitalists seek profit, and show concern for the freedom and well-being of their workers only if, and to the extent that, doing so would add to their profit margin. Workers have price, not dignity, for them. This has a systemic dimension as well, as capitalists normally throw their significant weight behind political agents and processes that sustain institutional schemes that cement their privileged position by making capitalist relations of production the law of the land. Capitalist exploitation is a social pattern of reduction of some human beings to mere instruments for the self-regarding benefit of others.

(ii) *Domination.* It could be objected that capitalist exploitation involves no dignitarian injustice because workers freely consent to the terms on which they interact with capitalists. They are not, like slaves, dragged to the factory or the office against their will. They sign contracts. But this objection ignores that the exploitation of workers happens in tandem with their domination. Consent that is given in circumstances of profound vulnerability and power asymmetry does not authorize its outcomes.

For consider, how is it that workers acquiesce to their exploitation? How come they enter contracts in which they produce and give away objects with more value than is expressed in their wages? Is it because they want to altruistically sacrifice their own well-being to make sure that the capitalists live in luxury? According to Marx, two conditions help explain workers' choice to enter a contract of exploitation: (1) Workers in capitalism (unlike in feudalism or slave societies) own their labour power, *but* (2) they do not own means of production. Given their dispossession (2), workers have no reasonable alternative to using their entitlement (1) to sell their labour power to the capitalists—who do own the means of production.[59] Because of the

---

[58] Goodin (1987).
[59] 'For the transformation of money into capital ... the owner of money must find the free worker available in the commodity-market ... free in the double sense that as a free individual he can dispose

80 Human Dignity and Social Justice

deep background inequality of power resulting from their structural position in a capitalist economy, workers accept a pattern of economic transactions in which they submit to the direction of capitalists during the activities of production and surrender a disproportional part of their fruits.

Again, Kant helps us understand what's wrong here. He deploys the radical idea of a human beings' 'innate *equality*, that is, independence from being bound by others to more than one can in turn bind them; hence a human being's quality of being *his own master*' (MS 6:237–8). This idea has important consequences for the assessment of relations of production in capitalism, as these involve domination and the dependence of workers on the discretion of capitalists' choices at three critical junctures. The first is the one we have already considered, which concerns the labour contract. Due to their lack of control of means of production, workers must largely submit, on pain of severe economic hardship, to the terms capitalists offer them. The second concerns the day-to-day interactions in the workplace. Capitalists and their managers rule the activities of workers by unilaterally deciding what the workers produce and how they produce it. Although in the sphere of circulation workers and capitalists might look (misleadingly, given the first point) like equally free contractors striking fair deals, once we enter the 'hidden abode' of production it is clear to all sides that what exists is relationships of intense subjection of some to the will of others.[60] Workers effectively spend most of their waking hours doing what others dictate them to do. Third, and finally, capitalists have a disproportionate impact on the legal and political process shaping the institutional structure of the society in which they exploit workers—such as the contours of legal property rights and labour law. Even if workers manage to obtain the legal right to vote and create their own trade unions and parties (which labour movements have eventually achieved after much struggle), capitalists exert disproportionate influence via greater access to mass media, the funding of political parties, the threat of disinvestment and capital flight, and the past and prospective recruitment of state officials in lucrative jobs in their firms and lobbying agencies. At the spheres of exchange,

---

of his labour-power as his own commodity, and ... he has no other commodity for sale ... [including] the objects needed for the realization of his labour-power' (Marx 1990: 272–3). But why do workers sell their labour power so cheap? Because they are weaker in bargaining power in general (given (2) above) and, besides, capitalism (through labour-saving technical innovations spurred by competition) constantly produces unemployment (the industrial reserve army of the unemployed), which weakens the bargaining power of individual workers further. Thus, Marx says that although workers voluntarily enter the contract of exploitation, they are 'compelled [to do so] by social conditions'. 'The silent compulsion of economic relations sets the seal on the domination of the capitalist over the worker .... [I]t is possible to rely on [the worker's] dependence on capital, which springs from the conditions of production themselves, and is guaranteed in perpetuity by them' (Ibid: 382, 899).

[60] Ibid: 279–80.

Production, and in the broader political process, workers are subject to the will of capitalists in the shaping of the terms on which they work. This is an affront to their dignity as self-determining, self-mastering agents.[61]

(iii) *Alienation.* The socialist critique of capitalism as a system of social relationships is complex. In addition to (and in combination with) the denunciation of exploitation and domination, it focuses on alienation.[62] This critical point can also be fruitfully articulated in dignitarian terms.

Marx uses the term 'alienation' to cover several phenomena.[63] Subjectively, alienation can appear as a sense of lack of meaning or worth in one's life. But for Marx, alienation has an objective aspect. People may be alienated even if they do not feel alienated. The key is the mismatch between people's existence—the way they actually live their lives—and their essence. Alienation occurs when the former fails to appropriately express the latter. More specifically, in Marx's view, people are alienated when they do not develop and exercise their human capacities. Marx concentrates on those aspects of human nature relevant for productive activity, such as the capacities for freely chosen and creative work, which is undertaken in cooperative ways, and which meets the needs of others.[64] Workers are alienated to the extent that their ability to develop and exercise these valuable capacities at work are

---

[61] Also relevant is Kant's view of the initial appropriation of external resources (such as land) as a matter of social convention and as calling for a justification that tracks the general will of all those affected rather than only the convenience of unilateral appropriators (MS 6:258–70). Kant does not specify the terms on which a general will would authorize acts of appropriation or types of property (e.g. private or collective). Some interpreters warn that we should not assume that a general will authorization requirement would turn property into an instrument of public policy. The point of property is not to foster the well-being of those affected by it, but to respect individuals as independent, purposive agents. (See Ripstein 2009: 154–5.) But it is not clear what the latter constraint really amounts to, or that a general will should not also have public policy aims. A dignitarian and socialist concern with the development and exercise of individuals' capacities would frame access to natural resources by recommending a scheme that optimally services that concern. As such, this public aim could be both embraced by a general will and satisfy the abstract idea of respecting individuals' purposive agency. Much would depend on the details of the scheme adopted, of course. But there is no general normative obstacle blocking a view of property in natural resources (and other means of production) as social devices to empower people to live free and flourishing lives. When defenders of capitalism protest, saying that socialized control limits the freedom of private agents, they must be reminded that 'private ownership for some ... [involves] non-ownership ... for others' (Marx 1991: 948). Capitalist property rights set limits to the liberty of workers to access means of production Cohen (2011: ch.7). The freedom question when resources are scarce is what feasible scheme offers, overall, the greatest freedom for all.

[62] This passage captures the charges discussed: '[W]ithin the capitalist system all methods for raising the social productivity of labour are put into effect at the cost of the individual worker ... all means for the development of production undergo a dialectical inversion so that they become means of domination and exploitation of the producers; they distort the worker into a fragment of a man, they degrade him to the level of an appendage of a machine, they destroy the actual content of his labour turning it into a torment; they alienate from him the intellectual potentialities of the labour process in the same proportion as science is incorporated in it as an independent power; they deform the conditions under which he works, subject him during the labour process to a despotism the more hateful for its meanness; they transform his life-time into working-time, and drag his wife and child beneath the wheels of the juggernaut of capital' (Marx 1990: 799).

[63] Elster (1986: ch. 3); Wood (2004: Part One); Wolff (2002: 28–39, 104–5, 122–5).

[64] Marx (1978c: 75–7, 80–93; 1990: 283–4).

82 Human Dignity and Social Justice

limited.[65] If, as seems plausible, these remarkable capacities are in the basis of dignity, then we can say that dignitarian norms are violated when workers are avoidably cornered in capitalism into work that is repetitive, stunting, toxically competitive, or that engages little initiative and decision-making.

When Kant discusses happiness, and the imperatives linked to its pursuit, he says that our inquiries would have to focus on figuring out empirically what causes happiness and then (conclude that we should) go for it.[66] But this ignores that there is a substantive, non-analytic but also not merely empirical or descriptive task of identifying certain ends in life as good, or as being constitutive of the agent's well-being. Marx's discussion of non-alienation and self-realization can be used to fill some of this gap.[67] The Marxian view of self-realization says that people add to their well-being when they succeed at engaging in the free development and exercise of their human capacities in solidaristic cooperation with others. This view provides a partial account of the good worth plugging into our moral framework as part of the metric of advantage to be taken into account when articulating dignitarian norms.[68] What we, individually or through our institutions, should not prevent others from accessing, or should enable others to access includes, inter alia, practices in which they can unfold their capacities so as to achieve self-realization. These ideas inform Marx's characterizations of a socialist society. Self-realization would occur once the 'realm of necessity' and the corresponding necessary labour to secure subsistence is circumscribed and people reach also a 'realm of freedom' in which 'the development of human energy which is an end in itself' unfolds.[69] This realm of freedom would involve non-alienated labour. In fact, such labour, enabling the 'all-round development of the individual', would become their 'prime want'.[70] Socialists call for a human emancipation featuring 'the development of the rich individuality which is

---

[65] Thus, when alienated, 'labour is *external* to the worker, i.e., it does not belong to his essential being ... in his work, therefore, he does not affirm himself but denies himself, does not feel content but unhappy, does not develop freely his physical and mental energy but mortifies his body and ruins his mind. The worker therefore only feels himself outside his work, and in his work feels outside himself. He is at home when he is not working, and when he is working he is not at home. His labour is therefore not voluntary, but coerced; it is *forced labour*. It is therefore not the satisfaction of a need; it is merely a *means* to satisfy needs external to it' (Marx 1978c: 74).

[66] See, e.g., G 4:418–9. Keep in mind the discussion in Section 2.2 (iii) above.

[67] Kant already claims in the *Groundwork* that people should seek to develop their capacities. '[A]s a rational being [a human being] necessarily wills that all his capacities in him be developed, since they serve him and are given to him for all sorts of possible purposes' (G 4:423).

[68] I agree with Wood (2004: 23–4) that we can interpret Marx's critique of alienation, and his ideal of self-realization, as relying on an objective conception of the good and of human happiness. As Wood also points out (Ibid: 281, n.1), such a conception can be used in a moral theory of justice to provide information about what kinds of opportunities or conditions people can reasonably make claims to in their social relations.

[69] Marx (1991: 957–9).

[70] Marx (1978i: 531).

Kantian Dignity and Marxian Socialism **83**

all-sided in its production as in its consumption'[71] and envision a 'higher form of society in which the full and free development of every individual forms the ruling principle'.[72]

3.3 The socialist project

How could the connection between the Kantian idea of equal dignity and the socialist views on socioeconomic justice be developed? We can proceed by envisaging the reshaping of socioeconomic relations so that they enact appropriate responses to the basis of the dignity of human beings involved in them. If people have equal dignity because of some features of them, then social relations should be shaped so that these features are given the support they deserve in each person. Consider the predicament of working people. When they are dominated, and exploited, their capacities for self-direction and for cooperating as equals with others are insufficiently respected. They are treated merely as means. And workers are not treated as ends in themselves when the economy is (avoidably) organized so that some of them do not have real opportunities to develop and express their talents for creative and meaningful production—and are thus alienated. Even if people have different (innate or acquired) talents, and as a result their efforts could not produce as much that is meaningful to them or others, they should still have equal chances to develop and exercise their valuable capacities and benefit from the contribution of others. This is what Dignitarian Socialism would suggest. As the flip side of the dignitarian critique of capitalism, it articulates Solidaristic Empowerment to recommend that we reorganize society so that it enables and supports each person's free development and exercise of their valuable capacities.

(i) *The Abilities/Needs Principle.* Marx never provided a detailed account of what a socialist society would be like. In fact, he was hostile to advancing blueprints, dismissing this as a form of paternalism (see (ii) below). It is obvious that such a society would involve a shift to the socialist aspects of organization mentioned in the contrasts stated in Section 3.1: the bulk of the means of production would be socially owned and controlled, production would predominantly be aimed at need satisfaction, and the division between bourgeoisie and proletariat would disappear. These points are consistent with different specific institutional frameworks. Indeed, there is a lively contemporary debate showing that a centrally planned economy is far from the only

[71] Marx (1973: 325). See also (1978e: 160).
[72] Marx (1990: 739.)

84 Human Dignity and Social Justice

option—for example, market socialism, the expansion of cooperatives, and the extension of democratic principles to the economy offer alternatives.[73] In this book, I will concentrate on a key general idea by Marx, which is that socialist organization would instantiate the slogan 'from each according to their abilities, to each according to their needs' (the Abilities/Needs Principle).[74]

The Abilities/Needs Principle can be understood as an elaboration of the dignitarian idea of Solidaristic Empowerment. As I argue in detail in the next chapter, we can develop it in terms of six general guidelines for economic organization that demand the creation of effective opportunities for productive activity in which workers can enjoy self-realization, the articulation of positive duties to cater for other people's needs, a specific requirement that people's basic needs for subsistence and for being able to function as political equals be secured, the generation of an ethos and a scheme of distribution of access to consumption goods that acknowledges a responsibility to cooperate in production on terms of fair reciprocity, a pursuit of differentiated provisions that target individuals' diverse abilities and interests, and a systematic affirmation of people's self-determination in shaping the terms of their economic life.

The Abilities/Needs Principle helps envision an economy of mutual affirmation amongst all producers and consumers. It takes the abilities and needs of all as the focus of negative *and* positive duties. As a result, it gives human dignity full recognition. Importantly, this vision combines freedom and solidarity. This, I think, is a Kantian point. Kant's moral philosophy obviously affirms rights concerning individual and collective liberty. But it also affirms duties to contribute to the freedom and well-being of others.[75] With the refinements proposed here, the Kantian dignitarian framework can escape the scorn Marx directed at the 'Robinsonades' of modern political theory.[76]

(ii) *Self-emancipation.* Some Kantians could criticize the view just outlined by saying that it risks a paternalistic imposition on workers of work they might not choose, even if it would involve self-realization. In response, notice four points. First, people are given real opportunities to engage in

---

[73] For extensive discussion see Wright (2010), and Gilabert and O'Neill (2019: sect. 4).

[74] Marx (1978i: 531).

[75] For example, Kant urges us to develop our own powers and make ourselves 'a useful member of the world' (which also 'belongs to the worth of humanity in [our] own person, which [we] ought not to degrade' (MS 6:446)).

[76] Marx (1973: 83–5) criticizes views that fail to capture the extent to which people are socially dependent on each other. He argued that '[i]ndividuals producing in society—hence socially determined individual production—is, of course, the point of departure' and that the 'independent, autonomous subjects' of many eighteenth-century theories are 'Robinsonades', 'illusions'.

Kantian Dignity and Marxian Socialism   85

non-exploitative, non-dominating, and non-alienating labour; they are not forced to do so. The scheme empowers workers; it does not force them into any final state. Second, the shaping of the economy would be subject to democratic authorization and contestation. Enjoying robust political liberties, people could collectively assess and reform economic arrangements of the kind proposed. Third, we should acknowledge that any society that has not completely eliminated material scarcity will need, and press, people to work. If this is so, it is only fair that they have opportunities to work in ways that engage rather than stunt their valuable capacities for free and cooperative production. Finally, the interest in the good of self-realization is linked to some of the capacities that give rise to status-dignity, and thus to the normative platform from which the paternalism objection itself draws its argumentative force. Responding to the dignity of people includes supporting their pursuit of a well-being involving the development and exercise of their valuable human capacities.

Despite popular misperceptions, Marx and many socialists inspired by him are quite hostile to paternalism. This is partly why, for example, Marx was opposed to developing detailed recipes for how socialist transformation should proceed.[77] He thought that 'the emancipation of the working class must be the work of the working class itself',[78] and that this self-emancipation would likely exhibit a radical democratic form (as his praise for the Paris Commune suggests).[79]

(iii) *Ideology and socialist politics.* Also important for the Marxian view of politics is the critique of ideology, of the attempts to shape the culture of a society so that the domination of some by others is deemed acceptable. Typical of ideologies is the presentation of the contingent as necessary, the historical as natural, and the conflictive as harmonious.[80] Ideology critique has a role in dissolving these presentations. It also shows that, often, what is presented as being in the general interest of all may in fact only serve the particular interest of the dominant class. Interestingly, this operation can work in tandem with the Kantian Social Contract Standard. We can see socialist politics as a radical democracy in which people engage in public debate to figure out together what the idea of the social contract would really amount to for them, and decide by themselves what to do about economic justice.

---

[77] Marx (1990: 99).
[78] Marx (1978j: 555).
[79] Marx (1978h: 634–6).
[80] See, e.g., Marx (1973: 87–8; 1978e: 172–5; 1978f: 487; 1990: 102–3).

86 Human Dignity and Social Justice

Ideology critique can even target deployments of the idea of dignity in capitalism which dissociate it from solidarity:

> The only comprehensible language we have is the language our possessions use together. We would not understand a human language and it would remain ineffectual. From the one side, such a language would be felt to be begging, imploring and hence *humiliating*. It could be used only with feelings of shame and debasement. From the other side, it would be received as *impertinence* or *insanity* and so rejected. We are so estranged from our human essence that the direct language of man strikes us as an *offence against the dignity of man*, whereas the estranged language of [commodity, economic] objective values appears as the justified, self-confident and self-acknowledged dignity of man incarnate.[81]

In opposition to a view of dignity that embraces possessive individualism to legitimize the asymmetric social power and disproportionate benefits enjoyed by the rich, the lucky, and the strong, socialists put forward a more humane project that relies on generally shareable reasons to have opportunities for the free and cooperative development and exercise of our capacities, to be offered support by others when we need it, and to give it when we can. This project charts a fitting practical horizon for the hope that human dignity always inspires.[82]

---

[81] Marx (1992: 276).

[82] We should 'develop the original predisposition to a good will within [us], which can never be lost' (MS 6:441—see also KpV 5:159; EF 8:355, 380; R:6:44).

3
The Abilities/Needs Principle

1. Introduction

This chapter offers an exploration of the socialist principle '*From each according to their abilities, to each according to their needs*'. The Abilities/Needs Principle (as I will call it) is arguably at the ethical heart of socialism but, surprisingly, has received almost no attention by political philosophers.[1] I will propose a dignitarian interpretation of the principle, and argue that it involves appealing ideas of meaningful work, solidaristic contribution, fair reciprocity, recognition of individual differences, and self-determination.

There is today a moderate revival of interest in socialism. In the aftermath of the global crisis of 2008, many people started to wonder whether there is a desirable alternative to the capitalist way of organizing economic life. Socialism provides the historically most important counter-tradition to capitalism. But how should we understand socialism today? To answer this question, we can think of a fully developed conception of social justice as having three key dimensions. It would propose a set of normative principles (DI), certain social institutions and practices that implement those principles (DII), and some political strategies of transformation leading agents from where they are to the social realizations implementing the principles (if these do not exist already) (DIII). Now, it is common to characterize socialism (or communism, a term preferred by many Marxists) in terms of dimension

---

[1] The principle was formulated in the following passage. 'In a higher phase of communist society, after the enslaving subordination of the individual to the division of labour, and therewith also the antithesis between mental and physical labour, has vanished; after labour has become not only a means of life but life's prime want; after the productive forces have also increased with the all-round development of the individual—only then can the narrow horizon of bourgeois right be crossed in its entirety and society inscribe in its banner: From each according to his ability, to each according to his needs!' Marx (1978I: 531). In contemporary debates, the principle is often referred to as the 'Needs Principle'. I call it differently, adding reference to 'Abilities', to emphasize that it addresses both the demand and the supply side. It states rights to receive, but also, and in conjunction, duties to give. For the historical linage of the principle in socialist thought, see Bovens and Lutz (2019). For an anarchist interpretation, see Spafford (2020).

Human Dignity and Social Justice. Pablo Gilabert, Oxford University Press. © Pablo Gilabert (2023).
DOI: 10.1093/oso/9780192871152.003.0003

88 Human Dignity and Social Justice

DII. Socialism is seen as a form of social organization in which economic class division no longer exists and in which workers control the means of production, shape the economic process, and benefit equally from it. I think, however, that this narrow focus on DII should be avoided, and that we should make discussion of DI more prominent. We cannot defend any specific version of DII as desirable without engaging the standards that DI illuminates.[2] Discussion of DI is also crucial because we cannot simply assume, as many socialists did in the past, that socialist transformations are inevitable. History need not move in a socialist direction. To move it in that direction, some political agents will have to become committed to socialism and pursue it in practice. Given the mistakes of past socialist politics, this point has real bite. Many people need to be convinced that socialism is desirable, and some also need to be convinced that socialism is not utterly undesirable. This requires moral argument and advocacy.

This chapter proceeds as follows. Section 2 briefly analyses the formulation of the Abilities/Needs Principle by Marx. Section 3 identifies the principle's initial plausibility, but shows that it faces problems (regarding scarcity, incentives, responsibility, diversity of metrics of advantage, and paternalism) that cannot be addressed without developing a fresh interpretation of it. The rest of the chapter provides such a fresh interpretation, deploying the Dignitarian Approach to support the specification, justification, and implementation of the principle. Sections 4.1–4 articulates the principle as yielding demands concerning opportunities for self-realization in work, positive duties to cater for the needs of others, sensitivity to individual differences, mechanisms of fair reciprocity, and structures of self-determination in economic life. Although it focuses largely on DI, this chapter also considers DII and DIII. Section 4.5 explores a practical implementation of the socialist principle, and Section 5 discusses some normative puzzles about the transition from capitalism to socialism. The chapter concludes with a response to the worry that the Abilities/Needs Principle could be used to inappropriately cajole people to work.

---

[2] I am not saying that we must proceed in a strictly linear way, from DI to DII, and from DII to DIII. Inquiry is of course more complex, involving epistemic back-and-forth between these dimensions in an ongoing search for reflective equilibrium. In this search, we should also pay serious attention to DIII, which may lead us to rethink our views of DI and DII. Thus, the mistakes in the history of communist politics in the twentieth century, especially the insufficient attention to civil and political liberties, should motivate the exploration of principles affirming those rights and of institutions implementing them.

The Abilities/Needs Principle **89**

2. The Marxian Platform

The Abilities/Needs Principle (hereafter 'ANP') was formulated by Karl Marx in a late text, the 'Critique of the Gotha Program'. This is one of the few occasions in which Marx is explicit about what socialism (or communism, in his words) would involve. Although my aims in this chapter are not exegetical, it will be helpful to summarize the key points in Marx's discussion.[3] They are of intrinsic interest, have been quite influential in socialist thought, and will be significant for this chapter's argument.

Marx presents two principles of distribution. The first is the so-called Contribution Principle (*To each according to their contribution*), and the second is ANP (*From each according to their abilities, to each according to their needs*). They are supposed to apply consecutively, in two phases of socialism. The second is evaluatively superior to the former. In the early phase, part of the distribution already caters directly for needs: the Contribution Principle is constrained by basic provisions concerning health care, education, and the reproduction of the infrastructure of the economy. But ANP goes far beyond such basic needs, catering for the conditions for everyone's human flourishing. ANP also interrupts the translation of inequalities in natural endowments into unequal access to consumption goods. The needs of each individual count equally regardless of the extent of their ability to produce. However, the principle's implementation is not feasible during the early stage of transition, as moral and political culture is still coloured by bourgeois principles (such as the principle of exchange of commodities with equivalent value—which disadvantages workers with lower natural talents), and there is not yet enough material abundance to support the more sophisticated needs of all. It thus makes sense to implement the Contribution Principle first. Although less intrinsically desirable, its implementation would ease the transition away from capitalism by delivering on its unfulfilled promise to reward productive output rather than simply reflect the greater bargaining power of those in superior class positions. Furthermore, it would pave the way for the creation of more desirable distributive schemes by introducing incentives to generate the level of material abundance that would make distribution according to needs viable and thus a real option.

---

[3] I concentrate on pages 528–32 of Marx's text. There is a debate as to whether Marx held substantive moral views about justice. See Geras (1989). As pointed out in Chapter 2, I agree with Geras that Marx did hold some such views even if he did not articulate them properly—or even fully recognized that he held them. I discuss the significance of the idea of rights for socialists (and for Marx) in Gilabert (2019a: sect. 4.2.2).

90 Human Dignity and Social Justice

3. Exploring The Abilities/Needs Principle

3.1 Initial appeal

I find ANP very appealing. Here are some initial (and related) reasons why:

(i) It involves an ideal of reciprocity. As a conjunction of requirements on economic life, the principle not only refers to the demand side (to distribution according to needs) but also to the supply side (to production according to abilities).

(ii) This idea of reciprocity is constrained by considerations of fairness. It involves similarity in effort, not equivalence of output or exchange value. If productive efforts are similar, it is fair that receipt of income and other means for need satisfaction be equal. This is important because people differ in their native abilities and social circumstances. Appealingly, the principle does not condone inequalities in capability to satisfy needs that depend on such morally arbitrary (and often unchosen) factors. Marx anticipated an insight of contemporary 'luck-egalitarianism'—the view that it is unfair for some to be worse off than others through no choice or fault of their own—when he criticized distributions that 'tacitly recogniz[e] unequal individual endowment and thus productive capacity as natural privileges'.[4]

(iii) The principle articulates an ideal of solidarity according to which we should produce and distribute with the needs of others (besides our own) in mind. Socialism involves positive duties to help make the life of others better, or, as Einstein puts it, 'a sense of responsibility for [one's] fellow men'.[5]

(iv) The principle involves a direct concern with people's well-being. Resources are only means to pursue well-being, and their distribution's significance is instrumental.

(v) Relatedly, the principle is sensitive to the fact that individuals differ in important ways both in their abilities and in their needs. So identical incomes or resources will not yield equality in the relevant

---

[4] Marx (1978i: 530). On luck-egalitarianism see Cohen (2008: 7–8). It doesn't follow that Marx must have also embraced the different thesis that we should not redress any inequalities resulting from people's choices. Thus, in his text Marx also calls for attention to the fact that some workers may need (and presumably be entitled) to more resources because they have larger families. To the extent that a luck-egalitarian view endorses the additional—and independent—thesis, it would differ from Marx's view as interpreted here. On this point, see Furendal (2019: n.3).
[5] Einstein (1949).

sense. Here Marx anticipated Sen's challenge to resourcist views of equality as facing the 'conversion problem' (the fact that, due to different personal, environmental, and cultural circumstances, people may not be able to achieve the same level of well-being even if they have identical resources).[6]

(vi) Marx's discussion of the principle addresses feasibility considerations to judge when its application is appropriate. Thus, when not enough cultural backing or material abundance is yet in place, the implementation of the lower Contribution Principle may be preferable. This exemplifies a general, appealing feature of the socialist tradition: its seemingly paradoxical—but in fact consistent and quite fruitful—effort to develop proposals for social change that are both ethically ambitious and realistic. Socialists invite both serious normative reflection (of the kind pursued in moral and political philosophy) and consideration of practical feasibility (as revealed by political experience and social science).

(vii) Within some strands of the socialist tradition, the principle has been interpreted as working in tandem with a demand for democratic control of productive resources and with public deliberation about how to specify the economic distributions it mandates. People can develop the ability, and arguably they also have the need, to be able to determine the conditions under which they live. Construed this way, the principle helps in the exploration of democracy at the level of the economy besides governmental institutions. Since people spend so much of their lives at work, it is important that they have opportunities to have a say on how their economic activities are shaped. Since inequality of economic power often translates into inequality of political power, it is also instrumentally significant to limit the former through economic democracy.

(viii) In the socialist tradition, the principle has been taken to require promotion of opportunities for self-realization through development and exercise of people's capacities in meaningful work and other activities. This is an important good (arguably a need) often missed in other political views that only focus on income and its use in acquiring consumption goods.

---

[6] Marx (1978i: 530–1). Marx's sensitivity to individuals' differences is missed in Rosanvallon's (2011: 175) otherwise insightful critical discussion of nineteenth century communism as involving a 'deindividualization of the world'. On the conversion problem see Sen (2009: ch.12). We can interpret Marx's criticism of talk of 'equal rights' for not tracking the specific needs of different individuals as a rejection of certain accounts of equality that do not address what ultimately matters (each individual's access to need satisfaction), rather than as a rejection of the idea that people have equal rights.

92 Human Dignity and Social Justice

(ix) The socialist view that needs ground entitlements to support by others helps challenge an extreme ideal of independence as self-reliance. That ideal is infeasible because nobody can flourish without substantial help, and it is undesirable because there is intrinsic value in mutual support.[7] As I see it, ANP expresses a view of people as producers and beneficiaries in inclusive society. There is no shame in getting more (to satisfy one's needs) than one produces (through using one's abilities) if one makes an appropriate effort to contribute when one can. Coupled with effective opportunities to participate and make decisions in production and politics, the positive right to support from others involves solidarity without disrespect for people's productive capacities and autonomy.

(x) A socialist concern with access to needs fulfilment has consequences for social design. It helps explain why 'pre-distributive' measures (such as egalitarian forms of property in means of production or access to training) to eliminate concentration of economic power are important but insufficient. It is important to directly focus on distribution that supports people's capability to lead flourishing lives. Furthermore, there is reason to rearrange production itself to offer producers a more cooperative and fulfilling experience.[8] Socialism always emphasizes solidarity besides freedom and equality, both at the level of production and distribution.

3.2 Is the principle trivial, redundant, or manifestly inferior to others?

Some might ask whether it makes sense today to even entertain a view of economic justice based in ANP. Kymlicka provides an instructive example of scepticism.[9] He raises a number of challenges to ANP. They can be summarized as saying that the principle may be trivial, redundant, or manifestly inferior to others. Triviality may arise if it just restates the familiar idea of equal concern for the interests of all without telling us anything specific about how to honour it. It may be redundant because we already have principles calling for equal consideration of the interests of all in liberal egalitarian

---

[7] Socialists praise social relations in which 'people care about, and, where necessary and possible, care for, one another, and, too, care that they care about one another' Cohen (2009: 34–5).

[8] Socialism may differ in these ways from property-owning democracy. See Rawls's (2001: 135–40) discussion of liberal democratic socialism and property-owning democracy. For new developments, see O'Neill and Williamson (2012).

[9] Kymlicka (2002: 187–90).

The Abilities/Needs Principle   **93**

theories (such as those of John Rawls or Ronald Dworkin). When we consider those theories we may find, furthermore, that ANP is manifestly inferior to them, as it does not include insights they lack and it lacks insights they have. Two examples of the latter insights are the account of the needs or interests that matter from the point of view of justice by reference to social primary goods (Rawls) or resources (Dworkin), and the circumstance/choice distinction that helps to establish a demarcation between inequalities that deserve to be combated from the point of view of justice (those resulting from circumstances) and those that do not (those resulting from choice).

To respond to this challenge, we can say several things. First, ANP was formulated before the recent liberal egalitarian theories that Kymlicka mentions, and Marx already captured some of the insights of those theories in his discussion of ANP. Marx, and socialists more generally, were worried about superficial views of equality that did not address material disadvantage. They demanded economic systems that actually worked equally to the benefit of all those living under them, challenging the absolute and relative deprivations capitalist institutions generated. In this respect, part of the appeal of contemporary liberal egalitarianism consists precisely in mobilizing socialist concerns that pre-date it. Furthermore, Marx anticipated the circumstance/choice distinction. As we saw, in the 'Critique of the Gotha Program' Marx criticizes the Contribution Principle precisely because it condones inequalities in the ability to satisfy needs which result from choice-independent differences in natural endowments. Arguably, ANP captures the liberal egalitarian concern for responsibility if we consider both of its clauses rather than only the second (as Kymlicka does). The first clause identifies a responsibility to contribute, and we can interpret the second (as I will below) as taking the justifiability of some demands on the social product as depending on one's making an appropriate effort to support its generation.

There is more. ANP, and the socialist tradition, provide fresh insights about how to think about the metric and duties of distributive justice. They include a rich account of 'abilities' and 'needs' as being multifarious, developing over time, and as partially dependent on the nature of social and political systems. They include a valuable emphasis on the significance of self-realization in work besides consumption.[10] And they display a fundamental concern for

---

[10] Meaningful work has been neglected in liberal political philosophy. Puzzlingly, Rawls acknowledges the importance of 'meaningful work in free association with others', but takes its 'definition' as not being 'a problem of justice' Rawls (1999: 257–8). However, recent proposals seek to justify reforms at the workplace through fresh developments of Rawls's theory. For example, Arnold (2012) argues that access to work involving authority, responsibility, and complexity is a social primary good to be regulated by the difference

94   Human Dignity and Social Justice

solidarity (as captured, for example, in the responsibility to produce to meet the needs of others as something that has intrinsic significance).

Recent liberal egalitarian theories are different from earlier liberal views of economic equality (which focused only on formal equality of opportunity) precisely because they have absorbed the historical contribution of socialism. It is liberalism that has moved towards socialist ideas. If contemporary socialists move towards the liberal egalitarian framework, they partly move towards greater understanding of their own historical contribution. As will become clear from what follows, I accept that there are serious problems in the Marxian formulation of ANP. I also accept that contemporary socialists have much to learn from liberalism. I think that a viable contemporary socialist view of justice must substantially overlap with liberalism, absorbing the priority the latter gives to certain civil and political freedoms. But the

principle. Arguably the fair equality of opportunity principle also has room for considerations about the intrinsic significance of labour activities. Thus, Rawls states that the principle 'expresses the conviction that if some places were not open on a basis fair to all, those kept out would be right in feeling unjustly treated even though they benefitted from the greater efforts of those who were allowed to hold them. They would be justified in their complaint not only because they were excluded from certain external rewards of office but because they were debarred from experiencing the realization of self which comes from a skilful and devoted exercise of social duties. They would be deprived of one of the main forms of human good' (Rawls 1999: 73). Furthermore, Rawls explores the importance of training and realizing their capacities. He formulates an 'Aristotelian Principle' according to which 'other things equal, people enjoy the exercise of their realized capacities (their innate or trained abilities), and this enjoyment increases the more the capacity is realized, or the greater its complexity' (Ibid: 374). This is a descriptive, psychological principle, not a normative statement about the good. But Rawls draws on it to make normative claims. For example, he says that 'in the design of social institutions a large place has to be made for it, otherwise human beings will find their culture and form of life dull and empty' (Ibid: 377). He also connects this principle to the 'thin' conception of the good to be used in articulating principles of justice (Ibid: 381). He links it to meaningful work in complementary activities fulfilling the idea of social union (Ibid: 363–4). He even refers to the principle when explaining the conditions of access to what he takes to be the most important primary good: self-respect and self-esteem (Ibid: 386–7). Given these considerations, the fact that work can be a major medium for the unfolding and enjoyment of realized capacities (or the stunting of them), and the quite general circumstance that work is a nearly unavoidable and time-consuming activity for most people in feasible economic systems, a requirement of access to meaningful work—work that features the unfolding of people's capacities—should have had a prominent role in his theory of justice.

It could be objected that this suggestion is blocked by Rawls's rejection of perfectionism (Ibid: sect. 50). Rawls defines perfectionism quite narrowly, as a conception of justice that (in its 'strict version') requires that we 'arrange institutions and ... define the duties and obligations of individuals so as to maximize the achievements of human excellence in art, science, and culture', or (in its 'moderate version') makes this requirement a consideration to be weighed by intuition against others (Ibid: 285–6). Now, as Wall (2015) notes, this characterization does not capture other variants of perfectionism that do not focus on the promotion of specific goods (such as art, culture, and science) but more generally on the development of people's diverse capacities, those with a satisficing rather than a maximizing structure, and those which have an egalitarian profile—valuing equally the perfectionist achievements of each person. The first and third of these possibilities could be combined with the Aristotelian Principle to generate a general requirement of access to meaningful work without implying the illiberal cajoling of individuals into activities that express a particular, thick conception of the good they reject. In any case, the suggestion made in the previous paragraph does not require accepting perfectionism as characterized by Rawls. An important remaining issue, however, is whether we should accept Rawls's subjectivist account of the good as the satisfaction of preferences formed with sufficient information and deliberation. I favour instead an objectivist view, which would recommend an articulation of the Aristotelian Principle as stating a normative fact about what people have reason to value in addition to a descriptive psychological report about what people have a tendency to prefer or enjoy.

The Abilities/Needs Principle **95**

socialist tradition has much to offer as well. An elaboration of ANP can yield important insights.

3.3 Need to develop an interpretation of the principle

Despite its initial plausibility, there are important worries regarding ANP that cannot be satisfactorily addressed without developing a fresh interpretation of it. In this subsection, I briefly identify the worries and say how we might respond to them. The rest of the chapter develops these responses.

(i) *Beyond justice?* Some say that when Marx depicts the future social-ist society, he assumes that in it there would be no serious conflict of interests or material scarcity. On this view, ANP is not really a nor-mative principle. It does not prescribe anything. Rather, it describes or predicts a situation beyond justice. Whether or not Marx thought this, we can entertain ANP as a normative principle for situations in which the circumstances of justice do hold.[11] It may be unrealistic to expect that we will ever be placed in a situation in which serious problems of distributive justice do not arise.[12] In any case, we need principles to guide our conduct in situations in which the problems exist. I will construe ANP as at least in part a guide to address them.

(ii) *Appropriate metric (and issues of scarcity, disagreement, and paternal-ism).* What needs should we recognize as giving rise to distributive entitlements? They must include more than very basic needs if ANP is to involve more than basic sufficientarian demands (which it cer-tainly does). But they cannot be equivalent to whatever people want or desire, given that scarcity remains. So, we need a criterion of reasonable demands. This is difficult to provide given that people disagree about what is good, and we should beware of paternalistic impositions by political institutions. These problems are real. But it is important to notice that they affect any egalitarian view of jus-tice. For example, advocating equality of opportunity or resources does not avoid them because we must determine which opportunities are worth guaranteeing politically, and make special provisions when equal resources yield unequal life-prospects (such as those regard-ing health) for people with different native endowments. In 4.2–3, I

---

[11] Geras (1989: 264–5). I agree with Geras that Marx did assume a view of justice when presenting the principle.
[12] Nove (1991: Part 1).

96 Human Dignity and Social Justice

recommend that we address these issues by developing a flexible yet substantive account of needs and by encouraging practices of public deliberation and democratic choice.

(iii) *Responsibility.* How should we respond to needs that are very costly to meet when the people who have them have chosen to act in ways that foreseeably generate them? This problem is common in egalitarian views. I will suggest that ANP can be sensitive to issues of responsibility. Given its concern with the supply side besides the demand side, it already assumes that each must be mindful of the effects of their choices on others. However, this will be qualified by other considerations. When what is at stake is access to basic goods necessary for subsistence and for participation in the political community, needs may give rise to unconstrained distributive obligations.[13] These points are developed in 4.1–4.4.

(iv) *Incentives.* Will people be motivated to be productive in a socialist economy? Why? Would they not choose instead to free-ride on the productive efforts of others? This is another typical worry. To address it, one could engage self-centred instrumental considerations, making it prudent for people to support a socialist economy to avoid financial losses or the shame provoked by the negative judgement or low esteem by fellow citizens. Another strategy is to cultivate a social ethos of solidarity and an appreciation of the intrinsic significance of self-realization in productive and meaningful work.[14] People could organize their working activities so that they develop and exercise their capacities and contribute, fraternally, to the well-being of others. It is interesting to consider the possible tensions between these considerations (including, for example, possible tensions between self-realization and solidaristic service). I develop these points in 4.4, 4.5, and 5.

(v) *Matching supply and demand.* Even if the incentives problem is solved, there is the issue of how to make what is produced and what is needed coincide. In a large complex economy this poses enormous informational problems. An option is to fashion economies that retain the efficient signalling mechanisms of markets without their inegalitarian distributive consequences. I explore this strategy in 4.5.

---

[13] See Gilabert (2012c). Cohen (2009) is hesitant as to whether demands of community are duties of justice, tending to view the latter as reduced to what luck egalitarianism commands. I take ANP to encode some demands of community as duties of justice.

[14] This was central in Ernesto 'Che' Guevara's view of non-alienated work as involving both self-realization and fulfilment of 'social duty' Guevara (1977: 10–1, 78–90).

4. Developing The Abilities/Needs Principle

4.1 ANP is not the only principle socialists should accept

I am focusing here on ANP. But a complete account of dimension DI of socialism should also include other principles, and if possible, identify their relations. For example, principles stating protections of civil and political liberties should be included, and these principles should be seen as typically outweighing ANP when their implications conflict. If people choose jobs in which they make poor use of their productive abilities they should not be coerced to do other work (except in emergencies[15]). People should obey (although they may campaign for changing) distributive arrangements generated by a legitimate democratic process even if they are unjust according to ANP (unless the injustices are extreme). In the interpretation I will formulate, the principle is normally constrained by basic civil and political liberties, such as freedom of conscience, choice of occupation, speech, association, and political participation. Thus, the form of socialism I envisage would be a version of liberal democratic socialism.[16]

4.2 ANP and dignity

The constraints regarding civil and political liberties flow naturally from the dignitarian perspective at the background of my exploration of ANP. On this perspective, as presented in the last two chapters, supporting secure conditions for individuals' self-determination has pride of place.

Furthermore, we can give ANP itself a dignitarian rationale. In particular, ANP can be seen as articulating some of the economic implications of the dignitarian ideal of Solidaristic Empowerment, according to which we ought to shape our social relations so that we do not block or destroy, and so that we enable and further, the development and exercise of people's valuable capacities (the ones that are the basis of their dignity). We should cater for other people's needs when, and because, those needs are interests in unfolding their valuable capacities (or are causally important for that unfolding).

---

[15] Stanczyk (2012) argues that work can be conscripted to enhance the well-being of others beyond emergencies. I take civil and political liberties to be normally, not absolutely, constraining; there is a presumption in their favour, but it can be defeated by especially strong reasons. Thus, my view is not necessarily incompatible with Stanczyk's. But it is hard to see how considerations of well-being that go beyond basic needs can outweigh central civil and political liberties (Stanczyk's own examples focus on basic health care—which caters for basic needs and the fair value of liberties themselves).

[16] On the possibility of a socialism that includes liberal principles, see Rawls (2001: 135–40). For instructive discussion, see O'Neill (2020).

98 Human Dignity and Social Justice

We should have (and use) opportunities to engage in productive contribution also because doing so would involve developing and exercising various valuable capacities for cooperation, creativity, etc., as well as the unfolding of our own moral capacities to enact respect and concern for others. An economy framed by ANP is an economy in which each participant gives and takes in ways that are appropriately responsive to the status-dignity of all individuals affected. Absent special reasons to do so, an economic structure which (foreseeably and avoidably) grants some no chance, or lower chances, to give and take in these ways, is an economy that does not fully respond to their dignity.

To be clear, I am not saying that this is the only way to defend ANP. There could be other defences of it, and their availability would only strengthen its appeal (as the subject of an overlapping consensus reached from different premises). I indeed hope that some of what I go on to say in this chapter about ANP and its implications could be retained by readers who prefer an alternative strategy for defending it. That said, I of course find the Dignitarian Approach compelling. In particular, I think that it provides a distinctively clear and sharp rationale for ANP's focus on engaging the abilities and needs of *each individual* as they arise *in their own specific configurations*, and this in a way that also affirms and explains people's equal standing, their claims to freedom, and their solidaristic responsibilities to support each other. As this chapter proceeds, I will point out various definite ways in which the Dignitarian Approach supports the specification, justification, and implementation of ANP.

4.3 Needs

When we develop our views about social justice, we must consider what is good for the people involved. Principles of equality, freedom, and solidarity cannot be given enough content otherwise. We face the questions such as 'Equality of what?' 'Freedom to do or be what?' 'Solidarity to help others get what?' The 'what' at stake, at least in part, concerns what is good for people to do or be. Goods are crucial as metric, or currency, of principles of justice. This general point applies to ANP. What needs should be recognized under this principle? Although I will not develop a full account of needs here, I will identify a general strategy that addresses three central questions concerning (i) how extensive the metric of needs should be, (ii) what kinds of items it should include, and (iii) how we might respond to worries about paternalism.

The Abilities/Needs Principle   **99**

(i) *Extensiveness.* How expansive should the metrics of needs be? It could be said that distributing according to needs involves some austere threshold of sufficiency. But since we are trying to articulate something akin to the Marxian ideal, which is concerned with human flourishing, we should not think about needs in this way. The relevant contrast should not be between needs and non-urgent wants. It should instead be between real and non-real, merely apparent interests or goods. ANP ranges over real interests in human flourishing. So the metric can be fairly expansive, without a fixed threshold, and such that having more is typically better than having less. The Marxian view that needs and abilities do, and should, develop and increase over time speaks in favour of this interpretation.[17] Given that people have equal dignity and that it is important to support their well-being, we can identify as an initial and presumptive focus the enabling of equal access to the highest feasible level of need satisfaction that can be reasonably secured for all, over their lives, in their societal context.[18] (In 4.4 I state some qualifications to clarify what 'reasonable' amounts to here, and to make sure that this presumption does not mandate requirements on production that are overdemanding.)

(ii) *Needs, capabilities, and self-determined self-realization.* A fruitful strategy for identifying the relevant needs, in a certain context, is to focus on the valuable capacities of individuals in that context. The needs would be constituted by what the individuals require to fulfil their interests in developing and exercising these capacities. The more people can develop and exercise these capacities, the more they can be said to have the power to lead a flourishing life.

An example of this strategy has been recently provided by the Capability Approach proposed by Amartya Sen and Martha Nussbaum.[19] On this approach, we can account for people's normatively significant needs by

---

[17] For exploration of the variety and dynamism of human needs and capabilities as characterized in Marx's texts, see Elster (1985: 68–74). Ultimately, Marx's ideal of human flourishing involves the 'development of the rich individuality which is all-sided in its production as in its consumption' Marx (1973: 325). We can drop the hyperbolic, infeasible Marxian depiction of scenarios in which people develop *all* their powers *fully*, but we can still envision cases in which they achieve a high level of development of some powers in certain desirable, chosen, and feasible schedule of activities. This point is developed further in this book's chapter on alienation.

[18] This desideratum (and the interpretation of ANP more generally) should be constrained by appropriate saving for future generations. This calls for further exploration, which will not be provided in this chapter. For convincing general arguments for why a sufficientarian account cannot cover all that matters for social justice and for the presumption that distribution of access to well-being should target the highest attainable equality, see Christiano (2008: ch. 1).

[19] Sen (2009); Nussbaum (2011). The Rawlsian account of primary goods as what free and equal cooperating individuals require to develop and exercise their moral powers of rationality and reasonability and to pursue their specific conception of the good over their complete lives is arguably a quite general case of this strategy. See Rawls (2001: sects. 17 and 51). However, Rawls's account is in one respect narrow, as it limits the scope of the principles of justice to people who have the two moral powers to a sufficient degree, and can engage in mutually advantageous cooperation. Clearly not every individual fits these conditions.

100 Human Dignity and Social Justice

considering what would constitute their 'capabilities' or agential power to engage in certain valuable 'functionings' (i.e. certain ways of being or doing they have reason to value). I think that this perspective is helpful for articulating ANP, and that the Dignitarian Approach can generate a distinctive version of it. The functionings people should be supported in gaining the capability to engage in are those through which the valuable capacities at the basis of their dignity are unfolded. Marx's view of socialism as securing the conditions for people's self-determined self-realization, itself construed as the development and exercise of various capacities, can indeed be seen as an instance of this strategy. In particular, the emphasis on capabilities for autonomous and cooperative activity at the workplace is an important contribution of the socialist tradition to the capability metric. Furthermore, in the Kantian dignitarian interpretation offered in this book, self-determination based on moral reasoning has a special significance, so that the capabilities linked to it have pride of place.[20]

Nussbaum (2006: ch.3) thus presses Rawls's account for its neglect of the claims of people with severe cognitive impairments.

[20] Nussbaum (2000: 13, 70–4; 2006: 74–5) acknowledges a debt to Marx in her development of the idea of capability. For further discussion on the relation between capabilities as people's configurations in which they have the power to live in ways that involve the development and exercise of the valuable capacities at the basis of their dignity, see this book's chapter of domination, Section 3.4.

Further discussion of the Capability Approach would distract us from the main tasks of this chapter. I survey the approach in Gilabert (2013), and I will return to aspects of it in Chapters 4, 6, and 7. Let me however state succinctly some important connections between it and the Dignitarian Approach (DA) explored in this book. There is, on the one hand, much that I endorse from the Capability Approach. In particular, DA embraces its exploration of capability as a suitable notion to articulate the central metric for considerations about the good for a theory of justice, its direct and pluralistic view of the significance of a variety of valuable features of people that include items other than rationality, and its recognition that some duties of justice involve unidirectional help to others and cannot be reduced to corollaries of the pursuit of mutual advantage. Furthermore, and like Sen (although this is not clear in the case of Nussbaum), DA sees the site of justice as concerning not only the institutions of the state, but more broadly social practices (what Sen's call 'social realizations'). Finally, like Nussbaum, DA sees dignity as based on an open-ended, disjunctive list of basic capacities, so that people can equally have (status-) dignity even if they are quite diverse. They have dignity when they have some of the capacities in the list, even if the sets of capacities they have are not identical. This diversity among people must be tracked by the support they are given to form capabilities to reach various functionings.

There are, however, some significant differences. First, DA unpacks the idea of dignity in much more detail and more systematically. It illuminates the network of dignitarian notions and their structure, showing how what I call status-dignity, the basis of dignity, condition-dignity, dignitarian norms, dignitarian virtue, and the circumstances of dignity, differ and relate to each other. Second, DA distinguishes sharply between the capacities for prudential and for moral practical reasoning, and gives the latter (when present) normative priority. Third, DA is formulated as a form of deontology. Nussbaum (2011: 93–6) presents her view as a 'cousin of consequentialism'. She takes condition-dignity, and I take status-dignity, as the more fundamental dimension. Whereas her approach is outcome-orientated, mine is reflective or response-based. The organizing question, for me, is what we owe to each other if we are to respond appropriately to our status-dignity. The list of capabilities and prospective states of condition-dignity to be fostered lie downstream. (We share, however, a wariness regarding the reliance on aggregative reasoning that is common in utilitarianism.) Fourth, and relatedly, DA, through the Bridge Principle, accounts more fully for how to traverse the gap between interests (or judgements about well-being and the good) and rights (or judgements about what is owed to others). Fifth, DA explores the extension of dignitarian considerations to requirements of social justice that go beyond minimal or basic thresholds. In particular, it explores the more demanding norms of democratic socialism. Finally, DA does not use a notion a 'species norm'. It does

The Abilities/Needs Principle **101**

There are two kinds of work in Marx's view: work that merely secures subsistence and work that involves the extensive unfolding of workers' various capacities. The second is the kind of work that includes self-determination and self-realization. It involves activities in which workers cooperate with each other as equals, have powers to choose what to do and how to do it, and acquire and deploy skills through interesting, challenging, and enjoyable performances. It is the opposite of alienated labour, which involves dull or distressful tasks and servile or hostile relationships.[21] Now, these two kinds of work are respectively picked out in two common interpretations of the significance of work in Marx's view of socialism, the 'higher form of society ... in which the full and free development of every individual forms the ruling principle'.[22] One interpretation draws on Marx's contrast between the 'realm of freedom' and the 'realm of necessity', which seems to locate all work in the latter, and envisions self-determined self-realization as occurring outside of it.[23] The other draws on Marx's characterization of work as 'life's prime want'.[24] Here the general access to self-determined self-realization at work is viewed as a primary achievement of socialism.

Arguably both forms of work are important, although in different ways. Access to work involving self-determined self-realization should count as one of the needs satisfied in socialism. As described in the previous paragraph, it strikes me as a significant intrinsic good. If the design of a just society is to focus not only on distributing the outputs of an economic process but also on its internal shape, it should have room for work of this kind. On the other hand, a duty to do one's fair share regarding some forms of instrumentally necessary but not intrinsically desirable work is obviously part of what a duty to contribute according to one's abilities should include.

---

not take an Aristotelian picture of 'the human being', of its 'nature' and 'characteristic' features and activities as being necessary for developing lucid moral judgements (even in the broad, evaluative account of them suggested by Nussbaum—see Nussbaum 2006: 179–95, 362–6). (Notice, furthermore, that requiring reliance on a species norm is in tension with the strand of Nussbaum's views—deployed when she criticizes aggregative reasoning—that emphasizes the importance of responding to the dignity of each individual as a separate unit of moral respect and concern.) Generalizations about people are not of fundamental normative significance, but have only a derivative, and mostly pragmatic, role. What ultimately matters is to respond to the dignity of individuals as they are, given *their own* features and predicaments. For more on this point, see Gilabert (2022).

[21] In alienated labour, workers experience their relation with their productive activity, its products, and other economic agents as meaningless or even as antagonistic. Marx (1978c). See the more detailed discussion in this book's chapter on alienation.

[22] Marx (1990: 739). See also Marx (1973: 488).

[23] Marx (1991: 957–9). Although Marx argues that 'the true realm of freedom, the development of human powers as an end in itself, begins beyond' the realm of necessity, he thinks that some freedom in the latter can be achieved when 'associated producers' 'govern he human metabolism with nature in a rational way, bringing it under their collective control instead of being dominated by it as a blind power; accomplishing it with the least expenditure of energy and in conditions most worthy and appropriate for their human nature' (Ibid: 959).

[24] Marx (1978i: 531).

102 Human Dignity and Social Justice

Of course, there are needs that go beyond work. Needs regarding consumption goods and the pursuit of intimate relationships are clear examples. When it comes to those Marx's framework is often limited, and we must look elsewhere.[25] For example, recent research in the capability approach provides excellent ideas concerning what further categories of needs and associated capabilities we should explore.[26]

The capability metric, on a dignitarian construal of it, emphasizes various dimensions of freedom. It recommends that we foster people's positive freedom to develop and exercise various capacities.[27] Second, it commands respect for people's choices by not forcing them to engage in any specific productive activity. Finally, it gives especial importance to political liberties (such as voting, organizing, protesting, deliberating) that enable people to identify, try, contest, and revise political accounts of important capacities and distributive schemes supporting their unfolding. I want to stress the limits, and importance, of this last point.

In a deliberative democracy, people can reasonably develop and revise their own views of what needs should be socially supported. But we should not conflate democratic procedures of choice and substantive criteria about what needs deserve to be supported. Thus, for example, Geras considers the problem of identifying a 'standard of reasonableness' of needs (given that we should avoid accounts that are too minimal—they are undesirable—and too maximal—they are infeasible).[28] He entertains three options: unilateral imposition by a state-type body, a standard that emerges spontaneously without reflection, and social norms people come to agree upon. He says, plausibly, that the third option is the best. But notice that his discussion moved from substantive to procedural issues. Some might say that we should adopt a constructivist view and think that how distributive schemes are chosen provides the conditions that make them right. I find this suggestion intuitively problematic because it is liable to a version of the powerful

---

[25] Cohen (2001: 346–50) provides instructive critical comments on Marx's philosophical anthropology as failing to account for people's need for 'self definition', and its fulfillment through special associations.

[26] Nussbaum (2011: 33–4) suggest that we explore people's capabilities with respect to (1) life, (2) bodily health, (3) bodily integrity, (4) the use of their senses, imagination and thought, (5) the engagement of their emotions, (6) the use of their practical reason, (7) the development of social affiliation, (8) the concerned relation with other species, (9) activities involving play, and (10) the control of their political and material environment. Work can of course display many of these, but it is not the only relevant medium. We should also have a broad view of what counts as 'contribution' under the Contribution Principle and ANP. For example, it should not only include work in factories and similar sites of formal labour. As feminists have emphasized, for example, it should also include domestic and reproductive labour. Furthermore, many abilities should be recognized as productive from a social point of view. For example, people with certain handicaps may still have important abilities to contribute in several ways (and technological development increasingly makes this easier).

[27] This is also a salient point in the theory of positive freedom advanced in Gould (1988).

[28] Geras (1989: 264).

Euthyphro question: Is a distributive decision right because we make it, or should we make it because it is right? And, independently of the truth or falsity of constructivism, procedural principles do not provide substantive guidance as we try to think lucidly about what to propose, criticize, and agree to in a public debate about needs if we join it.

The questions 'What is the politically legitimate procedure for deciding what needs will be met?' and 'What are the correct entitlements of need?' are different. The reference to democratic liberties answers the first question without necessarily settling the second. The Dignitarian Approach can orient us when approaching both questions. The second question, which regards the specification of the content of ANP, can be answered by deploying the Schema of Dignitarian Justification proposed in Chapter 1 (Section 2.2.1). In identifying rights to support for need satisfaction, we can consider whether their implementation through certain economic arrangements is either necessary for, or strongly contributes to, the feasible and reasonable support for interests regarding the maintenance, development, and exercise of the valuable capacities at the basis of their dignity. We would then explore how to support, in feasible and reasonable ways, individuals' capacities for sentience, self-awareness, practical reasoning and choice, knowledge, empathy and concern, cooperation, aesthetic appreciation, and creativity. We will pursue this line of exploration in 4.4.

The Dignitarian Approach can also help us recognize the great importance of democratic liberties for the implementation of ANP. First, these liberties are intrinsically valuable: their recognition involves respect for people as agents with capacities for self-determined moral judgement, which are central to their status-dignity. Deploying their moral reasoning, people are able, as they should, to shape their social life on terms that are duly responsive of the dignity of all. Second, their use is epistemically significant: people can enhance their knowledge about what needs are important by testing and correcting their political beliefs in public debate. Third, they are also instrumentally valuable by enabling people to keep accountable others whose political choices affect their needs. Thus, even if the standard of reasonable needs is independent, democratic liberties are important for discovering and applying its contents in autonomous, lucid, and effective ways. This is why we have a strong pro tanto reason to organize the implementation of ANP so that we support the needs recognized through democratic processes of debate and decision-making.

(iii) *Paternalism.* Since ANP is meant to track human flourishing, it clearly goes beyond anything like basic needs, and we can say that it concerns important interests more generally. But wouldn't social policy centred on some interpretation of these interests be unconscionably paternalistic?

104 Human Dignity and Social Justice

There are two immediate and important responses to this worry. The first is that, as we saw, the application of ANP is to proceed within a framework of democratic deliberation and choice. The presence of this framework limits the extent to which agents are subject to standards they do not themselves accept. They may, of course, be part of a minority. But the second response addresses this case. The distributive focus is on securing certain *real opportunities* or *capabilities*, not their exercise (i.e. people's 'functionings'). Everybody has a civil liberty against being forced to engage in specific activities or states judged good by others when they choose not to do so. In addition, the standards of needs can be quite general to allow for diverse interpretation and elaborations by individuals, thus giving them more liberty (such as about what work to pursue if any). Even if we have an expansive view of the good when developing our account of relevant needs, we should be mindful of the prospect that people will disagree about the details.

It might be objected that in a social scheme implementing ANP people's liberty is unduly limited because the generation of the selected opportunities is costly, and everyone is made to pay for it whether they use them or not. However, the imposition is justified if all feasible social schemes have consequences in terms of promoting and limiting opportunities. If our normative assessment of schemes is sensitive to consequences on people's opportunities to live flourishing lives (as it should be), and different feasible schemes promote different opportunity profiles, then we should (other things being equal) support the scheme with the best feasible consequences overall. It may include some opportunities that not everyone uses. But their presence is important to those who do use them, and it enhances the effective freedom of those who don't by offering them a wider palette of real options to choose from. Furthermore, and to repeat, the scheme would be constrained by strong civil and political liberties which entitle people to refrain from using, and empower them to challenge and change, existing opportunity profiles.[29]

Some might suggest that we deflate anxiety about paternalism by adopting a less controversial, sufficientarian reading of ANP, according to which we should empower people to meet their most urgent, or basic needs. But why not embrace a more ambitious ideal that targets equal opportunities to the highest levels of well-being that are reasonably feasible? After all, is it not part of responding to people's dignity to support the extensive unfolding of their valuable capacities (which would certainly involve more than fulfilling basic

---

[29] See Section 3.3 of Chapter 1, and 4.2–4.6 of the chapter on alienation for further discussion on how the dignitarian perspective can reflect reasonable pluralism about conceptions of the good.

needs), and is it not unfair to uphold a socioeconomic system in which some people can flourish less than others through no choice or fault of their own? If we secure civil and political liberties, why not pursue the more ambitious project? The remainder of this section develops this project further.

4.4 The demands of ANP

In this subsection I propose an articulation of the demands or requirements of ANP. I also offer an initial exploration (to be developed further in later chapters) of how ANP relates to important socialist concerns about alienation and exploitation and helps respond to worries regarding individuals' responsibility and their different personal needs and choices concerning self-realization, consumption, and leisure.

Regarding the first task, I suggest that we understand ANP as generating a set of demands on the organization of a system of economic cooperation. Its point is to call for an organization of economic activity that implements the Dignitarian Approach, engaging and responding appropriately to the status-dignity of each individual by being egalitarian, solidaristic, and sensitive to difference. The organization is egalitarian because in it everyone's level of burden and benefit matters equally. It is solidaristic because with it agents express their commitment to taking each individual's capability to flourish as an end. And it is sensitive to difference because it enables each individual to pursue their well-being in ways that are fitting given their own singular characteristics. These demands, combined, should shape the economic system. *Both* parts of the principle (from each according to their abilities, to each according to their needs) should be simultaneously operative.

What are the demands? At least the following five seem to me to be crucial:

(a) **Opportunities for self-realization in work:** There should be effective opportunities for productive activity that involves self-realization. People have valuable capacities to engage in complex, cooperative, creative, and socially useful work. They should have real chances to engage in this kind of work. Arguably, having such options would serve an important human need. These opportunities would be effective in that mechanisms would be in place to offset morally arbitrary differences between workers that affect their accessibility. For example, excellent education and training would be available to all, and the workplace would be designed so that workers with different talents and bodily restrictions can thrive.

106 Human Dignity and Social Justice

(b) **Positive duties:** There should be institutions, and a social ethos, which enable and encourage people to produce to meet other people's needs—thereby supporting the human flourishing of all. Each should envisage a reasonable level of development and exercise of their powers to produce in this way.

(c) **Securing basic needs:** Some instantiations of the positive duties mentioned in (b) are particularly urgent and stringent. They concern the satisfaction of basic needs for subsistence and for being able to function as a political equal.

(d) **Fair reciprocity:** There should be an ethos and a scheme of distribution of access to consumption goods that recognizes a responsibility to cooperate in production on terms of fair reciprocity. Nobody should take advantage of cooperative efforts of others without making their own, similar effort if they can. Similar effort is not equivalence in output (which might depend on morally arbitrary differences in native endowments), but a matter of the proportion of contribution given one's abilities.[30] Above the threshold marked by (c), those (but only those) who make an equal effort (when they can) should have equal access to consumption goods.

(e) **Sensitivity to individual differences:** Individual differences in abilities and needs are normatively important, and should be factored in when appraising appropriate levels of contribution and access to consumption. Each should be allowed, and enabled, to pursue their well-being in ways that are appropriate given their own characteristics.

(f) **Self-determination in economic life:** Respect and concern for individuals in their diversity should also be supportive of their self-determination. Absent conflict with very strong competing considerations (such as basic positive duties to respond to emergencies), everyone should be entitled to choose whether, and how, to work, and each should be entitled to choose whether, and how, to consume. For example, each should be allowed to form their own schedules of trade-offs between self-realization at work, leisure time, and consumption.[31] Furthermore, the contours of the social structure within which people

---

[30] See Castoriadis's (1978: 394) articulation of the idea of 'geometric proportionality', according to which an individual's ratio of contribution over ability may be the same as that of another even if their specific contributions and abilities are not identical. Thus, a worker with a ratio of contribution over abilities of 2/4 is on a par with another whose ratio is 3/6. An evaluation of contribution that proceeds in relative terms (indexing to abilities) can be used to criticize meritocratic views that condone inequalities of income and wealth that benefit some people simply because of their greater native talents. See also White (2007: 75–7).

[31] To avoid misunderstandings, I note that self-determination is not the same as self-ownership, if self-ownership is incompatible with recognizing positive duties of justice. It is also different from independence, if independence is understood as self-reliance. Self-reliance is infeasible and undesirable. Everyone

The Abilities/Needs Principle **107**

produce and consume should be subject to authorization, contestation, and change by all the members of society through democratic mechanisms of opinion—and will-formation.

The demands stated in (a)-(f) are ambitious but limited. It is not expected that people's productive contribution will be maximal, that all their valuable capacities will be fully developed and exercised in production, that all of their needs will be fully met, or that every important individual difference will be honoured. The requirement is, in each case, to achieve an arrangement that is feasible and reasonable (i.e. one whose requirements can be met and do not involve unjustifiable sacrifices—given important considerations such as individuals' personal prerogative to cater for their own needs—when compared to the feasible alternatives).

As I said in 4.1–2, the goal of framing an economic system so that it fulfils ANP should be weighed against other normative pro tanto considerations that will normally be stronger, such as the protection of civil and political rights and their fair value. My formulation of the demands associated with the principle incorporates aspects of those liberties, such as the freedom from forced labour and certain democratic political rights affecting the regulation of economic institutions and practices, both of which are captured by (f). Notice also that the sufficientarian principle of support for the provision of certain basic needs (health care, education, etc.) that are necessary or causally important for subsistence and effective citizenship is included in component (c).[32] These considerations could also be seen as separate requirements that weigh against a narrower formulation of the demands of ANP. Either way, they express the dignitarian emphasis on the importance of individuals' self-determination. An economy that, avoidably, does not fulfil them is one in which people are turned into mere cogs in a machinery that sucks their contribution without being properly responsive to their wills.

Notice also that we can, and should, understand demand (b) in a limited way. There is no assumption that society must adopt a hyper-productivist orientation. This is so because the needs that matter are not only the ones

---

depends on others for the pursuit of their own flourishing, and nobody should feel shame if they are helped, or guilt if they help others, to flourish.

[32] Requirement (c) could also be justified as stating what is due to members of society who (even though they can work but choose not to) contribute to the maintenance of a just social system by complying with its rules, participating as active citizens, and so on. See on this Freeman (2007: 229–30). Consider also Rawls's (1999: 477–8) remarks on the importance of a secure social status as an equal citizen for the furtherance of people's sense of self-respect. Note as well that Rawls (2001: 44n.7) allowed that provision for basic needs could be seen as a requirement that is prior to his first principle of justice. I also agree with Rawls (2001: sects. 14 and 18) that we should avoid confusing distributive justice with allocative justice, and that the former need not require maximal production. The scheme of cooperation framed by (a)–(f) does not, above the threshold specified by (c), involve an injunction of maximal productivity.

108 Human Dignity and Social Justice

that would be satisfied by productive activities (and some may be set back by an overextension of the latter—such as the need for leisure time and what it enables). In addition, we must avoid construing (b) in a way that turns out to be oppressive. Although there is a stringent duty to contribute to secure the floor of sufficiency targeted by (c), the positive duty stated in (b) is weaker and more indeterminate. It is open to reasonable specifications that do not involve maximal production. Through their democratic powers, the citizens of a society can choose to shape the structural setup of their economy in such a way that they produce in more frugal ways. This does not involve relapsing into a procedural answer to the substantive question challenged in Section 4.3 (ii), however. Although (b) is somewhat indeterminate in that it allows for a range of reasonable implementations to be selected through democratic politics (and see Section 4.5 for how this could be instantiated), it is not contentless because it requires that all items in the range should be chosen with an eye to catering for people's various needs beyond the threshold of sufficiency identified by (c).

Furthermore, the schemes of production implementing (b) must also respect the personal prerogative of each to choose how to engage in production in their own fashion, having (as per (a)) opportunities to do so in ways that are self-fulfilling and (as per (e)) fitting their singular predicament given their own individual abilities and aims, and also (as per (e) and (f)) so that they have leeway to choose to engage in production less than others do.

Finally, the demand of fair reciprocity, (d), kicks in once production as envisioned socially and personally is underway: it does not require that we produce beyond what is needed to fulfil (c), or to select a maximalist interpretation of (b), but that if we do produce beyond the threshold specified by (c) (as to some extent we should, if we can, given (b), appropriately interpreted as we see fit) that we share the proceedings fairly, without turning some of us into mere instruments for the flourishing of others.

Specified through requirements (a)–(f), ANP also helps honour the common socialist normative concerns for an economy that is orientated to satisfying needs, non-alienation, and non-exploitation. The first two concerns are captured in the shaping of the productive process so that it implements the duty to help produce objects and services that can be used to meet needs and includes effective opportunities for self-determined self-realization in work. The concern for non-exploitation is partly captured by the standard of fair reciprocity. I will provide an initial elaboration of these points, suggesting that their articulation avoids pitfalls in other interpretations of the ideas captured. A more detailed exploration is offered in Chapters 5–7.

First, consider non-exploitation of workers. Component (d) captures the relational wrong of taking advantage of the efforts of others without appropriate reciprocation. This contrasts with a libertarian construal of exploitation, and with a view that sees its significance as wholly derivative from the initial distribution of economic assets. The former sees the wrongness of exploitation as a matter of depriving workers of the product of their labour (to which they are entitled). The latter sees it as a symptom of the unjust inequality in control of means of production, which gives capitalists more bargaining power than workers.

The principle of entitlement to the product of one's labour is problematic because it makes it unjust to impose the redistribution of some of it to meet the basic needs of those who cannot work. It thus violates component (c) of the account, which for example requires the provision of basic resources to people who cannot work because they are infirm. The principle also prohibits redistribution to people who work but are (because of having less natural talent) less productive despite exerting similar effort. We should then seek to construe the wrongness of exploitation in a different way.[33] The proposal presented here can help. An intuition that seems to support the entitlement principle is that when workers have made an effort and borne costs to produce something, they have a prima facie claim to commensurate rewards.[34] The force of this intuition can be captured by the requirement of fair response to the efforts of others in (d). A crucial idea behind the condemnation of exploitation is that there is a duty to avoid taking unfair advantage of others. In my interpretation, ANP encodes an ideal of non-exploitation: we should not take advantage of need satisfying activities by others that benefit us without doing our share in producing advantages that can meet needs of others when we can. If we can do our share and we don't, and we receive from others who do their share, then we could be exploiting them. (d) is an ideal of reciprocity in cooperation, according to which everyone should put in corresponding levels of effort if they can when they benefit from the effort of others. Furthermore, since the proposed account includes (b) and (c), it also makes reference to positive duties to support others, which provides a key consideration missing in, and threatened by, the libertarian view. Notice that (b) and (c) need not conflict with (d): the needy who cannot work and

---

[33] A possible reply is that although some individual workers might not be fully paid when this distribution occurs, they would not be forced, because they belong to the class that collectively controls economic resources and policy (in a socialist society). See Holmstrom (1977: 363). For discussion see Kymlicka (2002: 204 n.11).

[34] Geras (1992: 60–1).

110 Human Dignity and Social Justice

are helped do not engage in unfair advantage-taking. A conflict may arise, however, if some make claims on the work of others without working when they can. I address this case below.

The second view of exploitation mentioned above (the one construing it as a symptom of unequal distribution of productive assets) captures the important points that unequal control of means of production affects bargaining power, and is in any case unfair given that nobody should start their life as an economic agent with fewer external productive assets than others. Now notice, first, that we can take ANP to generate this judgement given its egalitarian profile as described in the second paragraph of this subsection. Alternatively, of course, we could see it as a theorem of an independent, 'luck-egalitarian' principle. Furthermore, the issues could partly be handled through the democratic process envisioned in (f). Such a process could, and if (f) is to be fully implemented it arguably should, require forms of collective control of means of production, or severe restrictions on private control of them, to shape bargaining conditions appropriately, so that they do not unduly compromise the self-determination of the people involved in economic activity.

Second, the view under discussion misses the specific *relational wrong* involved in exploitation. Initial inequality of resources enables this wronging, but does not fully account for what constitutes it. The accounts of positive duties and fair reciprocity proposed here can partly explain what is missing. The problem with the exploitation of workers by capitalists, for example, is not only that their initial unequal access to means of production is unfair. There is also the problem that some (the capitalists) use their resulting superior bargaining power to get others (the workers) to benefit them disproportionately, instead of creating cooperative ventures that equally support all those who make similar efforts within them. The proposal advanced here also partly explains the possible wrongs involved in relations between people who start with, or currently have, equal access to means of production. Their differences in natural endowments (intelligence, vigor, charisma, creativity, etc.) may by themselves make their bargaining power unequal, and this inequality may enable the better endowed to shape economic interactions so that they gain disproportionately from them. Outcomes of this sort involve some agents taking unfair advantage of the relative weakness of others. A social ethos and institutions of solidarity and fair reciprocity of the kind envisaged in (b) and (d) would require that they be avoided.[35]

---

[35] For a survey of the first two views of exploitation see Kymlicka (2002: 177–87). I say that my proposal helps 'in part' to account for the relational wrong of exploitation. There is room for other accounts

The Abilities/Needs Principle **111**

Let me add a final comment regarding component (d). An important question is how the two parts of ANP are to be related. Is there any conditionality, however partial? For example, if workers A and B have the same level of ability and need, resources to meet needs are scarce and flow from productive activity, and A chooses to contribute more than B, would A be entitled to claim more resources to fulfil their needs than B? As I interpret ANP (as a conjunction referring to duties of contribution and rights to consumption), it does not involve a complete severing of the link between work and distributive entitlements.[36] That severance might make sense if we assume lack of material scarcity or ignore that goods for consumption are the result of productive efforts by people. As long as there is scarcity, some things that people need will not be readily available. If workers have freedom of occupation (as they should), and they can be more or less productive, then certain needs can be more or less satisfied depending on how much people choose to work. In this context, it seems intuitively problematic when an individual makes claims on scarce consumption goods without having contributed to the economic process by using their abilities. The problem would be one of lack of fairness towards those who have contributed but will receive less because of the lower economic input resulting from others' lack of contribution.[37]

This conditionality does not make ANP a version of the Contribution Principle, however. In circumstances of scarcity, the former, like the latter, is sensitive to contributive efforts[38] But components (e), (b), and (a) make ANP a different principle.

Thus, first, ANP recommends that we take individual differences into account when we appraise contribution and needs. Given similar amounts of labour input—assuming it can be provided—individuals A and B are not thereby given access to equal amounts of consumption goods. Instead, they are equally enabled to access goods that are appropriate for them *given their needs*. ANP is flexible at the level of principle as to how much in the way of consumption goods to allocate. Recognizing equal need claims by A and B, who exert equal effort given their abilities, is consistent with giving more

that are independent from ANP and capture additional problematic features of exploitation. For example, Vrousalis (2013) suggests that economic exploitation is a form of domination of others for self-enrichment.

[36] Here I differ with the interpretation by Nell and O'Neill (2003: 84–5).

[37] The worry about 'expensive tastes'—that some people may cultivate preferences that are very costly for others to fulfil—can also be partly addressed by mobilizing these consideration (which yield the responsibility of each to avoid making unfair demands on others).

[38] What is significant, normatively speaking, is effort in a system of fair reciprocity, not actual output, the generation of which partly depends on morally arbitrary differences in endowments (such as native talents) and other circumstances (such as opportunities for productive work) whose presence is independent of agents' control. The Contribution Principle arguably partially encodes a concern for fair reciprocity as well, as under it contribution is measured quite generally by the amount and intensity of work, and some support is given to those unable to work (Marx 1878i: 530–1).

112 Human Dignity and Social Justice

stuff to A than to B if A needs more than B. (We thus capture Sen's important point about the conversion problem, and his related normative insight that equal capability is not only different from equal resources, but also what is ultimately really important.) At the level of core ideals, and before difficult issues of implementation are tackled, dignitarianism calls for an equality that is people-centred rather than lot-centred. In this spirit, what is crucial for ANP is not that everyone has the same amount of stuff, but that everyone has the same chances to flourish given their specific bundles of valuable capacities and the needs they have regarding their unfolding, which may require different amounts of stuff for different people.

Second, labour-contribution is not the ground of the duty to expand others' access to consumption goods, but a condition on generalized support in circumstances of relative scarcity. Needs are still what primarily give rise to economic duties. To repeat, the conditionality in ANP holds where complete abundance is absent and consumption goods are the result of productive efforts. If consumption goods were manna falling from the sky, then distribution would not have to track productive efforts. Another caveat: the conditionality considered here assumes focus on consumption goods that meet needs above a basic threshold of subsistence and of whatever is required for people to function as political equals. Everyone should get support to secure those unconditionally (if feasible). To state the points succinctly, we can say the following. Each individual should equally be subject to this complex constraint on their access to consumption goods that result from social labour and lie above the basic threshold protected by demand (c): provided that they can contribute, they may claim such access (i) according to their needs and (ii) in proportion to the extent to which they have deployed their abilities to contribute.[39]

Finally, on the present interpretation ANP is of course quite different from the Contribution Principle because it involves a direct concern with self-realization. This engages the traditional socialist theme of non-alienation, to which I now turn.

The ideal of self-realization (or non-alienation) is obviously catered for by component (a) of the proposal presented here. The socialist view that economic systems should incorporate opportunities for self-realization in work has been subject to challenge, however. Some have argued that a conception of justice appealing to self-realization in work might arbitrarily disregard other goods or preferences concerning consumption, leisure, or the

---

[39] See further discussion in 4.5 below.

The Abilities/Needs Principle   **113**

cultivation of personal relationships.[40] Why not let people work less if this gives them more time to devote themselves to leisure and personal relationships, or work in ways that do not involve self-realization if this gives them more income for consumption? This is an important challenge. But the view presented here can answer it.

First, it is important to note that where there are time constraints, material scarcity, and multiple desiderata, *any* economic system will force people to make trade-offs between various goods. So the issue is what system offers the best balance overall, and whether it gives people real options and conditions of self-determination to choose from them. Capitalist societies fail badly in these respects. Economic necessity forces many people to work long hours in unsatisfying jobs for low salaries. Second, as presented in (a), work involving self-realization is an opportunity, not an obligation. Other forms of work are not banned. What is crucial is that workers are treated fairly by being given real alternatives to unfulfilling work. The objective is making available self-realization that is self-determined. Third, even including opportunities for self-realization, the length of standard full-time work can be reduced. As per (f), citizens shaping the rules of their economic system can impose that reduction to free up time for other activities. Fourth, self-realization can indeed also be pursued outside of productive work. Endorsing ANP does not require denying the importance of those other goods, or blocking their pursuit. Finally, given its components (e) and (f) demanding proper responses to individual differences, this proposal would support personal prerogatives for people to judge how to balance the multiple opportunities and obligations they face. As acknowledged, the desideratum regarding self-realization is limited.[41]

---

[40] Kymlicka (2002: 190–3); Arneson (1987). Notice that this charge, and responses to it defending (a), can be made both within objectivist and subjectivist frameworks by referring, respectively, to a plurality of objective goods and subjective desires or preferences. Each of these frameworks allow for different variants. Thus, an objectivist framework may or may not be perfectionist, and a subjectivist one may or may not impose constraints of information and deliberation on the relevant desires or preferences.

[41] Elster (1986: ch.3; 1989) provides the most systematic exploration of the ideal of self-realization. Elster defines the Marxian ideal as follows: 'self-realization is the full and free actualization and externalization of the powers and the abilities of the individual' (Elster 1989: 131). He shows that this formulation involves an infeasible ideal and must be changed by dropping reference to the 'fullness' of self-actualization, re-characterizing its 'freedom', and exploring various ways in which it might succeed in work and politics. My interpretation of ANP recognizes these limits. Elster also emphasizes the contrast between self-realization and consumption. Activities involving self-realization yield raising marginal utility: they are often painful at the beginning, but as capabilities are developed and actualized, they become increasingly enjoyable. Consumption displays the opposite trajectory (from excitement and delight to satiation and boredom). This is also an important point. But I think that there is a risk of overshooting the mark here. Consumption should not be underestimated. Besides the obvious point that it is enjoyable as far as it goes, its significance is often a necessary condition for self-realization in productive labour. As Elster himself explains, self-realization is often partly dependent on the significance of the outputs of the activities in which it arises. Since often the output is consumption goods to meet needs, a lowering of the significance of consumption could threaten the significance of the corresponding productive activities.

114 Human Dignity and Social Justice

We can add that creating opportunities for self-realization in production might well expand the feasibility of meaningful activity outside of it. Capitalism generates a ferocious pressure to make as much money as possible and to build one's self-esteem through competitive triumphs over others. Countering this selfish, hyper-competitive ethos, socialism might help generate a culture that supports rather than undermines deep relationships (such as friendship) that involve genuine care and sincerity. If production is not thoroughly framed by rapacious competition and profit maximization, it might also be easier to reduce working time and increase access to other activities and goods.

Still, production does have a central significance as a general enabler of pretty much every activity. In any economy that is not fully automated, work will have to occur if subsistence and opportunities for human flourishing (inside and outside the workplace) are to be extensive. Any society will put mechanisms in place urging people to work. It is only sensible that societies accompany this demand with policies that shape a significant number of opportunities to work in ways that enable self-realization.[42]

An interesting aspect of ANP, which makes the promotion of working activities more palatable, is that it encodes an interaction between needs and abilities. Needs are envisioned in the requirement regarding abilities, and abilities are envisioned in the requirement regarding needs. Thus, on the one hand, ANP calls people to produce with (inter alia) the end of helping meet other people's needs. The development and use of our abilities have in part a need-centred orientation. On the other hand, on the present interpretation of it, when ANP calls for enabling people to satisfy their needs, this also includes the generation of real opportunities for them to cultivate and actualize their abilities, including their productive abilities, in working activities featuring self-realization. Hence, we have a potentially virtuous circle here.

That said, there is potential tension as well. In the allocation of job opportunities, ANP links to two desiderata, one engaging people's abilities to produce to meet the consumption needs of others, and the other engaging people's need to gain self-fulfilment in working activities. These desiderata might conflict, as an individual may be less effective at a certain job than another

---

To make it more significant, we can also think of ways of making consumption more sophisticated. As Elster (1989: 136) recognizes, some forms of consumption (such as reading poetry) themselves involve self-realization, with its upward trajectory of enjoyment.

[42] When assessing the implications of ANP, we should not ignore that any feasible system of distribution depends on the existence of a system of production (as Marx 1978i: 531 points out). Relatedly, in capitalist societies, most people are not effectively free to opt out of work. They have to work to make a living. Work is imposed on them by the social circumstances they face, and this makes the duty to offer options of meaningful work more pressing on liberal grounds. See Roessler (2012: 76–81).

The Abilities/Needs Principle **115**

individual, but enjoy it more. The first desideratum centres on benefitting consumers (although in its fulfilment it also adds to workers' self-esteem, as a byproduct). The second desideratum caters for the well-being of workers. To appraise the possible tensions, we must consider the standpoints of both positions (of people as consumers and as workers) and find an appropriate balance in the contexts under consideration as we formulate policies and personal choices. As with the previous discussion of the extent of demandingness of (b) given the importance of personal prerogatives, there is a range of possible arrangements that might be reasonable. This indeterminacy is understandably frustrating, but it is also the natural result of recognizing that there is a plurality of important moral considerations that must be taken seriously. Simpler views might be less indeterminate but at the unacceptable price of ignoring some of these considerations. The complexity we are dealing with is a feature of the moral territory itself. On the other hand, this complex view can be made more determinate in practice as we make choices at the level of implementation, to which I now turn.

4.5 Implementing ANP

I have been developing a dignitarian interpretation of ANP that addresses the puzzles identified in 3.3. My discussion has proceeded at a fairly abstract level to focus on dimension DI of the socialist ideal. Of course, much more should be said, but I hope I have showed that the principle is appealing and worthy of future elaboration. Its neglect in contemporary social and political philosophy is unwarranted. But what about dimensions DII and DIII? I will tackle DIII in Section 5. In the remainder of this section, I will address DII by refining what to my knowledge is the only detailed proposal of an economic system that implements ANP. I will identify the main points in Joseph Carens's proposal and then suggest some amendments.[43]

(i) *Aims.* Carens seeks a way to make equality compatible with freedom and efficiency. His proposed implementation of ANP pursues this goal by mobilizing the freedom of choice and the informational virtues of markets without the motivational and distributive features they display in capitalist societies. By doing this, Carens addresses

---

[43] Carens (2003). I focus here on the Carensian proposal because of its explicit focus on implementing ANP. For a survey of recent accounts of dimension DII of socialism, see Gilbert and O'Neill (2019: sect. 4).

116 Human Dignity and Social Justice

several of the problems mentioned in 3.3, including, notably, those concerning incentives and the matching of production and demand.

(ii) *Full implementation.* Carens proposes implementations of both parts of ANP. The 'for each according to need' part is implemented via two requirements: equal post-tax income for all and direct provision targeting 'differentially incurred needs' (such as special health care needs). The 'from each according to ability' part is implemented via requiring from each person who can work (and only from them) that they take a full-time job and make good use of their talents in it. People are free to choose whether, where, and how much to work. They are not legally coerced to work. There is, however, a social expectation, a recognized social duty, that they work full-time and choose lines of work that are socially beneficial. People are not expected to choose jobs that maximize their level of contribution.[44] They have a personal prerogative such that they may choose not to take up jobs they hate. It is up to them to strike an appropriate balance between their social duty and other considerations that are important to them.

(iii) *Social ethos.* An economy that implements the principle is efficient because in it there is a strong social ethos such that people voluntarily choose to fulfil their social duty. It includes labour markets as we know them insofar as different pre-tax incomes vary, signalling the extent of social demand for different economic activities. But the distributive function of markets disappears, as after-tax income is the same for all. People use these signals to identify where to contribute with their ability (i.e. to choose some of the jobs they can do well which carry high pre-tax income). By doing it even if they will not get more after-tax income than others, they enact their ethical choice to fulfil the social duty to produce to equally support the needs of all. The incentive to work hard is moral, not pecuniary. People develop this strong sense of solidarity through socialization and by experiencing the benefits of living in a socialist society that affirms the equal importance of everyone's well-being.

(iv) *Fairness and freedom.* Finally, Carens addresses possible complaints regarding whether this proposal honours ideals of fairness and freedom. Concerning fairness, he says that the socialist principle draws on an intuitively appealing idea of sharing the burdens of cooperation in proportion to our abilities (all should do their part, but the part

---

[44] Here Carens departs from the earlier statement of his proposal in Carens (1981: 25). In that text, Carens takes the social duty to involve a maximal contribution, although he assumes that agents will balance this consideration against others (Ibid: 34–5).

The Abilities/Needs Principle **117**

each should do depends on what they can do, so that, for example, if we are moving stones from one place to another, if you are stronger than me you should carry heavier ones). He considers the worry that his approach is insensitive to the need to offer compensation to those whose work imposes greater hardships, or prefer to work less and devote themselves more to leisure, or prefer to work longer for a higher income to consume more. Carens recognizes that his proposal does not necessarily yield exactly equal access to conditions of well-being for all. But he retorts that in practice we cannot find a generally agreed upon and impeccably reliable way to balance all these considerations. Central planning systems and capitalist market economies would likely do worse. For example, the former would be seriously deficient at gathering fine-grained information about demand, and in the latter higher salaries would often track relative scarcity of certain talents, not burdensomeness of the work done. Although he acknowledges that his scheme is not perfect, Carens says that all things considered it is 'the best we can do'.

Regarding freedom, Carens considers the complaint that the social duty to produce according to ability is too demanding, leaving people too little room for doing what they want without facing social pressure. In response, he says that overall effective freedom is in fact comparatively maximized in his socialist economy. In a capitalist economy many people have fewer consumption options outside of work (given their lower income). His proposal does not force anyone to work, and it recognizes a personal prerogative so that people are morally entitled to choose jobs they enjoy rather than hate. This option is not always really available in capitalist economies, where people are forced by circumstances to take jobs they hate to pay for food and housing and other basic necessities. The socialist ethos would not be too confining. Furthermore, we should not think that other systems, including capitalism, do not secrete constraining social expectations of their own.

Carens's impressive proposal provides an excellent starting point to explore the implementation of ANP. In what follows, I introduce some critical comments and propose some amendments.

(i) *Principles and implementation.* Carens sometimes confuses the dimensions of principles (DI) and of implementation through specific institutions and practices (DII). For example, to say that it is difficult to find a publicly shared and reliable way to identify what is important for different people in terms of their relative packages of work satisfaction, consumption, and leisure may be a reason not to mention specific packages in the institutional

118 Human Dignity and Social Justice

implementation of a principle of distribution according to need, but is not itself an objection to seeing that principle as sensitive to these interpersonal variations. Other things being equal, if (and to the extent that) we could track those variations in an appropriate way, then surely we *should* introduce schemes that offer the right combination to each person. A principle stating this goal as a general requirement would guide agents by instructing them to shape institutions and practices so that they offer the overall best specific scheme they can figure out for their relevant contexts.

(ii) *Fairness in tracking diverse evaluations of work, consumption, and leisure.* At the level of implementation of the demand to cater equally for the needs of all, we can add to the two policies proposed by Carens (equal post-tax income for all and direct public provision regarding differentially incurred needs). I suggest three additions. First, since people are expected to spend a lot of time working, we could shape some workplaces so that those who care about having managerial power and self-realization at work have opportunities to enjoy them.[45] Second, since some people may value leisure, or consumption, more than others, we could organize the economic system to allow different schedules, so that to accrue different set levels of equal income people would have to work a different number of hours. Thus, the democratic identification of a standard full-time workload would constitute our initial standing policy regarding the extent of demandingness of requirement (b) in our society. But we can also introduce some flexibility, by allowing that those who want to have access to more money to consume more can work longer hours and get a higher salary, and those who want more leisure can work fewer hours and get a lower salary. The social ethos could be shaped so that people have a duty to work, should in principle aim to work full-time with equal salaries at that set level, but are free to depart from such social focal point to work more if they want to consume more or less if they want more

---

[45] It could be objected that organizing workplaces along these lines would hamper efficiency. But in complex modern economies a greater involvement of workers may actually increase productivity. Some argue that 'the information revolution is replacing one kind of management (command-and-control) with another (based on self-organization networks)' *The Economist* (2013). Second, given environmental threats posed by current forms of growth, insisting on productivity as the decisive evaluative factor may be unreasonable. In fact, ANP can help us figure out when and to what extent material development of the productive forces of a society might be desirable. It may be desirable when it enables the fulfilment of people's material needs, and when it involves occasions for people to unfold their abilities to create in cooperation with others. On the other hand, material development may not be desirable if it does not really cater for material needs or does not support people's self-realization. We can then give historical materialism's thesis that productive forces tend to develop over time an accompanying, normative dignitarian ideal about when and why this development is a good thing. By the same token, we can prevent thoughtless forms of productivism which make it into a fetish. Finally, the idea of efficiency is parasitic on some views of what is to be efficiently delivered. Productivity is not the only relevant consideration to be catered for. Increasing satisfaction in work is surely important, as are other considerations (such as expanding leisure time).

The Abilities/Needs Principle **119**

leisure. Considerations of reciprocity and equality would still be honoured by equalizing the incomes of those working the same number of hours. With these clear guidelines, everyone could see the scheme as fair. These modifications help service demands articulated in 4.3. They provide cases in which, through exercise of the democratic control envisaged in the dimension of component (f) regarding collective self-determination, we can affirm positive duties to cater for the needs of all (component (b)), provide opportunities for self-realization at work (component (a)), and recognize diverse individual needs and choices concerning work, leisure, and consumption (as per components (e) and the dimension of component of (f) concerning personal self-determination).[46]

A third amendment conflicts with a feature of Carens's view as formulated in *Equality, Moral Incentives and the Market*.[47] Carens does not explicitly take an individual's access to their equal income share to be legally (as different from ethically) conditional upon their actually working (full-time or at all). This would readily prompt the objection that the Carensian scheme would unravel due to free-riding tendencies. Carens responds that it is unlikely that many people would choose not to work, or work very little, because of the social pressure they would suffer from others, and their own sense of shame and guilt. I don't know if this speculative prediction is warranted. But, in any case, it does not seem wrong, when the problem of free-riding is real, to introduce legal conditionality in the system.[48] Two further points would make this amendment stronger by linking it to other desiderata mentioned above. First, the equal income rule could be made not only conditional upon people working but also sensitive to the number of hours worked, to allow work schedules that go above or below the standard full-time one (as discussed in the previous paragraph). So equality remains in that all those working the same number of hours would get the same income, but different egalitarian profiles could arise reflecting people's free choice to work more or less. This would give people the opportunity to fulfil different preferences regarding leisure and consumption while retaining the egalitarian spirit of the proposal.

---

[46] Carens is in principle open to modifications like the ones I suggest. For example, he acknowledges that income and consumption could be traded against other concerns and that society might democratically impose constraints on the market economy to allow different trade-offs (Carens 1981: ch. 3).

[47] Carens (1981: 131).

[48] I introduce legal conditionality to deal with the free-riding problem. If and when this problem does not in fact arise, I am happy to withdraw it. Notice also that the conditionality does not mean that people would be coerced to work. The legal scheme says that they may not get the equal pay at a set level without working, not that they must work. Given component (c), they would still receive the basic pay and direct provisions for basic needs even if they do not work. Notice also that even with the conditionality, it is still up to people's choices to determine how much effort they exert at work.

120 Human Dignity and Social Justice

It would also service the concern for reciprocity which free-riding violates. Thus amended, the Carensian scheme can better simultaneously service components (b), (d), and (e) of the interpretation of ANP proposed in 4.4. A second point should be added to prevent outcomes that are too onerous, and thus to cater for component (c). Everyone, regardless of whether they work or how much they work, would have access to a basic level of income and services. This would secure everyone's basic needs and general conditions of citizenship.[49]

To avoid misunderstanding, notice that even with these conditionalities, the implementation of ANP would not collapse into a version of the implementation of the Contribution Principle, because it is still catering for (a) (via the support for workplaces facilitating self-determined self-realization) and because it still encourages people, through the promotion of a solidaristic social ethos, to work to fulfil the basic and non-basic needs of others independently of the pay they get when they do so.

A factor this framework (and Carens's) does not fully account for, however, is that the ability to make an effort, and to derive satisfaction from work, may vary from individual to individual due to circumstances beyond their control. The same number of hours, or the same working activities, may not involve the same level of burden for everyone. I do not know how to fully solve this difficulty. Perhaps all realistic implementations of ANP are partially subject to Marx's criticism of the Contribution Principle as not fully responding to all important individual differences. Barring unlikely scenarios of complete abundance and lack of conflict of interests, it may be practically impossible to reliably allocate job satisfaction, income, leisure, etc., in ways that perfectly track all important personal differences and render everyone exactly equally and maximally well-off overall. Our social arrangements might have to be better or worse approximations without being perfect implementations. Some possible fine-tunings are the following. If each worker identifies work's burdensomeness, external devices like incentives could sometimes be avoided.[50] Second, the burdensomeness of work could be partially reduced as opportunities for self-realization in work are made available. Third, the amount of equal income accrued to those working beyond the set full-time

---

[49] The further flexibility in the framework that I suggest would also help if people want to devote themselves to forms of work that are not recognized as standard work, such as work at home or in the community. We can also recognize these forms of work as counting towards the calculus of the income each would receive. To the extent that measurement problems are overcome, this might be a good option. It is important to recognize the value of the capacities engaged in these kinds of work (such as empathy and creativity), to support their development and exercise, and to facilitate their fair allocation across gender groups. I thank Lisa Herzog and Adam Hosein for their comments on these points.

[50] I owe this suggestion to Kristi Olson.

The Abilities/Needs Principle **121**

workday could be reduced via increased taxation the proceedings of which are used to extend further the direct social provision regarding public goods and differentially incurred needs. Finally, compensatory payments could be added to defray the burdens undergone by people who spent time in specialized education and training—even though some of this time may have involved intrinsically valuable experiences.[51]

So, it seems that we should be exploring how to implement something like the following requirement: 'From each according to their abilities, while also taking into account the burdens of the work they do'. The measurement in terms of hours is only a rough proxy. It could, and probably should, be complemented with other indices to approximate the recognition of effort relative to ability and of hardships experienced at work and training. It is important here to note that much will have to be left to individual choices and to the creation and sustenance of an ethos of responsibility in contribution. Regarding this last issue, we can also explore mechanisms that bolster the ethos of social contribution. Some people might be unconditional altruists who will contribute independently of what others do. But many might (especially beyond occasional sacrifices or emergencies) only be conditional altruists, and might need to believe that sufficiently many others are doing their fair share to feel that they are really required, and to form the intention, to do their part. How can a social environment be shaped so that conditional altruism (solidarity constrained by fair reciprocity) is triggered in an effective way? Much depends on creating information mechanisms that signal to each conditional altruist when others are doing their part. One possibility here is to imagine that the hours contributed by each worker (and the overall level of effort and hardship, if reliable measurement of them exists) are counted and made public (say, through various computer devices anyone can use to get aggregate data for sectors of population and economic activities). Each agent can then see the extent to which others are contributing when they choose whether, and how much, to contribute themselves. If something like this could be implemented at reasonable cost, and especially without individualized and intrusive surveillance, it might be a good idea.[52]

(iii) *Role of government.* I share Carens's rejection of a centrally planned economy, and his scepticism about government bureaucrats being able to make accurate fine-grained assessments of diverse people's needs. But we should not exaggerate.[53] Even in Carens's scheme, the government has to make

---

[51] I owe this point to exchanges with Carol Gould and Peter Dietsch.

[52] I thank Erik Wright for discussion on these issues.

[53] For example, we certainly want government to continue delivering standard forms of control concerning safety of workplaces and products for consumption, even if their details are not uncontroversial.

122 Human Dignity and Social Justice

controversial decisions about what are the 'differentially incurred needs' that are to be serviced directly, and what and how much to do to meet them. Think here about public policy about priorities in health care provision. It also has to determine the length of a standard workload (how many hours an individual has to work to qualify as working 'full-time' and thus be morally entitled to receive equal post-tax income). These decisions are bound to be controversial too, and they already involve evaluative trade-offs concerning the value of consumption and leisure, for example. Carens acknowledges that there would be controversial choices here, but says that they would be subject to democratic debate and choice. Now, the same can be said about the policies I suggest. They do not involve a fully centrally planned economy. They recognize that government has a role in securing a fair, level playing field for workers without imposing an excessively narrow (and harmful) focus on income and consumption, as Carens's regime ends up in fact having. Furthermore, and pursuant to (f), they are framed by democratic procedures and allow for individual's specific choices.

Even if we have a reasonable picture of what would render the implementation of ANP workable and stable, we still have to explore how such an implementation might be feasible in terms of accessibility.[54] I now turn to this issue.

5. Transition

We considered how socialism could be construed at dimensions DI and DII by entertaining an interpretation of ANP and an amended version of the Carensian implementation. But how can we move from here to there? How is a socialist economy realizing ANP accessible from the current capitalist one? This is the question of transition pertaining to DIII. It gives rise to many issues about the relation between feasibility and justice in general,[55] and about the achievability of socialism in particular.[56] In this section, I concentrate on the

---

[54] Carens (1981: 21) explicitly brackets the issue of transition, but does not deny its importance. Another difficulty he does not address is that of staffing socially indispensable but generally undesired jobs, such as garbage collection. How would chores be allocated when they cannot be fully automated and not enough people readily choose to engage in them? See Wolff (2004: 96–7). In response, one could argue that if people in a socialist society have gained, through experience and socialization, a strong attachment to it, they will recognize that they should devote part of their time to these tasks. Perhaps we could require 'every able-bodied person, say from nineteen to twenty, to take his or her turn at a fair portion of the necessary unpleasant jobs' Nielsen (1985: 287). This could be a case in which restricted forms of (democratically scheduled) compulsory work is justifiable. See note 15 above.

[55] I tackle these issues in the next chapter.

[56] See also Gilabert (2011a). For discussions of problems and strategies of political transformation (spanning the spectrum between insurrectional and incremental approaches), see Elster (1986: 163–6);

The Abilities/Needs Principle **123**

specific issue of how the current capitalist ethos could be transformed into the socialist one orientated by ANP. An immediate answer is that people can become motivated to honour that principle by being socialized in families, schools, and economic institutions that subject them to expectations based in it. This answer is helpful, but does not go far enough. We have to figure out how a generation of people may arise that choose to socialize new generations in this way for the first time.

As we saw (in Section 2), Marx did not propose ANP as the immediate target for social reorganization. Instead, he suggested that we start by implementing the Contribution Principle (hereafter 'CP'). Implementing CP generates an incentive centred on self-advancement, and does not (beyond provision for basic needs) incorporate a wide positive duty to produce to meet the needs of others who cannot produce as much as oneself. Marx had thus a two-stage view of socialist transition. Is a view like this plausible? In this section I will advance three reflections. The first two introduce puzzles concerning the two-stage structure of transition. I do not fully solve them, but I articulate general and structural considerations that are fruitful to address them. My last reflection is more positive. It suggests that we deploy the powerful idea of dignity to increase ANP's motivational traction.

A clarification is needed before proceeding. To coherently explore the sequence from the implementation of CP to the implementation of ANP, if we see (like Marx) the first stage as having dissolved the capitalist class structure, then we must also see the second as not displaying this structure. This may require some further elaboration of the Carensian proposal introduced and amended in the last section. So, even if in that proposal there would be people occupying various roles in the management of firms and in the financial sector, there would not be a class of capitalists that is different form a class of workers. Means of production would be socially owned and all economic roles would be taken up by workers using but not privately owning those assets.

(i) *Immediate vs. deferred approximation.* The first puzzle concerns the issue whether CP and ANP work as maximal approximations of the same key ideals in different contexts or as a teleologically articulated sequence where only the final stage enacts the ideals. On the first interpretation, CP is as far as we can go in the early stage of socialism, and ANP states how far we can go later

---

Wright (2010: Part III); and Gilabert and O'Neill (2019: sect. 5). My discussion of transition in this section is avowedly partial. Important issues not addressed include the problems of emigration and capital flight, international pressure, and violent resistance. I also acknowledge that different transitional paths may be appropriate in different contexts, depending on the course of democratic argument and struggle. What follows are some suggestions about what to propose within that process.

124 Human Dignity and Social Justice

on (which is a lot further, arguably all the way). There are some underlying ideals (concerning self-realization, freedom, equality, solidarity, etc.) that are common. Each principle identifies the contextually maximal approximation that is feasible in each phase.

On the second interpretation, CP is not implemented because it provides the maximal approximation immediately available, but because it helps (1) complete the transition away from capitalism and (2) create the feasibility preconditions for the introduction of the higher phase of socialism. It is only in the latter that a real approximation to the ideals occurs. In the early phase, what is crucial is only (1) and (2). First, we ensure that we leave capitalism behind. This is done by finally fulfilling a key promise which capitalism makes but violates. Capitalism is often justified through the ideal of exchange of equivalents, but in it workers give more than they get, and capitalists get more than they give. By contrast, in the early phase of socialism framed by CP, each gets in proportion to what they give. This pattern would motivate those who endorse the ideal of exchange of equivalents to move from capitalism to the early phase of socialism, and to not go back. Second, the fulfilment of CP gives people a strong self-centred incentive to work (as they would be rewarded in proportion to how much they work). They would thus create the great material abundance that is necessary for the socialist ideals to be really approximated in the higher phase.

The two interpretations motivate an interesting general puzzle for sequential pictures of transformation in which different principles are recommended for different stages. They involve two different rationales for selecting principles in the first stage of the two-stage sequence. The interesting issue arises because the two rationales may conflict. It could be that if we follow the first rationale (and maximize approximation to the constant ideals in each stage), then we might choose social realizations that are not optimal for enabling the following stage in the sequence. Path-dependence could set in, with a local maximum that does not lead to the global maximum.[57] People socialized in the value of exchange of equivalents may not want to move to a society in which that principle is dropped. There is then the option of going for the second rationale (and choosing what would maximize the chances of eventually moving to the situation in which the constant ideals could find

---

[57] The problem of path-dependence becomes clearer when we consider the institutions generated to implement the distributive principles. If the state becomes larger in the first stage, it may itself become an obstacle for further change (which, in Marx's ideal, would involve decentralization and autonomous decision-making at the level of productive units). Perhaps choosing a form of market socialism would reduce the problem. For an influential proposal of market socialism, see, e.g., Roemer (1994). For criticisms, see Cohen (2009: sect. IV). The Carensian proposal (with the amendments I suggested) would be a form of market socialism that addresses Cohen's worries. See Chapter 8 for more discussion.

The Abilities/Needs Principle **125**

their maximal approximation overall). But then there is the moral problem of choosing social organizations for the first stage that are harmful to people, or not as good as they could be at the time. The worse the situation in the early phase of transition, the worse (other things being equal) this strategy is. Things get even more problematic when the calculation of what is necessary or most likely to produce the conditions for the higher phase is uncertain. Why take the step backward when it is not certain that this would enable us to take the envisioned two steps forward? The more uncertainty, the worse (other things being equal) this strategy is. These problems would be mitigated (but not dissolved) if people apply these strategies through their own democratic choice.

(ii) *Inclusion vs. contradiction.* Another puzzle when determining how to proceed regarding the two stages is this. We have to consider two possible valences of the first stage in relation to the second: (1) the first involves a less extensive realization of the relevant ideals than the second (*inclusion*); (2) the first violates the ideals realized in the second (*contradiction*). The early stage of socialism, by comparison to the higher stage, exemplifies both (1) and (2). The implementation of CP is accompanied by the requirement that certain basic needs be met, and it increases overall resources available to expand people's well-being beyond those basic needs. This is a case of (1). It could be said that to implement CP is to partially implement ANP: distribution according to contribution gives people (who can and do contribute) part of what they need, and the part of it that they can feasibly get in the early stage of transition. But it condones inequalities of access to means of consumption (and well-being more generally) that result from morally arbitrary differences (such as differences in native endowments and in social circumstances).[58] This is a case of (2).

It could be asked: Since the implementation of CP involves a case of (2), why not adopt another transitional principle? For example, Jon Elster suggests that a better pragmatic choice in the early stage is some version of Rawls's Difference Principle (which accepts only those inequalities that work to the maximum benefit of the worst-off—or, in a weaker version, make the worst-off better off).[59] Elster might be right, but we should not ignore the problem of feasibility that Marx is addressing. As we saw, CP involves some continuity with the bourgeois moral culture that is being targeted for transformation (the principle of exchange of equivalents is consistently applied), whereas the Difference Principle seems more remote. In fact, Rawls himself

---

[58] Both of these points are mentioned by Marx (1978i: 531–2) to explain why the early stage is still afflicted by a 'bourgeois limitation'.
[59] Elster (1986: 99–100; 1985: 230).

126 Human Dignity and Social Justice

acknowledges that it is quite a radical departure from the status quo.[60] If this is true, then it might be a good idea to explore a *three-stage* schedule of principles: CP, the Difference Principle, and ANP. The second stage would be introduced as the inequalities in access to consumption goods resulting from morally arbitrary differences in productive capacity condoned by the first become ethically and politically salient, and the third would be introduced once the incentive problems that the second addresses become less pressing. As material scarcity is reduced and people are no longer pressed to quarrel over resources to fulfil urgent needs, they are less likely to be so self-centred, and these changes in moral culture might succeed.

It is important that the Difference Principle in its weaker version is not the final destination. It involves a relatively feeble version of fraternity. Rawls says that it expresses fraternity as 'the idea of not wanting to have greater advantages unless this is to the benefit of others who are less well off'.[61] But we can envisage a stronger form of fraternity that involves more than consoling the worse off by enabling them to have more than they had before we came to have more that we ourselves had before. We can also wonder whether we should want to have more than them to begin with, and thus whether we should benefit them only if we get more than they do. Why not share the new advantages we help bring about equally with them instead? ANP involves a more exigent, and egalitarian, form of solidarity.

What about the strong version of the Difference Principle, which calls for maximization of the condition of the worst-off but does not require equality? Offhand, it is not clear why such a maximization would not simply coincide with the highest feasible equality. If everybody indeed honours the ideal, then nobody would say that they would not work in ways that benefit the worst-off unless they end up with more than them, as they could choose to benefit all equally (and thus maximize the condition of the worst-off by comparison to the contrastive scenario that would result if they pursued self-serving inequalities instead). They recognize, for example, that moving from an initial equal division of advantages between them and others which amounts to, say, 5 (for them) and 5 (for others), to another featuring (7, 7) is morally more appropriate than invoking a self-centred incentives-based scheme yielding (8, 6).[62] Of course, as we saw, ANP can be interpreted to

---

[60] Rawls is less optimistic about the widespread endorsement of his Difference Principle than about his other principles requiring equal civil and political liberties and fair equality of opportunity. See, e.g., Rawls (2001: 95).

[61] Rawls (1999: 90).

[62] See the discussion in Cohen (2008: 78–80, 100–3, 106–9, 118–24). Cohen argues that because of the moral arbitrariness of differences in talent and other unchosen circumstances (which, in the Rawlsian view, provides a rationale for seeing equal distributions as the initial benchmark—see Rawls 1999: ch. 2),

The Abilities/Needs Principle **127**

permit some specific inequalities in income or access to consumption goods that is based on compensation for differential levels of effort and hardship at work and to defray costs of training (and in this way it tracks considerations of desert and/or overall equality of benefits and burdens). But it is hard to see how ANP could justify inequalities on the basis of Rawlsian incentives (which are independent from such considerations). In the end, the Difference Principle seems less morally compelling than, or simply collapses into, a principle that requires the highest feasible equality for all (assuming, as we do throughout this discussion, that justified liberties and personal prerogatives are respected). As I see it, ANP straightforwardly calls for that equality.

Interestingly, Rawls himself considers whether Marx could have adopted the Difference Principle instead of CP, but judges that he would have rejected it because he held left-libertarian commitments. Those commitments require equality of access to external productive resources, but beyond that they prohibit involuntary transfers from more to less advantaged producers. The Difference Principle would coercively impose such redistributions (for example through taxation).[63] I think that Rawls's interpretation is defective. There may be a left-libertarian strand in Marx, but it is absent in the 'Critique of the Gotha Program'. In this text, CP is accompanied by requirements to provide health care and education for all and support for people unable to work. Marx says that those services will expand as the socialist transition deepens. These redistributions involve enforceable positive duties to help others.[64] They are incompatible with libertarianism.

With the ANP and its dignitarian rationale we can also render the common idea of basic equality (according to which every individual is owed equal respect and concern) compatible with accepting certain social and economic inequalities. Here is how this combination is seen as possible in Rawls's theory of justice. His basic equality constraint is that everyone in a society who has the capacities for a sense of justice and a conception of the good within

---

the especially talented should not ask, to use their talents in a way that benefits others, that incentivizing inequalities of reward be put in place so that they end up better off than them. For the further argument that the ideal of countering inequalities resulting from morally arbitrary differences would clash with the content of the Difference Principle itself, see Cohen (2008: 156–61). Similar considerations could be applied to Rawls's discussion of reciprocity. If this idea gives us reason to reject distributions that increase overall income and wealth boosting the position of the better off at the expense of the worse off, it would also give us reason to reject inequalities that would result from an incentivizing scheme promising greater benefits to especially talented people who are productive. As Rawls recognizes, the talented are already benefitted by the natural lottery by having their talents and they are further benefitted through an economic structure affirmed by others (including the less advantaged) which enables them to take up certain desirable positions which others do not or cannot occupy. (See Rawls 2001: 126.) Why ask, on top of that, to have more income and wealth than others who also work at similar levels of effort (even if they are less blessed by luck in terms of their talents)?

[63] Rawls (2007 367–8).
[64] Marx (1978i: 528–9).

128 Human Dignity and Social Justice

a certain range are owed equal rights of justice.[65] But his second principle of justice allows for inequalities in positions of authority in the economy, and for unequal income, so long as the inequalities work to the maximal benefit of the worst-off and proceed against a background of fair equality of opportunity. The first principle is assumed to apply as well, establishing equal civil and political liberties for everyone (with the range properties). So, inequalities of income and economic positions are allowed here. As noted above, the permission of inequalities in income by the Difference Principle can be disputed as not fully honouring basic equality. But notice that even the principle of fair equality of opportunity condones certain inequalities. For it accepts that certain positions in the economy will not be held by all. And, even if competition for them is fair, the positions themselves may be such that they are beyond reach for some, as not everyone will really be able to do the jobs available. The competition will proceed on the basis of candidates' abilities and motivations, and candidates will not be equal with respect to them. The principle secures fairness in that access to the positions is not determined in a nepotistic way, or on the basis of wealth and social power, and in that society makes sure (for example through public education) that everyone has a real chance to develop their natural capacities regardless of their initial social situation (their family's wealth, cultural resources, social contacts, etc.). But society would be permitting, and creating, positions that not everyone will have the ability to occupy. By doing this, it would be taking steps, including the use of scarce resources, to create paths of life which will foreseeably constitute real options for some but not for others. So, some people with the range properties but with lower levels of overall ability than others with respect to some activities will be effectively excluded from some positions socially created. (This would of course also be happening regarding people who do not reach the minimum level of the range properties.) So again, society would be creating paths that are effectively accessible to only a subset of the population. For examples, think about certain positions requiring rare motivational or cognitive abilities, such as those of a supreme court judge, a leading researcher in quantum mechanics, or a neurosurgeon. How can these social and economic inequalities be compatible with the idea of basic equality?

A dignitarian framework can help understand why this prospect could be coherent after all. For the equality it would demand is a matter of equally

---

[65] Rawls (1999: sect. 77). Rawls (2001: 55) recognizes that 'any modern society, even a well-ordered one, must rely on some inequalities to be well-designed and effectively organized', and so we must ask 'what kinds of inequalities a well-ordered society would allow or be particularly concerned to avoid'. See the illuminating discussion of 'basic equality' (to be distinguished from 'surface equalities' regarding various social and economic advantages such as jobs, income, and wealth) in Waldron (2017).

The Abilities/Needs Principle   **129**

catering for the flourishing of all individuals in view of what *their* valuable capacities are. Those capacities will often be different in kind and degree, and as a result catering for them will demand the creation of different opportunities. But since all of them would be given the appropriate responsiveness they call for, all their carriers would, in a relevant sense, be treated equally. Furthermore, if ANP is honoured, the positions would be shaped and adopted with a spirit of solidarity, so that their occupiers act for the sake of the well-being of others besides their own. The creation of opportunities that it would not be feasible for all to take up would be good for the ones who are able to take them up—it would foster their flourishing at work. But it would also be good for those who cannot—by enabling the workers occupying those positions to improve the life of others when they engage in the activities they gain entry into. So, in a more abstract sense of opportunity (more abstract because it focuses on the general opportunity to flourish given one's capacities rather than, more specifically, on this or that opportunity to engage in this or that activity), the schedule would give equal opportunities to all. We can see here how the dignitarian focus on responding appropriately to the singular configurations of each individual (highlighted in demand (e) of ANP, and discussed in Chapter 1, Section 2.2.5) finds its expression.

(iii) *Human dignity and the move from exchange of equivalents to mutual affirmation.*[66] The inspiring idea of dignity is central to (at least) modern moral and political culture. Its core is that human beings are owed forms of respect and concern that show proper appreciation of and support for their valuable capacities. As agents capable of sentience, self-awareness, practical reasoning, knowledge, aesthetic appreciation, creativity, and social cooperation (amongst other basic capacities), human beings should be granted rights to what they need to develop and exercise these capacities in their social life. Human rights identify the most urgent claims of human dignity.[67] But as pointed out in Chapter 1 (Section 3), social justice, including economic justice, goes further, recognizing that human dignity gives rise to equal entitlements to the conditions for leading a flourishing life, not only a decent one.

Shaping economic life under ANP involves a double affirmation of individuals as producers and receivers of products. As receivers, people are affirmed because their consumption-needs are seen as directly significant: it is worth working to meet them. They are also affirmed as producers, because the organization of production makes available to them activities in which

---

[66] In these final reflections I develop points stated in 3.1 (ix–x).
[67] Gilabert (2019a).

130 Human Dignity and Social Justice

their capacities for cooperative, creative, and satisfying labour can be developed and exercised, and this in self-determined ways. When multiple agents honour the principle in their economic relations, the double affirmation is reciprocal and general.[68] The economy becomes a system of mutual affirmation in which the well-being and autonomy of each participant are viewed as equally significant. In this economy, the dignity of everyone is respected, as each individual's free pursuit of well-being in production and consumption is protected. In addition, dignity is seen as giving rise to positive duties of solidaristic support. To show concern besides respect for the dignity of others we must help promote, not just refrain from hampering, the conditions in which they can flourish. Socialism takes the abilities and needs of all as the focus of negative *and* positive duties. As a result, it gives human dignity full recognition.

The socialist outlook of mutual affirmation, involving both negative and positive duties, goes beyond the ethos of capitalism, which involves widespread selfishness. In capitalist economic life, the needs of others are normally relevant for me only if, and to the extent that, catering for them would work to my own advantage. This attitude does not take the dignity of other human beings seriously. The idea of exchange of equivalents is also problematically self-centred. Why should we think that people are not entitled to objects whose exchange value is higher than the exchange value of the objects they themselves produce? This ignores the direct significance of their needs, and the mutual affirmation that solidarity embodies. The idea of exchange of equivalents gets whatever appeal it has from its association to the idea of fair reciprocity. But fair reciprocity is an altogether different idea, which, as we saw, is already captured by ANP. It requires mutuality in productive effort we are able to exert, not that only identical exchange values be swapped.

The socialist Abilities/Needs Principle gives human dignity its due. However, this point is obscured by a common, ideological construal of human dignity. On that construal, getting support from others is a source of humiliation or shame, and giving it involves arrogance or motivates guilt. This is an ideological outlook because it twists the idea of dignity to reproduce existing relations of inequality, exploitation, and indifference. Once we move beyond conditions of severe scarcity, the injustice of these relations cannot

---

[68] Here I engage, and develop further, the idea of 'double affirmation' expressed in Marx (1992: 277–8). I am also echoing Marx's apt worries about the detachment of the idea of dignity from solidaristic support, as apparent in the passage cited at the end of Chapter 2. Marx challenges a view of dignity that sees claims to that support as humiliating and offers of it as arrogant (Ibid: 276).

be ignored, and the inspiring call for the mutual affirmation of our dignity may finally gain the motivational traction it deserves.

6. Ideological Manipulation and The Duty to Contribute

I hope to have said enough in this chapter to show that ANP can be given an appealing interpretation, and that in any case it deserves to be taken seriously and explored further in future research. As a handy short statement of the agenda for further inquiry regarding ANP, I state below some interrelated questions such an inquiry could seek answers to.

- Q1. What are the *normative considerations*, such as the *requirements* or *demands*, or, less strongly, the *reasons*, involved in the principle (i.e. what ideas of equality, sufficiency, reciprocity, self-determination, etc. is the principle meant to capture)?
- Q2. Who are the *agents* to whom the considerations are addressed (i.e. who is to act to fulfil them)?
- Q3. Who are the *subjects* of the considerations (i.e. to whom are they owed)?
  (Answers to Q2 and Q3 give an account of the *scope* of the considerations, saying to what entities they apply.)
- Q4. What are the *objects* of the considerations (i.e. what is the currency or metric of the principle—or, more specifically, what are the relevant abilities the principle asks people to form and deploy, and what are the needs that their deployment should help fulfil)?
- Q5. How do the considerations flowing from ANP *interact* with each other, and with other considerations independent of ANP? These considerations might compete, so that they weigh against, undermine, undercut, cancel, constrain, etc. each other. If so, what is the relative weight, strength, or standing of the considerations flowing from ANP? The interactions among these considerations could also be positive, so that they enable, strengthen, intensify, or complement each other. If so, what are these positive linkages? As we explore these questions, we can develop a holistic picture of how ANP fits within our overall views about morality and justice.
- Q6. What is the *site* of the considerations? Do they apply to individual agents, groups, institutions, social systems, and to which ones in each case in what kinds of occasions?

132 Human Dignity and Social Justice

- Q7. What are the *feasibility* parameters that are relevant for assessing the implementation and strength of the requirements and other reasons flowing from the principle?

The sketch I have offered about how to understand ANP no doubt requires much further elaboration to give a satisfactory systematic answer to these questions. For example, an important challenge is to develop a fuller account of how to identify individuals' relevant needs and abilities. We want an account of them that can both track what is importantly different in each individual and devise a unified framework of description and assessment. The first point is relevant in order to cater for the desideratum of responding to individual diversity, which is one of the most important insights in ANP, and is very much in line with the individual-centred focus of the Dignitarian Approach. But the second point is also relevant when hard choices have to be made, in circumstances of relative material scarcity, about how much of the scarce resources should be given to different people (or to the same person on different occasions). The second point is significant as well when we face the task of having to measure and compare levels of appropriate contribution by different people given their sundry abilities for and burdens experienced in various forms of work. We need indices of needs and contributions that are fine-grained enough to appreciate the important diversity among people, but also coarse-grained enough to allow for appropriate comparisons between them for the purposes of reaching social agreements about the allocation of tasks and access to advantages.[69]

The discussion in this chapter allows us to note that there are two forms of recognition potentially at play in the use of ANP—one morally appropriate and the other morally objectionable. Regarding recognition of the appropriate sort, I argued that the plausibility of ANP can be explained in part by the fact that it illuminates how we should enact morally fitting responses to the dignity of participants in economic cooperation. I articulated this view by drawing on the Dignitarian Approach and its companion ideal of Solidaristic Empowerment. On the dignitarian perspective, ANP calls for an organization of economic relationships in which the institutions and practices of production, exchange, and consumption are made to be equally supportive of the unfolding of the valuable capacities of each person involved. As noted, ANP

---

[69] As Markus Furendal pointed out to me (in private communication), we should also recognize the implications of our epistemic limitations in the development of these indices. Since we are unlikely to know exactly how much people exert an effort and contribute, we should be cautious in how we praise or criticize them. As Furendal suggests, our sanctioning institutions should correspondingly be nonharsh.

The Abilities/Needs Principle **133**

also caters for human diversity, enjoining us to notice and engage people's various abilities and needs in their specificity and singular configurations. ANP is thus appealing in shaping economic relations so that participants in them express a mutual recognition that is simultaneously responsive to their equality and diversity.

On the other hand, we might worry that ANP could be used to articulate other forms of recognition that are in fact quite problematic. It might be deployed to push people to work at unfulfilling jobs in which they do not enjoy enough self-determination and self-realization, or to pressure them to seek the satisfaction of alleged needs they do not really have. These uses of ANP enact morally objectionable forms of recognition in which people are expected and incentivized to occupy certain social roles and choose certain personal pursuits that involve harmful hierarchies and cement unfair distributions. However, I think that the same normative ground—human dignity as a moral status—that we relied on to defend the plausible interpretation of ANP can be successfully marshalled to criticize its problematic deployments. The latter involve the generation of conventional social statuses that appear to support, but in fact undermine, the conditions in which the deeper and normatively more important dignitarian moral status of individuals is appropriately responded to.[70]

Let me conclude the chapter by exploring further the worry that ANP could easily lend itself to being used in inappropriately cajoling people to work. Recall that ANP combines demands of distribution with demands on contribution. It does not only ask who should get what—how the benefits of cooperation should be distributed. In addition, it asks who should do what—how the burdens of cooperation should be allocated. It thus addresses the supply side besides the demand side. The focus on demands of contribution as springing from concerns about solidarity—including aid and fair reciprocity—puts socialists at odds with traditional views that construe the agenda of social and political philosophy as variations on the theme 'Get off my back!' It prompts us to think about the theme 'Let me have your back!' or 'What can we do to help each other?' There surely is something of the former theme at play in socialist theory and practice too, of course. Workers get their bosses too much on their back, and should have access to a different economic environment in which they are free from their domination and

---

[70] Conventional statuses attached to certain social roles (such as that of a wage worker in a capitalist system) are tied to an economy of social esteem and disesteem in which fulfilment of the roles is appraised. But such statuses and roles can be criticized by reference to morally more weighty reasons regarding what we owe to each other as persons. Moral recognition regarding the latter constrains, and should help shape the terms of, social appreciations regarding the former. See on this Wallace (2019: sect. 4.3).

134 Human Dignity and Social Justice

exploitation. But socialists are certainly engaged with the second theme as well. They are keen to figure out how we could act to foster the flourishing of others besides our own.

Thus, according to requirements (b) and (d) of ANP, people have a duty to contribute to the social product from which all depend to lead flourishing lives. It is pro tanto wrong to be indifferent to the well-being of others and refrain from fostering it through one's work, or to draw from the social product without doing one's fair share to generate it when one can. Accordingly, a just society should create opportunities for people to contribute. This enables the production from which all benefit, and supports the self-respect of those who take up these opportunities—allowing them to see themselves as having integrity (as achievement-based dignity) when they do their part in sustaining the just social scheme.

But this line of argument, which is correct, can be used in a twisted way to manipulate people into taking up jobs which are odious to them. Consider a society that could, but does not, generate opportunities for jobs which, in addition to contributing to the social product, are also ones in which domination, exploitation, and alienation are minimized. Instead, this society makes available only, or mostly, jobs in which contribution proceeds under domination, exploitation, and alienation. Add that this society does not secure people's access to some goods necessary for a minimally decent life (such as food, medical care, education, housing, etc.) unless they work. Finally, imagine that a societal moral culture is nurtured which urges people to take up one of the jobs available or face the stigma of being shirkers and freeloaders who fail to fulfil their duty to contribute. This constellation will cajole people into doing odious jobs, on pain of severe material distress and personal shame, while enabling some employers to dominate and exploit them. If this setup is indeed avoidable, if alternative social institutions and cultural codes are feasible in which jobs would be organized differently, then what we find here is in fact a form of ideological manipulation of people to get them to adapt to an unjust social system. The sound ideas that there is a duty to contribute and that opportunities to do so should be socially generated is twisted to convince people that they must accept certain opportunities of suboptimal moral value. It likely also operates as a cover to enable others to benefit unfairly from the work that they do.[71] Contemporary capitalist societies display something very close to this pattern.

It is important, however, to see that this ideological setup is not really supported by ANP as we have articulated it in this chapter, and that in fact

---

[71] This is a case of the 'ideologies of contribution' mentioned in the last section of Chapter 1.

The Abilities/Needs Principle **135**

ANP gives us what we need to criticize it. In addition to the positive duties to contribute and to do one's fair share, envisioned in (b) and (d), ANP, as interpreted here, also envisions, in its requirement (c), that a floor of basic needs satisfaction for all should be socially secured. Since this requirement is unconditional, the provision for basic needs may not be withheld and made conditional as an indirect way to get people to work.[72] Furthermore, if we take seriously ANP's demands (a), (d), and (e), then there should be opportunities for work in which people can avoid exploitation, alienation, and domination. The setup described in the previous paragraph would violate these concerns.

Thus, to effectively criticize the ideological setup, we need to imagine a better way to implement the duty and the opportunity to contribute that eliminates, or reduces to an overall reasonable level, the presence of exploitation, alienation, and domination in production. A just society would, to the extent that it is reasonably feasible, give everyone genuine opportunities to contribute through practices that feature fair cooperation, self-realization, and self-determination. This is what solidaristic empowerment calls for, and what the workers' enjoyment of condition-dignity would involve. Chapters 5–7 will explore each of these desiderata in detail. But before engaging in that exploration, we need to pause to discuss the significance of feasibility for ambitious approaches to social justice like the one envisioned here. This is the topic of the next chapter.

---

[72] Recall also that requirement (f) supports people's self-determination. Coercive recruitment of work is excluded except in extreme or highly circumscribed cases. Furthermore, as noted throughout, people have a personal prerogative so that they may choose forms of work which are not optimific in terms of the consequences for the well-being of all but are significantly better in terms of their own personal fulfilment. No enslavement of the talented is envisaged here. For illuminating discussion of the relations between this personal prerogative and socialist egalitarian ideals, see Cohen (2008).

4
Justice and Feasibility

1. Introduction

Should we bring about a radically egalitarian, or socialist society in which everyone has extensive and equal access to what they need to lead a flourishing life? Any conception of social justice like this, animated by ambitious principles, faces the common worry that what it prescribes is unrealistic. There are at least three kinds of response to this worry. The first is to make the normative principles of the conception less ambitious and thus more practicable. The second is to dismiss practical concerns about feasibility as irrelevant to the truth of theoretical claims about what justice demands. These responses face further challenges. The first risks surrendering in the face of a morally rotten status quo, and the second fails to illuminate the relation between principles of justice and their fulfilment in the real world. Although I address ways in which these two strategies could be defended against these challenges,[1] in this chapter I focus on the constructive task of developing a third strategy that combines normative ambition and feasibility. I propose a *dynamic approach to the relation between justice and feasibility*. Some feasibility constraints are 'soft' rather than 'hard': they are malleable over time (e.g. several cultural, political, and economic mechanisms are soft, while logic and physical laws, when true, are hard). When demanding principles clash with soft rather than hard constraints, an appropriate response may be one that neither deems the principles null nor disengages feasibility considerations. We can use our *political imagination* to envisage alternative ways to fulfil principles in different contexts, and recognize *dynamic duties* to expand our ability to fulfil those principles over time. We can thus retain idealism about

---

[1] Defenders of the first strategy can say that their focus is only on what to do here and now (Sen 2009); defenders of the second strategy can say that their focus is not on what to do, but on the truth of fundamental normative principles (Cohen 2008). For responses see, respectively, Gilabert (2012b) and (2011a). Wiens (2012) argues that ideal theories of justice are irrelevant for solving practical problems. For a response see Herzog (2013). For an overview of the debate about ideal and non-ideal theory, see Valentini (2012). On feasibility, see Southwood (2018).

Human Dignity and Social Justice. Pablo Gilabert, Oxford University Press. © Pablo Gilabert (2023).
DOI: 10.1093/oso/9780192871152.003.0004

138 Human Dignity and Social Justice

principles and realism about feasibility and combine them in a way that is practically consequential.

I have identified some scattered elements of this approach in previous work.[2] Besides identifying elements missed before, in this chapter I present a systematic articulation of the approach, and illuminate its significance for the development and defence of ambitious conceptions of social justice like the one favoured in this book. In Section 2, I explain what feasibility is, why we should care about it, and how we should take it into account when developing normative judgements. In Section 3, I propose the dynamic approach to the pursuit of justice, which is focused on the importance of political imagination and the expansion of agents' power to realize ambitious normative principles. This chapter presents a program. It offers a conceptual framework to think about the relation between justice and feasibility and a substantive approach to normative problems concerning that relation. Inevitably, some details regarding the issues addressed will not be fully settled. But I hope that this deficiency is offset by the novelty and fruitfulness of the account proposed. Despite the importance of the topic for political philosophy, there is to my knowledge no other similarly systematic account of the relation between justice and feasibility. Considerations about feasibility were already marked as relevant for the Dignitarian Approach (for example in the identification of the circumstances of dignity and the justification of specific rights, in Chapter 1, Sections 2.1 and 2.2.1). In Section 4, I state succinctly how dignity relates to dynamic feasibility.

2. The Nature, Importance, and Role of Feasibiity

In this section I explain how considerations of feasibility should be incorporated into our normative deliberations. I propose a framework to guide a form of inquiry that is practical. It is concerned with shaping how we choose to act in the social world. I anchor my exploration in the deliberative stance of agents.[3] I organize my exposition by addressing the following three questions: What is feasibility? Why should we care about it? How should we handle feasibility claims?

---

[2] Gilabert (2008; 2009; 2011a; 2012a: chs. 4 and 7; 2012b). Gilabert and Lawford-Smith (2012). The current chapter is a significantly revised and expanded version of Gilabert (2017b).

[3] I assume throughout that moral reasons are normatively dominant in our deliberation about what to do, so that we never have conclusive reason to do what we have conclusive moral reason not to do, and if we have conclusive moral reason to do something that is the thing for us to do. Furthermore, I concentrate on reasons of social justice, which are central in politics, but what I say could be couched in more general moral terms.

2.1 What?

The expression ' … is feasible' is often used when considering political processes involving individual or collective agents seeking to bring about certain outcomes or states of affairs in certain circumstances. It is used to address the issues whether, and to what extent, the agents in the circumstances have the ability or power to bring about the outcomes they might seek.[4] Thus, feasibility is a relational concept of power or ability that connects three basic elements: an agent, certain outcomes, and certain circumstances. A possible schema to articulate this concept, which I explore in this chapter, is the following. An agent A has the power to bring about an outcome O in circumstances C if and only if O would occur if A tries, in C, to bring it about (and A can indeed so try). When we consider specific processes, it is often useful to break down the variable for outcomes into several components. Three such components are (i) the agent's deciding, or forming the intention to act; (ii) the agent's acting; and (iii) the action's producing the desired consequences. Thus, when we consider the feasibility of a group of workers obtaining a salary raise by means of strike action, we explore the ability of various workers who support the strike action to form the intention to strike, to initiate and continue the strike action throughout the appropriate period of time, and to obtain through their actions the concessions from managers they were aiming at.

As in previous formulations, I understand feasibility claims as involving a conditional: they say what would happen if agents take certain initiatives.[5] But I now emphasize that this account should be phrased more carefully: we should adopt a complex view of outcomes and include the assertion that agents can take the relevant initiatives. This makes sure that various important issues are not rendered invisible. Thus, there may be feasibility issues regarding the three aspects (i)–(iii) mentioned in the previous paragraph. To show that certain desired consequences are feasible for an agent to produce it may not be enough to show that the agent would produce them if they engaged in the relevant actions. One may also have to show that the agent

---

[4] In this chapter I use the terms 'ability' and 'power' interchangeably.
[5] Gilabert and Lawford-Smith (2012). The conditional approach is proposed in Brennan and Southwood (2007). I am not assuming that feasibility can only be analysed in this way. For further discussion on feasibility and motivation, see Lawford-Smith (2013a). In the previous paragraph (and also in Section 3.4 of Chapter 7), I indeed present the notion of ability in terms of a conditional analysis, but I modify it to address a common worry. The worry is that a conditional analysis does not provide sufficient conditions, because there are possible cases in which A would bring about O if they tried but A faces insurmountable obstacles to forming that volition. (See, e.g., Maier 2021: sect. 3). I dealt with this worry by adding a clause that says that A can form the relevant volition. Alternatively, it could be said that the analysis is restricted only to cases in which the pursuit of O is within the domain of agency of A.

140 Human Dignity and Social Justice

has the power to engage in such actions. Furthermore, to show that performing certain actions is feasible for an agent it may not be enough to show that they would perform them if they decided to do so. One may also have to show that the agents would be able to form the intention to act and sustain the intention to act through the duration of the relevant actions. There are at least three points of discussion about the feasibility of agents' bringing about certain outcomes, concerning whether the agents are able to produce what is mentioned in (i), (ii), and (iii).[6]

Not noticing this complexity may make our moral judgements and our political deliberations poorer, as these often rely on assumptions about what agents are able to achieve regarding (i) and (ii) besides (iii). Here are two examples. We should hesitate to say that it is feasible for Pedro to brush aside the spider that is on the table and is about to attack his helpless friend if his arachnophobia would make him unable to form the decision to engage in the close contact with the spider that is necessary to brush it aside, *even if* he would easily brush aside the spider if he did decide to approach it. If Peter should save his friend, he might do better by asking for assistance from someone else. The challenges the workers would face to get their salary raise once striking may be importantly different from the challenges they would face when seeking to get their collective action of striking off the ground. Particular workers may find these challenges to be of different levels of difficulty. John may find it hard to bargain well with management (e.g. to express himself boldly and compellingly), and Maria may find it hard to join the strike (e.g. to overcome her tendency to free ride). John and Maria may still be able to do what is so hard for them, but the degree of feasibility of doing it is affected by the psychological phenomena mentioned. Surely these considerations matter as strike action is planned.[7]

---

[6] A further clarification. As explored later in this section, claims about ability can be made more precise by using probability thresholds and scales. S's ability to determine O may involve there being a sufficient probability that S will determine O if S tries, and the scalar variation above the threshold (the existence of degrees of ability) may indeed be relevant for some purposes of discussion.

[7] Estlund (2011) considers whether there are any motivational constraints on requirements of justice. He accepts for the sake of argument that 'ought' implies 'can do' but explores, and rejects, the different view that 'ought' implies 'can will'. He claims that there are cases in which an agent ought to do something even if they cannot will to do it. Even if some people are so selfish that they cannot bring themselves to place the garbage in the right place and avoid littering when this costs them some extra effort, we think that they ought to do it and do not take their motivational incapacity to block the requirement (see e.g. Ibid: 219–20).

A problem with Estlund's argument is that the examples he picks are not intuitively clear cases in which an agent 'can't will' to do something. The littering case is not obviously a case of 'can't will'. It seems instead to involve a prediction that the agent 'won't will' or / and 'won't do' something, which is not obviously requirement blocking. Estlund puts aside what he calls 'clinical cases' (involving phobias and other powerful psychological mechanisms—see Ibid: 219). But these are the most promising examples of 'can't will'. And he allows that they may block requirements. The cases Estlund focuses on (concerning selfish tendencies) do not seem to be genuine cases of incapacity, but rather cases where willing to do something is hard

Justice and Feasibility   **141**

Feasibility claims often have this form: 'A (an individual or collective agent) has the power to bring about O (a certain outcome—possibly quite complex, as in (i)–(iii) above—in circumstances C'. This formulation takes feasibility to allow (like possibility) for presence or absence but not degrees. Now, there is a sense of feasibility that is indeed *binary*. It sharply says that an agent is able (or unable) to achieve certain results in certain circumstances. But we also need to capture another sense of feasibility that is *scalar*. This sense is not an 'on / off' one, but is graded. Claims of scalar feasibility have this form: 'A has the power to bring about O in circumstances C to the degree, or with probability, P'.

Both senses are relevant for moral and political deliberation. The binary sense is used to conclusively rule out certain outcomes. Feasibility parameters involved here concern, for example, laws of logic and nature. When true, these laws impose *hard constraints*. The strikers cannot succeed if they aim at securing for all workers in a country at time t1 a salary higher than the average salary for workers in the country at t1. The scalar sense engages different feasibility parameters. They are *soft constraints* involving, for example, various economic, political, and cultural mechanisms. These are soft because they are not insurmountable. They affect instead the probability of success of the pursuit of certain outcomes. Labour activists are more likely to succeed at unionizing workers in a country where there is a strongly solidaristic political culture than in a country where competitive individualism is rampant even if they are not, strictly speaking, unable to reach high levels of unionization in either context. The previous example concerning John and Maria also engages scalar feasibility. Despite its great importance (discussed below), the scalar sense of feasibility has been neglected in political philosophy. As a result, feasibility claims are often phrased in binary terms when they should instead be phrased in graded terms.[8]

---

or unlikely, and so they do not provide a clear counterexample to the claim that 'ought' implies 'can will', and when he does consider better candidates for motivational incapacities (as in the case of phobias) he allows that they may block requirements (thus potentially confirming rather than challenging the claim).
    A deeper problem is that it is not clear that accepting that 'ought to do' implies 'can do' is consistent with denying that 'ought to do' implies 'can will to do', as Estlund hopes (Ibid: 213). The problem is that 'can do' seems to imply 'can will to do' if the *doing* we focus on is *intentional*. Intentional action is indeed the focus of Estlund's discussion (see note 10 below). If the agent cannot will to do something, they cannot intentionally do it. Regarding intentional actions, 'ought to do' implies 'can will to do' if 'ought to do' implies 'can do', because 'can do' implies 'can will to do'.
    [8] For the introduction of the scalar sense, see Gilabert (2012a: chs. 4 and 7); Gilabert and Lawford-Smith (2012); Lawford-Smith (2013b); Gilabert (2019a: Appendix II). I do not claim that binary feasibility cannot be formulated so as to include cultural, economic, or political parameters. It could be said that some outcomes are infeasible if the probability that the relevant agent would produce them if they try is below some threshold. The gist of the discussion that follows, however, is that in those cases the scalar use is the more basic one (as it is the one that assigns probabilities), and that thresholds, if needed, are fixed contextually by drawing on concerns that often are not merely descriptive. Regarding threshold fixing, it

142   Human Dignity and Social Justice

2.2 Why?

In what circumstances, for what purposes, do we talk about feasibility? There may be different occasions and aims, which would affect the account of feasibility we go on to develop. Here I focus on issues of justice, and in particular on shaping our normative political reasoning regarding how we should act.

We have, I think, the twin intuitions that we should be weary of both naïve idealism and conservative realism. The first surfaces when we pursue outcomes that are desirable but whose feasibility is extremely low, and the latter surfaces when we surrender to a morally rotten status quo, taking as fixed what we could change through lucid action. Political history is full of examples of both failed voluntaristic radical strategies and successful revolutionary changes. These intuitions are important aspects of a desideratum of ethical responsibility and serious care for what we bring about (or do not prevent) through our actions (or omissions). To honour these intuitions, and to make ethically responsible choices, we should use feasibility considerations that include both the binary and scalar forms.

Binary feasibility claims can be deployed through the familiar 'ought implies can' principle.[9] When we are unable to produce a certain outcome, we take any requirement to produce it to be null. This helps us engage the worry about naïve idealism. It may also help us engage the worry about conservative realism. We can refuse to automatically drop the search for outcomes that are hard, but not such that we are strictly speaking unable to get. The use of scalar feasibility claims deploys a more diffuse, 'feasibility affects all things considered choices' principle. It engages the worries about naïve idealism and conservative realism in further, more complex ways.

Since the force of binary feasibility is obvious, I will say more about the use of scalar feasibility claims in the responsible generation of all things considered choices. This is a crucial area of normative reasoning. Scalar feasibility is

---

is important to note that even when we decide to introduce one, it may be reasonable to vary its precise location from context to context. What counts as a person able to fight in a war for a military official recruiting from a pool of civilians would vary depending on whether the official is recruiting in times of peace (or when a war has almost been won) or during war. If catastrophe is impending in the latter case, then the bar for recruitment will likely be lower: some candidates will be deemed able to fight who would not have been so characterized in the other scenario. Now, notice that the degrees of probable success in fighting (however that is measured) may have remained constant. So here the binary notion of feasibility is a combination of descriptive scalar assessments of probability and a judgement about what level of probability counts as sufficiently high in a certain context, given certain preoccupations that are salient in it (such as the importance of not losing a war). Often, the threshold is identified through a judgement of the form 'the level of probability of success x is sufficient for making an adequate contribution to achieving purpose y in context z', where the value of x varies depending on variations concerning y and z.

[9] I do not challenge this principle here. For the debates see Vranas (2007) and Graham (2011). Southwood (2016) argues that deliberation about what to do is constrained by what can be done.

important because practical deliberation often involves comparative assessment of strategies on account of their prospective potential for success. The strikers may wonder whether to ask for a 20% raise or a 10% raise. None of the final outcomes (the raises) may be impossible to achieve, but the probability of success may be different. And this may have normative significance. Imagine that the probability of getting the 20% raise is very low and the probability of getting the 10 % raise is very high. If the workers face circumstances of severe economic deprivation, then knowing these probabilities would support a choice of settling for a 10% raise. If their situation is not onerous, taking the risks and going for 20% may seem less problematic. It could be that in both cases the higher raise is in itself the more desirable outcome. However, the probabilities of success are also important in deciding what to choose.

Consider another example. Celeste is the leader of a political party. She has great political talent and a wealth of experience, and she is committed to the best views about social justice. She has been the leader for a very long time. She is now considering whether to step down. If she does, Delia will become the new leader. Delia is committed to the same views about justice. But she is less talented and experienced than Celeste. If they performed at their best, Celeste would help the party advance social justice more than Delia. However, given her long tenure in a position of power and certain psychological weaknesses, Celeste justifiably fears that she is far more liable to become corrupt than Delia, and thus to end up advancing the cause of social justice less. To make her choice, Celeste has reason to consider not only what she and Delia can achieve in a binary sense, but also the extent to which, in a scalar sense, each is likely to succeed at fulfilling the ideals they cherish if they are party leaders.

Conflict with hard constraints renders a putative duty of justice infeasible, and makes its prescriptive force null. Conflict with soft constraints renders a putative duty less feasible to fulfil than it would otherwise be, and might make a dent on its prescriptive force. When we consider soft constraints and scalar feasibility, our question is not whether normative requirements are blocked. We move beyond the application of 'ought implies can'. Our question is how, if at all, the probabilities of success in fulfilling various normative ideals if we take various initiatives to do so should bear on our choices about what to do. To avoid naïve idealism, we may sometimes have to avoid paths of action that have low probability of success. To avoid conservative realism, we may sometimes have to pursue those very same paths. Soft constraints are real, and they can be overcome. Responsible choice turns on weighing appropriately the importance of both points in the relevant circumstances.

144 Human Dignity and Social Justice

To engage in responsible choice, it is important to resist the temptation of imposing fixed thresholds on scalar feasibility assessments to turn them into binary ones. This would not be a good idea as a general conceptual policy. The problem, from a deliberative standpoint, is that doing that would disable some fine-grained comparative assessments we need to make when choosing between options that are above or below the threshold. Thus, two options that are above the threshold would count as binary feasible, but we would not focus on whether one is more feasible than the other. However, this is something we have reason to do to choose lucidly between them (to avoid wasting resources that could be used in valuable ways, for example).

Some might want to use a binary idea of feasibility to apply the principle that 'ought implies can' in a way that captures a certain view of agents' abilities. For example, they might recognize that the concept of ability is different from that of possibility, but characterize ability in binary terms as an agent's tendency to succeed at producing the outcome they seek to produce.[10] A tendency to succeed could be characterized by referring to what is at or above some threshold of probability. But I think that we should handle this suggestion with care. Sometimes it may be possible for someone to do something even if they are not able to do it (in the binary senses of possibility as not violating hard constraints and of ability as having a tendency to succeed given hard and soft constraints). It is important to consider such cases because some obligations may exist in them. Imagine that a psychopath says to me, 'I will kill your son unless you draw a jack of hearts from this shuffled deck in a single draw'. If the threat is credible and my only relevant options are to pick a card or not to pick one, that there is a possibility but not a tendency that I will draw the jack of hearts when picking a card might make a claim that I have an obligation to draw a jack of hearts awkward, but would not block my obligation to try by picking a card. Extremely low probability below the threshold may keep some obligations running.[11]

---

[10] Here is an example: 'A person is able to (can) do something if and only if, were she to try and not give up, she would tend to succeed'. On this view, ability is different from mere possibility. It would be possible for someone to draw a jack of hearts from a shuffled deck in a single draw, although we would not say that they are able to do so. Estlund (2011: 212). For more discussion on probability thresholds see footnotes 8, 11, and 18 in this chapter. See, further, Gilabert (2012a: sect. 7.6). For exploration of different levels of ability (involving differences in the extent to which agents have control over outcomes), see Mele (2003).

[11] Alternatively, the notion of ability may be characterized contextually, with thresholds of 'tendency to succeed' varying on the basis of various considerations, including value-based ones (e.g. imposing lower thresholds when the stakes are high). But this would involve a mixed concept of feasibility that smuggles desirability considerations. It is better to keep the notions of feasibility and ability descriptive rather than normative, to include a scalar dimension, and to see the combination with value-based considerations as a separate exercise to be undertaken explicitly in ways appropriate to the context at hand.

2.3 How?

How should we incorporate considerations of feasibility into a conception of justice? I will propose a general strategy in the next section. Here I introduce two key distinctions that will enable that strategy. The first is the distinction between *evaluative* and *prescriptive* judgements. As I construe the distinction here, both components make claims about what ought to be done, but they differ in how they handle feasibility conditions because they answer different questions. Schematically, and respectively, the questions are the following: 'Ought I to bring about O if it is feasible for me to do so?' 'Ought I to bring about O given the actual feasibility constraints I currently face?'[12]

We use evaluative judgements to compare the intrinsic moral desirability of various states of affairs. To do so, we neutralize consideration of feasibility by assuming that we have the power to bring them all about. We can further assume that the probability of our reaching the outcomes if we seek them is 1

---

[12] My characterizations of 'evaluative' and 'prescriptive' are stipulative, and do not seek to grasp the semantic wealth of ordinary usage. (A similar distinction between 'evaluative' and 'normative' appears in Barry and Valentini 2009.) The key difference between the evaluative and the prescriptive concerns how they relate to feasibility conditions. But consistent with that difference, the evaluative can be construed in various ways. In this chapter I focus on evaluative claims that range over what one ought to do, and in particular on 'oughts' of justice. Notice that these need not have a consequentialist form (they could, as I illustrate later, include pro tanto deontological requirements).

I introduced the distinction in 'Feasibility and Socialism' (Gilabert 2011a) to articulate and discuss several claims made by Gerald Cohen, in particular his view that there could be demands of justice that are infeasible. Although I agree that evaluative judgements are important, I do not share Cohen's tendency to downplay the importance of prescriptive judgements in political philosophy. The latter are of great importance for normative reasoning, and we need a philosophical understanding of how they are properly formed and justified. Thus, Cohen underestimates the task of identifying what he calls 'rules of regulation' (which derive from ultimate, fact-insensitive principles of justice together with facts and/or values other than justice). But rules of regulation are often not something we 'adopt' in a weak sense that involves their being 'optional' (Cohen 2008: 265–7, 277). Some rules may be worse than others. There may be some that we have most reason to follow in a contest. The search for the right rules to 'adopt' may be as strict as the search for the fundamental principle to 'believe'. There is also the issue of judgements of articulation that move from general and hypothetical statements about what ought to be done to specific and categorical ones about what some people ought to do in certain circumstances. The move involves substantive claims that come intertwined with descriptions and evaluations of existing facts, and is not an exercise of mere deduction. A lot of crucial work in political philosophy gets done at that level. Think about the identification of what specific liberties should be protected under a general principle demanding equal civil and political liberties.

A final, clarificatory remark. Evaluative judgements are not contingent upon the feasibility of what they recommend, but they may nevertheless be sensitive to certain facts. Fundamental, evaluative principles of justice identify certain ideals we should strive for. But the content of those ideals involves normative responses to certain valuable features of human beings (or other entities). Thus, principles of liberty may be responsive to the fact that human beings are able to make self-conscious choices. (On the general point that fundamental normative principles can be construed as 'reflecting', or telling us how to appropriately 'respond to' certain features of human beings—or other entities—see Kagan (1998: sect. 7.4). The Dignitarian Approach, as explored in Chapter 1 of this book, has a reflective structure. See also Gilabert (2019b: 44–6). Thus, although I agree with Hamlin and Stemplowska (2012: 51) that there is a useful contrast between a 'theory of ideals' that identifies various feasibility-independent principles and a continuum between 'ideal' and 'non-ideal theory' that handles their application once considerations of feasibility are brought in, I do not think that this contrast can fully account for the relation between facts and principles. There are some forms of fact-sensitivity that go beyond issues of feasibility.

146 Human Dignity and Social Justice

(the maximum). For example, we can compare three distributive arrangements in which income accrues to workers in the context of (a) a highly de-regulated competitive economy; (b) an economy where there is competition for jobs but where there are mechanisms securing that those who come from economically poorer backgrounds get support to develop their talents (e.g. via excellent public education); and (c) an economy in which, in addition to the measures in (b), mechanisms are in place to supplement the wages of the less talented. If we endorse luck-egalitarianism (the view that it is unfair for some to be worse-off than others through no choice or fault of their own), we would judge that (c) is superior to (b) and that (b) is superior to (a). This judgement is not contingent upon feasibility parameters.

On the other hand, we use prescriptive judgements to identify what we should do once we factor in actual feasibility. For example, if only (a) and (b) are feasible, then it is (b), not (c), that we should go for. The two kinds of judgements involve two different senses of the idea of *injustice*. In the first, there is an injustice whenever the state of affairs that occurs is not among the morally best. In the second, there is an injustice when agents (or agent-controlled institutions) fail to bring about a morally desirable state of affairs they could (and ought to, in the prescriptive sense) bring about.[13]

Both kinds of judgements are crucial. The importance of prescriptive judgements is obvious: they provide a straightforward basis for determining what to do. But evaluative judgements have several important roles as well. Here are four. First, they help us develop the right attitude and demeanour towards others. The evaluative judgement that (c) is the best state of affairs would give us reason to approach interpersonal relations under (b) in an appropriate way. If (c) is superior to (b), then those who end up better off should be somewhat circumspect, and show humility, in their interaction with those who end up worse-off. The inequality, given that (c) is not feasible, may simply be the result of the natural lottery. Second, if we cannot achieve the best outcome in our evaluative rankings, the rankings may help us determine how to choose among the remaining outcomes that are feasible. The

---

[13] The two cases can come apart. The presence of (b) and the absence of (c) would involve an injustice from the evaluative standpoint but not from the prescriptive standpoint. Both senses are important for justice. Definitions of justice that range only over states of affairs, or only over feasible actions, would thus miss part of the picture. An example of the former occurs in Gheaus (2013: 448). This kind of definition, which disconnects justice from feasibility, has the advantage of unshackling our exploration of ambitious normative views. The cost is that we do not illuminate how they shape our reasoning about what to do in the real world when feasibility is taken into account (as eventually it must). Keeping the distinction between evaluations and prescriptions while seeing both as relevant for justice allows us to be normatively ambitious *and* practically lucid. Our ethical sense of responsibility requires both. To be clear, I do not claim that Gheaus's account is false, but that it is incomplete: it does not address (although it does not exclude) the prescriptive sense of injustice.

ranking (c)>(b)>(a) helps us choose between (b) and (a) when (c) is infeasible. Third, keeping this ranking in mind may be helpful if the infeasibility of (c) is temporary. Perhaps in the future (c) may become feasible. We will then be ready to straightaway go for (c). Finally, (c) may be such that it may become feasible (or more feasible) in the future if we take certain steps in the present to make it so. If we keep (c) in view, then we will be on the look-out for the relevant steps to make (c) accessible. The strategy I will propose in the next section exploits these points at different levels of reasoning in the pursuit of justice.

Notice that by engaging in both evaluative and prescriptive considerations, and by connecting them, we service the intuitions springing from the ethical sense of responsibility and care for the results of our actions (see Section 2.1). If we only focused on evaluative judgements, we would risk naïve idealism. If we only focused on our immediate prescriptive judgements, we would risk conservative realism. If, instead, we engage in both kinds of judgements *and explore their relations*, we can combine normative ambition and political realism, and enable ourselves to choose the best strategies of action for the present and the future. As we do this, we take soft constraints seriously, but also consider whether to go against them (and as we will see, sometimes this may be what we should choose to do).

The second key, enabling distinction is more familiar, and can be presented succinctly. It is the distinction between *pro tanto* and *all things considered* judgements. A pro tanto judgement that we ought to do A is not final. To identify what, conclusively, we ought to do in certain circumstances C, we need to factor in feasibility considerations and the full palette of pro tanto judgements that may bear on the choice in C. Prescriptions are all things considered judgements, the result of the balancing of various considerations. Thus, there is much debate amongst political philosophers as to whether we should, all things considered, go for (c) (i.e. what luck-egalitarianism demands).[14] It could be that (c) is infeasible because we have no epistemic access to the differences in people's natural talents, or to how they affect productive output. It could be that this knowledge is accessible, but to get it we would have to force people to engage in forms of 'shameful revelation', or that using that knowledge to make public decisions would be humiliating to those deemed to have 'inferior' native talents. Obviously, what is happening here is that in addition

---

[14] For the challenges to luck-egalitarianism, see Anderson (1999), Scheffler (2003), and Wolff (1998). Defenders of luck-egalitarianism acknowledge the tensions, and emphasize the pro tanto nature of it. See, e.g., Cohen (2008: 7–8, 271), Gilabert (2012c: 101–21), and Swift (2008: 382–7). For epistemic issues involved, see Herzog (2013: 279). On how egalitarians can be pluralist about normative grounds, see Temkin (2009). For analysis of the notion of a 'pro tanto *ought*', see Reisner (2013).

148 Human Dignity and Social Justice

to the pro tanto judgement about fairness supporting luck-egalitarianism, we may hold *other* commitments regarding liberty, privacy, respect, etc., which, given feasibility considerations, may lead to conflicting demands. So to move from various evaluations along different axes of appraisal to prescriptions about what to do in certain circumstances we need to balance various pro tanto judgements, given feasibility considerations, to reach all things considered judgements. I will say more about this below. But it is important that recognizing this complexity does not debunk the importance of making evaluative judgements that do not depend on feasibility. We would not be fully alive to this complexity without them (as they identify the relevant ideals that make the cases complex). And the complexity is morally engaging and the resulting conflicts tortuous because the evaluative judgements track important reasons of justice.

Let me illustrate the significance of the distinctions made in this section by considering an interesting type of cases for practical judgement. Here agents have to determine whether to pursue a path leading to a morally desirable outcome when its achievement collides with soft but not with hard feasibility obstacles. This situation of choice may be hard to deal with. Recall Celeste. She has reason to choose to stay as leader (she could perform at her best and help achieve more social justice than Delia). She also has reason to step down (she could, and in fact is likely to, become corrupted and help achieve less social justice than Delia). What should she choose to do, all things considered?

My intuitions are in tension here. On the one hand, I want to avoid a line of thought that lets agents off the hook and is too deferential to the status quo that is morally rotten. That people will not do something that is morally desirable, or have a very low probability of success even if they try, is not something that can simply dissolve a duty to do it. Only strict inability would have that upshot. Celeste *could* succeed. She ought to go for it. On the other hand, choosing to do something when one is unlikely to, or will not, do it may be morally irresponsible. One should be mindful of the harm one may cause, or fail to avert. Predictably, Delia will go further in the pursuit of social justice than Celeste. Celeste ought to get out of the way.

How can we address this situation, in which these two conflicting moral conclusions seem warranted: (i) Celeste ought to choose to stay as leader, and (ii) Celeste ought to choose to step down? It would not do to say that (i) is superior to (ii) because it honours moral reasons. Even if moral reasons are decisive in practical reasoning, (i) need not win. This is because (ii) is also backed by moral reasons. The worry about irresponsibility is a worry about harm or failure to bring about what is right (in this case, social justice).

It is also relevant in this situation that we are not just talking about an act, but about an initial choice, a subsequent set of acts, and a certain final outcome. The possibility of failure arises if one chooses to act in a certain way, does some of the necessary acts but not all, and the final outcome fails to materialize. Things would be less complicated if the issue was whether to bring about the final outcome by just pressing a button when one already has a finger on it and could just press it. Extended active processes (such as Celeste's activities as leader of the party) include numerous occasions for the agent's will to weaken or lose the right orientation.

An interesting phenomenon here concerns the adoption, by the agent engaging in deliberation, of two perspectives. When Celeste selects (i) she mainly sees herself from the first-person perspective, as a free agent. When she selects (ii) she hesitates, steps back and sees herself as it were from sideways on and predicts that she will fail to achieve the outcome if she goes for it. There is something troublesome, morally speaking, about the third-personal detour. She *can* do it after all. Seeing oneself in the way one sees a stone helplessly falling from a cliff seems both inaccurate and morally faulty. It is *up to her* to try hard and avoid corruption, isn't it? And yet, one's will is not all-powerful. It would also be a failure of self-knowledge not to notice one's vulnerabilities and weaknesses. Celeste may still act freely when she chooses (ii). But she does so in a way that takes notice of how free choice (if there is such a thing) is surrounded by obstacles and risks such that it may fail to hit its favourite targets.[15]

Even if the right choice, all things considered, were not to try to bring about the evaluatively best final outcome, agents would not be off the hook. First, they should feel regret or some remorse when not going for that outcome. Second, they could train themselves to become better persons who are more likely to follow through in the pursuit of the right goals. Third, they could reshape their circumstances to make this pursuit easier in the future. Thus, Celeste could choose to step down, but also seek help to strengthen her resolution to avoid corruption, and work to change the internal rules of her party and of the political system more widely to disincentivize corruption. This choice to change feasibility prospects over time involves the kind of attitude

---

[15] In our interactions with others, we take a double perspective. We expect them to sometimes do what is rational for them to do, and to sometimes be overwhelmed by physical or emotional forces. We also approach ourselves this way. We expect ourselves sometimes to act rationally and sometimes to act irrationally. Given these expectations, it is rational for us to organize our lives in a way that assumes that sometimes we will act irrationally, and provide ourselves with strategies to respond in such cases. This kind of meta-rationality at the prudential level can be used for moral purposes. One reason why we accept coercive backing of just laws is to provide ourselves with extra, prudential reasons to do what we have moral reason to do.

150 Human Dignity and Social Justice

a dynamic approach to justice seeks to articulate. I turn now to developing this approach.

3. The Pursuit of Justice: A Dynamic Approach

How should evaluative and feasibility considerations interact in the pursuit of justice? How can this interaction proceed in a way that normative ambition and practical realism are both catered for in a responsible way? This section answers these questions, developing a dynamic approach to the relation between justice and feasibility.

3.1 Three dimensions of a conception of justice and deliberative reflective equilibrium

The first step in the development of the dynamic approach consists in explaining, in a systematic way, how normative desirability and feasibility interact at different levels of deliberation about the pursuit of social justice.

If we seek to articulate a conception of social justice that can guide political practice, then we have reason to identify demands that are both normatively desirable and feasible.[16] We are aiming at identifying all things considered prescriptions whose fulfilment would produce the expectably best results given our best efforts of inquiry about what is desirable and feasible. How can we go about pursuing such a target? We can proceed by trying to find a maximally satisfactory combination of truths about desirability and feasibility for each of the different dimensions of a conception of justice. These dimensions involve normative claims about:

DI: Core principles—including evaluative principles or ideals (DIa) and prescriptive principles (DIb).
DII: Institutions and social practices.
DIII: Processes of transformation.

Once our conception is worked out, there will be an explanatory order among the three dimensions, with the contents of DIII depending on the contents of DII, which in turn depend on the contents of DI. We demand institutions and social practices that would implement our core principles, and

---

[16] Goodin and Pettit (1995: 1).

strategies of reform that would lead agents from where they are to a social situation in which the appropriate institutions and practices are in place (if they are not already there). As we move from one dimension to the next, we decrease the level of abstraction, and entertain desirable specifications and implementations of the demands of previous dimensions in more circumscribed circumstances. Binary feasibility concerning hard constraints is of course relevant for all three dimensions, but as we will see considerations of scalar feasibility addressing soft constraints involve important variations.

I will state the targets for each dimension and illustrate them by using elements of Rawls's familiar theory of social justice.[17] At DI, we identify a set of pro tanto evaluative principles (DIa) and formulate the prescriptive combinations of them (DIb) that are most appropriate for the range of social contexts we wish to address (which may be fairly wide). Take Rawls's two principles of justice, the first demanding an extensive set of equal civil and political liberties and the second economic distributions that maximize the prospects of the worst-off against a background of fair equality of opportunity. They constitute a prescriptive package (with the first principle having priority over the second) that balances various evaluative ideals concerning equality, liberty, efficiency, and reciprocity. These evaluative ideals involve pro tanto principles that respond to general features of human beings (such as their capacities to form, revise, and pursue conceptions of the good life—i.e. be rational—and to impartially entertain and honour conceptions of what is right—i.e. be reasonable). Their articulation into a structured set of conclusive, prescriptive principles is sensitive to facts that make their fulfilment feasible, such as the 'circumstances of justice' involving only moderate material scarcity and conflict of interests and certain relevant features of human psychology and social organization. The circumstances of justice involve soft constraints. There have been stages in human history where material scarcity was extreme rather than moderate, and it is not impossible that extreme scarcity may reappear in the future (e.g. as a result of massive climate change). The probability of achieving the circumstances of justice, or of moving away from them, may vary. But Rawls's prescriptive articulation of the two principles takes them as fixed for modern contexts in the foreseeable future. The circumstances of

---

[17] See Rawls (1999: 266) for the two principles; Ibid: sect. 22 on the 'circumstances of justice', and Ibid: sect. 77 on the capacities of rationality and reasonability as the 'basis of equality'. I use Rawls's theory only for illustration purposes. Alternative interpretations are of course possible. What follows revises the statements in Gilabert (2008: 412–4; 2012a: 122–4), and Gilabert and Lawford-Smith (2012: 819–21). DI is reformulated by addressing DIa and DIb, the 'circumstances of justice' are characterized differently, and the relations between DI, DII, and DIII are explored further.

152 Human Dignity and Social Justice

justice thus operate, for all practical purposes in a certain subset of possible contexts, as a hard constraint.[18]

As we move to DII, we notice that there are various candidate social arrangements. The task is to identify some that are no worse than any alternative when it comes to implementing the principles from DIb in certain specific contexts. To do this, we engage again in considerations of desirability and feasibility. Social arrangements are desirable to the extent that they fulfil the principles from DIb. They are feasible to the extent that they are *stable*. A social arrangement is stable to the extent that once established it is likely to remain in place. (Stability contrasts with accessibility—discussed below—which is paramount at DIII.[19]) For example, Rawls discusses five specific candidates for contemporary societies: property-owning democracy, liberal democratic socialism, laissez-faire capitalism, welfare state capitalism, and state socialism with a command economy.[20] When discussing these alternatives (holding constant, it seems, some facts about the likely functioning of a modern economy), he argues that only the first two are appropriate implementations of his two principles. This preference is based primarily on desirability considerations. Laissez-faire capitalism and welfare state capitalism would condone unacceptable levels of economic inequality and would not secure the fair value of citizens' political freedom, while state socialism with a command economy would unacceptably limit civil and political liberties.[21] The choice between the remaining arrangements depends on scalar feasibility. The political culture of certain countries may make one more realistic than the other, and agents should choose between them accordingly. For example, Americans are more likely to embrace property-owning democracy.

---

[18] This is a case in which we can contextually identify thresholds of probability regarding soft constraints, constructing binary feasibility claims out of scalar ones (see note 8). I do not claim that there would be no obligations of justice in situations of extreme scarcity. Besides dynamic duties to overcome them, agents would have other prescriptive principles to immediately fulfil. These prescriptions articulate evaluative pro tanto principles in ways that may differ from the articulations for circumstances of moderate scarcity.

[19] The accessibility question is 'Can we move from here to there?' and the stability question is 'Can we stay there?' See Cohen (2009: 56–7). The former is arguably also relevant for selecting items at DII—as its prescriptions might be dented by difficulties in accessing what they demand. And stability at DII is relevant for DIII, as the decision to embark in a transition may be affected by beliefs about the stability of the destination. Furthermore, very general facts about human psychology may make some prescriptions at DIb unstable (e.g. Rawls (1999: 119, 153–5) argues that utilitarianism leads to instability by demanding excessive self-sacrifice). This would differ from the more specific forms of instability arising from certain institutions in some specific situations at DII.

[20] Rawls (2001: 135–40).

[21] These three regimes can also be criticized on feasibility grounds. If people care enough about the liberty and equality they would depress, they would be motivated to move away from them. Notice that this is different from a challenge on moral grounds. The latter is based on the actual moral costs of those regimes, while the former refers to believed moral costs.

When we turn to DIII the task is to identify a trajectory of political reform producing the social arrangements from DII that is all things considered reasonable. Again scalar feasibility and desirability considerations are necessary. Regarding feasibility, a social arrangement is *accessible* to the extent that agents are able to reach it from where they are. The desirability of a process of reform depends on the moral appeal of its results (whether it turns out to be what DII calls for) and the severity of the moral costs that would be involved in the process. Dimension DIII is the least explored in political philosophy. Rawls had little to say about it, although he did emphasize the importance of combatting the 'curse of money' in politics, which slants the political playing field so that it is very hard for poorer citizens to promote reforms leading to the regimes selected at DII. He also emphasized that we should use principles from DI to identify priorities, and measure moral costs, in the processes of reform involved in DIII.[22]

To summarize, the targets of each dimension of a conception of justice are the following. At DI, we select a prescriptive package (DIb) that is maximally satisfactory in terms of honouring fundamental pro tanto evaluative principles (DIa) given general facts about human beings and social organization and the societies we seek to regulate. At DII, we select a set of institutions and social practices that is maximally satisfactory at implementing the principles from DI in the set of specific contexts within the societies we are considering. At DIII, we select a process of political reform that is maximally satisfactory at reaching the social arrangements from DII without imposing unreasonable moral costs. Each of these targets is the result of comparative judgements where alternatives are assessed in terms of feasibility and normative desirability.[23] Of course, the inquiry tracking these targets is fallible. What we expect to have maximal normative value may not actually have it. We can

---

[22] Thus, if liberty has priority over other demands of justice, then we should take the establishment of liberties (and their fair value) as the first goal and pursue further reforms only if they do not collide with liberties if we can secure them (Rawls 1999: 132, 215–8). Rawls of course did not think that the priority of liberty holds in all conceivable circumstances (see, e.g., Ibid: 267).
    Unlike stability, Rawls did not explore in any detail the issue of accessibility. But he was aware of its importance and complexity. Thus, he recognized that 'there is a question about how the limits of the practicable are discerned and what the conditions of our social world in fact are; the problem here is that the limits of the possible are not given by the actual, for we can to a greater or lesser extent change political and social institutions, and much else' Rawls (2001: 5). Unfortunately, he added that he would 'not pursue this deep question' in that text. He did not do it in other texts either. I hope that the dynamic approach to feasibility offered here goes some way towards addressing the 'deep question' Rawls states in this passage.
[23] I phrase the targets in terms of what is maximally satisfactory (i.e. no worse than the alternatives) rather than in terms of what is optimal, because we may sometimes be unable to rank certain options (e.g. two options may be equivalent in their overall normative value). To simplify my formulations, I sometimes talk about our 'best' views regarding DI–DIII, but the reader should keep in mind that in cases in which the set of the best includes more than one view we should revert to the more cumbersome, 'maximizing' formulation.

154 Human Dignity and Social Justice

(and should) revise our beliefs as we continue our moral and scientific inquiry and learn from political experience.

There is a gaping hole in political philosophy when it comes to DIII. I will take steps to fill it in Section 3.2. But before proceeding, let me characterize the methodology for the articulation of the three dimensions. Since it shapes the deliberation of acting agents, this methodology is also an essential aspect of the dynamic approach to justice and feasibility.

The foregoing presentation might make it seem that the inquiry into the components of a conception of justice is strictly sequential, that one first fixes the contents of DI and only then proceeds to DII, and that one fixes the contents of DII and only then turns to DIII. In epistemic practice things are more complicated. The development of a conception of DI–DIII is in fact a matter of a fallible, ongoing search for *deliberative reflective equilibrium.* This means, first, that the content of each dimension is taken as open to change by considering its relation with the contents of the other dimensions. We already saw how variations at DII might respond to what results at DI, and how changes in DIII may be guided by results both at DI and DII. But notice that changes can also proceed in the opposite direction. One may wish to revise the principles at DI as a result of one's inquiry regarding DII. Libertarians could revise their sweeping prescriptions regarding economic liberty after noticing that limiting some economic liberties of owners of capital may be crucial to realistically secure effective political freedom for all at DII (a value they may already hold, or have come to accept). Changes at DI and DII may result from consideration of issues regarding DIII. Socialists could add explicit requirements of civil and political liberty to their view of DI and to their institutional designs at DII as a result of exploring undesirable consequences of some of their historical experiments in which those liberties were trampled with. Anarchists might revise their criticisms of democratic political theory and practice when they notice that creating a political organization of society that includes no coercive mechanisms has an extremely low score of scalar feasibility. Thus, what we have reason to do is pursue an ongoing inquiry in which changes at each level may motivate changes at other levels. We should be open to continuous revisions yielding successive reflective equilibria.[24]

---

[24] 'The method of reflective equilibrium consists in working back and forth among our considered judgements (some say our "intuitions") about particular instances or cases, the principles or rules that we believe govern them, and the theoretical considerations that we believe bear on accepting these considered judgements, principles, or rules, revising any of these elements wherever necessary in order to achieve an acceptable coherence among them' Daniels (2011).

My account of three dimensions of a conception of justice differs from Rawls's (as presented in Rawls 1999: sect.31) 'four-stage sequence' (including selection of principles, a constitution, legislation, and individual decisions). Both envision progression from more abstract to more specific prescriptive judgements. But there are differences. First, I do not take the characterization of DI–DIII to work within the

Justice and Feasibility **155**

Second, the reflective equilibrium we should aim at is 'deliberative' in two senses. To begin with, it is not a description of our existing beliefs, but an attempt to form and integrate the best we can muster. We are not merely trying to make explicit what we already believe to be feasible or desirable. We are trying to determine what *to* believe.[25] Further, we could ideally seek a reflective equilibrium that is intersubjective, involving various agents for whom the issues at stake are relevant. This includes, of course, political agents on the ground. But it would also include social scientists engaging in feasibility assessments, philosophers of science reflecting on how those assessments are methodologically framed, and political philosophers seeking to articulate core concepts and principles of justice. This intersubjective pursuit is difficult, and often missing.[26] It is difficult because the parties may have different practical exigencies, use different methods, and be unfamiliar with each other's activities. But these are not reasons to avoid the intersubjective exercises. We need them for at least two reasons. One is epistemic. Each party has something to contribute which the others are unlikely to provide on their own in the most satisfactory way. Political philosophers are not particularly good at making feasibility assessments, and would thus benefit from interaction with social scientists when it comes to the identification of appropriate institutional proposals. Philosophers can be provoked by political actors to formulate conceptual and normative questions that have real political significance. Social scientists may benefit from normative theories and political agents on the ground to formulate questions of research that are interesting rather than trivial. They may also need help from philosophers to articulate their core concepts in perspicuous ways, and to gain awareness of the epistemological strengths and limitations of their research. Citizens and activists

---

thought-experiment of the original position. Second, Rawls's sequence has no explicit place for the issue of accessibility. Third, I emphasize the epistemic back-and-forth when determining what to accept as the content of each dimension. I should note, however, that Rawls himself is not always consistent. When he introduces the idea of the four-stage sequence, he says that what is figured out at each stage coming after the first 'inherits' the results of earlier stages (it must be consistent with the latter, and apply their results to more specific circumstances) (Ibid: 175–6). But at one point (Ibid: 174) Rawls says that we will find the 'best constitution' by '[m]oving back and forth between the stages of the constitutional convention and the legislature'. This is incompatible with a strictly sequential view. I think that on reflection Rawls would agree with a not strictly sequential view of the relation between the stages in the order of knowledge given that for him reflective equilibrium is the ultimate epistemic test. Thus, Rawls (2001: 136) notes the importance of exploring the institutional implementation of principles to figure out whether to endorse them.

To avoid misunderstanding, I emphasize that when I talk about a back-and-forth I focus on the order of knowledge. There is a sense in which I agree that there is a strict sequence. As I say at the beginning of this section, when an overall conception has been settled, the final product has to exhibit a sequential order: DIb articulates the evaluative principles of DIa into a prescriptive package, DII implements the principles of DIb, and DIII targets the process that generates what DII demands.

[25] Scanlon (2003)

[26] Herzog (2013: 284).

156 Human Dignity and Social Justice

on the ground would also profit from the work by philosophers and scientists. Arguably that work is a technical continuation of considerations they already engage in when they wonder about what makes their situation unjust, what ideals to strive for, and what are some reasonably feasible ways to act in a complex social world where causal mechanisms are not always transparent. These cooperative exercises are also important for normative reasons. We should shape our politics democratically. It is important that the agents who will endure the consequences of important political decisions are able to have a say on them. To do this they need (inter alia) real opportunities to form lucid opinions on the matters at stake.

I do not want to give the impression that the difficulties in reaching deliberative reflective equilibrium are not serious. A source of difficulty is the increasing fragmentation, both at the epistemic level (within and between groups of social scientists, philosophers, policy makers, etc.) and at the political level (for example between citizens, political parties and leaders, and bureaucrats). On the other hand, successful interactions have existed and can be fostered. I also do not want to overestimate the value of actual agreement amongst the parties involved in the plural conversations aiming at reflective equilibrium. Sometimes the best contribution will be one that undermines agreement in the short-term. To illustrate, new social movements often formulate new grievances that are not in the radar of mainstream philosophical and scientific research, but can help reshape them. Think about the consequences of working-class and feminist movements, and, more recently, the revival of discussion on inequality sparked by the Occupy movement in 2011. Another example is when some philosophers stubbornly insist that ambitious ideals of justice be explored even when their practical fulfilment appears to have very low feasibility prospects in the here and now. It is part of the job of political philosophy to keep ambitious ideals clear and visible, and to criticize a political culture when it becomes complacent and superficial. In what follows, I focus on unpacking the importance of these forms of insistence.

A third way in which reflective equilibrium regarding DI–DIII may be deliberative is that it is related to how each of us, as political agents, decides to act. A problem here is that there may be multiple reflective equilibria held by different people. There may be no theoretical solution to this problem. Each one of us has to act in the social world, and each will have to do it on whatever balance of reasons seems best to them after inquiry. We can hope for, seek, and achieve more convergence. But the convergence may not materialize in time. There may be a meta-feasibility issue here. As we choose how to act, we may have to think about the feasibility of our converging on our normative and descriptive views, and determine the significance of the results in our overall practical reasoning. The deliberative nature of the reflective equilibrium leading to choice is basic in the sense that we cannot unload the task to others.[27]

3.2 Transitional standpoint, political imagination, and dynamic duties

3.2.1 Transitional standpoint

After identifying the dimensions of a conception of justice, their relations, and the methodology of their articulation and revision, I proceed to explain the features of the dynamic approach that directly orientate political action in a way that enables us both to remain ambitious in our normative aims and to think lucidly about what practical steps to take. The first move is the adoption of a *transitional standpoint*. This is the standpoint of political agents in the process of changing central features of the institutional and cultural environment in which they act. It involves envisaging paths of action from the status quo to social arrangements in which principles of justice are fulfilled. What should happen at DIII is that political agents entertain trajectories of political reform such that social arrangements are (more or less suddenly, more or less gradually) transformed to reach the implementation of the principles envisaged at DII. Various considerations are relevant from this perspective. But it is crucial to remember that these are much more specific as we move from DI to DII, and from DII to DIII. As we move from one dimension to the next, the agents, actions, and circumstances envisioned in our political considerations become more circumscribed spatially and temporally. Once the transitional standpoint is taken, the dynamic approach involves two further practical features. First, no single failure at DII is sufficient to warrant dropping the principles from DI. We can imagine alternative social configurations that do implement the principles. Second, no temporary inability at DIII to achieve the implementations envisaged for DII warrant their abandonment as political aims. We can entertain successive steps that expand our feasible sets of political action over time so as to eventually access the implementations envisaged. DI sets a wide and long-term political horizon for DII and

---

[27] Even philosophers and scientists have to act as political agents. The best bet is to shape philosophical and scientific work so that it illuminates the choices of political agents. In this way, philosophers and scientists can retrace their activities to the aim of illuminating the praxis of changing the social world to make it more just.

158 Human Dignity and Social Justice

DIII. In what follows I explore these two key moves involving, respectively, *political imagination* and *dynamic duties*.[28]

3.2.2 Political imagination

It is important to keep in mind the distinction between DI and DII, and to recall that the task of DII is to find a way to implement the evaluative and prescriptive principles of DI in a certain context. These points might sound obvious, but political theory and practice are awash with failures to honour them. There is a tendency to fetishize certain institutional proposals, taking the truth or relevance of the underlying principles of justice to be inextricably tied to their success. Sometimes the overall conception is simply identified with what it says at DII, with DI dropping out of view. This impoverishes political debate and unduly narrows our practical options. Some implementation of a prescriptive principle must work (on desirability and feasibility grounds) for that principle to be successful (as a prescriptive principle), but we cannot infer that the principle fails when any single implementation does not work. A typical example occurs in the socialist tradition, with its common fixation on construing the socialist ideal in terms of state control of productive assets. Many historical experiments involved high levels of inefficiency (given the deficiencies of states' agencies when gathering and processing information about supply and demand in a complex modern economy), and also worrisome limitations of citizens' ability to control the economic and political processes (given extensive centralization of decision-making in the hands of a bureaucratic elite). It is not uncommon to hear that the socialist ideal is dead because a centrally planned economic system is inefficient and oppressive.

But we should explore the possibilities opened up by the fact that there are different levels of generality within normative political judgement. We can use our *political imagination* to envisage alternative specifications at DII of the principles of DI. If we find a candidate at DII wanting (for feasibility or desirability reasons), then we can move up to DI and then back down to DII by imagining alternative implementations of the principles. This argumentative triangulation helps us distance ourselves from problematic political proposals without having to drop the principles that ultimately should animate our political practice. Thus, instead of fetishizing a particular institutional design, socialists should first notice that what animates their practice is a set of principles and then imagine better ways to put them into

---

[28] The dynamic approach has an important consequence for the debate between ideal and non-ideal theory: it vindicates ambitious principles as important for DI, and thus as framing the content of DII and DIII.

Justice and Feasibility   **159**

practice. Arguably what motivates their critique of capitalism is a set of commitments to deep forms of equality, freedom, and solidarity. The institutions of central command socialism were problematic because they did not implement those ideals. Alternative designs are conceivable, such as various forms of market socialism, including the recent proposals by David Schweickart, John Roemer, and Joseph Carens, and they might work.[29]

Another problem that can be addressed through political imagination that is both attuned to ambitious principles and specific feasibility considerations is the tendency to take a social design that works in some context as valid for every other context. There is room for political imagination at DII partly because the 'circumstances of justice' of DIb can take (at DII and DIII) multiple more specific forms. We can call those 'situations of justice'. Thus, as mentioned above, if indeed property-owning-democracy is as good as liberal democratic socialism at fulfilling the principles of justice as fairness, then there is no loss in taking the former rather than the latter as the institutional objective in the American context. Things could be the opposite in many countries of Asia, Europe, or Latin America. If both designs are normatively equivalent as far as DIb is concerned, when in a certain situation we are finding it hard to implement one we may have reason to imagine and pursue the other.

As political agents, political philosophers, and social scientists envisage alternative feasible implementations of ambitious principles, they face ideological beliefs that clog the arteries of political imagination. These take some social configurations to be unavoidable, have transhistorical significance, or cater equally to the interest of all when they are in fact avoidable, of limited historical significance, and beneficial to some at the expense of others. Examples are the tendency to seek the indefinite accumulation of money (or some other economic means of exchange) and the tendency to construe self-respect as what results from winning in competitions for advantageous economic positions. These operate as soft, not hard constraints. They are arguably contextually specific to capitalist societies. But they are commonly presented as fixed facts that any conception of social justice should accommodate or draw on. Thus, we are often told that we should accept some inequalities in rewards because they involve necessary incentives for highly talented or productive people to work hard. Now, it is obvious that it is infeasible for everyone to

---

[29] In market socialism, the class division between capital owners and workers having to work for them is dissolved, but markets mechanisms in goods and services, with their allocative efficiency virtues, are retained. For different versions, see Schweickart (2011); Roemer (1994); Carens (2003) (and the amended variant in Chapter 3 of this book). For surveys of socialist proposals for the organization of economic systems, see Corneo (2017) and Gilabert and O'Neill (2019: sect. 4). I say more about market socialist proposals in Chapter 8, Section 4.

160 Human Dignity and Social Justice

be at the top and gain self-respect from being there (unless, implausibly, we could devise as many competitions as individuals), and we need not link expansion of productivity to inequality. Furthermore, we could imagine, and perhaps achieve, other forms of incentivizing talented people to develop and use their natural gifts. The self-realization that comes from the development and deployment of one's abilities in challenging work, and the satisfaction of increasing the material opportunities of one's fellow human beings, might be strong motivational forces. As we saw in the previous chapter, we could interpret the socialist Abilities/Needs Principle ('From each according to their abilities, to each according to needs') as including these ideas.

These operations of political imagination are possible partly because those engaging in them accept principles that are more abstract than their implementations. This means that, despite some complaints about it, abstraction, when handled properly, is in fact a positive tool in politics. We have reason to identify high-level values and facts when we track true and important features of human beings and their social life. They enable us not to get stuck when some of our specific designs do not work. Principles range over many possible implementations, and without having a clear view of the former we are unable to shift from one implementation to the other in thought and thus fail to identify alternatives we could, and perhaps should, pursue in practice. When we adopt a set of principles, we envision an ethical and political *project*. A political project is different from a *program*, or a *plan*. The latter involve specific designs of institutions and practices. A project does not formulate its own application. It provides, instead, the core guiding standards by reference to which the programs and plans are to be drawn up, evaluated, and revised.

As I said, abstractions are valuable when properly handled. We would not handle them properly, however, when we neglect facts about human beings and social organization that are significant for the desirability and feasibility of principles or their implementation. Let me illustrate this point by exploring the Abilities/Needs Principle further.[30]

This principle has been interpreted in many ways. On one interpretation, it merely describes, or predicts, a state of affairs in which the circumstances of justice have disappeared as a result of superabundance. On another interpretation, which I prefer, it is an evaluative principle that can be used to handle situations of moderate scarcity and conflict of interests in certain (prescriptive) ways. I think that the merit of this principle is that it foregrounds the importance of fair reciprocity, positive duties of solidarity, and meaningful

---

[30] The principle was formulated in Marx (1978i: 531). For detailed discussion, see Chapter 3.

Justice and Feasibility **161**

work. Briefly, the key ideas are the following. In a just economy people contribute through productive activities if they can. Since productive abilities are partly based on unequal native endowments, the levels of productivity are likely to differ. But if productive efforts are similar, receipt of income and other means for need satisfaction should be equal. Opportunities for meaningful work are important. Work can be meaningful in at least two ways. First, it is itself a satisfaction of needs when it involves development and actualization of workers' abilities (e.g. for creative and cooperative problem-solving). Second, it contributes instrumentally to the satisfaction of other needs by creating goods that people can use and enjoy.[31] Since any functioning economy that is not completely automated needs labour input, it should recruit it somehow. If, furthermore, human beings have a legitimate interest in meaningful work, then there is reason to make available to them forms of work that are meaningful.

Thus interpreted, the Abilities/Needs Principle assumes that many human beings are interested in self-direction and self-improvement, that they can find self-direction and self-improvement in productive activities, that they have different native capacities that affect their abilities to produce, and that they are profoundly vulnerable and dependent on the help of others to live flourishing lives. These are facts that call for normative responses and set feasibility boundaries on principles and institutional and cultural configurations.[32] When we pay attention to them, the socialist view becomes more appealing, while other views turn out to be disappointing. For example, a view centred on radical independence that only prescribes negative duties not to depress the opportunities of others to direct their own affairs and improve their own life conditions may then appear either undesirable or hardly feasible (or both). To neglect the features of human social life socialists insist on would be to engage in improper abstraction.

Finally, keeping in mind the distinction between DI and DII, and taking into account the internal complexity of DI, enable us to respond to the important charge that ambitious theories of justice that sketch pictures of the perfectly just society are of no help when choosing among immediately feasible alternatives, none of which is the perfectly just society envisaged. This charge has been pressed by Amartya Sen.

Sen anticipates the likely response that the picture of the perfect society could be useful to rank the immediately feasible ones through identifying their relative distance from it. A first problem with this response is that the

---

[31] On the first point, see Elster (1986: ch.3). The second involves socialism's affirmation of positive duties of solidarity or, as Einstein (1949) puts it, 'a sense of responsibility for [one's] fellow men'.
[32] See note 12 for the various roles of facts.

162 Human Dignity and Social Justice

imperfect societies may differ from the perfect one in different ways, and we may be unable to tell which way is more important. The second problem is that 'descriptive closeness is not necessarily a guide to valuational proximity'. Sen illustrates this point with an analogy: 'a person who prefers red wine to white wine may prefer either to a mixture of the two, even though the mixture is, in an obvious descriptive sense, closer to the preferred red wine than pure white wine would be.'[33]

Sen's complaints lose force if we keep in mind the distinction and the relation between DI and DII. An ambitious theory of justice does not only seek to imagine maximally desirable social institutions and practices (at DII). It also seeks to identify the principles that make them desirable (at DI). It is largely those principles that determine what 'descriptive features' are relevant, and what comparative importance they have. In fact, descriptive proximity may be quite significant if the descriptive features we track are the relevant ones (or the most important ones in the exercise) given our valuational commitments. (Something similar happens as we judge wines; perhaps colour is less important than consistency of taste.)

It is also important to notice the internal complexity of DI. It could be that a preferred prescriptive combination (at DIb) of pro tanto evaluative principles (from DIa) is not feasible to implement in some situations. To decide between the alternatives, we look for other combinations of the pro tanto principles appropriate to the situation. Thus the Abilities/Needs Principle may have different weight in different situations, and may have to be combined with, or be interpreted so as to include aspects of, other principles (such as a principle of free choice of occupation to make sure that the demand for meaningful work is a matter of opportunity rather than forced activity). Evaluative principles help us articulate the appropriate prescriptive principles given general feasibility considerations, and the latter help us select social institutions and practices given more specific feasibility considerations. If we

---

[33] Sen (2009: 16). This discussion touches upon the 'problem of the second-best'. See Goodin (1995: 37–56) and Swift (2008). Swift (2008: 372–8) also criticizes Sen for failing to pay attention to how normative principles affect relevant descriptions. Goodin (1995: 53n.45) notes that the problem of how to choose when some of the items from the ideal package are unavailable resurfaces when dealing with principles. My comments on the complexity of DI partially address this issue by saying that evaluative principles (DIa) may help us choose between different packages of prescriptive principles (DIb). If the worry were reapplied to the set of fundamental evaluative principles, it is hard to think what could lie beyond them. Intuitive balancing seems all one can do then. And it is possible that the absence of an item of the preferred package forces us to reconsider what principles bear on our choice, and what their relative weight in the circumstances is. It could be, however, that the evaluative principles can be tied together as dimensions of a unifying ideal, within which their relations can be explored in a more systematic way. The Dignitarian Approach advanced in this book goes some way in this direction, but the complexity of appraising and weighing the relative significance of the various capacities at the basis of dignity as they are engaged in different contexts by different people still calls for intuitive balancing.

Justice and Feasibility 163

look behind the perfect instances to identify the (evaluative and prescriptive) principles animating them, we can remain normatively ambitious. It is true that it is difficult to rank different axes of comparison. In justice as in other areas of practical reasoning, we may lack a general algorithm. But the relation between DII and DI, and the internal complexity of DI, provide us with consequential resources.

3.2.3 Dynamic duties

In addition to the transitional standpoint and political imagination, the dynamic approach to justice and feasibility involves a third, crucial practical feature. According to the dynamic approach, we should focus not only on what is immediately feasible, but also on the long-term and on our role in shaping it.[34] Perhaps perfect (or significantly less imperfect) social arrangements may turn out to be (more) feasible in the future. Focusing only on immediate feasibility may lead us to miss the point that our abilities for political action, involving soft rather than hard constraints, are open to temporal variation. What is not feasible (or has very low feasibility) now may become feasible (or be significantly more feasible) in the future if we take some steps to expand our political abilities. Consider the situation represented by this chart in Figure 4.1:

Make the following assumptions. R is the perfect outcome. From the status quo P, R is not immediately feasible. The two immediately feasible options from P are Q and S. S is intrinsically more desirable than Q. R would not be immediately feasible from S, but it would from Q. (To make formulations less cumbersome, here and in what follows I sometimes use binary phrasing for feasibility claims, but the reader should remember that scalar claims can and often should be made as well.) What should one choose? If one focuses only on the immediately feasible at P, then S should be chosen. But if one also factors in the long-term, then Q may be all things considered preferable. Thus, imagine that Celeste has to choose whether to form an alliance with a less progressive party for the coming elections. If she does, the alliance will win the election and go some way towards implementing policies of social

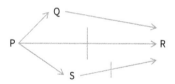

Figure 4.1 Dynamic Feasibility Chart

---

[34] This provides a further response to the challenge by Sen mentioned in 3.2.2.

164 Human Dignity and Social Justice

justice; but since in the alliance the other party will be dominant, the political agenda will be so shaped that deeper reforms will become very unlikely for the foreseeable future. If instead she decides not to join the alliance, to concentrate on extending the increasing reach of her party, to wait until the next election and, let us assume, that an alliance in that election will be under her party's hegemony, then again an election win is likely but much deeper reforms will be undertaken. To make a responsible choice, Celeste has reason to look beyond what is immediately feasible.

So when we face soft constraints, we should explore their temporal variation. Celeste's party can work to reshape the political culture in its country and become a stronger force for social change. In general, we may have what I call *dynamic duties*. Unlike normal duties, dynamic duties are not focused on achieving certain desirable outcomes within current circumstances. Their point is to change those circumstances so that certain desirable outcomes become achievable (or more achievable). Thus, dynamic duties direct a change, often an expansion, of an agent's power to bring about certain outcomes.[35] *Power* can in general be defined as follows. In certain circumstances C, an agent A has power with respect to whether some outcome O occurs to the extent that A can voluntarily determine whether O occurs. Now, dynamic duties involve a companion form of *dynamic power*, which we can define thus: A has dynamic power over A's power with respect to whether some outcome O occurs to the extent that A can, in current circumstances C1, voluntarily determine whether C1 change into different circumstances C2 so that A becomes more (or less) able to voluntarily determine whether O occurs.[36]

---

[35] I say 'often' because one could also entertain dynamic duties to reduce one's power to do certain things. Sometimes one may have a duty to make oneself *less* powerful. The elimination of nuclear arsenals may be an example. In this chapter I focus on the case of expansion (i.e. empowerment).

[36] We can add time indices to make the account of power more explicit: we can talk about A having power at time t1 with respect to O in tn, where tn coincides with, or comes later than, t1, and A acts in that period. See Goldman (1986: 160–1). Also helpful is the notion of 'indirect diachronic abilities' (e.g. to speak Italian in a year if I start studying it now). Jensen (2009). The idea of expanding feasible sets is explicitly used by economists (e.g. Sen 2009: 384). For the more general idea of change in potentialities or abilities in metaphysics see Vetter (2013: 11–2). When I introduced the notion of dynamic duties in Gilabert (2009), I did not state the companion idea of dynamic power.

It is important that my claims about dynamic duties calling for changes in the feasibility set faced by an agent assume that the actions populating such a set are relative to agents placed in certain circumstances. Consider the following scenario: in circumstances C1, the agent is not able to do A, in C2 the agent is able to do A, in C1 the agent is able to do B to change the circumstances C1 into C2. In a circumstances-relative sense of feasibility, the feasibility set of the agent in C2 is different from the feasibility set in C1 (A is included in the former but not in the latter). Now, the agent has control as to whether C2 comes about. It is perfectly intuitive to say that by doing B in C1, they generated an ability to do (in C2) something (A) they were not able to do before (in C1). Someone may challenge this characterization by appealing to another according to which the feasibility set is fixed at the outset. On this view, at the outset it is already feasible for the agent to do A later if they first take appropriate means (do B). I do not deny that this characterization is intuitive as well. Both characterizations are used in ordinary talk. We talk about

Within a conception of justice, dynamic duties come into play at DIII, when we consider how to generate the social institutions and practices that we prefer at DII. This is the issue of *accessibility* of a just society, which is different from its *stability*. Although there has been some work in political philosophy on stability, accessibility has been largely ignored. But accessibility cannot be ignored when we adopt a transitional standpoint, which we must adopt to fully assess proposals for social change. There are some issues that are relevant to both stability and accessibility, such as motivational problems regarding free-riding, but their treatment would differ. For example, a society implementing the Abilities/Needs Principle might be stable in dealing with free-riding by socializing its people into a strong ethos of solidarity and by imposing financial penalties on non-compliance. But when it comes to accessibility those mechanisms will not yet be in place, and different strategies would be appropriate. The relevant institutions and ethos must first be created.

At DIII, political agents consider what dynamic duties they have given their dynamic powers. They ask themselves what processes of transformation they (and their successors) should pursue to implement their principles from DI through successive social institutions and practices to eventually instantiate their long-term goal concerning DII. A historical example is workers mobilizing for their inclusion in the political system through expansion of the franchise and then, with their voting power, pressing for the realization of basic socioeconomic rights (regarding minimum pay, reduced working hours, workplace safety, etc.). More ambitiously, some socialists, following Marx, have envisaged the trajectory towards full socialism as taking two phases. In the first, after some resources are put aside to secure the maintenance of economic infrastructure and satisfy basic needs (e.g. regarding health care and education), distribution of access to consumption goods follows the so-called Principle of Contribution ('To each according to their contribution'). In the second, distribution is based on the Abilities/Needs Principle. This principle is evaluatively superior. But it is not feasible during the early stage of transition, as moral and political culture is still coloured by bourgeois principles (such as the principle of exchange of commodities with equivalent value—which disadvantages workers with lower natural talents), and there is not yet enough material abundance. Introducing the less

---

developing new abilities, and we also talk about the ability to achieve certain ends through certain means. The discussion here seems merely terminological, and in fact the two approaches are compatible (as taking means to an end may involve developing a new ability, so that the feasibility of the end is a function of this development). But I think it important to highlight the first characterization because it illuminates the substantive issues addressed in this chapter (concerning empowerment and dynamic duties). I thank David Estlund for discussion on these matters.

166 Human Dignity and Social Justice

intrinsically desirable scheme first would, however, ease the transition away from capitalism (by delivering on its unfulfilled promise to reward on the basis of productive activity rather than class position and power) and towards more desirable distributive schemes (through incentives to increase productivity that would make distribution according to needs more viable and thus a lively option).[37]

Are large-scale sequential projects of this kind worth pursuing? If so, how should the required all things considered normative political judgements be framed? I don't know whether an algorithmic decision procedure can be identified. But I will suggest four points that would help in forming those judgements.

First, we can adapt some guidelines from decision theory. For example, we can compute the expected value of alternative paths of transition (as well as the status quo) by considering their intrinsic desirability and probability of success and favour ones with maximal score. We can also factor in the moral costs and risks that the processes might incidentally produce. Thus, the sequence P-Q-R may not be a case of 'one step forward, then another step forward'. Q may involve violations of basic civil or political rights. 'One step backward, two steps forward' is sometimes an unacceptable strategy that sacrifices the rights of some for the benefit of others (or the same people) in the future. Another difficulty is path-dependence: Q may be more likely to become self-replicating than to give way to R. Also, it could be that besides rendering R accessible, Q involves a serious probability of leading to T, a catastrophic outcome. If Q involved a form of economic growth that could unleash deep environmental destruction, then perhaps the standard of equal access to conditions for a flourishing life should be catered for in different ways. Failing this, perhaps S is after all the preferable alternative. We have reason to engage in prospective choice seeking to maximize expectable normative value, guiding ourselves by the normative standards from DI, and the aim of approximating the realization of the preferred social formation at DII.

---

[37] Marx (1978i: 528–32). See the fuller discussion in Chapter 3, Section 5. Another possibility is to envision a sequence with Roemer's coupon market socialism first and Carens's proposal second (see note 29). The latter is arguably more desirable than the former because it addresses inequalities resulting from different natural endowments, but it may be less immediately feasible. (Roemer sees market socialism as a transitional proposal.) The socialist tradition is particularly rich when addressing the relation between justice and feasibility because it has displayed both highly ambitious ethical ideals and a hard-nosed sensibility to factual considerations. The inevitable tensions and dilemmas that result can be more fully thought through if socialists avoid an unfortunately common philosophy of history according to which whatever is desirable is feasible, and whatever is desirable and feasible is necessary (Elster 1986: 3). For surveys of debates among socialists regarding DIII, see Gilabert and O'Neill (2019: sect. 5) and Wright (2010: Part III 2015b; 2016). Also valuable is Antonio Gramsci's discussion of how social transformation involves not only struggles to control the coercive power of the state, but also to gain 'hegemony' in the shaping of moral views in civil society. See Gramsci (2000: 195, 205–6, 211–2, 249, 306–7, 333–4, 345).

Justice and Feasibility   167

The full palette of options and ethically relevant issues would not even be visible without entertaining this ambitious normative project.

The foregoing considerations assume that we can assign probabilities to outcomes. But this of course is not always immediately achievable, in which case when comparing different paths of action we may have to appeal to other typical strategies of choice under uncertainty. For example, if the stakes are extremely high, a 'maximin' rule selecting the path whose worst possible outcome is among the least bad may be appropriate. When the stakes are low, taking risks with a 'maximax' rule selecting the path whose best possible outcome is among the highest may be appropriate. What we may not do if we are to make responsible choices is simply ignore the future.[38] Uncertainty about the future is no reason to disregard it. Notice that uncertainty could also affect the status quo. We may be unable to ascertain whether the current social situation will endure into the future, and what moral costs it will involve. So omitting the envisioning of alternatives to the status quo may itself amount to choosing an uncertain path. Notice also, and this is the second main point I want to make, that epistemic limitations are themselves soft constraints we may have dynamic duties to overcome. If we keep our aims high even when they are not immediately realizable, and imagine social realizations at DII that would implement our principles from DI, then we will approach the tasks of transformation at DIII in a more serious way. We can engage in social-scientific work to learn more about political history and the dynamics of social change. There are numerous examples of scientific research that was sparked by political debates and fed back into them to make alternatives less indeterminate.[39]

The two final points I want to make concern the problem (mentioned in 3.1) of incongruence between views held by different agents regarding what should be done. How should Celeste approach political agents who disagree with her proposals for social transformation? Should she argue from

---

[38] We should take seriously the worries captured in the famous Keynes's line that 'in the long-term we are all dead'. But we should also remember that in the long-term future generations are born. We owe them something.

[39] De Swaan (1988) reports how history and social science helped shape the introduction of the welfare state. Ostrom (2009) explains how social science can help solve the 'tragedy of the commons' in dealing with common-pool resources. Sen (2009) shows how social choice theory and normative political philosophy can shape anti-poverty development policy. Wright (2010) outlines how sociology can help identify feasible strategies for socialist transformations. I am not suggesting that social scientists and philosophers can provide fully detailed blueprints for action. I agree with Berlin (2000: 139) that in the end virtuous political agents 'behave like artists who understand their medium'. But, as Berlin would agree (see Ibid: 140), we should avoid an artificial dilemma between comprehensive scientific planning and choices only based on personal hunches. Science and philosophy cannot provide the former, and the latter may be the output of erroneous prejudices and irresponsible indifference to genuinely illuminating research. I thank Bob Goodin for discussion on these matters.

168 Human Dignity and Social Justice

an internal point of view that builds only on what they already accept or should she adopt an external approach? The former may be motivationally more appealing but lead to less profound social transformations, while the latter may target deeper transformations but be less motivating. In response, I think that two moves are important. The first is to focus on situations of crisis. In those situations people are sometimes more open to envisaging deeper political projects. Their self-regarding interests are threatened by the status quo, and the normative principles they already hold dear are seriously underserved. Situations of crisis may also be such that people are more open to revise their normative commitments, and thus the external approach may get a hearing as well. For example, during a deep economic crisis, the positive duties of solidarity and fair reciprocity involved in the Abilities/Needs Principle may become appealing.

The second move is to seek institutions and practices of egalitarian political empowerment. To see the importance of this, agents can take not only the first-personal and third-personal attitudes discussed above (See 2.3), but also a second-personal attitude in which they seek to generate conditions in which they can argue with each other and decide together in a fair and inclusive way.[40] This is a desirable configuration of their dynamic power. If the principles at DI and the ideal social structures at DII involve deep democratic self-determination, then shaping the practices of political transformation at DIII in ways that include egalitarian political empowerment would begin to instantiate the change agents are aiming at. Additionally, although processes of transformation may involve painful choices where each option involves some loss, these are less troublesome if they are made by the ones having to live with their consequences. When we think about what we, together, should do to pursue justice, it is important that the 'we' be inclusive, taking people as protagonists of their own political history.[41]

4. Feasibility and Dignity

In this chapter I proposed a program of inquiry about the relations between justice and feasibility. When we pursue justice, descriptive considerations about what we are like and what we are able to do are important. They trigger application of our principles of justice, they identify features of human beings that give rise to normative responses, and they illuminate our ability

---

[40] On the importance of the second-personal standpoint, see Darwall (2006).
[41] For further, illuminating discussion of the standpoint of agents pursuing justice, see Laurence (2021).

to implement them. Feasibility affects our power to change the social world to make it more just. We should pay attention to feasibility if we are to make responsible choices. But we should distinguish evaluative claims of justice that focus on what we should do if we were able to do whatever we preferred and prescriptive ones that focus on what we should do given what we actually are able to do. We should take the former as our ethical compass when we factor in descriptive claims to articulate the latter. Prescriptions of justice operate at different levels, with different feasibility constraints. Principles involve more general constraints than their implementation, and the latter involve more general constraints than the strategies of reform leading to them. These differences are important to develop a dynamic approach to facts blocking the pursuit of justice. We can imagine alternative implementations of principles, and we may have dynamic duties to reshape feasibility constraints over time. When we adopt this dynamic approach, our deliberations about how to pursue justice take a long-term transitional standpoint in which we are both normatively ambitious and hard-nosed about the realities of social life.

The tension between the ideal and the real is typical of political practice. As I see it, the job of social and political philosophy is not to help us escape from this tension by focusing only on evaluative principles without paying attention to feasibility, or to dissolve it prematurely by tying principles to specific and changeable feasibility constraints. Instead, philosophy should help us relate to this practical tension in a lucid, hopeful, and effective way. The dynamic approach to justice and feasibility that I propose offers a way to do this. It might be objected that it makes the best an enemy of the good, encouraging agents to rush for ideal projects that are likely to fail, only to then recoil from political action, turn apathetic, and fail to bring about less ambitious but valuable changes they could easily secure. But since the approach I propose has built into it an ethics of responsibility that factors in the probabilities that various strategies would succeed, this consequence is not encouraged. Furthermore, we should not make the good an enemy of the better, or even the best. We can aim high if we pay attention to how to get there.

Let me conclude by noting that the dynamic approach to feasibility is congenial if we view social justice from the dignitarian perspective proposed in this book. Consider first the twin intuitions linked to ethically responsible choice. An attitude of conservative realism fails to give dignity its due because it tends to pass up opportunities to alter the conditions that block human flourishing, and it does not do enough to harness people's valuable capacities for practical reasoning and imagination. These capacities are at the basis of people's dignity. A dynamic view of feasibility, by contrast, helps people

170 Human Dignity and Social Justice

unleash their potential for creative and ameliorative agency. The intuition regarding the shortfalls of naïve idealism is also significant for a dignitarian politics in that it alerts us to the fact that the circumstances of dignity and justice are such that people's agency is embodied, facing serious limitations and displaying disvaluable capacities in addition to valuable ones (see Chapter 1, Section 2.1).

Feasibility considerations were recognized as key when formulating the Schema of Dignitarian Justification (see Chapter 1, Section 2.2.1). According to this schema, rights of justice are justified not only when their implementation might conceivably support the unfolding of people's valuable capacities, but also when, and to the extent that, such a support is feasible.

The Dignitarian Approach also coheres well with the characterizations of stability and accessibility entertained in this chapter. Regarding stability, we can anticipate that a social order that affirms people's dignity as the source of their entitlements would have a tendency to be robust. In it, people's respect for each other, and their own self-respect, would be quite secure. It benefits from the public recognition of the value of the features at the basis of their dignity, which does not depend on their class, ethnicity, nationality, or other conventional or less morally significant properties. The systematic support for each individual's singular unfolding of those capacities—through their own path of self-determination and self-realization—would give them the sense that they matter. People would not seek to undermine a social order that puts them at the centre of its mission in this way, or at least there would be less of a tendency for instability than in other societies which do not give them this kind of affirmative treatment, but instead ignores or downplays their interests.

A dignitarian approach to social change also combines well with the dynamic view of accessibility. A dignitarian culture would foster stability, but it would be more likely to emerge in the first place if the process of social transformation already affirms and engages the value of the capacities at the basis of dignity. When the critique of domination, exploitation, and alienation is coupled with forms of political action that make a serious effort to avoid them, then a society that minimizes these problematic patterns is more likely to develop. If, for example, socialists and liberal egalitarians organize their politics in ways that feature paternalistic and highly centralized decision-making, the self-serving manipulation of activists to foster the careers of party bosses, and the neglect of the specific needs and talents of participants, they would be reproducing in their political practice the injustices they are trying to overcome. The shape of a process of emancipation should, as far as possible, anticipate the characteristics of the society that is desirable to build. Thus, for example, emancipatory politics, to cater for dignity, should have a deeply democratic form. The Dignitarian Approach, with its emphasis on self-determination (foregrounded in Chapter 2), would indeed insist on the significance of democratic practices when accounting for dimension DIII of a conception of justice.

There are deep connections between dignity, critique, imagination, and hope. A politics of dignity challenges forms of social life that ignore or crush people's valuable capacities, but in doing so it engages precisely some of those capacities. Agents undertaking this critique can use their creativity, moral judgement, and cooperative powers to envision a society that unleashes these abilities even further. Because these powers are very much part of who they are, they can reasonably hope that a dignitarian politics will be effective. When they stand up to contest social injustice, and search for a society which (as per the Abilities/Needs Principle discussed in Chapter 3) gives each a chance to advance their own, and each other's, freedom and well-being, people affirm their status-dignity and, enacting dignitarian virtue, envision the condition-dignity that they deserve.

This chapter completes the articulation of the theoretical framework to social justice offered in this book. In the remaining chapters, I will deploy this framework to explore particular topics in the socialist critique of injustice in contemporary capitalist societies.

PART II
RETHINKING THE SOCIALIST CRITIQUE OF CAPITALISM

5
The Critique of Exploitation

1. Introduction

In January of 2018, the provincial government of Ontario in Canada raised the minimum wage to $14 an hour. The response by many firms' owners was not to accept a cut on their profits, but instead to impose the (perceived) costs on their workers. Thus, an owner of franchises of the successful and iconic firm Tim Hortons sent their workers a letter including the following lines:

> I'm sure some of you have wondered that with such a dramatic increase in wages if some or many of you will be laid off or lose your job. I want to assure you we are doing everything we can to eliminate that concern.
>
> Unfortunately when wages rise at such a fast pace we cannot raise our prices at the same rate to offset the costs and something has to give.
>
> Effective January 1, 2018 we will no longer be able to provide the benefit of paid breaks.[1]

Further responses by franchises' owners were to reduce benefits and to downgrade the status of their workers from salaried employees to independent contractors. Other businesses planned to increase automation, laying workers off. The bottom line is that when 'something has to give', it will mostly be workers' interests, not their employers'. This systematic prioritizing of the interests of powerful economic agents at the expense of the interests of the less powerful agents working under them is typical of class societies, and of the phenomenon of exploitation they secrete. It was obviously present in slavery and feudalism, and it is pervasive in contemporary capitalism—from the clothing factory sweatshops of Bangladesh and the 'zero hours' contracting of workers in the Global North, to the employment of better paid and more

---

[1] Saltzman (2018b). A worker told a reporter, 'I feel that we are getting the raw end of the stick', and asked to remain anonymous for fear of being fired. The owners of this franchise, heirs to the founders of the firm, were safe from the cold Canadian weather in their winter home in Florida Saltzman (2018a).

Human Dignity and Social Justice. Pablo Gilabert, Oxford University Press. © Pablo Gilabert (2023).
DOI: 10.1093/oso/9780192871152.003.0005

176 Human Dignity and Social Justice

secure and yet asymmetrically vulnerable salaried blue-collar workers—and even white-collar ones—the world over.

This chapter offers a new exploration of what exploitation is and of what is wrong with it. The focus will be on the critical assessment of the exploitation of workers in capitalist societies. Such exploitation is wrongful when it involves a contra-solidaristic use (and perhaps even allocation) of power to benefit oneself at the expense of others. Wrongful exploitation consists in using your greater power, and sometimes even in making others less powerful than yourself, in order to get them to benefit you more than they ought to. This account of exploitation is superior to others because it simultaneously captures three morally significant dimensions of exploitation: its material and social background, the relational (interpersonal and systemic) attitudes it enacts, and the final distributive results it generates. Exploitation is indeed a multidimensional social process. The flipside of the proposed critical characterization of this process is a positive ideal of solidaristic allocation and use of economic power, which this chapter articulates in terms of the socialist Abilities/Needs Principle ('From each according to their abilities, to each according to their needs!'). The Abilities/Needs Principle, as discussed in Chapter 3, is a fitting specification of the Dignitarian Approach for matters of socioeconomic organization.

This chapter has the following structure. After some preliminary points and caveats, I present in Section 2 the contra-solidaristic use of power account of exploitation and a framework to display its application. In Section 3, I develop the content and normative force of this account through a conception of solidarity based on the idea of dignity and articulated in terms of the Abilities/Needs Principle. In Section 4, the proposed approach is summarized and contrasted with the main alternatives to show that it avoids their pitfalls, captures their insights, and articulates important points missed by them. I do not pretend that this discussion *establishes* its claims about exploitation, solidarity, and dignity. My goal is to say enough to show their originality and initial plausibility, and to reveal the fruitfulness of their relations—thereby motivating future research to develop them further. A unified statement of the emerging research program is provided in Section 4.2. The chapter concludes by addressing some objections regarding agency and structure.

Exploitation has been characterized in many ways. A first strand is (a) descriptive. In its most general and neutral sense, exploitation is simply the extraction of benefits from some source. In the specific context of human work (which is my focus here), exploitation is a feature of socioeconomic processes in which some people benefit from the work (the productive efforts and activities) of others. Some Marxists have a more specific, technical definition

The Critique of Exploitation **177**

of exploitation as an unequal exchange that features the extraction of workers' surplus labour.[2] A second strand of characterization is (b) normative. Thus, it is common to take exploitation to involve a wrongful, unfair, or unjust taking advantage of others. When combined with (a), (b) yields the category of cases in which exploitation is the wrongful benefitting from the work of others. The aim of this chapter is to develop this normative characterization. I will address the following questions: 'When incidents of exploitation in the descriptive sense are wrong, what makes them so?'[3] And: 'What ideals and principles justify this normative judgement?' My answer to the first question will be that wrongful exploitation of workers involves benefitting from their work through contra-solidaristic use of greater power, and my answer to the second question will be that we have reason to assess economic schemes, and judgements about exploitation, on the basis of the (solidaristic and dignitarian) Abilities/Needs Principle. A wrongfully exploits B when and to the extent that A benefits from B's work by using greater power in ways that flout the Abilities/Needs Principle.[4]

Before proceeding, let me enter a few caveats. First, when talking about A, the exploiters, and B, the exploited, I will take A and B as variables ranging over individuals, corporate groups, or more diffuse coalitions of agents.[5] Furthermore, exploitation can arise in occasional encounters, but I will largely focus on extended, and regular, social relationships. Within them, we will consider exploitation both from interpersonal and systemic angles. The significance, and difficulties, of these different renderings of the variables and the contexts of their relations are sometimes important, and I will address them when necessary (and prominently in Section 5).

Second, my claims about exploitation will be limited in the following two ways. Exploitation will be characterized as a pro tanto consideration in the assessment of an economic system. I do not claim that, all things considered, exploitation may never be engaged in—there could be other competing considerations that have more weight in some circumstances. An upshot of this is

---

[2] One definition of surplus labour in the technical account is that it is that part of workers' labour which goes beyond the amount of labour embodied in the consumption goods they can access with their salary or as some other form of remuneration for their work. I will not rely on this characterization to avoid being saddled with the problems of the labour theory of value, but I will try to capture the point that the exchange between exploiter and exploited is unequal (with the former obtaining surplus benefits).

[3] Exploitation in sense (a) does not logically imply exploitation in sense (b).

[4] In the remainder of this chapter, when I use 'exploitation' I mean it in the normative sense. When disambiguation is needed, I use 'wrongful exploitation'. This chapter thus differs from the chapters on alienation and domination in that it proceeds directly to the exploration of the normative version of the idea rather than starting with a discussion of its merely descriptive version.

[5] The exploitation relation is often articulated by reference to classes. Marx (1978g: 205) said workers 'belong not to this or that capitalist but to *the capitalist class*' (they must sell their labour power to *some* member of the capitalist class).

178 Human Dignity and Social Justice

to circumscribe the assessment of Marxist views on exploitation and justice. Thus, I disagree with Roemer when he takes Marxists to hold the view that there is social injustice if and only if there is exploitation.[6] He is right that this view might generate 'false positives' (as some instances of exploitation in the Marxian technical sense are not unjust) and 'false negatives' (as some social injustices are not instances of exploitation). But only the problem of 'false positives' exercises me. The problem of 'false negatives' does not worry me because, like many Marxists and socialists, I recognize the importance of criticizing capitalism on other grounds as well (such as on account of its tendency to generate domination and alienation, which are explored in other chapters of this book).

Third, the normative account I offer states only sufficient conditions for wrongful exploitation. Although I argue (in Section 4) that this account is fruitful and fares better than others, I do not claim that no other account could exist that also explains the wrongness of exploitation satisfactorily.

Fourth, I will largely focus on exploitation in capitalist societies, and address the contrast between them and socialist societies (or hybrid forms of capitalism incorporating socialist elements). Furthermore, when characterizing economic systems like capitalism and socialism, I will characterize them not only in terms of their institutions of property or control of economic assets, but also in terms of the social ethoi that orientate agents making choices in social environments featuring those institutions (and this includes, inter alia, their tendency to embrace or challenge them, and to select among the possible forms of behaviour compatible with them).[7]

Fifth, when comparing the levels of advantage different social arrangements provide to the people entangled in them, I will adopt a relatively broad view that includes not only access to consumption goods and leisure time, but also to self-realization in creative and cooperative activities, social contribution benefitting others, and self-determination in one's economic life.[8]

Finally, it is important to keep in mind the distinction between the three dimensions of a conception of social justice: the proposal of certain core ideals and principles (DI), the identification of the social realization or implementation of those principles through certain institutions and social practices (DII), and the strategies of transformation to move from here to there—from the status quo to the configurations envisaged in DII when these are not already in place. My focus is largely on DI, although I will introduce some remarks about DII and DIII.

---

[6] Roemer (2017: 263).
[7] On the importance of social ethos, see Cohen (2008).
[8] On the metric issue, see Cohen (2011: chs.1–3).

The Critique of Exploitation   **179**

2. Exploitation as Contra-Solidaristic use of Power

We can say that an agent has power with respect to a certain outcome or state of affairs to the extent that they can voluntarily determine whether it occurs. Applied to social contexts, this definition leads (inter alia) to the view that an agent A has power over another agent B to the extent that A can get B to act in ways A desires. A is able to achieve certain outcomes by getting B to do things A wants B to do, which B would not do (or would not do in the same way, for the same reasons) if A did not have the influence they have over B. If they disagreed about how to organize their interactions, the will of A would likely prevail.[9] Now, when A exploits B, A wields power over B. The wrongful use of power account of exploitation (the *WP account*), builds on this point. According to WP, you exploit others when you use your greater power (i.e. take advantage of their weaker power) to get them to give you more than they should. More formally:

WP

A exploits B when A uses A's greater power to get B to benefit A more than relevant normative considerations would justify.

WP must be developed further to identify the relevant normative considerations that make certain uses of asymmetric power morally problematic. I propose an account of exploitation as contra-solidaristic use of power (the *CSP account*), which further specifies WP by stating that the wrongfulness of exploitation consists in its contra-solidaristic nature.

CSP

A exploits B if A benefits from B through a contra-solidaristic use of A's greater power.[10]

According to CSP, to ascertain the wrongfulness of exploitation we should combine judgements about two issues: the wielding of asymmetric power and the generation of distributive outcomes. In some cases, we may want to add consideration of a third issue: the allocation of power. We may want to scrutinize the very fact that A is more powerful than B, asking how this asymmetry

---

[9] For this account of power see the Appendix I to Chapter 7. On this account, the power of A over B may proceed through various mechanisms (such as threats, promises of rewards, moral persuasion, etc.). It is useful to start with a broad definition of power, and identify relevant variants depending on our specific normative and explanatory purposes.
[10] WP and CSP are stated here quite generally. To apply them to the case of the exploitation of workers, we should add that the surplus benefit A gets from B comes from B's work.

180 Human Dignity and Social Justice

has come about. Exploitation may arise as the culmination of a process that features misallocation of power besides a misuse of it. A's treatment of B looks in one sense worse if the power A wields over B has a tainted history in which A has taken steps to make it the case that B turns out to be vulnerable to A's exploitation. Think about the history of colonialism—featuring invasions and then imposition of exploitative terms of production and exchange on the people colonized—or predatory lending—in which indebted people or countries are made more vulnerable and readily available for subsequent economic interactions in which the lender preys on them. These historical processes yielding asymmetric power allocation may be problematic even if, although the result was foreseeable and avoidable, the agents generating it did not have the intention to render others more vulnerable (although when those intentions exist the result is even worse). To avoid misunderstandings, I note that judgements on the first two issues are necessary in this account, while problems regarding the third are a significant worsening factor but not a necessary component. Exploitation consists in using your greater power to get others to benefit you more than solidarity would justify. Exploitation is worse when the power asymmetry you benefit from is also one you yourself have generated. This exploitation features misallocation of power in addition to misuse of it.

I will explain my understanding of solidarity in Section 3, but for now let us say that it involves acting for the sake of other people's freedom and well-being besides our own. In the remainder of this section I introduce a framework to represent practical situations in a way that is relevant for the application of CSP to the systematic exploitation of labour. The key elements are the following.

a. Technical feasibility (given the current state of development of productive forces).
b. Institutions of ownership and control of productive forces (means of production and labour power).
c. Individuals' beliefs and preferences (prudential and ethical). We include here the strands in a society's moral and political culture, or social ethos.
d. Social power configurations (resulting from a–c and prospects for their dynamic change).
e. More or less socially feasible economic scenarios regarding who does what and who gets what (given a–d).
f. Agents' strategies in their economic relationships (interpersonal and societal; short term and long term).

The Critique of Exploitation   181

Regarding (a)–(d): Modes of production, social formations, and classes.[11] To understand people's choices regarding exploitation, we should pay attention to the circumstances in which they act. To describe such circumstances, we need first to note what is technically feasible—i.e. how much of what is valuable to people can be produced. Next, we should identify the mode of production that is typical in the context under discussion. In broadly Marxist terms, a mode of production has two important components. The first is the relations of production, which concern certain social forms of ownership and effective control over productive forces—in particular the labour power deployed by workers to produce and the means of production they use to do so, such as land, raw materials, and tools. In different modes of production, different types of relations of production are dominant. Thus, in slave societies, slaves own neither the means of production nor their labour power, while masters own both; in feudal societies, serfs have some control over the means of production and some control of their labour power, with the remainder being in the hands of the lords; in capitalism, wage workers own fully their labour power but the means of production are owned by capitalists; in socialism, workers control both their labour power and the means of production. The second component of a mode of production concerns the typical orientation and motivation of the agents who are engaged in production. In capitalism, for example, capitalists typically seek to maximize their profit, workers seek an optimal combination of wages and leisure time, and both tend to give some weight to the intrinsic satisfaction they get in their economic activities and to accept values affirming individual negative liberty and meritocracy. This characterization is of course highly stylized. Actual social formations involve the stated features to different degrees, and often in hybrid configurations. Thus in some contemporary capitalist societies there are important public and social economy sectors (for example in the provision of health care services) in which capitalist ownership is not dominant and in which economic activity is undertaken in a spirit that is significantly solidaristic.

It is noteworthy for our purposes that most important cases of systematic exploitation arise in modes of production in which the relations of production feature class division between workers and other agents who direct their work and extract a surplus benefit from it. Slavery, feudalism, capitalism, and state 'socialism' under an authoritarian bureaucracy or one-party rule

---

[11] To state the historically typical background conditions of systematic exploitation of labour, I rely on Cohen (2001), Elster (1985), and Roemer (1996).

182 Human Dignity and Social Justice

all involve class division of this kind.[12] Of course, these class divisions typically occur together with class tensions and struggle, which precisely centre on sustaining or challenging exploitation. It is important, however, that this conflict proceeds against a background of significant power asymmetries. To summarize, where there is systematic exploitation of workers, the following three background conditions typically hold: means of production are relatively scarce, they are unequally controlled, and those who control them (or have more control of them) are more 'powerful and able to extract surplus benefits from direct producers who do not control them (or have less control of them). Presumably, a socialist mode of production would eliminate, or minimize, exploitation, by altering these circumstances. We may add consideration of a fourth circumstance: inequalities in talents (which affect labour power) can also contribute to extraction of surplus benefits, and this even in the absence of the second circumstance. Socialism would also have to address how best to handle this asymmetry.

Regarding (e): Scenarios and baselines of comparison. Let us now canvass some technically feasible (but more or less socially feasible) economic scenarios and the pay-offs agents would get in them. In the description of the pay-offs we focus only on self-regarding preferences—a restriction we later drop. Four important scenarios are the following:

S1: B works to A's greater benefit.
S2: What would happen (independently of A's actions) if B did not take up S1.
S3: What A would make happen if B did not take up S1.
S4: What A could (together with B) make happen but chooses not to.
We assume the following preferences. For B: S1>S2, S1>S3, S4>S1. For A: S1>S2, S1>S3, S1>S4. Furthermore, S2 and S3 are significantly worse for B than they are for A.
Some illustrative payoffs for A and B: S1 (7, 3). S2 (3, 2). S3 (2.5, 1). S4 (6, 4).

In S1 (the exploitative scenario), A offers and B accepts a deal in which B works to A's greater benefit. Now, S1 is better for B than scenarios S2 and S3. That's why B accepts to be exploited. There is, however, a fourth feasible scenario, S4, in which A and B cooperate on terms that are less unequal than

---

[12] There are exceptions, such as exploitative trade between differently endowed independent producers in a simple commodity production society, and the 'socialist exploitation' by the talented in early stages of socialist organization. On 'socialist exploitation' concerning the handling of unequal talents, see Roemer (1996: 107–8).

The Critique of Exploitation **183**

in S1. That scenario would be best for B, but not for A. Even if A were to fare better in S4 than in S2 or S3, A would rather extract surplus benefits from B. Missing the exploitative schedule S1 by allowing B to proceed as B would without engaging A, and even more, perhaps, having to impose penalties on B for not acceding to S1, would be costly for A, but it would be significantly more so for B. This is why, although there is room for negotiation between A and B, A has superior bargaining power. The bargaining is constrained differently depending on the absolute and relative payoffs. If S2 and S3 are below a certain threshold of subsistence, or (less minimalistically) of decent living, for B, then A has an extremely strong hand to play. If S2 and S3 are above those thresholds, it would be harder for A to get B to settle for S1 rather than hold out expecting A to go for S4 in the next move during their negotiations. The bargaining would then be focused on how inegalitarian S4 (or a new version of S1) will end up being. But even then, A is in a stronger position, as waiting it out is less harmful for A than it is for B.

Regarding (f): Strategies. The scenarios just discussed inform the strategies that A and B might choose as they relate to each other. In the case of A, there are two exploitative strategies:

I. *Forced and coercive cooperation*: A offers S1 to B, threatening S3 if B declines.
II. *Under-supportive cooperation*: A offers S1 to B, and B faces S2 as the alternative—even though A could offer S4 instead.
A different, less-exploitative or more solidaristic strategy would be the following:
III. *Solidaristic cooperation*: A proposes S4 to B.

In strategy I, A makes it the case that B has no acceptable alternative to the scheme put forward by A. A can do this by eliminating alternatives altogether—brute force—or by threats that make them unacceptable to choose—coercion. An example is the relationship between slave-owners and slaves. Slave-traders remove people from the territory in which alternative forms of life were available, and slave-owners threaten physical torment if slaves do not work as they demand. Another example is the power capitalist employers have over their workers to get them to exert more effort (and thus to increase profits) through threats of dismissal or non-renewal of contracts.[13] There are more indirect forms of strategy I. A might contribute

---

[13] Since, normally, in a capitalist economy, even in competitive equilibrium, labour markets don't clear (i.e. there is involuntary unemployment), and labour contracts are incomplete, this form of power is effective. Bowles and Gintis (1992).

184 Human Dignity and Social Justice

to a complex causal process that eventually makes it the case that B has no acceptable alternative to S1.[14] The difference here is that A does not directly threaten B with unacceptable scenarios, but is instead actively involved in a process that has the result that B does not have acceptable alternatives. A historical example is the 'enclosures'—the concerted efforts to deprive people of commonly accessible land, who as a result become readily available for exploitative employment as wage labourers. Another example arises when capitalists push governments to eliminate unemployment benefits or other income security programs, or undersell or otherwise undermine the prospects of worker-owned cooperatives.

Turn now to the contrast between strategies II and III. A could, at reasonable cost, adopt strategy III and pursue S4 with B, but in strategy II A chooses instead to take advantage of the relative weakness of B to drive a hard bargain leading to a division of the fruits of cooperation that is more beneficial to A. The difference between strategy II and strategy I is parallel to the distinction between allowing and doing. In strategy II, A is directly or indirectly responsible for the fact that B does not have acceptable alternatives through omission rather than through (actual or threatened) commission. A does not *deprive* B of an otherwise available option, but fails to *provide* them with an otherwise non-available option. A could adopt strategy III and help generate the more beneficial S4 for B. A could do so directly or indirectly, for example by offering B a better deal within the current economic relationship, or by helping change the background circumstances that make the bargaining power of B so weak. So, strategies II and III, like strategy I, can have more or less direct versions. The direct versions of II and III are illustrated when we compare capitalist employers who choose to offer low salaries or other benefits to their workers (as is common in sweatshops or in precarious jobs) and others who choose to offer better deals. Examples of the indirect versions arise when we compare capitalists using some of their profits to support reforms that strengthen workers' abilities to defend their interests (for example, by funding leftist parties) and others refraining from doing so.

Marxist scholars sometimes say that exploitation occurs when workers are coerced by their bosses, or compelled by the circumstances, to take up employment under their direction and surrender surplus benefits to them.[15] These cases are covered by the categorization of strategies just mentioned.

---

[14] Notice that in this case the distinction between S2 and S3 is blurred as, historically, B's status quo is the result of A's coercive agency.

[15] Elster (1986: 82–3). Marx (1990: 899) talks about workers in capitalism as voluntarily taking up employment under capitalists while also being subject to the 'silent compulsion of economic relations'.

The Critique of Exploitation **185**

Thus, the direct version of strategy I includes the relation between slave-owners and slaves, which is directly coercive. The case of capitalist exploitation is covered by a combination of I and by II: capitalists may not violently coerce workers to work, but they can get them to work harder through threats of dismissal and by shaping the circumstances faced by workers so that they have no acceptable alternative to working under them. They can also fail to offer better terms at the point of hire, more humane treatment at work, or support for the creation of a broader social environment in which workers' power increases over time.[16]

Of course, there are strategies open to B as well. In particular, B could engage in collective action making it the case that S2 and S3 are less bad for B, or are worse for A, than before. Think about unions and their ability to organize strikes, the formation of influential socialist parties, changes in labour law and, at the limit, the transformation of economic structures. After all, changes within modes of production, and radical transformation generating new ones, are historically familiar. These changes alter the prevalence of the three strategies we canvassed. Thus, in sequences of change moving from slavery or serfdom to capitalism (in which the total or partial property rights in other people's labour power ends, and a market economy featuring competition between firms flourishes), some cases of A being entitled or able to dish out S3 become blocked. A tends to use milder forms of strategy I and to deploy strategy II. In turn, sequences of socialist change within and beyond capitalism could include, over time, or suddenly, the generation of hybrid social formations featuring social provision for unemployment, public health care, a universal basic income, worker-owned and managed firms, and the socialization of the means of production in large sectors of the economy. Here S2 improves for B and becomes less unequal between A and B. As a consequence, versions of strategy III (exploring a range of pay-offs from, say, (6, 4) to (5, 5)) are increasingly engaged.[17]

To understand these changes, we should take into account that people are not only moved by self-interest. They also have certain social and normative preferences. Within capitalism, certain exploitative deals may be undesirable, even for some capitalists, when they flout the ideal of meritocracy (if, for example, they feature bosses wielding inherited fortunes and paying low

---

[16] Given the point about thresholds mentioned above, it might be a mistake to say that when B faces fallback options above the thresholds of subsistence or decency they are coerced or compelled to work for A. And yet, if the options are significantly worse for B than the deal offered by A, and significantly worse for B than for A, then A may still manage to impose an exploitative schedule.

[17] On paths of socialist change, see Wright (2010) and Corneo (2017).

186 Human Dignity and Social Justice

salaries to poor but very hard-working employees), or when they are sustained through the violation of civil and political liberties (if, for example, deeply unequal distributions of wealth and income are defended against protest by the poor through intense surveillance and repression of their political action). And pushing beyond capitalism, a new social ethos might emerge in which a solidaristic concern for the self-determination and well-being of all makes versions of S4 more appealing than S1 for increasing numbers of people.

The asymmetric social power of A over B (the greater ability of A to get B to do what A wants) is based on their different abilities to access valuable objects for themselves, and to make inaccessible or accessible those objects for the other. Often, these differences are the result of institutional structures, such as the relations of production discussed above. When A has greater control than B over certain desirable resources, A can bargain from a position of greater strength and get B to work to benefit A more than A benefits B. The injustices involved here, if there are any, would at least have to do with these power relations. The injustices might regard the morally objectionable use of this asymmetry in social power and sometimes the very existence of it. Specifically, the CSP account of exploitation condemns extractions of surplus benefits like those envisioned in strategies I and II, which, by contrast with strategy III, are at odds with solidarity. We can call for the reduction of power differentials, and for a use of whatever differentials remain in which the people involved enact proper concern and respect for each other. This is the solidaristic perspective, to which I now turn.

3. Dignity, Solidarity, and the Abilities/Needs Principle

The CSP account says that there is wrongful exploitation in cases in which the exploiter goes for an exploitative scenario (such as S1) rather than a solidaristic one (such as S4). But we still need to understand when the former is wrong and the latter right, and the significance of solidarity itself.

3.1 Dignity and solidaristic empowerment

We should make explicit what guides our critique of exploitation as presented in the CSP account. There are three levels of discussion here. Level 1 concerns the CSP account itself. Level 2, in turn, concerns principles of economic justice that shape it. Finally, at Level 3 we consider the moral grounds justifying

The solidaristic perspective urges us to allocate and use power in a solidaristic way. An articulation of this perspective can be provided through elaboration of the appealing idea of human dignity. According to the Dignitarian Approach proposed in this book, we have reason to organize social life in such a way that we respond appropriately to the valuable features of individuals that give rise to their dignity.

Recall some key ideas of this approach discussed in Chapter 1. People have *status-dignity*. This is a moral status such that certain forms of respect and concern are owed to them. To the extent that people get this treatment, they enjoy *condition-dignity*. The distinction between status-dignity and condition-dignity is important (and often overlooked). Workers toiling in a sweatshop—getting minimal pay, working very long hours, being routinely humiliated by managers, and threatened with loss of their job if they try to organize to defend their interests—enjoy little condition-dignity. But they retain status-dignity, a non-conventional moral standing which ought to be recognized even if it is not in fact recognized, and on account of which condition-dignity must be aimed at. The kinds of respect and concern owed to people in accordance with their dignity is specified through *dignitarian norms*. Such norms state what the appropriate responses to people's status-dignity in various relevant contexts are. To develop the content of these norms, we need to consider what lies in the *basis of dignity*, i.e. the valuable features of people in virtue of which they have the deontic standing that status-dignity marks. Dignitarian norms will identify the appropriate responses to those features in the relevant social arenas. I will say more about these norms and features in a moment. But recall that the norms range over institutions and more diffuse social practices. They state guidelines for designing property regimes, labour law, and market regulations, as well as ways of addressing and communicating with others, for example. Relatedly, we can recall the idea of *dignitarian virtue*. Agents have this virtue to the extent that they shape their sensibility, practical reasoning, and behaviour on the basis of dignitarian norms. A dignitarian ethos is important to render dignitarian institutions and practices accessible and stable—or to make their accessibility and stability more robust. Agents with virtuous dispositions are more likely to create these institutions and practices, and to sustain them over time.

Let me conclude this summary of the Dignitarian Approach by recalling that dignitarian norms can be articulated as specifications of the following ideal.

188   Human Dignity and Social Justice

Solidaristic Empowerment
We should support individuals in their pursuit of a flourishing life by implementing both negative duties not to destroy or block their valuable capacities and positive duties to protect and facilitate their development and exercise of these capacities.

If we recognize that people have status-dignity in virtue of having certain capacities, then we should also see that we have reason to shape our social life with them in ways that enact appropriate respect and concern for the development and exercise of these capacities. If people have the valuable capacities for self-determination based on their prudential and moral reflection and judgement, for example, we should organize our common political institutions and practices with them in such a way that they have effective opportunities to participate as decision-makers and not just as decision-takers. People who work have these features, as well as others such as capacities for creative and cooperative production, and for meaningful personal and social activities outside of work, which should be given appropriate recognition and support when figuring out how economic systems should be organized. I explain the idea of solidarity further in Section 2.2.2 of Chapter 1, and return to some details in Section 3.2 of this chapter.

A final point in this discussion of Level 3 is to note that the suggested dignitarian account of solidarity supports a radical version of egalitarianism. Its metric of advantage ranges deep to support people's abilities to flourish by developing and exercising their various valuable capacities. Furthermore, it simultaneously includes a relational attitude in which we regard and address others as beings with equal dignity, and a distributive aim to generate and sustain social arrangements in which each has equal and effective opportunities to flourish—or power to unfold their valuable capacities in ways they choose. This is more than what some relational egalitarians call for because there is a directly distributive concern regarding people's opportunities to (freely) pursue well-being. It is also different from luck-egalitarianism, as basic positive duties are acknowledged which require supporting others to overcome certain hardships even when those hardships arise through their choices rather than their circumstances. Thus, unless we would have to face unreasonably severe costs, we should help other people escape grievous situations in which they cannot achieve subsistence, or exercise their political rights as equal citizens.

To further clarify my dignitarian approach to solidarity, let me contrast it with the recent account offered by John Roemer.[18] Roemer acknowledges that

---

[18] Roemer (2017: 307–10). Roemer discusses the important views on community that Cohen provides in *Why Not Socialism?* (2009). I examine them in Gilabert (2011a) and (2012c).

The Critique of Exploitation **189**

a socialist perspective must include not only a radical requirement of equality of opportunity (according to which nobody should have less access to productive assets than others through no choice or fault of their own), but also a solidaristic and cooperative ethos that urges people to shape their behaviour by the slogan 'We all stand together or we each hang separately'. Roemer says, however, that such an ethos does not need to include an altruistic element, which in any case would be, he thinks, supererogatory. In contrast, I think that an altruistic component is important, and not supererogatory.[19] First, its residual aspect regarding basic positive duties (mentioned in Chapter 1, Section 2.2.2) helps capture what we owe to others when they are in dire straits even as a result of their choices. Second, it may explain why we should not bargain as hard as we can with them when they become vulnerable as a result of their choices (a point to which I will return in Section 4).

Third, an altruistic element seems relevant to support Roemer's own favoured principle of socialist equality of opportunity. The currently more naturally or socially endowed might not accept surrendering benefits to the less endowed—to compensate for initial inequality of opportunity—if they did not directly care about their human flourishing. A similar remark applies to Roemer's preferred view of the cooperative ethos. Roemer says that such an ethos would be shaped by a protocol of 'Kantian optimization' that requires that 'each takes the action he would like all to take'. This protocol is contrasted with a purely self-centred one that allows each to take care only of themselves—so that each takes the action that, given what others are doing, is the best action for him or her. Now, Roemer says that to prefer the Kantian optimization protocol, I do not need to rely on altruistic reasons; it is enough to notice that it would be good for *me* if I and the others followed it. But it is not always best for me to do what I would like everyone to do. When I am more powerful, I may succeed at getting others to benefit me more than I benefit them, by pressing others to make choices I do not myself make.[20] The gains of free-riding may be greater for me than the gains of cooperation. I might have to care about them, for their own sake, to not pursue terms of interaction that are exploitative. As it turns out, even the Kantian protocol, as stated by Roemer, is open to egotistic abuse. If I am more powerful, I may want everyone to act on a rule that permits exploitation. I will be the

---

[19] I do not deny that some forms of altruism are supererogatory.

[20] It could be objected that Roemer's argument grants this, that his cooperative ethos only works under reasonably egalitarian social conditions and is, he claims, a necessary complement to the socialist equality of opportunity. But the background conditions would not dissolve all important power differentials, and the defence of them, and the ethos, involve some altruism. See also Vrousalis's (2021b) charge that Roemer's ethos is in tension with his principle of equality.

190 Human Dignity and Social Justice

one doing the exploiting. To avoid this abuse, I would need to adopt a partly altruistic perspective that takes others as ends in themselves.

The Kantian protocol can be reformulated to prevent the abuse and make clearer that each agent's perspective is central to it. I propose a revision that requires that *each takes the action everyone concerned would like (or better: rationally prefer) all to take.* This reformulation asks each to take up the perspective of others besides their own when determining what patterns of action to accept (after all, some of the actions A might like everyone to engage in—such as capitalist interactions—may not be the same as the ones a less powerful agent B might like everyone to engage in—as the former might feature B as a discarded destitute, or in the role of an exploited subordinate).[21] Socialist solidarity, as I see it, does indeed involve expanding the first-person singular perspective (the I-perspective) to assume an enlarged first person plural perspective (the We-perspective). It is also a matter of exploring, in a respectful and concernful way, the second and the third person perspectives—singular and plural. It involves also the I—you, and the I—she or he or them perspectives. These additional standpoints improve the We-perspective, making it more fully responsive to the dignity of the people in it.

3.2 The Abilities/Needs Principle and exploitation

Turning now to Levels 2 and 1 of our account of exploitation, we ask: What is the upshot of the dignitarian perspective on solidarity regarding economic principles? And how do these principles help us make judgements about

---

[21] Those who will need (partially or fully) unreciprocated help will not rationally choose schemes of social life devoid of altruism. My reformulation of the Kantian protocol is akin to the proposal of Kantian Contractualism as elaborated in Parfit (2011: sects. 49, 52).

We can say that this formula also better captures the spirit of Kant's Formula of Humanity, demanding that we treat persons as ends in themselves, not merely as means. I argue elsewhere that this core Kantian idea includes positive duties. See Gilbert (2010), and Chapter 2, Section 2.2 (iii) of this book. Now, exploitation can be seen as flouting an appropriate interpretation and application of the formula as framing economic behaviour and structures. Exploitation is a paradigmatic case of failure to respond appropriately to the human dignity of workers. It involves treating them merely (or excessively) as means, as mostly a bundle of resources, or not treating them sufficiently as ends. Capitalism may do better in some respects than, say slavery, by recognizing some negative liberties—workers may not be made to work without their consent. But it is insufficient because workers are not granted much in terms of real opportunities to access work that is not exploitative. Capitalism may even twist the idea of freedom insidiously, by casting the exploited as responsible for their own exploitation.

Parfit (2011: ch.9) helpfully notes that we should refine our understanding of the Formula of Humanity to avoid making it unduly lenient—it would be easy not to treat others *merely* as means by taking them as ends just a little bit while neglecting them in every other respect. One way to do this is indeed to deploy the Kantian idea of a Realm of Ends, in which people identify norms that everybody concerned would, simultaneously, rationally accept. This is the Kantian Contractualist protocol mentioned above. Of course, we need to also explore what substantive principles could rationally be chosen, and the generic reasons for choosing them. The Abilities/Needs Principle I propose is one such principle, and the interests in developing and exercising the capacities at the basis of dignity provide relevant generic reasons.

The Critique of Exploitation **191**

exploitation? Let us start with the first question, and ask, more precisely, what are the relevant duties and rights regarding work, income, leisure, and the provision and consumption of other goods?

The socialist Abilities/Needs Principle (ANP) (*from each according to their abilities, to each according to their needs*[22]), as interpreted in Chapter 3, provides a fruitful account of the economic requirements of dignitarian solidarity. Although this is contentious, I argued that we should see ANP as a principle of justice. In general, this principle requires that the organization of an economy (its relations of production and its social ethos, among other features) be such that each participant benefits *and* contributes solidaristically. Assuming that economic resources are scarce, the distribution of access to advantages should in principle be equally sensitive to the needs of all and be attuned to their diversity. Furthermore, nobody should make claims on the social product without contributing to it if they can, and as they can given their diverse abilities. As with solidarity, and given technological feasibility constraints, I do not take ANP to require maximal contribution and complete need satisfaction. ANP has a dignitarian justification. It can be defended by appealing to the dignitarian principle of Solidaristic Empowerment, according to which we ought to shape our social relations so that we do not block or destroy, and so that we enable and further, the unfolding of people's valuable capacities (the ones that are the basis of their dignity). We should cater for others' needs at least when, and because, those needs are interests in developing and exercising their valuable capacities (or are causally relevant to that development and exercise). We should engage in productive contribution also because doing so would involve developing and exercising our various valuable capacities for cooperation, creativity, etc., as well as our moral capacities to act with respect and concern for others besides ourselves.

Recall the six core demands of ANP (which provide further specification of the ideal of Solidaristic Empowerment for an economy):

(a) **Opportunities for self-realization at work:** There should be effective opportunities for productive activity that involves self-realization. People have valuable capacities to engage in complex, cooperative, creative, and socially useful work. They should have real chances to engage in this kind of work. Arguably, having such options would serve an important human need. These opportunities would be effective in that mechanisms would be in place to offset morally arbitrary differences between workers that affect their accessibility. For example, excellent

---

[22] The ANP is stated in Marx (1978i: 531).

192 Human Dignity and Social Justice

education and training would be available to all, and the workplace would be designed so that workers with different talents and bodily restrictions can thrive.

(b) **Positive duties:** There should be institutions, and a social ethos, which enable and encourage people to produce to meet other people's needs—thereby supporting the human flourishing of all. Each should envisage a reasonable level of development and exercise of their powers to produce in this way.

(c) **Securing basic needs:** Some instantiations of the positive duties mentioned in (b) are particularly urgent and stringent. They concern the satisfaction of basic needs for subsistence and for being able to function as a political equal.

(d) **Fair reciprocity:** There should be an ethos and a scheme of distribution of access to consumption goods that recognizes a responsibility to cooperate in production on terms of fair reciprocity. It is wrong to take advantage of the productive efforts of others without making our own, similar effort if we can. Similar effort is not strict equivalence in output (which might depend on morally arbitrary differences in productive abilities), but a matter of the proportion of contribution given one's abilities. Above the threshold marked by (c), those (but only those) who make an equal effort (when they can) should have equal access to consumption goods.

(e) **Sensitivity to individual differences:** Individual differences in abilities and needs are normatively important, and should be factored in when appraising appropriate levels of contribution and access to consumption. Each should be allowed, and enabled, to pursue their well-being in ways that are appropriate given their own characteristics.

(f) **Self-determination in economic life:** Respect and concern for individuals in their diversity should also be supportive of their self-determination. Absent conflict with very strong competing considerations (such as basic positive duties to respond to emergencies), everyone should be entitled to choose whether, and how, to work, and each should be entitled to choose whether, and how, to consume. For example, each should be allowed to form their own schedules of trade-offs between self-realization at work, leisure time, and consumption. Furthermore, the contours of the social structure within which people produce and consume should be subject to authorization, contestation, and change by all the members of society through democratic mechanisms of opinion—and will-formation.

The Critique of Exploitation **193**

An economy that honours ANP would instantiate these demands. Since they fairly cater for general interests shared by all, and these are interests in the unfolding of capacities at the basis of their dignity, the Dignitarian Approach would recommend that ANP be adopted. For the same reasons, the demands of ANP could be rationally chosen (using the revised Kantian protocol) as guidelines for economic life. Now, as it turns out, an exploitative economy would flout some or all of these demands. Here are the links. When A exploits B, A uses their greater power in ways that fail to solidaristically support B's flourishing. A fails to appropriately respect B's self-determination, appreciate B's efforts, or further other needs of B (such as access to consumption goods). Thus, the failures of solidaristic support in exploitation involve a benefitting from others which flouts at least some of (a)–(f). Since ANP (in my account) has a dignitarian rationale, the fact A uses their greater power to benefit from B in a way that flouts ANP implies that A fails to respond appropriately to B's dignity.[23]

I have articulated ANP at a fairly abstract level. We could formulate various implementations of it (thus moving from dimension DI to DII in a conception of justice—see Section 1). An example would be a modified version of Joseph Carens's proposal of market socialism.[24] Carens seeks to combine equality with freedom and efficiency, proposing a radically restructured market system. His scheme retains the information function of markets (which often are better than central planning at identifying matches between supply and demand) without some of their typical distributive upshots (which often involve problematic inequalities) and motivational configurations (which are often quite egotistic). In this scheme, pre-tax income varies widely, signalling demand. But post-tax incomes are equal, so people choose jobs on the basis of a social duty to contribute to the needs of others (as well as some personal, self-regarding preferences). A second sector of the economy would feature direct public provision for individually differentiated needs (such as

---

[23] Notice that the dignitarian solidaristic perspective captures concerns about both freedom and self-realization or well-being—given their connection with important human capacities. Thus, it links up to the critiques of domination and of alienation in the articulation of the critique of exploitation (even though the former critiques also range beyond the latter). Exploitation involves insufficient regard for the freedom and well-being of the people exploited. Exploitation arguably involves domination because the extraction of benefits from the exploited is accomplished by the use of asymmetric power by the exploiter, who imposes their will on the exploited. Exploitation also involves alienation because the exploited are less able to develop and exercise their valuable human capacities (i.e. achieve human flourishing) than they would if people pulled their powers together with the aim of fostering each other's human flourishing rather than with the aim of extracting from each other asymmetric benefits. So the dignitarian solidaristic perspective illuminates the fact that for socialists the critique of exploitation is connected to, and forms a package with, the critiques of domination and alienation. We should also think about what unifies these three critiques. I think that the Abilities/Needs Principle and the dignitarian ideal of Solidaristic Empowerment, help illuminate the common basis.

[24] Carens (2003).

194 Human Dignity and Social Justice

in health care). This scheme does quite well regarding the demands (b)–(f) of ANP. In Chapter 3, I have argued for a modified version that makes it better in catering for these, and other demands. Two of the modifications are the following. First, to cater for demand (a) and to better cater for (f), some workplaces would be generated in which opportunities for self-realization and self-management are available. Second, to better cater for demands (c), (e), and (f), a flexible system of different tiers of equal income schedules could be introduced, in which a standard full-time workday is identified, but in which people are also allowed to work more (and earn more) if they especially value consumption and work less (and earn less) if they especially value leisure. This would allow people to strike their own judgement about the relative significance of various goods for them, without exploiting others in their pursuit.

4. Exploitation as a Multidimensional Social Process

4.1 Contrast with other accounts

According to the account offered here, wrongful exploitation involves a contra-solidaristic use of power, as stated in CSP. I gave more substance to CSP by characterizing the kind of solidarity that is relevantly flouted in exploitation by reference to the demands of ANP (which, in turn, was given a dignitarian rationale). We can now further clarify the account of the exploitation of workers shaped by ANP through a comparison with other accounts. These views have already been discussed by others. I thus survey them only briefly (although I spend more time with the last one because, being more recent, it has received less critical discussion, and because it is close to the view I propose). The main objectives of this exercise are to tease out desiderata for an intuitively satisfactory account, and to show that the contra-solidaristic use of power account (CSP), when shaped by ANP, satisfies them.

Unequal exchange account. On this account, A exploits B if and only if in their exchange A gets more than B does. This account leads to seeing the normative idea of the exploitation of labour as extensionally equivalent with the technical notion. Thus, in a common Marxist formulation, A exploits B, when B works for A, if and only if the amount of labour embodied in the goods A can consume thanks to the economic transaction with B is greater than the amount A contributes, with the opposite being the case for B (i.e., the goods accessible to B embody less labour than the labour B contributes in B's

The Critique of Exploitation **195**

economic transaction with A). The insight of this account is that it captures the significance of reciprocity. The CSP account can do so too by drawing on demand (d) of ANP regarding fair reciprocity. Now, an important difficulty of the unequal exchange account arises from its normative focus on exchange of goods with equivalent value (measured in terms of socially necessary labour or market price). It unduly accepts the results of morally arbitrary differences in economic agents' natural endowments. B, through no choice or fault of their own, might produce less than C despite exerting the same amount of effort or spending the same actual time at work, thus being entitled to less.[25] The account would imply that redistributing from C to B would be exploitative. This result would be avoided by CSP if based on ANP, as the demand of fair reciprocity focuses on ratios of effort to abilities, not to average labour or market value.[26]

Furthermore, the unequal exchange account is insufficient because it would imply that redistribution from workers to people who cannot engage in production (because of certain handicaps, for example) would involve wrongful exploitation.[27]. If based in ANP, CSP would not yield this counterintuitive result because ANP affirms positive duties (demand b), and, especially, basic positive duties which are not contingent on contribution (demand c). And, in any case, someone flouts the norm of fair reciprocity only if they *can* give more than they are actually giving.

The labour entitlement account. On this account, A exploits B if and only if A benefits from B in a way that is forced or coerced.[28] Workers are entitled to the product of their labour. They are exploited when they are compelled by socially created circumstances to surrender it. Thus, in a common Marxist formulation, B is forced to surrender surplus labour when B has no acceptable alternative to doing so. The imposition is social when the fact that B faces unacceptable alternatives to the exploitative scheme is the result of social institutions and practices. A's forcing or coercing of B could be more or less

---

[25] It could be said that a modified version of the unequal exchange account that requires perfect competition would avoid this objection. But it is not clear that perfect markets would eliminate unfairness resulting from unequal natural endowments (such as talents and bodily abilities). The salaries and other rewards which low skilled workers fetch in a perfect market may still be too low from a moral point of view. See Arneson (2016).

[26] This holds at the level of principle. However, as noted in Chapter 3, it is difficult to operationalize fair reciprocity to measure levels of effort and abilities. This is a shared concern for the CSP/ANP account and for the unequal exchange account. Furthermore, B and C may work for the same hours and with the same effort, but one experiences more drudgery than the other. This does not make the account break down, however (as Elster (1985: 202) suggests). The proportionality of income to time or effort at work can be held as a pro tanto consideration, with special considerations about relative disutility of work being added when desirable and feasible. The modification of the Carensian scheme suggested in Section 3 provides resources to address these issues but is far from perfect. More work in this area is needed.

[27] Arnsperger and Van Parijs (2003: ch.III); Vrousalis (2018: sect. 4.2).

[28] Holmstrom (1977); Reiman (1987).

196 Human Dignity and Social Justice

direct—it can operate through threats to B if B does not accept the exploitative deal or through the creation and maintenance of certain institutional frameworks, such as property rights in means of production, which render propertyless people like B unable to fend for themselves. In the framework discussed in Section 2, A exploits B when A offers S1 while threatening S3 or generating a S2 that is intolerable for B.

The insights of this account are the recognition of workers' contribution and the critical examination of force and coercion. But if based in ANP, CSP can capture these points as well. The demand (d) of fair reciprocity gives workers standing to reject some forms of surplus extraction, and the demand (f) regarding self-determination warns against economic frameworks which cast workers as mere puppets of the will of others.

CSP/ANP can also avoid the problems of this account. The first problem is that it does not provide sufficient conditions for exploitation. As a response to morally arbitrary inequalities resulting from disparities in natural endowments, it would not be wrong to transfer benefits from able-bodied workers to the handicapped people who cannot work. So, either there would be no exploitation here or there would be exploitation in the technical sense but not in the normatively loaded one (the extraction of benefits would not be wrongful). Again, positive requirements (b) and (c) of ANP help avoid the problematic results.

This account also fails to provide necessary conditions. Exploitation can occur without force or coercion. For example, A may have sophisticated means of production which were legitimately acquired, hire B to work on them, and get a rent out of this, which B voluntarily accepts despite having acceptable—although less advantageous—alternatives.[29] This problem is also avoided by CSP when it draws on ANP's demand (d), which challenges surplus extraction facilitated by inequalities in assets even in the absence of force or coercion.

The unfair distribution of productive endowments account. On this account, workers are entitled to a fair share in means of production (and other productive endowments). It is unjust when they are disadvantaged as a result of having less access to them than others. They are exploited when they have smaller shares than others, benefit the latter with their labour, but end up less well off (with less access to leisure time or income, for example). In capitalism, workers have little or no control of means of production while capitalists enjoy effective control of them. Workers are hired by capitalists, and transfer to them more benefits than they would if the distribution of means of

---

[29] Roemer (1996: ch.4).

The Critique of Exploitation **197**

production were less unequal. One way of formulating this account is by saying that A is an exploiter, and B is exploited, if and only if A gains from B's labour and A would be worse off, and B better off, in a hypothetical economic environment in which the initial distribution of resources was equal (with everything else remaining constant).[30]

This account carries two important insights. First, it illuminates the importance of background inequality of opportunity in access to productive assets. Second, it recognizes the significance of the responsibility of agents for the choices they make regarding the use of what they control. Both points can be captured in ANP thanks to its egalitarian profile regarding access to economic preconditions of human flourishing, and through the demands (f) and (d) which call for an economic system that empowers workers to shape its terms, and which, to some extent, allows some agents to refrain from benefiting others who do not reciprocate in appropriate ways.

However, although CSP/ANP recognizes the significance of fairness and responsibility, it does so in a way that avoids an important problem of the unfair distribution account. As pointed out by Vrousalis, this account generates counterintuitive results which make it unfit for the identification of necessary conditions for wrongful exploitation. In Vrousalis's *Pit* case, A encounters B in a pit from which B cannot get out. B is in that pit through (bad) option luck—say, after choosing to go skiing in a mountain with known risks posed by pits in it. It is not the result of brute luck such as an unfair initial division of economic advantages. Now, A could easily rescue B by throwing a rope, but chooses to drive a hard bargain offering the rope only if B signs a contract to work for A in a sweatshop for life.[31] This is wrongful exploitation, but it involves no unfair background distribution. This result would not arise with CSP if it relies on ANP because, in addition to concerns about fairness and responsibility, ANP includes basic positive duties to rescue others in dire straits (demand c). ANP also calls for appreciating the specific circumstances of individuals and the importance of a self-determination in economic affairs that is real rather than merely formal (demands e and f), which in cases like Pit should call for aid rather than opportunistic profiteering. Pit also displays a violation of demand (a), as in it A boxes B indefinitely into a situation in which self-realization in work is unavailable.

Another problem of this account is that it seems explanatorily deficient. It tells us something about what enables A to exploit B, but not what exploitation consists in. (Alternatively: it makes exploitation a wholly derivative issue,

---

[30] I base this formulation on Roemer (1996: 110).
[31] This is a simplified version of the case in Vrousalis (2013: 148–9).

198 Human Dignity and Social Justice

holding the distribution of productive assets as the only really significant issue). Even if all and only the cases of exploitation could be identified by using the device of hypothetical comparison with counterfactual situations of equality of endowments, we would get extensional equivalence but not sufficient understanding. The relational dimension regarding the inappropriate instrumentalization or contra-solidaristic treatment of others when wielding social power over them is not captured.[32]

The domination for self-enrichment account. The relational dimension is addressed by accounts that view exploitation as a case of taking advantage of the vulnerabilities of others. This chapter's view of exploitation as a misuse of power to get others to benefit you more than they should is indeed a variant of this perspective, although developed in a specific way. As Vrousalis notes, in its initial versions the instrumentalization of vulnerability account is insufficiently discriminative. Surgeons benefit from the sorry health of their patients, but getting paid for their services need not involve exploitation.[33]

Vrousalis has a proposal to fill in the details. According to his 'domination for self-enrichment' account, 'A exploits B if A benefits from a transaction in which A dominates B.'[34] The added point here is that A subordinates B, getting B to act on reasons that are not independent from A's power over B. Exploited workers transfer benefits to their exploiters not because they are generous or to fulfil the exploiters' needs, but because they are at their mercy.

This account captures the importance of power differentials, and the relational odiousness of using them egotistically. (CSP also obviously covers these points by, respectively, drawing upon ANP's demands (f) and (b)–(e).) But the domination account is itself insufficiently discriminative. Some exchanges involving domination might not involve exploitation, and some may be more exploitative than others.[35] The account does not deny these points, but the problem is that it cannot explain how these variations bear on exploitation without drawing on additional considerations about appropriate distributive outcomes—something the CSP account does and is for that reason better. To notice and measure the exploitative abusiveness of power use

---

[32] For a survey of Roemer's various formulations of his exploitation theory which discusses this problem (which has also been addressed by others), as well as an argument that Roemer's distributive account is insufficient because it does not properly illuminate the centrality of power asymmetries in relations of exploitation, see Veneziani (2013).

[33] Vrousalis (2018: sect.6.1). For a seminal discussion of exploitation as abuse of power over the vulnerable, see Goodin (1987).

[34] Vrousalis (2018: sect.6.2).

[35] Some economic arrangements might involve subordination and some extraction of benefits without exploitation as their rationale. The ruling agents in Orwell's *1984* seem to be in the game for the perverse joy of lording over others, not to extract material advantages from their subjects.

The Critique of Exploitation 199

we need a distributive principle. Just saying that freedom is set back by domination while benefits are extracted is not enough. Solidaristic Empowerment includes additional vital considerations.

To clarify this challenge, consider Vrousalis's discussion of Roemer's critique of exploitation as only a matter of unjust inequality in initial distribution of assets. Vrousalis deftly shows that the latter is not necessary for exploitation, as exploitation can arise even when the current inequality has a clean pedigree—one that reflects choices by agents initially situated in fair conditions. His *Ant and Grasshopper* case is telling. In it, Ant and Grasshopper start with equal endowments, but while Ant works hard before the winter, Grasshopper lazes about. When the winter comes, Grasshopper lacks enough resources to survive, while Ant has plenty. Ant can now choose to (i) ignore Grasshopper, (ii) give Grasshopper shelter on condition that Grasshopper signs a sweatshop contract to work for Ant, or (iii) give shelter to Grasshopper at no cost to Ant. If Ant chooses (ii), Ant would be exploiting Grasshopper, and this against a background of inequality in assets that is not unjust. The resulting payoffs in terms of the relevant metric of advantage are:

(Ant, Grasshopper)

(i): Do nothing: (10, 1)
(ii): Sweatshop: (12, 2)
(iii): Shelter: (10, 3).[36]

Vrousalis is right that there is wrongful exploitation in (ii), and that unfairness understood on the luck-egalitarian way is unnecessary for it.[37] But it would be helpful to explore further scenarios of wage labour that proceed not only in (ii) sweatshop conditions but also in (iv) non-sweatshop conditions (with pay-offs of 11.5, 2.5 for example), and where case (iii) is not available (i.e. when instead (iii)* Ant would bear costs when sheltering Grasshopper— yielding pay-offs of 9, 3 for example). There could be many versions of (iv), and to ascertain their acceptability we need considerations of distributive justice or fairness which Vrousalis's account does not provide. Here reciprocity and individual responsibility would be relevant, I think. Some instances of (iv) may not be wrongful if A worked hard to reach the current state while B chose to enjoy more leisure time.[38] Without considerations like these, we cannot know when the terms Ant offers to Grasshopper really involve an affront

---

[36] Vrousalis (2013: 150).
[37] It is not helpful, however, to reduce (as Vrousalis does) the use of 'fairness' to what a luck-egalitarian would characterize as unjust. The notion is often used more widely.
[38] This case of (iv) could still involve domination, but not wrongful exploitation.

200 Human Dignity and Social Justice

to Grasshopper's status or dignity, or how serious that affront is. We need some substantive distributive principle regarding either initial positions or outcomes (or both) to know when domination or misuse of power features exploitation (to know when there is too much that is being taken by the exploiter), and how bad that exploitation is.

Vrousalis says that 'exploitation constitutes procedural injury to *status*, and status-injury is not reducible to distributive injury.'[39] If I am right, however, we need a combination of procedural and distributive considerations. It seems to me that this combination is already assumed in Vrousalis's formulation of exploitation as 'domination for self-enrichment'. Here the procedural notion (domination) is coupled with a distributive one (self-enrichment). After all, since exploitation is an agential process, its teleological dimension—regarding distributive outcomes—must be addressed squarely. One possibility going forward is to constrain power differentials in economic power. This can be done by prohibiting unequal control of productive assets, or by allowing some which have a 'clean pedigree' while blocking ex ante, or redressing ex post, some uses of them that would generate unacceptable distributive results. ANP supports this through the considerations of self-determination (f), fair reciprocity (d), and basic positive duties (c), for example. The CSP/ANP account promises a more textured discussion of exploitation because the Dignitarian Approach providing its rationale precisely takes off with a fuller understanding of what it is to appropriately respond to the moral status of people.[40]

4.2 A multidimensional process

Each one of the alternative views of exploitation discussed captures important points but misses others. The CSP account informed by ANP can avoid the problems of these accounts and capture their insights (as well as some others, such as the importance of positive duties). In particular, CSP/ANP illuminates the fact that the wrongfulness of exploitation is complex. Exploitation involves a combination of features regarding three dimensions, and CSP/ANP meets the challenge of illuminating their significance and relation.

---

[39] Vrousalis (2013: 151).

[40] Vrousalis construes his account of respect for people's moral status along the lines of the ideal of democratic equality proposed by Elizabeth Anderson, which downplays distributive considerations. My dignitarian account of respect and concern is different. Solidaristic Empowerment has distributive implications, and ANP articulates them.

The Critique of Exploitation **201**

(i) *Background material and social circumstances (including initial distributions).* The first dimension concerns the material and social background against which exploitation takes place. A key feature of this background is the asymmetry of power between the relevant agents, or the disparities in the extent to which they are vulnerable to each other. This asymmetry may be due to psycho-physical features of the agents and their circumstances or to social structures that agents have created (such as certain private property institutions).

(ii) *Relational attitudes, treatment.* The second dimension is attitudinal, expressive, or procedural. It concerns how agents treat each other. Exploitation involves a problematically instrumental treatment of the exploited by the exploiters. This has both interpersonal and systemic or structural instances (a point I return to in Section 5).

(iii) *Final distributive results.* The third dimension concerns the final results of the exploitative process. The distributive upshot of this process is that the exploited get less, and the exploiters more, than what they could justly claim.

The three dimensions are analytically distinct and can come apart. Thus, (ii) can hold without (i): it is possible for A to form instrumentalizing intentions in their relation with B even if A is not powerful enough to get B to do what A wants. (i) can in turn hold without (ii): A may be more powerful than B but not use that power to instrumentalize B unduly, pursuing instead forms of cooperation that yield fair (or less unfair) distributions. Next, (i) and (ii) can hold without (iii): A may use their power over B to try to get B to yield surplus benefits for A, but due to other factors (such as the intervention of another agent C, or some natural phenomenon) fail to generate the distribution that gives A more than B. Finally, (iii) can arise without (i) and (ii) as an unintended consequence of interactions by initially equally endowed agents.

The dimensions are nevertheless typically connected. For example, the power asymmetry in (i) enables A to effectively instrumentalize B in (ii). Together, the background in (i) and the treatment in (ii) help explain how the morally problematic distributions in (iii) come about. And the distributive disparities in (iii) reproduce the background power asymmetries in (i), and enable the problematic treatment in (ii), over time.

Now, the solidaristic perspective can be developed so that it targets each of these dimensions. Targeting (i), it can call for reducing interpersonal or structural power asymmetries. This would remove conditions that enable exploitation. Targeting (ii) (and, simultaneously, (iii)), solidarity can call for using whatever asymmetries remain in ways that enhance the personal power

202 Human Dignity and Social Justice

of agents (and in particular the weaker ones) to achieve flourishing lives. And targeting (iii) (but not interpersonal cases of (ii)), solidarity can call for the introduction of institutional mechanisms that incentivize people to act in ways that will cause just distributions even if the motivations to act in those ways do not themselves include reference to the prospect of producing those effects (some frameworks combining market competition and redistributive taxation might be defended in this way). Arguably, the ideal project would be to target all the dimensions simultaneously. But it could be that in some junctures this ambition is not sufficiently likely to succeed. It could be, for example, that in a particular context a reduction of power asymmetry targeting (i) would produce more rather than less instrumental treatment, or worse rather than better distributive effects. A challenge for future research on CSP/ANP is to explore the various possibilities opened up by this analytic framework. What is clear is that those possibilities are firmly on the agenda once we see exploitation as a multiple failure to take the dignity of others seriously.

Pulling together the various strands of the discussion offered in this chapter, we get the following picture:

Level 1: The contra-solidaristic use of power account of exploitation (CSP).

Level 2: The Abilities/Needs Principles (ANP) and its implications for the three dimensions regarding background circumstances, relational attitudes, and distributive results.

Level 3: The Dignitarian Approach with its ideal of Solidaristic Empowerment, and the (revised) Kantian protocol.

The CSP accounts says that A exploits B when A benefits from B's work through a contra-solidaristic use of A's greater power. To figure out when wrongful exploitation indeed occurs, we mobilize substantive standards to shape the content and application of CSP. That is the task of Levels 3 and 2. Deploying the Dignitarian Approach and the revised Kantian protocol proposed in Section 3, we ask: Is the allocation and use of power under examination one which those affected by it could, ex ante, prospectively authorize if they envisioned what terms of social cooperation to establish while treating each other's dignity seriously?[41] The relevant terms will have to rely on grounds that all can rationally accept as responding to everyone's dignity.

---

[41] Recall the contrast between the cases (ii) and (iv) in the Ant/Grasshopper case. Using the Kantian protocol, both Ant and Grasshopper could rationally authorize, ex ante, the prospect of asymmetry of power and its use in (iv), but not in (ii).

The ideal of Solidaristic Empowerment guides the search for those grounds by directing people to figure out how to support the unfolding of the features in virtue of which they have dignity. Those generic considerations are then articulated further into an economic outlook through the Abilities/Needs Principle. ANP has implications for each of the three dimensions stated in this section. By working out the details of this approach, we can explain why some interactions, or even some social structures, contribute to wrongful exploitation. Future research should illuminate these details for relevant contexts—to operationalize the application of ANP to assess cases of transfer of surplus benefits from workers to others. This chapter has certainly not provided such details. Its task has been the more foundational and philosophical one of outlining the core normative structure of the approach.[42]

5. Agency and Structure

I conclude by briefly discussing some possible objections. They all target complexities regarding the agency of A and B as individual or collective agents variously affected by other agents and social structures. The objections can in principle be answered, but they also point to the need to develop the CSP/ANP approach in future work.

It could first be objected that it is not really problematic that there is interpersonal exploitation if at the aggregate level the upshot is desirable. A system allowing for exploitation might be more efficient than a system without (or with less of) it. Witness the dramatic increase in productivity that capitalism has generated. In response, consider three points. First, from a principled perspective, it is important to keep the intrinsic odiousness of exploitation in view. The intense instrumentalization of other human beings which exploitation involves is in itself an awful way of shaping human relationships, even if all things considered people end up better off as a result. We should keep asking: Could we imagine ways of getting equivalent levels of advantage without having to treat each other in this way? Second, it is not clear that increases in productivity require contra-solidaristic treatment. In fact, in its current phase capitalism has been incorporating reliance on personal initiative and solidarity among workers forming teams and pursuing projects

---

[42] Although I present Solidaristic Empowerment as a specification of the Dignitarian Approach, I do not say that the former could not be defended differently. A similar caveat applies to the relation between the items in Level 3 and ANP, and between ANP and CSP. The relations stated in this chapter are strong enough for my purposes, but readers could accept some items falling downstream while formulating other grounds they find more appealing. I thank Vida Panitch, Lucas Stanczyk, and Nicholas Vrousalis for discussion on these points.

204   Human Dignity and Social Justice

within firms (especially those involved in knowledge-intensive and innovative tasks). These workers are still exploited, but their new experiences may be pointing towards future possibilities in which their practices of autonomy and cooperation shatter the exploitative mould within which they have been unleashed. Third, assuming (contrary to the second response) that a trade-off is unavoidable, we should rethink how important it is to insist on greater material output when it comes at the expense of serious relational deficits (as well as environmental risks, of course). Efficiency is parasitic on the utility variables being maximized. Once high levels of production are already achieved, improving human relationships may be more important than getting even more stuff to consume.[43]

A second objection is that it might not be so problematic that there are power asymmetries and domination at the workplace or in the labour market if there is self-determination at the political level. A might be using power contra-solidaristically in day-to-day economic life, but A and B, together, might be political equals in a democratic system. If as equal citizens they choose an economic framework involving exploitation, then it is not clear that anyone is wronged, as that framework is self-imposed. I agree that self-determination at the macro-societal level is important. Demand (f) of ANP requires it. But it also affirms the importance of the self-determination of individuals in their daily economic life. A collective, societal permission of economic exploitation would depress individual self-determination. The democratically selected regime might be legitimate, but it would still be unjust. It would make sense for citizens to keep campaigning within the democratic process to reach better decisions. An additional, familiar, but very important answer is that the inequality of wealth that results from exploitation infects the political process so that those with greater economic power wind up having disproportional influence on the political process (through lobbying on law-makers, campaign finance of politicians, the offering of corporate jobs before and after they are in office, and through the threat of disinvesting and capital flight if policies lower their profit margin). Democratic complacency towards exploitative schemes is self-destructive—it depresses the prospect for effective political equality, which is at the heart of the dignity of individuals as citizens, and of the value of democracy. For this reason, it also weakens the indirect authorization of exploitation that democracy is said to provide.

---

[43] These points engage the significant issue of the subjective schemas sustaining practices of exploitation. Often A are cast as leaders and inciters, and B as contributors and consumers. Now, when B become involved in the design of production and engage in horizontal cooperation, A appear rather parasitic and manipulating, and their exploitation becomes more evident and appalling.

The Critique of Exploitation **205**

A third worry concerns the relation between individual agency and social structure. It might seem inappropriate, on reflection, to focus on the moral condemnation of the relation of exploitation between A and B, if A and B are individuals. First, it is not evident that B is at the mercy of A. B could choose another job, and eventually even exit the working class by starting a small firm. Second, it is not clear that A is capable of treating B differently. Facing stiff competition, A might go out of business if A does not maximize profit through exploitation.

Although familiar, this worry is not convincing. Regarding the first point, we can note that even if some workers can, in a tight labour market, get better deals because of their rare skills, their normal condition is one of having to accept subordination and exploitation by some capitalist or other. Furthermore, changing jobs often imposes significant personal and financial costs. Employers benefit from this general condition and use it in their dealing with any worker they hire. As for exiting the working class altogether, this is a prospect that is very unlikely indeed for individuals who are not extraordinarily endowed or motivated,[44] and in any case is not possible—within capitalism—for all or most of them simultaneously.[45] For most individual workers, their predicament remains as discussed in Section 2. Only collective action, deep reform, or structural change offer them a significantly better prospect in which they reject S1 by falling back on a solid S2 from which they can confidently demand S4.

Regarding the second point, I concede that individual capitalists are affected by competitive pressures. In particular, the owners of small business, such as the Tim Hortons franchise in the example opening this chapter, have less power than other capitalists with controlling shares in massive corporations like Amazon. The point, however, should not be exaggerated. Unlike most workers, who must take up wage employment to make a living, most capitalists do not need to hire and exploit other people to do so (they could be wage workers themselves). Additionally, each capitalist may choose to amass less personal wealth to reduce the exploitation of their workers.[46] Furthermore, capitalists routinely engage in collective action—for example, through business associations—to shape economic, political, legal, and cultural conditions. They indeed have significant causal responsibility regarding their

---

[44] Elster (1985: 208–16).
[45] Cohen (1983).
[46] Must the owners of the Tim Hortons franchise have a winter home in Florida while their workers are struggling to pay their rent back in Ontario? Contrast this with the owner of Gravity Rainbow choosing to dramatically increase workers' salaries and reduce his profits. P. Chen (2015).

206 Human Dignity and Social Justice

generation. And, given their greater power to affect them over time, they have sharper normative responsibilities than the workers they exploit.

An important issue, however, emerges from this discussion. It concerns the significance of avoiding an exclusive focus on interpersonal rapports, and the need for illuminating the relational stance as it concerns the larger systemic or structural dimension (as well as for linking both aspects of the second, relational dimension in the framework identified in Section 4.2 with the other dimensions concerning initial and final distributions). Besides exhortations for occasional acts of individual decency and abnegation, it is especially important to focus on generating societal structures in which power is allocated in more egalitarian ways that express and facilitate solidaristic treatment as a regular feature of economic life. Agents act within structures, but they can also change them over time. This is precisely what the CSP/ANP perspective proposed in this chapter encourages us to do. Imagining and pursuing alternative, solidaristic social structures is, I think, what dignitarian virtue would mostly consist in.

6
The Critique of Alienation

1. Introduction

The topic of alienation has fallen out of fashion in social and political philosophy. It used to be salient, especially in socialist thought and in debates about labour practices in capitalism. As Castoriadis once put it, capitalism has the peculiarity of having (more than any previous economic system) made work utterly central to people's lives while at the same time having the tendency to render it 'absurd'—a site of frustration of people's self-determination and self-realization rather than a medium for their expression.[1] Famously, Marx criticized capitalism for constituting a form of economic life in which workers are not at one with themselves and with others. They do not control their productive activities, their talents and creative potentials are stunted rather than unfolded, and they relate to their bosses, other workers, and consumers in primarily instrumental and even hostile ways rather than on terms of mutual service or fellowship.[2] The lack of identification of people with their working lives—their alienation as workers—remains an important practical issue.[3] However, despite the obvious practical significance of alienation,

---

[1] Castoriadis (1979: 110).
[2] Marx (1978c).
[3] 'A Gallup survey [in 2018] found that, on average, only 15% of workers around the world felt fully engaged with their jobs'. This failure of firms to motivate workers does not only hold in the case of jobs involving repetitive, mechanical tasks, but also where more flexible and creative activities are called for. Although profitability is positively correlated with it, capitalist firms do not succeed at inspiring workers' commitment. The Economist (2019). (Interestingly, the same issue of this journal features, as its leading headline, 'The Rise of Millennial Socialism'.) It is true that the condition of contemporary workers is not the same as that of the nineteenth century depicted by Marx. But core inequalities of power and lack of well-being remain. For example, although hours of work are shorter, new technologies and management strategies have increased the intensity and repetitiveness of some tasks, imposing serious harms to workers' physical and psychological health. Coutrot (2018: 63). See Section 5 for further discussion on contemporary capitalism. For a survey of (and call for more) empirical research of alienation at work—understood as a psychological state of estrangement in which workers dissociate, or feel detached, from work—see Chiaburu et al (2014). This study considers job involvement, but also other attitudes (like job satisfaction and organizational commitment), as well as other outcomes regarding withdrawal, health, and performance. Various predictors are explored, including individual characteristics (such as need for achievement or control), role stressors (such as role conflict and ambiguity), leadership dimensions (such as supportive feedback and consideration), job design (articulation of tasks), and work context (such as levels of formalization and organizational support). For a survey of sociological research of alienation at work, see Edgell and Granter (2020: ch.2).

Human Dignity and Social Justice. Pablo Gilabert, Oxford University Press. © Pablo Gilabert (2023).
DOI: 10.1093/oso/9780192871152.003.0006

208 Human Dignity and Social Justice

normative engagement with it has been set back by at least four important worries.[4] First, the idea of alienation seems to presuppose a false essentialist picture of human beings as somehow having certain trans-historical, constant features that define them independently of how they shape and see themselves in their various social contexts. The Marxian picture, for example, involves claims about workers' existence in capitalism not coinciding with their human essence as capable of self-realization through freely chosen, creative, and cooperative productive activity. Secondly, it is not clear whether judgements about alienation are prudential judgements about the good life or moral judgements about right conduct and institutions, and how judgements of the two types should relate in the critique of alienation. Third, the critique of alienation might seem to lead to favouring paternalistic imposition of forms of life on those deemed to be alienated, and thus to disrespect their freedom to author their own lives. Finally, alienated work may not be problematic if the institutions underpinning it are democratically authorized. In this chapter, I seek a way to recast the critique of alienation that vindicates its importance for social and political philosophy and rebuts these charges. I do this by articulating discussion of alienation in terms of the ideas of positive freedom and human dignity. I argue that human dignity grounds a solidaristic requirement to support positive freedom, which enables people to counter alienation.

The chapter proceeds as follows. Section 2 offers a general framework to understand alienation—distinguishing its various definitional, explanatory, and normative dimensions. The Marxian discussion of alienated labour is a paradigmatic example (although the framework proposed can be extended to other topics). Section 3 explores the normative dimension of the critique of alienation by articulating it in terms of prudential and moral ideas of positive freedom regarding human flourishing and solidaristic empowerment. This articulation must be developed further to counter the four objections to normative engagement with alienation. This is done in Section 4 with the use of the Dignitarian Approach—the view that we have reason to organize social life in such a way that we respond appropriately to the valuable features of individual human beings that give rise to their dignity. In reflective equilibrium, the fact that the approach vindicates the critique of alienation means that it receives confirmation by illuminating a significant issue in social and

---

[4] There are also political causes, related to the failure of influential labour and leftist parties and movements to challenge Taylorist forms of organization of production. For a survey of this failure, of some exceptions, and a spirited call for focusing on the quality of work besides its duration and remuneration, see Coutrot (2018: 63). Another potential source of worry with the discourse of alienation is that a common target of it, the existence of market mechanisms, has come to be accepted by many leftists' views of a just society. I consider this point in Chapter 8.

The Critique of Alienation **209**

political philosophy, and also that the critique of alienation itself becomes normatively sharper. Section 5 concludes by addressing some changes in the organization of work in contemporary capitalism.

2. Alienation: An Analytical Framework

2.1 Basic definition

At a minimum, 'alienation' is used to refer to a state or process of separation or division—of lack of unity, harmony, or connectedness. This disunity occurs between a subject S and some object O in certain circumstances C. S is usually taken to be a person or an agent that is capable of self-knowledge and self-assessment. O, in turn, may be aspects of the natural world, other people, or the agent themselves. C, finally, may range over various material and social background factors.[5]

2.2 Subjective and objective alienation

Alienation may be subjective or objective. Judgements about subjective alienation make ineliminable reference to the attitudes of S (to S's desires, beliefs, or experiences). They say, for example, that S *feels* a lack of unity with O. Judgements about objective alienation, by contrast, say that there simply *is* a lack of unity between S and O, whether S takes that disunity to exist or not.[6] They say, for example, that S is at odds with themselves by failing to develop their talents.

As pointed out by Leopold,[7] this distinction generates four possible cases for consideration. There could be (a) subjective alienation and objective alienation; (b) no subjective alienation but objective alienation; (c) subjective alienation but no objective alienation; and (d) neither subjective nor objective alienation. In his discussion of modern society, Marx tends to focus on case

---

[5] I partly follow here the lucid analysis in Leopold (2016: sect. 1). My analysis differs in making explicit mention of circumstances C. Furthermore, it does not use 'problematic' when referring to the disunity stated in the basic definition, as I think that this obscures the distinction between descriptive and normative accounts, which I add as a separate point in my analysis. Although 'alienation' is often (perhaps typically?) used with normative intent, it is theoretically fruitful to make the distinction. Finally, I also distinguish between prudential and moral aspects of the normative dimension of alienation. I thank David Leopold for discussion on the moves made in this section.

[6] To the extent that the psychological life of S is part of what S is, subjective alienation is an instance of objective alienation: if S feels disunity with O, there is some disunity going on, at least at the level of psychological integration. But the distinction is important to capture cases in which S is alienated but fails to feel so, and when S's attitudes about themselves are inaccurate or fail to track independently true factual or normative considerations that apply to them.

[7] Leopold (2016: sect. 4).

210 Human Dignity and Social Justice

(a), in which workers fail to unfold their capacities for free and solidaristic cooperation and feel dissatisfied with such a condition. Hegel, in turn, tends to focus on (c), saying that agents fail to understand the reasonability of their predicament. Both Marx and Hegel yearn for a society in which (d) holds, but they construe the change leading to it differently, with Hegel seeing it mostly as a matter of change in self-understanding, and Marx as requiring also a change in material and social circumstances. Finally, case (b) has been explored by critical theorists from the Frankfurt School tradition, who are particularly attuned to scenarios in which agents fail to act autonomously and self-realize but happen to be rather content.

Let us consider in more detail Marx's account. He starts with objective alienation and explores the subjective responses to it. According to Marx, people are self-alienated when their actual condition is at odds with their human nature—whether they are aware of it or not.[8] Their actual condition is a set of activities in certain material and social circumstances, and their human nature is a set of capacities. In particular, Marx takes human beings to have certain capacities for activities that are freely chosen, self-conscious, creative, individually differentiated, sensuously sophisticated, and socially cooperative and beneficial. They face alienation when, and to the extent that the development and exercise of these capacities is frustrated. The paradigmatic case is alienated labour, which is productive activity in which workers:

(AL1) are dominated by others, and/or

(AL2) do not control (or even understand) the social process of production, its mechanisms, and results, and/or

(AL3) do not develop and exercise their creative powers and talents, and/or

(AL4) interact with others in ways that are not mutually supportive and cooperative, and/or

(AL5) do not count among the final aims of production the fulfilling of the needs of fellow human beings, and/or

(AL6) do not garner social appreciation or recognition.[9]

---

[8] Marx is most explicit about the links between alienation and human nature in his *Manuscripts of 1844*. Marx talks about a 'strife between existence and essence' (Marx 1978c: 84). He says that alienation arises in productive activity that features 'self-estrangement' (Ibid: 75), in which the worker 'is estranging himself from himself' (Ibid: 73). This activity 'does not belong to [the worker's] essential being' (Ibid: 74). This failure to be at one with oneself is sometimes presented as including a subjective experience in which the worker 'does not feel content but unhappy' and 'feels outside himself' (Ibid: 74). But this experience does not seem to be a necessary condition for alienation.

[9] This list tracks insights in Marx's overall discussion, but I do not present it as Marx's own list. For example, it is different from the canonical list in Marx (1978c: 71–7), which includes workers' alienation from the product of work, from working activity, from their species-being, and from others human beings. My list is more perspicuous, identifying items which are more clearly different and lie at the same level of analysis. Marx's canonical list is somewhat confused, I think. For example, alienation from others

The Critique of Alienation   **211**

According to Marx, wage workers are largely subject to the will of the capitalists that hire them. As owners of the means of production, capitalists have greater bargaining power, which they use to determine (much more so than workers do) the content and rhythm of production and the division of revenues resulting from the sale of what is produced. The activity of production is for the workers mostly of instrumental relevance (a means to get a salary to pay for subsistence and consumption goods). It is not intrinsically valuable because it does not offer a medium to cultivate and deploy their abilities. The instrumentalizing attitude is also paramount across the human relationships shaping economic life.[10] Other people are relevant mostly as means for self-advancement. There is a tendency to give only in order to receive, and to give as little as possible to get as much as possible. Economic competition is pervasive and ruthless, and production is primarily geared to profit maximization, not to need satisfaction. In this context, one is mostly appreciated by how much one owns and by the power one has over others, not by the intrinsic significance of what one produces and by the contribution it makes to the well-being of others. A social structure pushing people to live in this way generates alienation for everyone, including the oppressors—all are at odds with their inner tendencies towards freedom and cooperative sociality.

2.3 Descriptive and normative accounts of alienation

Descriptive claims about alienation report that there is disunity between S and O. Normative claims go further, adding that some disunities are worthy of criticism. Normative accounts of alienation assume, or explicitly put forward, views about the positive value of some instances of unity, and about what the components, form, and justification of the unity should be.[11]

includes aspects AL1, AL4, AL5, and AL6, which should be more sharply distinguished, alienation from one's species-being lies at a more general level than the other items and should not be listed on a par with them, and alienation from working activity seems to track all the items in my list. Notice that the list AL1-AL6 elaborates on the last four items in the list of interests I1–I5 mentioned in Chapter 1 (Section 3.2), and engages capacities in the basis of dignity (Section 2.1). This informs the dignitarian argument in 4.3 below.

[10] A society in which other persons only are relevant for us when they 'become a means for' our self-advancement is disparaged by Marx, and characterized as a terrain of 'mutual swindling and plundering' Marx (1978c: 101, 93).

[11] Some accounts of alienation seem to build the normative dimension into its very definition, saying that there is alienation if there is separation between S and O when there should be unity (Leopold 2016; Wood 2004: 3). I think it is better to capture the point these accounts try to make by saying that some (but not all) descriptions of alienation refer to cases of separation when there was, or there is some tendency for S and O to be together. This is different from saying, normatively, that S and O should be together. There is a difference between the 'should' of expectation or prediction and the 'should' of evaluation or obligation. The former is descriptive, the latter normative. Not every unity, however likely, is desirable.

212 Human Dignity and Social Justice

Some descriptive accounts also offer explanations of why the disunity between S and O exists. For example, Marx argues that facts about the background circumstances C help explain why workers are at odds with themselves and others as they produce. Marx highlights three important features of such circumstances: the property relations framing the control of productive forces, the orientation of production and consumption, and the level of technological development. There is alienation if the level of technological development is relatively low, the property relations are not egalitarian, and the orientation of production and consumption is predominantly instrumental and self-centred. In these circumstances, people tend to fight over scarce resources and to try to subordinate each other, and many people spend much of their time in activities which do not afford them intrinsic satisfaction. In turn, alienation is reduced as technological developments, coupled with more egalitarian relations of production and non-instrumental orientations, allow people to organize their production and consumption in ways that enable all to steer their own lives and flourish. Marx's contrast between a future socialist society and previous class-divided and technologically less developed societies coincides with his contrast between overcoming and undergoing systematic alienation.[12]

2.4 Prudential and moral variants of normative accounts

Normative accounts may be of at least two kinds: prudential and moral. Alienation may be criticized on prudential terms by saying that a lack of unity between S and O is a strike against S's well-being. By contrast, moral criticisms say that the disunity involves wrongdoing, that S is treated by other agents (and perhaps even by S themselves) in ways that contravene duties which are morally justified. An important question is whether, and if so how, prudential and moral accounts of alienation are related—a topic I will address later in the chapter.

There is controversy as to whether Marx has substantive views about ethics and justice, and I will not rehearse it here. He does make several normatively coloured statements about alienation and other problems in capitalism, and I interpret them, for the purposes of this chapter, as involving substantive

---

[12] Marx is sometimes interpreted as holding that alienation in capitalist societies is especially acute. But this interpretation would be false if it implies that for Marx the alienation in earlier societies was not great. The distinctive acuteness is a function of the fact that capitalism, thanks to its enormous technological development, makes feasible new forms of production featuring deep forms of self-determination and self-realization while, at the same time, frustrating their instantiation. I thank Jan Kandiyali for discussion on this point.

The Critique of Alienation **213**

prudential and moral ideas.[13] We can, in particular, identify the important proposal that activities displaying self-determination and self-realization are the positive flipside of self-alienation. There is *self-determination* when, and to the extent that, agents control their activities (choosing, understanding, and directing them). And there is *self-realization* when, and to the extent that, in their activities, agents actualize themselves by cultivating and employing their various talents and cooperative skills, and externalize themselves by producing objects others appreciate.[14]

These ideas are significant prudentially, as they identify aspects of human well-being. They are also of moral relevance if a just society requires fostering people's access to the conditions of their well-being. Thus, self-determination and self-realization would arguably be unleashed in a better (socialist) society. Thanks to extensive technological advancement and the rational organization of the economy, the 'realm of necessity' and the corresponding indispensable but onerous toil to secure subsistence would be circumscribed, and everyone would reach also, and expand, a 'realm of freedom' in which 'the development of human powers as an end in itself' unfolds.[15] This realm of freedom would feature non-alienated labour. Labour can be 'repulsive' when it is '*externally forced labour*', and this is generally the case with 'slave-labour, serf-labour, and wage-labour'. But it can also be 'attractive'. It can be a medium for the individual's 'self-realization' and 'real freedom'.[16] Marx depicts an advanced socialist society as one in which people honour the slogan 'from each according to his ability, to each according to his need', and take non-alienated labour involving the 'all-round development of the individual' as a 'prime want'.[17] Marx indeed invokes the ideal of 'the development of the rich individuality which is all-sided in its production as in its consumption',[18] and envisions a 'higher form of society in which the full and free development of every individual forms the ruling principle'.[19]

---

[13] For example, Marx (1990: 798–9) condemns capitalism as involving alienation, torment, exploitation, and domination of labourers. For a masterful critical survey of the interpretive debates, see Geras (1989). For a recent discussion of Marx and alienation, see Kandiyali (2020).

[14] This statement partly draws on Elster (1986: ch.3) and Schacht (1970: ch.3). Elster construes self-realization (including self-actualization and self-externalization) and autonomy as the positive ideals underlying the critique of alienation. And Schacht characterizes Marx's view of human nature as focusing on capacities for activities involving individuality, sociality, and cultivated sensuousness. My definitions of 'self-determination' and 'self-realization' are stipulative. We could construe self-realization more broadly to include self-determination as a sub-dimension. But using the terms as I propose is fruitful for identifying different kinds of alienation.

[15] Marx (1991: 958–9).

[16] Marx (1973: 611).

[17] Marx (1978i: 531). See Chapter 3 on the Abilities/Needs Principle for further discussion.

[18] Marx (1973: 325).

[19] Marx (1990: 739).

214 Human Dignity and Social Justice

2.5 Dynamic patterns

Alienation is illuminated by a dynamic account of feasibility of the kind offered in Chapter 4. Thus, to complete our analytical framework, let us note that claims about alienation often take a dynamic form, to illuminate temporally extended processes. These processes often are (but need not always be) cast in a positive normative light, as involving progress. A common pattern in Hegelian and Marxian discussions includes the stages of undifferentiated unity, differentiated disunity, and differentiated unity.[20] Thus, for Marx, primitive communism displays communal relations, but also a lack of development of each person's individuality. Class-societies, and in particular capitalism, feature some assertion of individuality, but in ways that work to the detriment of communal relationships. The developed communist society of the future would display both individuality and community. The second stage in this process includes individuals' alienation from others (and from themselves as social beings), but it has a progressive significance in that it ushers into the emergence of personal differentiation, which is to be retained (and developed further) in the final, fully non-alienated stage. This final stage is not a mere return to the initial one, as in the initial stage individuals' personal development is stunted, but a richer form of sociality that involves greater, and more harmonious, unfolding of both individuality and community.

Another dynamic pattern focuses on personal (or collective) development in which agents move from a state of self-identification in which they are satisfied with their condition to a state of strife in which they feel at odds with it, to culminate in a third, new state of re-identification in which satisfaction appears again but as a result of changes in the agent or/and their circumstances. Interestingly, the overcoming of states of alienation often passes through subjective alienation. This is because only in these situations do agents engage in a reflective appraisal of their current configuration as being at odds with some alternative, better configuration they come to envisage. In exclusively objective alienation, the conflict is a more indeterminate, and psychologically not yet potent one, between their current condition and a disjunction of possible alternative paths that would fulfil the relevant normative criteria. Practically, the path from objective alienation to its overcoming would sometimes pass through stages in which subjective alienation arises and is processed.

An important theme from Marx concerns the relation between the alienated agents and their material and social circumstances. When agents are

---

[20] Cohen, 'The Dialectic of Labour in Marx', in Cohen (1988: 183–208).

The Critique of Alienation   **215**

alienated from themselves, there is the question of how they express their inner tendencies and the ideals linked to them. One possibility, which Marx takes to be common in religion, liberal politics, and capitalist economies, is to project the realization of their ideals onto some entities such as God,[21] the state or the political community,[22] and money or capital.[23] These entities are seen as embodying the ideals. In a mental act of sublimation, agents seek a substitute, indirect self-determination or self-realization by attaching themselves to those entities. This operation is indirect and a substitute, because it does not feature the agents directly enacting in themselves the fulfilment of the ideals they cherish. Marx favours, instead, a direct fulfilment of the ideals in people's daily lives. This requires changing the material and social circumstances so as to make the fulfilment more feasible. So, for example, if agents cherish self-determination and solidarity rather than hierarchy and cutthroat competition, then they would do well to change their economic systems to dissolve class structures, and increase material production to make competition for scarce resources less pressing and nasty. The central pattern in this discussion is that ideals tend to find expression in some way or other—they must find a medium of expression because they are central to people's motivational profiles—and when they do not find direct expression in the life of the agents due to hostile circumstances, the agents either change these circumstances to make them amenable to fulfilling the ideals in their daily lives, or, failing to do that, they construct a separate plane in which the ideals play out in ersatz form.

A significant, related point is that the dynamic duty to overcome alienation is for Marx a practical not merely a theoretical one. It is not a matter of simply concocting a different description of ourselves, but of changing the social and material circumstances that make alienated activity a widespread condition.[24] An interesting question here is how descriptive and normative accounts of alienation might interact. One important, dynamic relation is this. If the normative account is based on the value of certain human capacities, and if people have at least some tendencies to try to develop and exercise them, then the content of the normative account may help identify facts that contribute to explain, or predict, or at least increase the feasibility of, changes of social circumstances in the direction of greater opportunities for

---

[21] Marx (1978b: 53–4).

[22] Marx (1978a: 32–46).

[23] Marx (1978c: 101–5; 1990: 163–77). As Cohen (2001: 128) argues, recurrent in Marx's discussion of alienation and fetishism is the 'theme that division leads to duplication': when people are divided within or between themselves, they produce a surrogate, illusory domain in which integration appears (the state, religion, the market economy).

[24] Marx (1978c: 89). Compare Marx's (1978d: 145) famous Thesis XI: '[P]hilosophers have only *interpreted* the world, in various ways; the point, however, is to *change* it'.

216 Human Dignity and Social Justice

self-determination and self-realization. Normative advocacy may also partially affect the change. It would call people to appreciate certain valuable features of themselves, and to seize the tendencies to unfold them in decisive and transformative ways.

3. Human Flourishing and Freedom

The foregoing, brief discussion of Marx was meant to provide a salient example of alienation critique. My objective now is to articulate some core normative features of this kind of critique and its relation to freedom. The next section addresses four objections to which it is vulnerable by deploying the Dignitarian Approach.

3.1 The normative dimension of alienation

Are all instances of alienation bad or wrong? Maybe not. In the remainder of this chapter I develop a *normative* rather than descriptive account of alienation (that is, I am concerned with instances of 'not at oneness' that are bad or wrong). To identify normatively problematic cases of alienation, prudential and moral considerations must be introduced. Sections 3.2 and 3.3 do that. My discussion will focus on self-alienation—i.e. on cases in which when S is at odds with O, O is some aspect of themselves. But before proceeding, it is important to insist that descriptive and normative claims about alienation are indeed different, although they overlap in interesting ways.

The distinction is evident if we notice that there are cases in which a person may be alienated on account of features of themselves which, although they endorse or cherish, they have reason not to so endorse or cherish. A despot who has been removed from their position of power may feel at a loss in their new life, noticing that they cannot lord it over others anymore. But the condition of domination is not one to be celebrated, and the persons moving away from it should not regret its end. Or consider a boss who feels estranged with their new daily life in their firm after regulations have been put in place limiting heretofore common practices of harassment of workers. Not every instance of alienation is clearly bad or a mark of wrong-doing.[25]

---

[25] True, there may still be a regrettable feature in these cases, viz. that there is insufficient psychological integration. In this way, when there is descriptive subjective alienation, there often is some normatively problematic alienation. Thus, the claim that not every instance of alienation is bad should be qualified. But the key focus of the examples is on whether the *specific* disunity (rather than the fact of disunity just as such) is problematic. There is a difference between saying that S feels at odds with a particular O and saying that it is undesirable that S be at odds with that particular O. I thank Arash Abizadeh for discussion on these matters.

On the other hand, the sources of alienation and of the normative critique of it can overlap. People may feel alienated in contexts of domination. If they are the dominator, they may fail to be at one with themselves as beings with capacities for respectful and solidaristic cooperation with others—such capacities are neglected, and the social relationships their development and exercise would enable are missed. If they are the dominated, they may fail to be at one with themselves as beings with capacities for self-determination—such capacities are crushed as they are under the thumb of others. In these cases, a feeling of alienation is in fact a symptom that people understand that they should live on better terms with each other. Importantly, it is also a hint that they could do so. Alienation here marks both a problem and a motivational resource to overcome it (a point first broached in Section 2.5, and to be revisited in 3.2 and 4.7).

The overlap just mentioned is important for a moral and political conception that seeks not only to point out what is good or bad, and what is right or wrong. If that conception also wants to inform projects for better forms of social life which are feasible, then the overlap helps because it marks springs for ameliorative action.

3.2 Human flourishing and the prudential critique of alienation

A descriptive claim about self-alienation simply says that there is a lack of successful self-identification on the part of some agent (some deficit in their sense of identity). Normative claims go further, saying that what is lacking is a self-identification that is *appropriate*. I articulate these claims more specifically, by saying that alienated agents fail to be at one with themselves as self-determining and self-realizing persons. I thus argue for the presence of links between substantive values of self-identity, self-determination, and self-realization (with all three being relevant for well-being as human flourishing).

So, to state this position in more detail, I suggest that alienation contrasts with *successful and appropriate self-identification as a form of human flourishing*. Here are the components of the ideal involved.

- *Human flourishing* consists in conditions in which human individuals develop and exercise their valuable capacities in some activities. I take flourishing to be at least part of what constitutes people's well-being (of what has non-instrumental prudential value for them). (A caveat: I use the common phrase 'human flourishing' here, but see 4.2 below for my considered view that there is no need to refer to what is typically 'human',

218 Human Dignity and Social Justice

that what matters fundamentally is individuals' flourishing given their own valuable features.)

- The capacities engaged in human flourishing can be grouped into two categories. The first, concerning *self-determination*, involves the capacities underpinning autonomy, such as the capacities for technical, prudential, and moral judgement and choice. I understand autonomy here in a broad sense, to range over people's determination of their acts, the motives on which they act, and the consequences of their acts.[26] The second category, which concerns *self-realization*, involves capacities regarding creativity, social cooperation, knowledge, pleasure, and aesthetic appreciation.
- Self-determination and self-realization are related but also different. In particular, self-determination should (and thus in fact might or might not) be used to foster self-realization. When people determine themselves, they ask how they have reason to live, and 'pursuing self-realization' is a fitting answer.
- *Successful self-identification* refers to mental processes and states in which people achieve a satisfying, positive sense of their own predicament. Self-identification is *appropriate* when it tracks the development and exercise of one's valuable capacities—i.e. one's flourishing. Here the ability to self-identify is an unfolding of the valuable capacity of self-awareness as it combines with the other capacities mentioned above. It is thus relevant to well-being.[27] But it operates at a higher level than self-determination and self-realization. Its roles are to ascertain whether the latter are indeed at play, and to spur their operation. (It is not redundant, however—a life involving successful and appropriate self-identification is better than another in which there is the same level of self-determination and self-realization but in which the person can but does not identify with these achievements.[28])
- Appropriate self-identification does not require the total or complete development and exercise of one's capacities. Only valuable capacities are included in the relevant list. Furthermore, it is infeasible to fully

---

[26] On various dimensions of autonomy, see Mackenzie (2014).

[27] It is important to people to address the question 'Who am I?' The development and exercise of other capacities is to be pursued in such a way that it fits within an overall project of self. This project need not be fixed once and for all, and can be fairly complex, but it matters to people that there is some such project (or perhaps projects), which features some level of complexity and coherence.

[28] I add that the attitude involved in self-identification is not only cognitive but also conative. Through it people see themselves in a way that carries positive emotions and feelings of appreciation, elation, joy, etc. Someone who displays the cognitive but not the conative component is missing something important for their well-being. I thank Serena Olsaretti for discussion on this point.

The Critique of Alienation   **219**

develop and exercise all capacities.[29] To be plausible, the Marxian ideal of workers' self-determination and self-realization has to be understood with these limitations in mind. However, I take the ideal of appropriate self-identification to require the pursuit of some maximal overall schedule of self-determination and self-realization in which the agent achieves a combination of them that delivers as much overall flourishing as it is feasible and is not defeated by other, more weighty considerations, such as some moral constraints.[30] Of course, there can be several such schedules available to an agent to choose from (such as different work activities).

On this account, the truth conditions for self-alienation can be stated as follows. A person S is self-alienated if and only if, and to the extent that, (i) S is capable of self-awareness and self-identification; (ii) S has capacities relevant for self-determination and self-realization; (iii) either S does not successfully self-identify or does self-identify successfully but not appropriately (due to actual deficiencies regarding the development and exercise of the capacities in (ii), or epistemic mistakes about noticing these deficiencies). People facing working conditions including AL1–AL6 (see 2.2), for example, do not achieve self-determination and self-realization because they spend most of their waking hours doing what others dictate them to do, and what they do does not allow them to adequately cultivate and express their talents. These people will likely feel somewhat frustrated with this predicament, but even if they did not, they should recognize that it is not fully satisfactory.

Some important caveats are in order. The list of valuable capacities given above is not meant to be exhaustive. Furthermore, I do not assume that human flourishing is all that human well-being involves (although this could be argued for). Finally, I do not assume that self-identification must be present for there to be human flourishing. If some people are unable to self-identify, but have other valuable capacities, they could have human flourishing regarding these other capacities even if they do not accompany it with self-identification. Self-alienation is a specific failure to achieve human flourishing.

The link to ameliorative action may not be readily apparent if the alienation that occurs is objective but not subjective, i.e. if S does not develop and exercise their valuable capacities but is not worried about it. To use an apt phrase by Elster, they do not experience a sense of a lack of meaning but,

---

[29] See on this point Elster (1986: 43–4).
[30] Here I differ from Elster's account in that I use an objective rather than a hedonistic account of prudential value, and I highlight the issue of self-identification.

220 Human Dignity and Social Justice

instead, display a lack of a sense of meaning.[31] We could add here that, in some such cases, there is a presence of a sense of meaning that is mistaken or problematic—as when people identify with what they should not identify with, besides not noticing the failure to pursue projects they should pursue. Now, not experiencing subjective alienation in a situation where there is objective alienation is one of the first things that critical reflection and debate should address. The critic sometimes has the role of helping people (themselves or others) to come to experience subjective alienation, as a step in their becoming active agents in their amelioration. This critique involves an operation of *de-identification* with respect to conditions that are objectively alienating (and thus the generation of a moment of subjective alienation), and an act of *re-identification* with respect to prospective conditions which are objectively not alienating (and thus the generation of a project whose fulfilment would yield an appropriate subjective sense of self-identification).

3.3 Freedom and the moral critique of alienation

The moral appraisal of alienation and its opposites, including self-determination and self-realization, can be approached in terms of the idea of positive freedom.

Non-alienation may be characterized as a *capability* to live in certain ways or as the *functionings* resulting from the *exercise* of this capability.[32] Agents avoid alienation on the first characterization to the extent that it is feasible for them to flourish—i.e. to the extent that they would engage in activities featuring self-determination and self-realization, and achieve successful self-identification related to that engagement, if they tried (and could try). In contrast, as an exercise notion, non-alienation refers to a condition in which agents successfully pursue the forms of life they have capabilities for. The more they choose this pursuit, and the more they succeed, the more they enjoy a non-alienated condition. Opportunities for, and achievement of non-alienation should not be conflated. For example, we cannot infer from

---

[31] Elster (1986: 41).

[32] I follow here the 'capability approach'. A person's functionings are certain ways of being and doing. A person's capabilities are their ability to engage in such functionings. Capabilities are a form of substantive or real freedom. Sen (2009: 231–4); Nussbaum (2011: 20–5). Of course, not all capabilities and functionings are valuable. Some are unimportant and others should be disvalued. Having enough to eat is valuable for all, being able to brush your teeth in five rather than in six minutes is indifferent for most people, and being extremely effective at torturing others should be disvalued. As a normative perspective, the capability approach focuses on capabilities and functionings agents have reason to value. As the main focus for social justice, Nussbaum helpfully suggests the idea of 'combined capabilities', which are made up of certain developed internal capacities and surrounding material and social conditions (such as opportunities) enabling their exercise. For more on the capability approach and its link to the dignitarian perspective, see Chapters 3 and 7. The ideas of 'real freedom' or 'effective freedom' are common amongst socialists. See Van Parijs (1995: 21–4); Arnold (2016: sect. 6); and Gilabert and O'Neill (2019: sect. 3).

The Critique of Alienation **221**

the fact that two individuals enjoy equivalent levels of achievement that that they have equivalent opportunity sets.[33]

As we saw, non-alienation can feature as a prudential ideal of the good life. But it can also feature in a moral ideal regarding right conduct. In the latter case, the focus is on what duties people have, on what forms of treatment they owe each other (and perhaps also themselves). A specific type of moral requirements concerns *social justice*, and states the rights people have against each other in their social life. Non-alienation is indeed significant in both normative dimensions. I may have prudential reason to determine the conditions of my own life, and to shape it so that I achieve self-realization. But I may also have reason to do my part in securing that everyone has the capability to do these things. Some of these reasons may correlate with rights implemented in the institutional structure of a political and economic system.

The two dimensions can be combined in substantive views of justice. The prudential value of non-alienation can inform part of the metric (or the currency) for the articulation of the content of moral requirements. Thus, a conception of justice could say that we have duties not to deprive, and also to further, each person's prospects for a non-alienated life by securing that real opportunities to work in self-determining and self-realizing ways are available to them in the economic system. Given the critical importance of self-determination—both as a prudential and as a moral value—it is likely that the best view of justice will predominantly focus on requiring the generation of capabilities to enjoy flourishing lives rather than final outcomes in which such lives are lived. It should be up to each agent to exercise their capabilities—to decide whether, and how, they shape the specific contents of their lives. What is morally obligatory is to make sure (to the extent that it is feasible and reasonable to demand) that each is given real opportunities to do so.

The ideals of self-identification, self-determination, and self-realization can be stated as favouring certain forms of *positive freedom*. As I see it, a positive freedom to x can indeed be defined as the power or capability to x. Importantly, negative freedom (as absence of interference by others in one's choices and acts) might contribute to, but does not exhaust the conditions of, overall positive freedom. Interference by others may depress your capability set by removing options, or by hampering your pursuit of some existing options. But your capability set may be limited by other facts—such as your

---

[33] This might be missed by some empirical studies on alienation. Thus, perhaps the kind of data referred to in note 3 is insufficient. Perhaps some workers are less satisfied with their activities than others but have greater opportunities to engage in alternative, more satisfying work: they have assets and skills that allow them to more easily quit their current job and get another. I thank Tom Parr for discussion on this point. See also Section 4.6 on unequal distribution of opportunity sets and trade-offs.

222 Human Dignity and Social Justice

psychological difficulties and a lack of external resources—which others could ameliorate but choose not to. This is why the social support for self-identification, self-determination, and self-realization would only be fully envisioned through an ideal that yields both negative duties to refrain from harmful interference and positive duties to provide help. I think that the following ideal fits the bill:

Solidaristic Empowerment

We should support people in their pursuit of a flourishing life by implementing both negative duties not to destroy or block their valuable capacities and positive duties to protect and facilitate their development and exercise of these capacities.

Solidaristic Empowerment requires negative freedom, but only as part of the broader call for supporting the positive freedom of people to shape and pursue life prospects which are valuable.[34]

An important question regarding positive and negative freedom is whether some forms of negative freedom may justifiably be limited in order to increase positive freedom. For example, may the fostering of capabilities for self-determination and self-realization justify interference with some choices and acts regarding the control and use of external resources such as productive assets? On the account I propose here, the answer is yes.[35] Some claims regarding negative freedom can be defeated, or constrained, when this is necessary or highly important for securing appropriate levels of positive freedom for all. This, at any rate, is what the ideal of Solidaristic Empowerment that I propose suggests. This ideal also illuminates the Marxian picture discussed in Section 2. Marx's critique of capitalism, and his view of socialism, are often couched by reference to the idea of freedom. Capitalism is seen as involving lack of sufficient opportunities for workers to develop and exercise their capacities in spontaneous activity which is an end in itself (rather than a mere means to gain subsistence) and as featuring the domination of workers by capitalists at the workplace and in other social spheres. By contrast, an envisioned future socialist society of 'freely associated producers' is depicted as lifting these constraints. Socialism would give everyone (and not only, as in capitalism, a ruling minority) access to 'real freedom' through effective opportunities for self-realization and through novel forms of organization of production set on workers' own terms rather than on the dictates imposed by

---

[34] For the view that the value of negative freedom is parasitic on the value of positive freedom, see Raz (1986: 409–10).

[35] Property rights over external resources also restrict the negative liberty of people who do not own the resources (e.g. impoverished workers may be interfered with if they forage in the land a landlord controls). Cohen (2011: chs. 7–8).

The Critique of Alienation   223

a class that oppresses and exploits them. This picture includes not only limits to interference but also the social empowerment of each individual.[36]

The moral critique of alienation targets forms of alienation that involve failure to honour Solidaristic Empowerment. These are cases of morally problematic lack of freedom (or unfreedom) in which we can observe:

(PLF1) obstacles to positive freedom (*power or capability deficit condition*),

(PLF2) which are feasible to remove or reduce through human action and social institutions (*feasibility of change condition*),

(PLF3) and which some agents have reason to so remove or reduce (*desirability of change condition*).

Two comments on this characterization. Notice, first, that in (PLF1) and (PLF2), the obstacles to power or capability need not be, or result from, coercive or other forms of intentional action by others. They could be the unintended consequence of impersonal factors, such as natural processes, or the aggregation of many agents' acts, or institutions. What is crucial is that the obstacles can be changed socially. Second, in (PLF2) and (PLF3), the removal or reduction of obstacles may involve positive obligations besides negative ones. The obstacle to capability an agent suffers—their lack of empowerment—may result from the wrongful imposition of it by other agents, or have other causes but remain in place because other agents wrongfully refrain from acting to remove them when they could do so at reasonable cost. This view is controversial, of course (and I return to it in Section 4). But the affirmation of positive duties is indeed a crucial component of a solidaristic perspective. It is common to say that lack of freedom is a moral or political issue only when it reflects a social problem rather than merely being a case of inability.[37] On the account presented here, disempowerment is a social problem not only if the social context features some agents reducing the power of others, but also when it displays some agents failing to help others keep or develop their power. Additionally, the acts by other

---

[36] '[O]nly in the community ... is personal freedom possible' Marx (1978e: 197).

[37] A common worry about positive freedom accounts is that they fail to distinguish between unfreedom and mere inability: the former, unlike the latter, is said to entail the presence of normatively problematic social constraints. A powerful reply, offered by Schmidt (2016), is to introduce a new category of 'unfreedom'. Even if S's freedom to do something A is understood in the positive sense, as S's ability to do A, not every case of S's lack of freedom to do A—not every inability of S to do A—involves S's unfreedom to do so. The latter requires that the constraints on freedom/ability be constraints on a freedom/ability which would feature in an ideal distribution of freedoms/abilities, and for which other agents can be held responsible (through interference or failure to aid). An alternative way to make this point—which I pursue with conditions (PLF2) and (PLF3)—is to distinguish between wrongful and non-wrongful deficits of positive freedom (or lack of capability or empowerment).

224 Human Dignity and Social Justice

agents generating the change may be individual or collective, be punctual or involve an extended process, and be direct or indirect (through the change of institutions, for example).

4. Dignity

I will now address four objections that are commonly directed at the critique of alienation (understood as the alienation-based critique of capitalism and other social arrangements). They concern the risks of an essentialist view, a mishandling of the distinction between the good and the right, the risk of paternalistic impositions, and the significance of democratic authorization. Responding to these objections is important in its own right, and also enables us to develop further and sharpen the account of the critique of alienation provided so far.

4.1 The Dignitarian Approach

To answer the objections, I suggest that we develop the critique of alienation in terms of the Dignitarian Approach proposed in this book:

Dignitarian Approach
We have reason to organize social life in such a way that we respond appropriately to the valuable features of individuals that give rise to their dignity.

Let us recall briefly some of the main points in this approach.[38] *Dignity* is at the most fundamental level a non-conventional normative status of persons such that certain forms of respect and concern are owed to them. (The status is non-conventional in the sense that people have it independently of whether they are actually taken to have it in the society in which they live.) *Dignitarian norms* specify the appropriate treatment—the forms of respect and concern—that responding to such *status-dignity* requires. When people are treated in accordance to these norms, they enjoy *condition-dignity*. Now, people have status-dignity because of certain valuable capacities, which constitute *the basis of dignity*. The ideal of Solidaristic Empowerment, discussed above, can be used, and framed, as a device to render the Dignitarian Approach more determinate. It can be deployed to state dignitarian norms—the various duties not to undermine, and positive duties to facilitate, people's pursuit

---

[38] One purpose of this chapter is to further develop and prove the fruitfulness of the Dignitarian Approach. I do not claim, however, that no other normative framework could be similarly useful to account for alienation and freedom.

The Critique of Alienation   225

of a flourishing life in which they develop and exercise the valuable capacities *at the basis of their dignity*. The Dignitarian Approach, via Solidaristic Empowerment, thus requires a form of support for positive freedom.

People are alienated to the extent that they fail to be at one with themselves in their life activities. As we saw, a plausible way to explain alienation is to show that it involves deficits in people's ability to develop and exercise their capacities in activities featuring self-determination and self-realization. Now, when the relevant capacities are amongst the valuable capacities that give rise to status-dignity, and their development and exercise can be supported by others at reasonable cost, Solidaristic Empowerment calls for such a support, and its neglect wrongfully contributes to alienation.[39] An important case of alienation is the predicament of workers in capitalist societies. The critical point here is that the capitalist economy is organized in such a way that in it (foreseeably and avoidably) workers are insufficiently empowered to develop and exercise valuable capacities regarding practical reasoning and choice, creativity, knowledge, cooperation, and socially beneficial contribution, among others. Accounts of freedom focused only on non-interference fail to fully capture what is wrong with the alienation of labour. Alienation involves additional deficits of positive freedom—a hampering of people's power to live flourishing lives in which they develop and exercise their valuable capacities. Since the dignitarian and solidaristic perspective outlined in this chapter is well-positioned to explain concerns about positive freedom, it can also provide a normative basis for the critique of the alienation of workers in capitalism. According to Marx, for example, to move beyond the predicament in which workers are unable to realize their potential, radical changes are needed. It is not enough to raise wages. This 'would not conquer either for the worker or for labour their human status and dignity'.[40] Overcoming workers' alienation would only be achieved in a new society that lifts the constraints on positive freedom imposed by material scarcity and class division. This society would unleash self-determination and self-realization in production.[41]

4.2 Problematic essentialism?

The Dignitarian Approach provides a unified and powerful basis to answer the four typical worries about normative engagement with the topic of alienation. The first objection runs as follows. We characterized alienation

---

[39] Situations like this, in which applying dignitarian norms is both feasible and called for, are part of what I call the *circumstances of dignity*.

[40] Marx (1978c: 80).

[41] It would also feature a more sophisticated and appreciative sensibility and enjoyment in consumption. Ibid: e.g., 87–9.

226 Human Dignity and Social Justice

as a deficit of positive freedom. More specifically, we discussed deficits in people's self-identification regarding their self-determination and self-realization. Now, this discussion seemed to presuppose the view that there is a human essence or nature, a certain set of invariant capacities that people have. But views of freedom (and alienation) tied to the power to develop and exercise these capacities is problematic, for three reasons. (a) First, it is not clear that there is a human essence. If we look hard at the facts, what we encounter is great variation (biological, historical, and individual). For any allegedly universal feature, there are human beings who do not exhibit it. (b) Even if there were an essence, it would be explanatorily inert. The features would be too general to account for important cases of freedom or alienation. (c) Finally, essentialist views threaten the 'interpretive sovereignty' of reflective agents. For example, they push them to fit substantive, objective moulds of well-being which may not be appropriate for them. It would be better to deploy a procedural, formalist account of positive freedom (and self-alienation) which focuses not on *what* agents identify themselves with, but on *how* they do so.[42]

These worries can be answered. Regarding (a), notice first that a picture of human nature can be quite broad and flexible. It can state natural features of human beings which allow for diverse specific developments. We can distinguish, within the space of capacities and needs, between more or less abstract and specific instances. A general capacity, and need, for creative production, for example, can be unfolded in different ways in different contexts by different people. One can produce different objects, for different consumers, in different settings. The Marxian view precisely affirms this variation, demanding opportunities for individuals to chart their own singular projects of self-actualization and self-externalization. Successful appropriate self-identification does not entail fixation. Since agents are dynamic in the development and exercise of their capacities, they are dynamic in their self-identification. Continuity of self is consistent with diversity of its configurations. So long as change in configuration involves self-determination and self-realization, it need not carry alienation. Most importantly, however (and quite independently of Marx's views), the dignitarian approach to freedom does not require believing that there is a uniform human essence or nature. We can do without the idea of human nature and just rely on a disjunctive list of valuable capacities at the basis of dignity. We can even decide to talk about individuals' flourishing without having to add that it is *human*

---

[42] These worries are raised, e.g., in Jaeggi (2014: 27–35). (The phrase 'interpretive sovereignty' is used in Jaeggi's discussion.)

The Critique of Alienation   227

flourishing. As explained in Chapter 1, people have status-dignity whenever they have some of the capacities in the list, and they enjoy condition-dignity when these capacities are given appropriate responses. What the freedom of an individual S requires is that S be capable to develop and exercise the valuable capacities that S has, to whatever extent this is feasible and reasonable (whether these capacities are shared with every other human individual or not).[43]

Turning to (b), it is worth noting that being able to refer to relatively general valuable features of human beings (even if there is no human essence) may be desirable.[44] This reference allows us to gain distance from existing practices and conventions, and to criticize them as unreasonable because of failing to properly respond to something that is normatively more basic and important. Second, it helps formulate significant norms of solidaristic empowerment with expansive scope, such as human rights.[45] It also helps form judgements about historical change as involving progress or retrogression. Third, reference to relatively general features (valuable and not) helps us to develop historical explanations. We can identify relatively constant factors that operate in different ways in different contexts, to produce certain social outcomes. Perhaps the capacities and needs regarding non-alienated labour are an example of this. They may be the basis of robust *tendencies*. Fourth, these tendencies may even be relevant politically, in the present, to understand the conditions of feasibility of proposals for social change promoting their expression. The possibility of, and the hopes in, the critique of alienation lie in the fact that it seizes and unleashes valuable capacities and tendencies that seem deep and widespread. The dignitarian approach to human flourishing and solidaristic empowerment, and empirical research tracking the

---

[43] This allows us to address another worry about essentialism: (d) the risk of committing the naturalistic fallacy—in this case, the invalid inference from judgements about what people are like to judgements about what people should be like. Saying that alienation is normatively problematic because it features deficits of development or exercise of capacities that people have would involve the fallacy. But the Dignitarian Approach avoids it. It does not rely only on descriptive reports about existing capacities. It also deploys evaluative judgements to identify *valuable* capacities. For a fuller discussion of the problems of reliance on a picture of human essence, see Gilabert (2022).

[44] The following points are discussed in detail in Gilabert (2022: sect. 3.4).

[45] Even if he is right that Marx (unlike Hegel) paid insufficient attention to associative forms of self-identification, Cohen (2001: 354) overshoots the mark when he says that 'Marxist universalism suffers from the abstractness of the Enlightened universalism criticized by Hegel'. We can *both* relate to each other as members of specific associations and more generally as fellow human beings. Human identity can and should exist alongside, and be seen as normatively constraining, particular associative identities. Think about the moral and political culture of human rights. When someone in Canada campaigns against the sweatshop conditions in Bangladesh's factories, or against the mistreatment of refugees in the United States, they can meaningfully criticize the fact that a *fellow human being* is being unduly subject to hardship. They do not need to qualify this by reference to any other kind of fellowship. The cosmopolitan solidarity articulated by Enlightened universalism is a moral achievement worth holding on to, even if it has to be reformulated to take social embodiment seriously. Acknowledging good critical points made by Hegel should not make us forget other good points made by Kant.

228 Human Dignity and Social Justice

incidence of the features it zeroes in, can capture these points without the problems of essentialism.

Finally, regarding (c), I have three replies. The first is that the objection seems to presuppose an essentialism of sorts when it invokes the interpretive sovereignty of reflective agents. If the criterion of successful and appropriate self-identification is reflective acceptance by that agent, then the existence of such an agent, and the value of their capacities of self-assessment, are assumed. Second, a merely formal criterion of appropriate self-identification—if it aims at providing a test that is determinative rather than merely evidentiary or epistemic—faces a version of the traditional Euthyphro question: Is a configuration of myself good (or right) because I endorse it, or do I (or should I) endorse it because it is good (or right)? The reflective agent either relies on reasons for their judgement or they do not. If they do not, then their verdict is arbitrary and lacks normative force. If they do, then the reasons provide an external, substantive, and objective standard whose normativity is not reducible to the agent's attitudes. The approach faces the familiar problems of desire-satisfaction theories of the good and cultural relativist and conventionalist theories of the right. The problems are not dissolved by saying that agents' endorsement should be informed and reasoned—as the significance of these qualifications is in part precisely to alert the reflective agents to reasons they do not themselves construct.[46]

Third, and most importantly, the Dignitarian Approach can acknowledge the importance of the reflective agent's stance while avoiding both problematic forms of essentialism and a relapse into arbitrariness or subjectivism. The reflective agent has crucial epistemic and constructive roles (as well as decisional ones—see 4.4 below) even if the normative assessments they engage in track substantive, objective reasons. So, S may come to reject a configuration of themselves as F and envision and pursue an alternative one as G. Both F and G may be social or personal constructions, but their assessment by S relies in part on their search and recognition of reasons which are not themselves constructed. The latter can involve appropriate responses of concern and respect for the valuable capacities at the basis of the dignity of S (or other people). Thus, a worker may quit a job in a standard capitalist firm and join a cooperative, or advocate for societal opportunities for this kind of change. In justification, the worker can invoke the importance of being able to enjoy self-determination and self-realization at work, and explain that, in

---

[46] It could be objected that this 'qualified subjectivism' (Jaeggi's phrase) merely helps the agent gather information about how to implement their ground projects. But the latter need themselves to be justified. It is better to endorse a qualified objectivism instead, admitting external dignitarian reasons while allowing plenty of flexibility for the agent to chart projects honouring them in chosen ways.

The Critique of Alienation **229**

the relevant circumstances, cooperatives do better than standard capitalist firms in catering for these desiderata.

4.3 Gap between the good and the right?

Recall the points about problematic instances of lack of freedom (PLF1–PLF3) in Section 3.3. A worry here is that there is a gap between what is desirable in the sense of being good and what is desirable in the sense of being a matter of right. When we argue for the claim that people are entitled to opportunities for self-determined and self-realizing work by saying that they have an interest in accessing working activities with those features, a critic may say that there is a logical gap between having an interest in something and having a right to it. How do we traverse this gap?

The Dignitarian Approach, which takes rights to be grounded in status-dignity, helps bridge the gap by identifying interests with deontic standing. I explained how this works in Chapter 1 (Section 2.2.1), with the introduction of the Bridge Principle and the Schema of Dignitarian Justification. If the object of the relevant interests includes the development and exercise of certain valuable capacities, and these capacities are in the basis of dignity, then the support regarding the interests is potentially a fitting response to the status-dignity of the person who has them. If this response is feasible and imposes no unreasonable costs on the responder, then it may constitute a pro tanto duty correlated with a pro tanto right.[47] We are not taking others' dignity seriously if we deny that we have negative duties to avoid obstructing, and positive duties to facilitate, their self-determination and self-realization. More specifically, we can say that when conditions of alienation (such as AL1–AL6, listed in 2.2) set back valuable capacities which are in the basis of dignity, people have interests in the development and exercise of these capacities which morally calls for (feasible and reasonable) ameliorative action offering them real opportunities to avoid their alienation. The response envisaged would deliver the condition-dignity which the condition of alienation prevents and status-dignity calls for.[48] This is why access

---

[47] 'Reasonable costs' is an umbrella expression to be unpacked by reference to whatever would be agents' fair share (barring emergencies, which may be more demanding) in a just scheme of social life that implements the dignitarian norms in the relevant context (including but also going beyond appropriate conditions). The specifics of such a scheme are important to settle, but lie beyond the focus of this chapter. See 4.6 below.

[48] The Dignitarian Approach thus orientates the search for the metric of specific freedoms that are both prudentially significant and claimable as rights. By the same token, it helps avoid a sharp dichotomy between a 'moral', deontological approach to alienation focused on justice and rights and an 'ethical' one focused on recommendations for a good life. On this dichotomy (and a critique of Jaeggi's account for

230 Human Dignity and Social Justice

to self-determined self-realization at work featured as a key demand of the Abilities/Needs Principle as interpreted and defended in Chapter 3.

4.4 Paternalistic imposition?

Recall that one of the dynamic patterns in the critique of alienation consists in sequences involving initial identification, de-identification, and re-identification. What we find in the second, critical stage, is a situation in which, in circumstances C, S experiences a conflict between an ideal or desirable view of themselves as A and their actual condition as B. Emancipation here calls for S to move from realizing B to realizing A (perhaps by changing C to make this realization more feasible). Now, a typical liberal worry is that an account of freedom that calls for socially supporting this change in people's condition would unduly violate their liberty to live as they choose. It would involve a paternalistic circumventing of their will for their own good. But the Dignitarian Approach is not unduly paternalistic. It primarily requires effective opportunities for, rather than conditions of, non-alienation, and it sees agents as protagonists of their own amelioration.

In fact, a defence of the requirement to resource and protect real opportunities for activities featuring self-determination and self-realization could be mounted within a broadly liberal egalitarian framework. The two principles of freedom and equality can be marshalled to accomplish this task. To have enough content, such principles need to specify a metric, certain goods, which they range over. They need this to answer the questions 'Freedom from what to do or be what?' and 'Equality of access to what?' The defender of non-alienated labour can say that people should be free from undue interference in their pursuit of self-determination and self-realization at work, that this pursuit should be one they have the power, or capability, to fulfil, and that effective opportunity to engage in it should be made available to all on equal footing.[49]

---

missing it), see Forst (2017a). On my brand of deontology (dignitarianism) substantive considerations of access to self-realization are added to more procedural considerations of self-determination, and are morally significant. The distinction between prudential and moral normativity is important, but so is their connection.

[49] It could be objected that Solidaristic Empowerment is still unduly hostile to individual negative liberty because it requires everyone to fund certain positive freedoms for all, such as options of non-alienated work, even if they do not themselves want them. There are common replies to this kind of worry. People's inabilities regarding self-realization may result from restrictions to their negative liberty imposed by property conventions, and there could be more overall negative liberty without them (see note 35). The negative liberties infringed upon (e.g. to not be taxed to fund options of non-alienated labour) might be less weighty than the positive liberties enabled. The positive freedoms fostered may be authorized through

The Critique of Alienation   231

This move is significantly strengthened by justifying opportunities for non-alienation on dignitarian grounds. This is so because the idea of human dignity can be shown to give rise *both* to the general principles of freedom and equality *and* the goods of non-alienation. People are to be treated as equals, and afforded freedom from interference and positive freedom to pursue their projects, because they have status-dignity. Now, since people have this status-dignity because of their valuable capacities—the ones forming the basis of dignity—the freedom and equality owed to them should favour opportunities for developing and exercising these capacities. Activities featuring self-determination and self-realization at work are significant examples of such opportunities. They should, therefore, be targets for the implementation of liberal egalitarian principles.

Notice also that this view does not conflict with the liberal preoccupation with respecting reasonable pluralism regarding conceptions of the good. The Dignitarian Approach defends the idea that certain opportunities should be made available by taking the good they provide as reflecting the value of the capacities at the basis of dignity. But this perspective carries no oppressive imposition of a specific conception of the good, or of human flourishing, because, first, as noted, people are free to choose whether to use the opportunities they have. Second, they are also free when it comes to how to shape and use these opportunities. People can achieve self-determination and self-realization by organizing production (and other activities) in their own preferred and specific manners. The valuable capacities at the basis of dignity can be unfolded through different plans, and pursued in a variety of different ways. Finally, the normative platform of argumentation centred on dignity is itself such that it could be the focus of an overlapping consensus among people holding comprehensive metaphysical, religious, and moral perspectives that are quite different. In sum, the dignitarian perspective does not need, and it does not recommend, that the same detailed and exhaustive conception of the good be drawn up and fulfilled by everybody. Each person is to be supported as they pursue their flourishing in their own way.[50]

But who gets to say what opportunities should be made available? The answer is: In a way, nobody, and in another way, everybody. Nobody, because our interests and rights are not the decision of anyone.[51] Everybody, because

---

practices of political democratic freedom (within a constitutional framework enshrining basic individual liberties), and important for enhancing robust citizenship (e.g. via the linkage between practices of self-determination at work and in politics—see 4.5).

[50] I thank Itzel Mayans and Moisés Vaca for discussion on these points.

[51] We do not need 'immanent critique' to counter the paternalism objection. To be sure, that critique is possible and often fruitful epistemically and politically. For example, in contemporary firms, workers are simultaneously called to invest themselves in their work—and to some extent make some decisions about

232 Human Dignity and Social Justice

nobody has an epistemic crystal ball to grasp them and we should be the authors of our lives and the framers of our institutions. We all can form beliefs about our interests and rights, revise them in critical debate, and devise successive accounts which, we hope, improve over time, as they survive scrutiny. Self-determination has pride of place within the Dignitarian Approach. We, together or separately as appropriate, have to figure out what positive freedoms we shall support and exercise.

4.5 The two-level justification objection

An advocate for institutions and practices that support non-alienation faces another criticism that builds on the significance of political, democratic freedom. We can distinguish between two levels of social activity. There is a first, ground level at which people interact in their daily lives, such as when they transact in the market and produce at the workplace. And there is a second, higher level at which people decide what forms of first-level activities to permit, require, or facilitate. A clear example of second level activity would be the political process steering the state. Now, the objection is that alienated conditions at the first level would not be problematic if they are authorized in appropriate ways at the second level. If people, as citizens in a fair democratic process, decide to permit alienating activities in economic life, and to not facilitate robust alternatives to them (via, for example, support for cooperatives and the social economy sector or a high universal basic income enabling experimentation with novel forms of work), then there is no injustice taking place. Concerns about alienation thus have at most a personal significance. They do not rise to the height of concerns about social injustice.

In response, consider, first, that although procedural political legitimacy plays an important role in social justice, it does not exhaust the terrain. Norms that are endorsed democratically can still be unjust. The question 'Is this norm just?' is not settled by an answer to the question 'Who (and how) decides whether this norm is enacted?' Norms requiring access to opportunities for self-determination and self-realization in economic life may be substantively correct even if citizens choose not to adopt them. Citizens

---

what and how to produce with others. But they are also pushed harder to yield more goods and services in allotted time frames and to obey externally imposed standardized protocols, while facing greater insecurity regarding income, benefits, and maintenance of their jobs. (See Coutrot 2018: 63–5, 274.) As I discuss in Sections 4.6, 4.7, and 5, the tension between these aspects of workers' condition could be used for an internal critique (pivoting on the former to challenge the latter). But we would still need to explain what makes the sources of this critique normatively sound.

The Critique of Alienation **233**

might have made a mistake, which they should correct in future iterations of their political action.

Second, if widespread, alienation in economic life may undermine the quality of the democratic process which the objection invokes. What happens at the first level may affect what happens at the second in a way that subverts the latter's normative status. This is partly an empirical issue, but a hypothesis worth taking seriously is that when people go about their daily lives in a way that is systematically alienated, they may fail to effectively enjoy political equality. Apathy, ignorance, egotistic self-centredness, submissiveness, and other attitudes, which people develop in their economic practices, may stunt the development of attitudes of critical reflection, concern for others, and readiness to resolutely participate to address issues of general significance which seem crucial for a healthy democratic process.[52]

Third, and relatedly, we should distinguish between incidents of alienation at the first level that are occasional and incidents that are widespread. The former might not pose a serious problem, while the latter clearly do. The two-levels objection is often pressed by using examples such as competitive games. Such games may engage certain behavioural patterns and attitudes such as greed and aggression that are prima facie worrisome. But we could authorize them as occasional activities (while also constraining them through appropriate rules). We could even say that it is a good thing to have such games so that people discharge in them some nasty drives they would otherwise express in less contained, and in more dangerous, forms. But when a whole economy displays worrisome behavioural patterns in a systematic way, then the situation is quite different. The intrinsic and instrumental harms generated by an economy suffused with alienation are not easily reduced to occasional incidents. They are instead pervasive features of people's lives, of the many hours they spend working, five days a week. The moral significance of the harms is thus heightened and the absence of real opportunities to avoid them a clear problem of social justice.

Finally, it is important to insist that the case of work is special. For many people it is not a merely optional activity. Societies systematically push them to work on pain of failure to meet urgent needs of subsistence and social recognition. Furthermore, it is unlikely that many people will access enough self-realization outside of work. By urging the creation of opportunities for non-alienated work, Solidaristic Empowerment does not so much force people to be free as prevent their being forced to be unfree.

---

[52] On the relation between attitudes at work and in broader political action, see Fraga et al (2019).

234 Human Dignity and Social Justice

4.6 Further issues

I have responded to four central worries about alienation critique. My main purpose has been to use the Dignitarian Approach to identify and defend a core normative structure for this critique. But, of course, other important concerns should be addressed to develop the account more fully. Let me briefly mention some of them, with some indications about how they could be handled. The objective is not to settle them, but to offer some hypotheses for future discussion.

Solidaristic Empowerment enjoins us to support people's positive freedom to engage in non-alienated activities. Our negative and positive duties, I said, are to do what is feasible and reasonable to respond to people's status-dignity as they face alienating predicaments. The reference to what is 'feasible and reasonable' is an umbrella expression which must be unpacked to specify more determinate dignitarian norms that state who owes what to whom in the relevant circumstances under examination. These norms would take the support for non-alienated activity as a pro tanto consideration which has to be balanced against other considerations to reach all things considered judgements about what we owe to each other. This exercise would require, for example, that we say more about the division of labour, if any, between social institutions and individual and collective agents. I take dignity to require duties for both. Two societies with the same institutions, but in which agents make different choices about whether to support the dignity of others, are not equally just. But the precise scheme for the allocation of responsibilities certainly requires careful examination.

We will also want to illuminate distributive issues about people's freedom to avoid alienation. For example, should we accept a sufficientarian or some kind of egalitarian function? I think that dignity generates a presumption in favour of the highest equal distribution that is reasonably feasible. But a sufficientarian floor of condition-dignity may be identified as an important specification of Solidaristic Empowerment as well. Of particular importance would be to support the kinds of self-identification that allow people to gain a robust sense of self-esteem and self-respect in their social life—which they normally need to pursue their flourishing in a confident manner.[53] Other significant distributive issues concern the extent of duties to contribute to

---

[53] I thank Peter Dietsch for discussion on this point. See also the account (in Chapter 3) of a requirement to secure basic needs under the Abilities/Needs Principle. Another important issue is the metric of distribution. If what is crucial is catering for needs, then equal (or sufficientarian) distribution of resources may not be the key notion: what is key is to secure the power to meet the relevant needs given diverse conditions, which may justify different bundles of resources for different people. In the case of labour, for example, power to flourish may require specific arrangements supporting people with certain disabilities.

the flourishing of others, especially in the face of (likely) facts of partial compliance and unequal capacities, and given the ethical importance of a personal prerogative to give special weight to one's own projects and relationships. It might be unfair, for example, to demand that we take repeated steps to help others flourish when they consistently can but choose not to reciprocate. If resources are scarce, it might be wrong for me to ask for equal shares in the proceedings of social cooperation when I choose to contribute less than you do. Above some sufficiency threshold of the kind mentioned above, some requirement of reciprocity or responsibility regarding contribution seems appropriate, and should qualify the egalitarianism envisaged. This reciprocity, however, should itself be fair, by tracking not simply outputs of production but ratios of effort to given capacity. This, I think, is part of the spirit of the slogan 'From each according to their abilities, to each according to their needs!'; and I proposed a demand of fair reciprocity as a component of the interpretation of the Abilities/Needs Principle offered in Chapter 3. Other things being equal, if I put less effort into our shared cooperative venture than you do, then it seems that I am taking your needs less seriously than you are taking mine. This would be so even if the amount of output we produced is the same. If I had done my best as you did, we would have had more to share.

Some issues regarding conflicts and trade-offs would also have to be explored.[54] I have focused on successful and appropriate self-identification at work as an important need. But I do not deny that non-alienation is significant in other activities. Agents may reasonably choose to enact self-determination and self-realization in the latter, even if that costs them some alienation in the former. But we should be careful. Consider the view that the remedy for alienated labour is not so much to *improve* work, but to *contain* it, that the main demand should be to shorten the working day. I agree that self-determination and self-realization can be achieved outside of work. However, for most people in our current societies, this is not enough. Most people are pushed to work on pain of losing access to subsistence and social respect, and they will not get enough access to self-determination and self-realization in their daily lives unless options of non-alienated work are available. I also agree that we can reduce the amount of necessary but unsavoury work. We can also distribute it more fairly. However, we should be sceptical about the prospects of reduction of working time in capitalism. Workers in advanced

---

[54] I thank Sam Arnold and Jahel Queralt for discussion regarding the critical points that follow in this section. See also Nozick (1974: 246–50). Nozick illuminates some potential trade-offs, but ignores that realistic incarnations of a capitalist economy make some people much less able than others to bargain for self-affirming deals.

236 Human Dignity and Social Justice

capitalist societies work fewer hours than workers in the nineteenth century, but only after much political struggle by trade unions, socialist parties, and other progressive organizations. And the reduction has slowed or stagnated in the last fifty years even though productivity has skyrocketed.[55] Capitalism has displayed a strong bias against reducing the working day. The tendency is instead to use productivity gains to increase output to undersell competitors.[56] Finally, there is the issue of how to define 'work'. We should, I think, use a broad notion of work (as intentional activity to produce goods or services that meet needs or desires) to include some activities that are not typical 'jobs' and are often not categorized as work, such as homemaking and community service. They also provide potential mediums for non-alienated productive activity.

Reasonable trade-offs could arise not only within the space of non-alienation (between different activities), but also between non-alienated activity and other values. Some might prefer jobs that score lower in terms of avoiding alienation if that gives them more income to pursue other goods, such as leisure and consumption. Such trade-offs may indeed be reasonable. But, again, we should handle claims about them carefully. Consider the view that, given the efficiency of alienated work, there may be a tension between (a) getting more income and wealth and (b) achieving more meaningful work. Why not prioritize the former? Money is an all-purpose means allowing multiple desirable activities. Notice, however, that the need for the alleged trade-offs may be spurious. There is some empirical evidence that more self-realization and self-determination at work increases productivity. Workers identifying themselves with a job they help control and in which they unfold their talents may be able to generate more output.[57] The trade-offs must be shown to be really unavoidable. Second, even when they are necessary, their distribution should be fairly shared among people, rather than concentrated in some vulnerable groups. Third, it is also important to consider that beyond certain levels of income, and assuming that working hours remain long, having more money likely adds less to workers' well-being than meaningful work. Finally, many forms of meaningful activity outside of work do not require a lot of money. Good cultivation of friendship, for example, is not simply a function of how much money we spend on it.

My references to Marx's stark contrasts between capitalism and socialism may give the impression that I endorse them without qualifications.

---

[55] See data in The Core Team (2018: Unit 3). See: https://core-econ.org/the-economy/book/text/03.html#subheadline.

[56] Cohen (2001: ch. XI).

[57] Coutrot (2018: Part III).

The Critique of Alienation   **237**

But consider, for example, the challenges that socialism is not a necessary condition for self-determination and self-realization at work because non-alienated work is feasible in capitalism (especially with a welfare state, or with a high universal basic income). It is also not clear that socialism is a sufficient condition, as some unsavoury, alienated work will likely be needed even in a socialist economy. I do not mean to settle these issues in this chapter. My focus has been on identifying some core normative concepts and principles. The reference to Marx's critique of capitalism and advocacy for socialism is mostly illustrative. Surely comparing feasible forms of capitalism and socialism would require a careful argument that lies beyond this chapter's scope.[58] Still, consider some responses. Regarding necessary conditions, I do not deny that achievements in self-determination and self-realization are feasible under capitalism, for some people. But the main question should be: Does capitalism give everyone the highest equal chances to avoid alienation that are technically feasible and reasonably implementable? The answer may very well be no. Turning to sufficient conditions, I do not deny that some unsavoury work will have to be done in a feasible socialist economy. But it would at least display more self-determination if it is scheduled democratically (both at the macro-societal level and within the organization of the workplace). And regarding self-realization, socialism would likely be less exacting in terms of working hours devoted to unpleasant as opposed to fulfilling work. That is the point of talking about reducing the 'realm of necessity' (which is not the same as eliminating it) while expanding the 'realm of freedom' (which is not the same as making it saturate the space of work). But these are only promissory remarks. The issues are indeed complex and require detailed separate treatment. Socialist transformation may also involve long processes with uncertain feasibility prospects, which leads me to the last reflection in this section.

4.7 Dynamic patterns and the critique of alienated self-determination and self-realization

As pointed out (in Sections 2.5 and 3.2), people might respond to their alienation through two kinds of pathways: they might either find ways to reconcile themselves with it or they might seek to emancipate themselves from it. Schematically, what might happen is that, in circumstances C, some agent S undergoes a conflict between their ideal view of themselves as A and their

---

[58] For surveys of recent discussions on feasible socialist proposals, see Corneo (2017); Gilabert and O'Neill (2019: sect. 4). I offer some further reflections in Chapter 8.

238 Human Dignity and Social Justice

actual condition as B. In the face of this conflict, they might accept C but redescribe their predicament as B under a more desirable light which captures some of their concerns as A or, more insidiously, they might redefine A to make it fit B. Alternatively, and more progressively, they might seek to change C so as to actually overhaul their condition as B to turn it into a new configuration that really honours their commitments as A. Even better, they could do this while developing a reflectively and critically achieved account of these commitments.

It is interesting to explore these patterns further. An important issue, for example, is how they link up to the development of certain subjective schemas—such as the generation of social identities. Sometimes social roles are reshaped in a way that makes them seem desirable without threatening the existing social structures. Thus, capitalist bosses are cast as innovative trailblazers and socially beneficial entrepreneurs, while wage labourers are depicted as productive, responsible, and loyal employees and breadwinners. The critics of capitalism, in contrast, recast the roles as those of exploiter and exploited, the manipulator and the capable but oppressed. These critics challenge the objective alienation of people in capitalist societies, recoding their endorsement of their predicament as a form of *alienated self-realization*. A related example is when ideals of self are narrowly orientated to self-interest maximization. A self-understanding as a *homo oeconomicus* involves a failure on the part of people to connect with their actual tendencies as solidaristic beings. The homo oeconomicus is an objectively alienated agent.[59]

Other critical judgements target the forms of consent that obtain in contractual relations between workers and capitalist employers in the labour market. We find here instances of *alienated self-determination*. These can be cases of objective alienation in which the parties do not even notice that they are supporting schemes of social interaction that are deleterious of their freedom and well-being. There can also be cases of subjective alienation in which the despondent parties consent in view of social circumstances they think are inappropriate but also impervious to change in the immediate future.[60]

As we examine these problematic patterns, it is interesting to explore the relation between the critical appraisal of alienation and historical

---

[59] The search for self-realization can take egotistic forms, or be unresponsive to the well-being of others. It may also involve an excessive focus on quantity over quality, and on means rather than ends. For discussion of these 'alienated needs', see Heller (2018). See also Rosa (2019) on increasing incidences of burnout and depression and their link to an excessive focus on accumulation of resources in the face of heightened uncertainty.

[60] In these cases, the device of hypothetical consent, under critical and reflective conditions, could be used to challenge acts of actual but alienated consent—even if not always to morally override it. See Enoch's (2017: 27–8) discussion on 'depth' of consent.

The Critique of Alienation **239**

materialism. The latter illuminates the feasibility of change of various material and social circumstances over time. Marx imagined that a full suppression of alienation would arise in a technologically advanced, classless society to be built after capitalism (and that it would not be achievable within capitalism, although capitalism itself was necessary to generate the enabling conditions for the socialist transformation that would occur as it matured). One can disagree with the specifics of historical materialism. But a valuable insight is that in scrutinizing alienation, we should acknowledge that various material and social conditions both set limits to what is immediately feasible and are changeable over time. There is a dynamic view of feasibility operating here which is quite relevant for a robust critical analysis of alienation.

Indeed, some circumstances surrounding alienation—such as certain levels of material scarcity, class structure, cultural scripts, and political systems—may be more or less historically specific and malleable. To explore this point further, we can identify (a) certain tendencies of people regarding their important and valuable capacities and needs; (b) certain features of the material and social circumstances in which they live and act; and (c) certain practical instantiations in which they pursue the fulfilment of those tendencies in alienated ways. Let me give some examples. (a) Regarding the tendencies, we can pick out those concerning self-determination and those concerning creativity, singular self-expression, and cooperative sociality (which fall under self-realization). (b) Regarding material and social circumstances, we can identify, in capitalism, the presence of moderate material scarcity, the lack for many of secure access to means of subsistence (given that they do not control means of production), ownership of their own labour power, the use of markets for allocation of employment, investment, and consumption goods, and, given widespread market competition, the dominance of the motive of accumulation of capital or monetary value when deploying productive resources. (c) Turning to the alienated instances, we can identify the following predicament. Creativity is incentivized by competition and insecurity, but its instances are alienated because the intrinsic value of what is created is not really crucial. What is paramount is that what is produced is new and likely to be desired and purchased, not that it is worth desiring and purchasing. Self-determination and singular self-awareness are also partly incentivized by competition and market liberties, but their instantiation is alienated because what is most important is to come up on top of others. This is ultimately frustrating due to the impossibility of everyone being on top, the indifference to the well-being of others that this positional search encourages, and the anxiety it produces. Finally, consider sociality. Every economy requires cooperation and some form of reciprocity. But

240 Human Dignity and Social Justice

capitalism typically involves configurations that are excessively instrumentalizing. People approach others mostly as potential obstacles or as resources for self-benefit. This turns sociality into a vector of utilization instead of also a medium of joint self-realization. Capitalism does not require reducing others completely to means. Capitalist property rights, self-ownership, and market relations involve normative limits to what may be done to others (limits not present in slavery, for example). But capitalism fails to sufficiently honour the dignitarian idea that others are ends in themselves rather than mere means. Arguably, a socialist society would alter the circumstances mentioned in (b) to allow for the tendencies mentioned in (a) an expression that is less alienated than in (c).

Successful self-realization includes a process of self-actualization in which people develop and exercise their capacities, and a process of self-externalization in which the self-actualization of individuals meets with recognition by significant others.[61] (Recognition here involves both noticing and appreciating what others produce.) Now, in at least modern times, the search for self-realization is seen as a prerogative of all individuals, not just of a minority of them. In principle, this should make not only the self-actualization component more available, but also the recognition one more likely to succeed. As Hegel famously argued,[62] in hierarchical frameworks those who are at the bottom do not get to actualize themselves very much, and those at the top fail to get satisfactory recognition if it is obtained from subordinated people who are not reciprocally recognized. The modern, more egalitarian setting opens up a new cultural possibility of relations in which each can flourish, and in which the horizontal appreciation people give each other can succeed (as it is given by equals, not denigrated subordinates). However, capitalism upsets this promise. Although the crystalized hierarchies of masters and slaves and lords and serfs do not exist, other hierarchies effectively arise—such as the one between bosses and wage workers. Additionally, and more generally, the instrumentalizing egotism typical of intense market competition (which colours relationships between individuals in all walks of life) frames the search for singular self-identification as a matter of prevailing over others. This outlook of success as the putting down of others undermines the self-esteem and self-actualization of the losers, and their standing to give satisfactory recognition to the winners. It also condemns the winners to restless anxiety.

---

[61] As pointed out by Elster. See Section 2.4 above.
[62] Hegel (1977: ch. IV).

The very idea of dignity has shifted in modern times from its earlier understanding as a superior status held by minorities ruling over the rest in hierarchical social structures to a universally recognized status held equally by every individual.[63] But in capitalism this universalism and egalitarianism is twisted in a self-undermining way. If we understand dignity to yield an ideal of solidaristic empowerment, we can see what is wrong with the capitalist ways. The challenge then is to identify forms of social organization that do not generate this twisting. Socialism is the other great strand in modern political practice that can take the mantle of universalist and egalitarian dignity, including its affirmation of free and singular self-realization, without bleaching it in the alienating acid of egotism.

The foregoing reflections can also be used to respond to a common worry that the ideal of self-realization must lead to undermining community. Understood in the solidaristic, and socialist way, the trope of non-alienation can be made consistent with community—and with a community that is not hierarchical but richly supports the freedom and well-being of each member of it.

How could the critical stance towards alienation unfold? People can develop their contestation of alienation in different ways. Some are problematic. For example, they might adopt a thoroughly *voluntaristic* stance and, straightaway and without much concern for feasibility, seek to create an alternative condition that exactly matches their ideals. A possible result of voluntarism is *wishful thinking*—the refusal to form beliefs about feasibility prospects that reflect the evidence available, or to gather evidence at all. People might instead adopt a *tragic* attitude, forgoing attempts to change their circumstances because they think this is infeasible. This attitude is tragic because people do not lose sight of the ideals, and thus notice the gap between what they would like to be and what they think they can, or likely will, be. It differs from another accommodating attitude, which involves *adaptive preferences*—the lowering of people's ideals to match what they believe they can get.[64] The cognitive dissonance implicit in the tragic attitude is painful, and might lead people to escape it by eventually developing adaptive preferences. Adaptive preferences might also arise after voluntaristic endeavors in which people fail to fulfil their ambitious but unrealistic plans.

An alternative, reasonable development of the critical stance is to keep normative ideals ambitious, be hard-nosed in our feasibility assessments, and articulate social projects and experiments that dynamically push the

---

[63] Waldron (2012).
[64] Elster (1983: ch. 3).

242 Human Dignity and Social Justice

feasibility frontier over time. This is the dynamic perspective recommended in Chapter 4.[65] It would involve a form of political self-empowerment, or positive freedom, that gives our human dignity the hopeful response it deserves.

5. On Recent Developments in Capitalist Conditions of Work

This chapter has argued that a commitment to human dignity yields a solidaristic requirement of support for positive freedom and developed this normative point by exploring the issue of the critique of alienation, with an illustrative focus on the predicament of workers in capitalism. The chapter included four main moves. It started by offering an analytic framework to understand alienation. Second, the critique of alienation was revamped as part of an inquiry into the conditions for the successful pursuit of positive freedom. Next, I identified four objections to normative engagement with alienation concerning the problems of essentialism, a lack of articulation of the relation between the good and the right, paternalistic imposition, and democratic authorization. Finally, I responded to the objections by recasting the discussion of positive freedom and alienation in terms of the Dignitarian Approach.

I conclude this chapter with some remarks on a significant transformation in the organization of capitalist economic activity that has been taking place in the last decades.[66] The changes include a move from highly centralized, hierarchical, and stable economic units to more dispersed, cooperative, and fluid ones.[67] This change towards a so-called 'network model' gives some (not all) workers new liberties and opportunities for actively shaping their economic activity. But it also increases their insecurity and anxiety, and accelerates tendencies towards inequality of income and wealth. The new worries

---

[65] See also Wright (2010: Part III).

[66] For a detailed exploration of how these changes affect the organization of the workplace see, e.g., Boltanski and Chiapello (1999). It is common to identify three stages in capitalism: an initial, 'competitive laissez-faire' form featuring relatively small firms, low governmental regulation, and direct involvement of owners in management; a second, 'state-managed monopoly capitalism' in which large, often monopolistic firms engage life-long employees immersed in a highly integrated and hierarchical distribution of tasks, from management to deskilled jobs, while government imposes significant regulations and protections of workers' rights regarding income, retirement, and vacations; and, finally, a 'globalizing neoliberal capitalism' in which governmental regulation recedes while firms introduce more flexible schemes of production of the kind explored by Boltanski and Chiapello. See further Fraser and Jaeggi (2018).

[67] These changes are more prominent in rich countries. The Global South, on the other hand, has seen an increase in more traditional forms of industrial work (with sweatshop factories lacking many basic protections for workers that are common in the Global North).

The Critique of Alienation **243**

affect both white-collar and blue-collar workers, although in different ways. White-collar workers are particularly hit by the intensification of competition within and between firms, and by the anxiety regarding the prospects for successful development and marketing of their talents and skills in constantly changing economic activities. There is a relentless requirement that they continuously and personally invest themselves in the firms, identify with their values and mission, and display new and appealing aptitudes that are unique and at the cutting-edge. It is very hard for workers to remain successful over time, and the increased tendency to hold them responsible for their performance makes it also more likely that they will blame themselves (rather than the surrounding social circumstances) for any failure. Blue-collar workers, in turn, are particularly hit by the elimination of many jobs through automation, by the precarious nature of jobs that are available, and by the erosion (or 'flexibilization') of protective labour regulations (regarding salary, working hours, conditions for dismissal, vacations, etc.). Workers of all kinds are affected by the use of new information technologies that enable the intensification of the surveillance of their activity, increasing their insecurity.[68] Unions have lost power as jobs in their traditional base in the industrial sector shrink and the organization of workers in precarious jobs and in flexible economic networks turns out to be very difficult. Governments have been slow to react to these changes, and in many cases have yielded to pressure from capitalists (especially those from the financial sector) and reduced regulations of labour contracts, making it easier for employers to fire workers and to impose flexible and differential schedules of work and remuneration on them. Increased economic globalization has also generated a 'race to the bottom' in which states compete with each other to attract investment by weakening the regulations of their labour market (thus depressing protection of workers' rights further).

What is the significance of these changes for the dignity of workers? Some problems are inherent to the very nature of work under capitalist circumstances. On the one hand, the capitalist institution of the labour contract has given workers more freedom than they had under slavery and feudalism. The labour contract is a voluntary arrangement in which workers rent their labour power. They are not directly coerced by employers to work for them. Furthermore, capitalists and workers are equals as citizens, with the same civil and

---

[68] See the report of the condition of white-collar workers in the company Amazon in Kanto and Streitfeld (2015), and the depiction of the predicament of blue-collar workers in various precarious jobs in Thompson (2013). On the condition of workers in large factories in China, see Duhigg and Barboza (2012). On the impact on worker's rights of the so-called 'gig' or 'sharing economy' (as exemplified by Uber), see M. Chen (2015).

244 Human Dignity and Social Justice

political rights (although this is a recent achievement which required much political struggle by workers, and not a constant of every capitalist society). On the other hand, the labour contract ushers into a relation between workers and capitalists that involves subordination and hierarchy rather than freedom and equality. Employers and workers have deeply asymmetrical entitlements to determine what gets done at the workplace, and derive highly unequal benefits from economic activity. These inequalities of power and benefit are linked to a background inequality of condition, from which they partly result and which they reproduce over time. Labour contracts are the output of negotiation between highly unequal parties. Capitalists are able to successfully drive hard bargains on workers partly because the background inequality of resources between them makes it far more urgent for the latter to agree to what the other proposes than vice versa. So, if we think that respect and concern for human dignity requires equal empowerment and access to conditions of well-being in economic life, capitalism is in some respects inherently incompatible with it. It is characterized by asymmetrical bargaining among parties with unequal resources and power, and by resulting relations of subordination and exploitation. We have discussed these features in the last chapter, and will return to them in the next.

That said, the ongoing changes also involve some new issues regarding the dignity of workers that are especially relevant for our present discussion on alienation. Some examples revolve around mental health and well-being. In earlier phases of capitalism, it was perhaps easier for workers to psychologically dissociate themselves from their job, to distinguish between who they are and what they do for a living. As workers are increasingly expected to invest their self and identity in their work, it is harder for them to develop a sense of self-esteem when their working life does not go well. Furthermore, this investment of self in one's job may give rise to worries. As Barbara Ehrenreich says, there may be a loss in 'dignity' in having to 'sell oneself' besides selling one's skills and hard work. This happens to white-collar workers most often, as they are expected to identify fully with their company.[69] This tying of the self with work is potentially a good thing *if* work is organized in a way that is more conducive to human flourishing. But when the workplace involves relentless competition and anxiety, the legitimate concern with self-expression at work is twisted and manipulated to get workers to accept what is in fact harmful to them.

The new forms of labour under neoliberal policies, which involve precarious, flexible, and often low-wage work, have been legitimized by

---

[69] Ehrenreich (2005: 234).

The Critique of Alienation   **245**

selectively drawing on dignitarian concerns for autonomous choice and self-management on the part of workers. Boltanski and Chiapello have shown how these transformations exploited a strand of leftist thought—the 'artist critique' against Fordist forms of production, which challenges rigid, top-down management and the deskilled, monotonous, and uncreative forms of work it generated. The new forms of production, involving a 'connectionist' and 'project' based model, recruit (some, although by no means all) workers' responsibility and creativity. But they also destroy what earlier forms of leftist critique (the strand of 'social critique' emphasizing equality and compassion) and labour movements had achieved: robust institutions and practices of social security and solidarity.[70] A similar development has been identified by Nancy Fraser, who argues that neoliberalism resignified appropriate feminist concerns for the dignity of women's work to justify worrisome arrangements that generate precarious jobs. These jobs, often taken by women, were cast as examples of liberation from the traditional framework in which there was a male breadwinner working full-time and receiving a 'family wage' and a female homemaker performing unpaid work.[71] A third example is the invocation of personal freedom and the inclusion of minorities in the workforce in campaigns by companies in the gig economy (such as Uber and Lyft) to repel efforts to have workers recognized as employees rather than independent contractors, thus hampering workers' organization, collective bargaining, and benefits.[72] A challenge for a dignitarian framework is to rescue the valuable ideals of self-determination from these ideological uses, so that a synergy between those ideals and the ideals of solidarity and equality can be imagined and given political traction in the articulation of policies that really foster the greatest overall emancipation for workers that is feasible given current and foreseeable material circumstances.

Another problem linked with the new ways of organizing economic activity is that the increasing emphasis on personal responsibility fosters a heightened sense of shame and guilt in individuals who fail to get jobs, or who are not as productive as expected in the jobs they have. If the economic culture included a greater sense of social solidarity, and if it recognized that the causes of unemployment and 'underperformance' are often structural and social rather than the result of any single individual's volition, things would be less hard for workers. They would be less likely to blame themselves and experience shame and guilt for their condition. They would be more likely to

---

[70] Boltanksi and Chiapello (1999) urge leftists to reunite the two strands of critique (as they were, e.g., in Marx's use of them).
[71] Fraser (2009).
[72] Vicks (2022).

246 Human Dignity and Social Justice

feel instead dissatisfaction and indignation towards a social environment that generates the problems they face, and engage in collective action to change it. They would be more likely to participate in a union, join a political party, or protest. These would be healthier attitudes. The recognition of individual vulnerability would turn into an occasion to pursue dynamic forms of collective agency.

New information technologies could be used in promising ways. Some good examples already exist (a paradigmatic case is wiki platforms, which allow people to share knowledge in a cooperative fashion). But some current uses are harmful. An example is the intense surveillance of workers' level of output, which leads to exhaustion, heightened anxiety, and other forms of stress. Another example is the use of these technologies to enable and encourage workers to undercut each other. Managerial practices in Amazon provide an illustration. This company used the 'Anytime Feedback Tool ... [a] widget in the company directory that allows employees to send praise or criticism about colleagues to management. (While bosses know who sends the comments, their identities are not typically shared with the subjects of the remarks.) Because team members are ranked, and those at the bottom eliminated every year, it is in everyone's interest to outperform everyone else'. This generated 'a river of intrigue and scheming'.[73]

There is also an interesting dialectics exhibited by the invocations of singularity in the new patterns of production and consumption in contemporary capitalism. These patterns are praised as enabling individuals to be truly 'themselves' when they work. Workers are called to invest their personal perspective in the shaping of projects and to fashion their own unique engagement with the firms. Consumption is also 'personalized'. New information technologies allow consumers to develop their profiles and purchase items that fit their own tastes, selecting those which combine features in distinctive ways. But this emergence of singularity is Janus-faced. It does awaken in people a genuine interest in shaping their lives in personal ways. But it also tethers them more tightly to economic schemes that are not really under their control and do not leave them as well off as the new technologies, if handled differently, could. Workers are not just supposed to give their labour power and their time to the firm. They are expected to give it their own 'selves'. Consumption is also not just a means to achieve other ends, but an expected medium of self-expression and self-realization. But these processes happen under intense surveillance and manipulation by managers and marketers. Workers and consumers could instead seize their emerging

---

[73] Kanto and Streitfeld (2015). There is debate as to whether practices of this sort are even effective for increasing productivity. See *The Economist* (2015).

The Critique of Alienation **247**

sense of singularization in a way that links to freer, more stable, and more cooperative frameworks of production and consumption.

Something similar seems to be happening with the incitation to 'share'. Workers are encouraged to work in teams, to be caring towards their coworkers as they develop and implement their common projects. Consumption is also expected to proceed by developing communities of like-minded consumers, who cluster to enjoy together and give constructive feedback to the sellers to cater more closely to their common desires and needs. This invocation of solidarity happens, however, in a context in which workers are also pitted against each other in intense competition in the recruitment for productive teams, in the relation between any of these teams and other teams within a firm, and in the relation between their firm and other firms. Consumption also features a proliferation of tribes, internally cohesive and supportive, but externally disdainful or hostile. These dynamics increase the availability and readiness of workers and consumers to support and sustain the economic processes which syphon disproportionate wealth and power up to owners and managers of capital.

This situation is 'dialectic' in the sense that just as the incitation of singularity and solidarity is exploited for capitalist profit, it also creates tendencies which could lead to shattering the capitalist mould. Once awoken, the interests in pursuing lives that feature personal autonomy and intersubjective collaboration might point towards different social schemes that are more fully in line with them. The new practices of exploitation, domination, and alienation become potential occasions for contestation and progress.

The prospects for workers' dignity are indeed quite uncertain. Two authors provide helpful summaries of the difficulties of workers' current predicament:

> Despite the disagreements revealed ... by scholars, technologists, labor activists, business leaders, politicians, and policy analysts about what the world of work will look like in twenty years or so, a few clear outlines emerge. Whether robots eradicate human effort or assist it, advanced industrial economies are likely to have fewer and fewer high-end jobs, more and more service jobs, and a significant decrease in full-time occupations with benefits. In the developing world—indeed in the entire world—various forms of bonded labor and servitude are re-emerging. Where workers lack locations to congregate regularly—be it around water coolers, at dispatch halls, or in factories—collective action will need to evolve to ensure the kind of worker voice and pressure to which governments and politicians respond and that serve to promote the kinds of protections and tax systems Piketty advocates.[74]

---

[74] Levi (2015). Levi is addressing the situation of increasing inequality portrayed in Piketty (2014).

248 Human Dignity and Social Justice

> Many of the new service-sector workers are crowded into low-skilled, poorly paid and often somewhat demeaning jobs that offer little prospect of upward mobility; and even many of the more educated, better-paid service sector workers face pressing problems to do with perceived job insecurity, pension insecurity, work intensification and poor work-life balance ... The task for egalitarian politics is to persuade workers in both groups that these problems are best addressed through political programmes that rest on an ethic of solidarity, rather than through individual effort alone.[75]

As these statements emphasize, solidarity and collective action are essential for the improvement of workers' situation. The pursuit of dignity at work requires a renewed effort to imagine how politics can recognize and fulfil workers' rights—including their positive freedom to avoid alienation.

---

[75] White (2007: 156).

7
The Critique of Domination

1. Introduction

Domination is a recurrent phenomenon. In patriarchal societies, men dominate women. In capitalist economic systems, capitalist employers dominate wage workers. In authoritarian political regimes, ruling elites dominate the population. But what is domination? And what, if anything, is wrong with it? To answer these questions, I offer an account of the concept of domination and deploy the Dignitarian Approach to articulate the normative contours of the critique of domination.

There is an influential trend in contemporary political philosophy to treat domination as the master idea for the critique of social injustice. Because of this centrality of domination in contemporary political philosophy, it is important to both deepen the analysis of the idea of domination itself and to show in some detail why, although the idea is quite relevant for understanding injustice, it is insufficient to account for all of it. This chapter will thus be longer than the previous ones.

The first question is addressed in Section 3, which offers an analytical framework to understand domination. Domination is characterized as a highly asymmetric social power relationship between agents such that some (the more powerful, the dominators) are able to impose their will on others (the less powerful, the dominated) with respect to some issues or outcomes, in some circumstances. Several analytical dimensions of domination are identified, including its degree, range, sites, scope, depth, mechanisms, resources, and dynamic transformation. The idea of non-domination is also distinguished from the related ideas of self-determination and agential empowerment.

I turn to the second question in Section 4. There are serious difficulties with the trend presenting domination as the master idea to understand injustice. The ideal of freedom from domination itself needs to be clarified and justified, and this requires drawing on more fundamental concepts and principles. Such normative resources are also needed to explain why some forms

Human Dignity and Social Justice. Pablo Gilabert, Oxford University Press. © Pablo Gilabert (2023).
DOI: 10.1093/oso/9780192871152.003.0007

250 Human Dignity and Social Justice

of domination constitute injustices, and some forms of domination are more serious injustices than others. Furthermore, not all cases of social injustice are cases of domination. In addition to exploring these issues, I offer a positive account of the normative structure of the critique of domination by using, and developing further, the Dignitarian Approach. According to this approach, we have reason to organize social life so that we respond appropriately to the valuable features of individual human beings that give rise to their dignity. According to the companion ideal of Solidaristic Empowerment, we should support people in their pursuit of a flourishing life by implementing both negative duties not to destroy or block their valuable capacities and positive duties to protect and facilitate their development and exercise of those capacities. This approach illuminates the critique of domination by helping explain how domination conflicts with rights with a dignitarian justification. People have rights to access the conditions for their self-determination and self-realization, so that they can feasibly and reasonably unfold the valuable capacities at the basis of their dignity. Relationships of domination frustrate access to these conditions. Self-determination is directly hampered, as domination precisely consists in the colonization of the will of some by the will of others. In addition, domination's curtailment of self-determination poses an indirect threat to self-realization, by rendering agents' access to the resources needed for it less secure than it could and should be. The Dignitarian Approach indeed clarifies and justifies rights against domination. It also generates other requirements of support for people's empowerment which are independent of the avoidance of domination. As a result, the approach provides a systematic and unified perspective to simultaneously articulate the content, the grounds, and the limits of the critique of domination as an appraisal of social injustice.

As the main illustration of the theoretical points it makes, this chapter concentrates on the multilayered phenomenon of the domination of wage workers by capitalist employers. I present an initial characterization of this phenomenon in Section 2, and regularly return to it as the argument in the chapter proceeds.

2. The Case of the Domination of Workers in Capitalism

It will help our discussion if we identify a common and important case of domination. I focus on the salient features of the relation between capitalist employers and wage labourers, hereafter referred to simply as capitalists and workers—a stylization to refer, respectively, to people who are owners of

The Critique of Domination **251**

means of production and are able to hire others to work under their supervision, and people who are owners of their labour power but cannot afford a decent life unless they work under some capitalist employer for a wage.[1] My aim is to identify a context to develop the conceptual and the normative structures of the appraisal of domination provided by the Dignitarian Approach, not to make new empirical or social scientific points. For my description of this case, I rely on the recent work of other researchers.[2]

---

[1] This simplified analysis will not fully capture some important categories of people, such as the managers who have significant decision-making power but are not capitalist employers. This category is significant, although its incidence should not be exaggerated. For example, it is true that ownership and control may come apart. In some capitalist firms, managers exert regular control over wage workers, and have significant discretion in their relation with capitalist share-holders (who may be large and diverse group of people). But often some capitalist owners will have controlling shares in their firms and have ultimate power over what managers can do. Furthermore, sometimes managers will themselves be part of the owning group. There is also the case of worker-owned cooperatives hiring external managers to make certain decisions. But here workers-owners have the power to recall managers (which they do not have in capitalist firms). I also acknowledge that there is significant variety within the sets of capitalists and workers as defined—e.g. capitalists may be owners of big corporations or small businesses, and workers may be employed full-time, part-time, be subcontracted in the gig-economy, unemployed, and so on. I thank Joseph Heath for comments on these matters.

[2] Of course, the domination of workers is a central topic in Karl Marx's writings. I will not focus on Marx's views in this chapter. But, in this footnote, I offer a summary survey of Marx's remarks about how capitalism constrains the self-determination of workers.

Although it appears that workers are free and equal to capitalists in the sphere of circulation—e.g. when the labour contract is set up—once the 'hidden abode of production' is revealed, things are different (Marx 1990: 279–80). Marx describes the predicament of workers in factories as involving unfreedom in various ways. Workers are converted into 'automatons' controlled and stunted by machines and their rhythm (Ibid: 544–53). Workplaces are organized like military barracks in which bosses wield despotic power over them (Ibid: 544–53; see Marx 1978f: 479). In capitalism, workers are 'free' in a 'double sense'. They may sell their labour power as a commodity, but they are also free from (devoid of control of) means of production. Capitalists, who own the means of production, buy the labour power of the workers who do not and must thus sell their labour power to make a living (Marx 1990: 272–3, 874). This inequality regarding property in means of production shapes contractors' bargaining power in the sphere of circulation, so that in the end it also fails to display equal freedom. Wage-labour is only 'formally free' (Ibid: 928). More specifically, Marx says that although workers voluntarily enter the contract of exploitation, they are 'compelled [to do so] by social conditions' (Ibid: 382). 'The silent compulsion of economic relations sets the seal on the domination of the capitalist over the worker. Direct extra-economic force is still used of course, but only in exceptional cases. In the ordinary run of things, the worker can be left to the "natural laws of production", i.e. it is possible to rely on his dependence on capital, which springs from the conditions of production themselves, and is guaranteed in perpetuity by them' (Ibid: 899). Additionally, market processes at a large scale are far from being controlled or even understood by the individuals entangled in them (Marx 1978e: 163–4; see 1990: 163–77).

Marx is sceptical about the invocation of the idea of freedom to defend the capitalist organization of the economy. Thus, responding to the view that capitalist property rights are necessary for 'personal freedom, activity and independence', Marx (1978f: 484–6) argues that, effectively, a society framed by such rights deprives workers of freedom, as they are subjugated to the capitalists who appropriate means or production and the product of workers' labour. The liberty invoked in declarations of the 'rights of man', when coupled with rights to private property, turn out to be a 'protection of egoism' (Marx 1978a: 42–3; see also 34, 45–6). '[O]nly in the community … is personal freedom possible' (Marx 1978e: 197). The concepts of 'freedom, equality, etc.' are deployed by the bourgeoisie as an ideology to cement its dominance, as the aristocracy did before, in feudal times, with concepts such as 'honour, loyalty, etc.' (Ibid: 173).

Marx's rallying cry is to 'stamp out the despotism of capital over labour' (Marx 1978h: 652). When defenders of capitalism reject the socialization of the means of production by saying that this would limit the freedom of private agents, it is relevant to consider Marx's (1991: 848) point that 'private ownership for some … [involves] non-ownership … for others'. As Marx sees it, a society that socializes the means

252 Human Dignity and Social Justice

To understand the relationship between capitalists and workers, we should see how it plays out in three spheres: (1) the day-to-day relationship within the workplace, (2) the setting up of a labour contract, and (3) the broader political process. Thus, workers face capitalists in the sphere of production, where many issues not codified in the labour contract arise regarding the control of production (such as the pace of work, the introduction of labour-saving technology, the technical division of labour, and decision-making about how various productive activities are to proceed). Second, workers face capitalists within the sphere of exchange, notably in the labour market, where they negotiate the terms of the employment contract (such as salary and the number of working hours). Finally, like the capitalists, workers seek to influence the state's decisions that impact on the overall shape of the economy and their specific standing within the two previous spheres. Policies regarding minimum wages, taxation and benefits, unemployment insurance, funding for training, unionization rights, and, more deeply, property rights, are examples. For each sphere, we can consider scenarios of three kinds, involving a relatively pure capitalist economy, a reformed capitalist economy featuring policies that limit the power of capitalists and boost the power of workers, and more radical transformations altering the very structure of their relationship. We can in turn consider cases in which capitalists and workers act as single individuals and cases in which they act as part of larger sets of people, including collective agents (such as a union or a business association).

Start with a minimally constrained capitalist economy. In the sphere of production, capitalists have sweeping power over workers' lives. Capitalists give orders to workers regarding what they are to do at work, determine with whom they should do it, and how fast and in what ways their tasks must be performed. Capitalists' decision-making power is unilateral and not accountable to workers.[3] Capitalists can enforce their diktats by credibly threating to fire workers, or to make their schedules of activity more gruelling, isolating, or humiliating. The mere fact that capitalists have the ability to do these things may motivate workers to adapt to their wishes, without need for explicit threats.

The subordination in the first sphere may seem only apparent. Some might argue that it is authorized by the fact that capitalists and workers enter into their arrangement voluntarily through the labour market, in which they

---

of production can simultaneously affirm freedom and community. With the 'expropriation of the expropriators', communism transforms the means of production into 'mere instruments of free and associated labour' (Marx 1978h: 635). 'The veil is not removed from the countenance of the social life-process, i.e. the process of material production, until it becomes production by freely associated men, and stands under their conscious and planned control' (Marx 1990: 173).

[3] Anderson (2017).

The Critique of Domination   **253**

negotiate as free and equal bargainers. Furthermore, capitalists and workers can exit their relationship at will. Capitalism is not slavery. However, this equality in the second sphere is only apparent. With some exceptions (such as when a worker is exceptionally skilled, and the labour market is very tight), a worker would lose much more than their employer if they leave their job. It is difficult to find another job that pays at least as much. New jobs involve challenging learning curbs. Taking a new position might require moving to a new neighbourhood or city. The time spent searching might require use of savings the worker does not have or the use of which would increase their vulnerability in the future, or impose severe penury for family members. Some workers are also bound by 'non-compete' clauses that further restrict their room for manoeuvre. And so on. Entry into the capitalist class is also very hard given workers' lack of initial capital, the tendency for most small businesses to fail, and the competitive advantage of large firms which are already established. Even if a few might escape their status as wage workers, most will not, and they cannot all do it simultaneously within capitalism. By contrast, capitalists can hold out in a negotiation by relying on accumulated wealth. They can also hire and train other workers relatively quickly. Since the costs to workers are higher, the threat of exit is not credible, and thus bargaining on its basis not very effective. The capitalists with whom they negotiate are typically far stronger. Crucially, their bargaining proceeds against a background of inequality in access to productive resources. Capitalists own means of production and workers only own their labour power—or, if they own capital, it is not enough to allow them to avoid having to sell their labour power to get enough income to make a living. This inequality slants the playing field to the advantage of capitalists from the start.

Might this inequality not be acceptable, however, when it is the result of legitimate processes operating in the third sphere? Property rights in means of production, and the other legal underpinnings of the economy, are framed by the state. If capitalists and workers are equal citizens in a democratic political system, then the governmental framing of the second and first spheres might render their contours acceptable. Non-domination in the third sphere authorizes domination in the others. In response, the critic of capitalist domination continues their indictment by arguing that where there is domination in the first and second sphere, there is likely to be domination in the third. Even assuming that the political process has a roughly democratic form (which only has arisen, historically, after much struggle by working people to gain the right to vote in the face of stiff and often bloody repression), any capitalist has much more influence on it than any worker. Capitalists can offer state bureaucrats lucrative jobs in the private sector before and after they are in office, incentivize politicians through generous campaign donations, own

254 Human Dignity and Social Justice

mass media or pay for disproportionate access to them, employ highly skilled lobbyists to pester officials with detailed proposals, and signal to government that if restrictions on their power are imposed, they will move their capital abroad, thus depressing the tax base politicians need to fund popular policies and be re-elected. If capitalists coordinate through business associations, as they regularly do, their power is very significant indeed. Domination in the three spheres forms an infernal circle of mutual reinforcement.

Of course, contemporary reality is more complex, especially once we take into account that workers are capable of collective action. Erik Wright notes that in the three sites or institutional contexts identified, capitalists and workers struggle and sometimes reach compromises, and workers can generate and utilize associational power in each of them. In the sphere of production, workers can form works councils to have some say on how production is carried out (as they do in the codetermination system in German firms). In the sphere of exchange, workers can form trade unions to engage in collective bargaining. In the larger political sphere, they can launch political parties (such as labour, socialist, or social-democratic parties) to champion their interests in the crafting of legislation and public policy.[4]

Wright also helpfully distinguishes between *structural* and *associational power*. The former is the relative power that agents have in virtue of their class position within a class system. Workers have some power as owners of their labour force. They may not be put to work without their formal consent. Capitalists in turn have power as owners and controllers of the means of production. Capitalists can bargain with significant clout with workers. Since workers cannot directly access means of subsistence, they must seek employment under some capitalist, who normally seeks to maximize profits by maximizing workers' productivity and minimizing labour expenditures. On the other hand, both workers and capitalists can form associations which increase their relative power. In the case of workers, the development of associational power is very important given that their structural power as individuals is comparatively weak. Through works councils, unions, and political parties, workers can act collectively to elicit more convenient arrangements in their conflicts and negotiations with capitalists. Short of overthrowing the capitalist class system altogether, workers' best hope for increasing their self-determination and well-being lies in developing strong collective agencies of these kinds. Such collective agencies also enable them to pursue more ambitious trajectories of transformation leading to a post-capitalist society.

---

[4] Wright (2015a). See also Arnold (2017).

The Critique of Domination   255

The relation between increases in unionization and other forms of workers' associational power and the interests of capitalists is complex. There obviously is conflict, as increasingly powerful workers are able to limit capitalists' decision-making over the organization of production, wages, hiring and firing, and other crucial features of the economic process. On the other hand, as Wright also argues, if the associational power of workers grows beyond a certain point, it might actually function in a way that benefits capitalists. Collective workers' associations can solve a collective action problem for capitalists, ensuring that they all pay their workers decent wages that boost consumption and, with it, capitalists' profits. Furthermore, workers' associations may discipline their own rank and file, securing that protests and disruptions are limited, thus generating a predictable and stable environment for investment and profit. The following Table 7.1 summarizes Wright's key points.[5]

Wright also considers the possibility that if the associational power of workers along the three spheres extends to approach the limit of democratic socialism (in which workers control the means of production), then of course the synergy between the interests of capitalists and the expansion of workers' power ends.[6]

This leads us to the third and final kind of scenario, which concerns deeper structural transformations. The domination of workers by capitalists could

Table 7.1 Wright's key points.

	Characteristic forms of working class power	Capitalist class interests threatened by increasing working class power	Capitalist class interests facilitated by increasing working class power
Sphere of production	Works councils	Unilateral ability to control the labour process and job structure	Ability to elicit complex forms of vertical and horizontal cooperation; cheaper solution to information problems in production
Sphere of exchange	Trade unions	Unilateral ability to hire and fire and make wage offers	Ability to restrain wages in tight labour markets; ability to sell what is produced (Keynesian effects)
Sphere of politics	Political parties	Unilateral political influence over redistributive policies	Ability to sustain stable tripartite corporatist cooperation

[5] Wright (2015a: 210). (I reverse the ordering of the spheres of production and exchange in Wright's exposition).
[6] Ibid: 218ff.

256 Human Dignity and Social Justice

be challenged more decisively if it is the structural power of capitalists over workers that is targeted. One way in which this could be done is by introducing a high unconditional basic income. This policy would disable a crucial source of workers' vulnerability—their inability to access means of subsistence without taking employment under some capitalist owning means of production. Secure in their survival, workers could bargain on stronger terms with any capitalist, and wait it out until a better offer of employment is given. They could also engage in forms of work—such as community service and homemaking—which are highly meaningful and allow for more self-determination. Workers could also form worker-owned and run cooperatives which are more viable and stable. As their subsistence is guaranteed, they could stick with the cooperatives through the hazardous initial phase, and even in times of crisis; they could thus more easily attract new members and investment. More dramatically, workers could socialize the control of the means of production, dissolving the capitalist class structure to establish some form of socialism. If the structures of a socialist economy are democratic (avoiding the tyranny of an unaccountable state or a ruling political elite) they would maximize workers' social power, and eliminate their domination both by capitalists (a class that would no longer exist) and the state. The process of getting there could proceed abruptly or incrementally. The former path creates the risk that a militant elite comes to dominate the population through the state. The latter path, in turn, faces the difficulty of succumbing to counter-pressures by currently entrenched capitalist and political elites. A middle-way is to introduce and nurture experiments in non-dominated economic activity (such as those featured in the social economy sector). These experiments would combine state support (via a universal basic income, incentives, or direct investment), workers' management of firms, and the presence of stakeholders' oversight, and they could strengthen workers' social and political power to introduce further changes later on.[7]

3. Domination: An Analytical Framework

What is domination? In this section, I propose an analytical framework featuring a set of interrelated descriptive dimensions. Although deployed in them, this framework is independent from the substantive normative arguments advanced later in the chapter. A reader who does not find the

---

[7] For surveys of socialist proposals, see Gilabert and O'Neill (2019: sects. 4–5); Wright (2019); O'Shea (2020).

The Critique of Domination   **257**

normative arguments appealing could still find the analytic framework useful to articulate alternative moral assessments of domination.

3.1 Definition of domination

The plausibility of the characterization of a concept typically depends on the purposes of the theoretical or practical exercise in which it is deployed. There are three desiderata that I take into account when articulating my definition of domination. The first desideratum, the function of which is to ease communication, is that a definition of a term should try when possible to fit its ordinary usage in the relevant contexts in which it is employed, or justify any departures. Existing usage may not be always uniform, and when it is not, the proposer of a definition should explain why they choose one of the alternative usages, if any. Innovative usages may sometimes be appropriate, but, again, the proposer should explain why the innovation they suggest is fruitful. I will do this as I articulate the various dimensions of domination. Although the definition proposed here is fairly general, it is not thoroughly ecumenical, and this is so in part because of the other two desiderata, which explain why some departures from certain usages are justified. The second desideratum is that since my definition of domination is meant to enable and sharpen normative debates, it should help prevent circular moves within them. It is not a good idea to pack into the concept of domination controversial substantive claims about what is wrong with it; these should be explicit topics of normative argument. To help debaters avoid talking past each other, I offer a non-moralized definition of domination. I do not deny that 'domination' is often used with normative, and typically critical, intent. But not every use is of this kind. We sometimes say, for example, that a football team is dominating another in a match, without implying that there is anything morally wrong with that. And even for the cases in which we are using 'domination' in normative discourse it is best, I think, that we use a non-moralized definition that allows us to foreground substantive discussion about what makes the domination we criticize normatively problematic. Finally, the third desideratum is that a definition of domination should illuminate its agential dimension. There are important substantive normative questions as to how much power, and what kind of power, people should be allowed to have or exercise in their social relations. Since duties regarding domination, like any duty, can only be held by agents, it is reasonable to use a concept of domination that tracks possibilities of specifically agential power. I thus present domination as a form of agential power, although I also try to explain how the insights

258   Human Dignity and Social Justice

tracked by non-agential characterizations can be accommodated within the broader analytical framework.

Enough with methodological preliminaries. In the definition I propose, we can view domination as an inter-agential relationship consisting in a kind of social power configuration in which some agents have highly asymmetrical power over others such that, effectively, the will of the latter is subject to the will of the former. When you are dominated, someone else is able to ultimately determine much of what you do, why you do it, or what results from what you do. More formally: an agent A dominates another agent B with respect to some object—issue or outcome—O, in context or circumstances C, if and only if, and to the extent that, B's engagement with O does not ultimately reflect B's will but A's will. If A dominates B with respect to O in C, then B's engagement with O—the path of agency of B regarding O—proceeds on A's terms rather than B's. A's will sets the boundaries—with B's will only counting insofar as it does not conflict with A's will. Let us unpack these ideas in more detail.

The definition of domination just stated can be clarified by drawing on Philip Pettit's illuminating account, while introducing two important modifications of it. In Pettit's account, domination is exposure to uncontrolled power of interference by others, i.e. the subjection to their will.[8] A can interfere with B's choices by removing, changing, or misrepresenting the options that B faces, so that B's relation to their choice is ultimately shaped by A and not by B. I add 'ultimately' to capture Pettit's point that an interference involves domination when it is not authorized by the party suffering it. Pettit illustrates this point with his *liquor cabinet case*, in which someone asks their spouse to not give them the key to the liquor cabinet immediately after demanding it in order to help them control their impulse to drink. Here the terms of the interference are set by B, not A. Domination is different. In it, B is effectively subject to A's will regarding O, as the terms on which B relates to O reflect A's will and not at all, or not sufficiently, B's own. This is what is meant in saying that A has uncontrolled power over B with respect to O. Importantly, B's subjection to A's will does not require that A exercise this power. The mere fact that A could exercise it guarantees that what A wants will set the boundaries of what B does. Furthermore, the mere awareness on the part of B that A has this power likely leads B to adapt their behaviour to A's wishes. To illustrate this point, Pettit uses the *non-interfering master case*, in which (rather unrealistically) the master allows their slave much leeway to act as they please. Since the master remains able to interfere, the slave is

---

[8] Pettit (2012: 50).

The Critique of Domination   **259**

dominated—and likely develops a tendency to ingratiate themselves with the master to avoid harm.[9]

This is a fruitful account. But to make it more ecumenical, I suggest two modifications. First, we should allow that mechanisms other than interference are relevant for domination. For example, A could affect B's predicament in a dominating way through their power to provide B with something B needs but does not currently have (as different from depriving B of something B needs and already has). More generally, A can influence B through their ability to add options, not only through their ability to affect those which already exist.[10] A capitalist can come to dominate a worker by offering them the only employment that would allow them to pay for their bills. We can use the notion of *intervention*, which is wider than that of interference, to capture this additional possibility.

A second modification is in order, this time concerning the object of domination rather than its mechanisms. Pettit focuses on intervention regarding choices, but we can also take into account the psychological processes leading to choices and the results flowing from chosen acts.[11] Final results are indeed relevant, as people's freedom surely includes their ability to make certain things happen with their acts. Pettit seems to acknowledge this already when he considers that options can be described in different ways. He holds that some consequences may be part of the description of options—by suggesting that O includes doing x to bring about y, for example. But stating a separate category is useful for fuller treatment of the issues arising, such as those regarding the frustration of an agent's plans regarding the generation of certain consequences which also involves acts by other agents. Psychological states and processes are also important. Pettit acknowledges some of the relevant issues when he characterizes an agent's options as including not only an objective dimension regarding what agents can do, but also a cognitive dimension concerning the agent's beliefs about what they can do. But a

---

[9] A further insight in Pettit's account is that an agent's freedom, to involve non-domination, must be *robust*, i.e. B's ability to determine an outcome must be relatively constant across possible variations in B's and other agents' wishes. This is why Pettit rightly takes support for freedom to involve 'resourcing' and 'protection': agents must have what they need to take advantage of the relevant options without depending on the whim of others, and to avoid invasive removal, replacement, or misrepresentation of such options by them (Ibid: 69–70). Thus, consider the right to form trade unions as a protective measure for workers to defend themselves against abusive bosses. It is problematic (from the point of view of freedom as non-domination) to refuse to recognize a union by arguing, as reportedly an Amazon representative in the UK did, that the company 'already offers what they [the union] are requesting for employees'. The workers ought to be allowed to have their union to defend their current options should their powerful bosses change their mind. See *The Economist* (2020).
[10] This point is also made effectively by O'Shea (2019: 11–2). Pettit (2012: 53–4) acknowledges a version of this possibility in which the options added by A to B's feasible set are such that B cannot refuse them.
[11] I am here disagreeing with Pettit's restriction of the object of freedom to only act-options (see Pettit 2012: ch.1).

260 Human Dignity and Social Justice

separate and fuller treatment is necessary to address not only beliefs about the existence of an option but also attitudes regarding its prudential desirability or moral permissibility. Pettit is mistaken in taking 'psychological' freedom or 'autonomy' as beyond the purview of discussion of freedom in political philosophy.[12] Psychological freedom is relevant to explain and predict political acts. It is also normatively important to characterize some political choices as free in the sense of being the result of agents' self-determined reasoning. Furthermore, subjective issues are within the scope of influence of political institutions and choices. (Think about policies about education and attitudes about how to conduct political communication—through propaganda or other rhetorical devices, reasoned deliberation, etc. Think also about the phenomenon of ideology, or cultural hegemony, in which some groups shape what other groups come to see as justified social orders.) Finally, sometimes the invasion of other agents' freedom targets their psychological states as an end rather than merely as a means to steer their behaviour. Indeed, the point of domination is sometimes to shape how people feel rather than what they do. Think about political instances of cruelty in which some groups try to impose suffering and humiliation on others. The psychological dimension is relevant for understanding domination both indirectly, as it affects choices and thus acts, and directly, as an intended result of efforts to create conditions of domination.

When we can then understand domination more broadly, considering agents' *paths of agency*. A path of agency with respect to O in C is made up of the ways the agent might be involved in shaping O in C: the agent's motives, their acts, and the final results of those acts.[13] Thus, if we think of the relation between an agent B and an outcome O, and we understand O as a comprehensive outcome including not only the final result but also the process leading to it,[14] then we can identify three important junctures at which another agent A might have power over, and dominate, B:

a. A can affect B's motives or attitudes (their desires, beliefs, etc.) regarding the items in their option set, for example by influencing the cognitive and evaluative processes leading to the formation of B's intentions.

b. A can affect what B chooses to do *given* B's pre-existing motives and attitudes, for example by influencing B's option set—removing, changing, or adding items in it.

---

[12] Pettit (2012: 47–9).
[13] Elster (1986: 48–50) also helpfully identifies these three junctures as affecting autonomous agency or the lack thereof.
[14] See Sen's (2009: 215–7) distinction between 'comprehensive' and 'culmination outcomes'.

The Critique of Domination **261**

c. A can affect the final results arising from B's acts, by for example intervening in ways that facilitate, hamper, or frustrate the fulfilment of B's intentions.[15]

Domination exists when, at any of these junctures, it is A's will rather than B's will that ultimately shapes B's relation to O. For example, a capitalist can frustrate a worker's plan to strike and get a salary raise by persuading this worker that they have a duty of loyalty to their employer to work on the terms the latter states, by credibly threatening this worker with dismissal if they strike, by convincing sufficiently many other workers to not join the strike effort this worker is engaging in, or by refusing to give a salary raise to the striking workers.

Taking the two proposed modifications into account, we can define domination in a more ecumenical way as follows:

Domination: An agent B is dominated by another agent A with respect to some object—issue, outcome—O in circumstances C if and only if, and to the extent, that A has a highly asymmetrical power to intervene regarding B's path of agency concerning O in C such that it is A's will rather than B's that ultimately sets the terms of B's engagement with O. (This definition assumes a dyadic relationship, but it can be made more complex to account for polyadic relationships involving further agents C, D, etc.)

Notice four important features of this definition. First, the definition is non-moralized, as the definiens does not include any normative terms. Of course, domination might be wrongful. But whether this is so, and why, should be shown through separate, substantive moral arguments (a matter we take up in Section 4). Second, the definition of domination is procedural. It focuses on how the wills of A and B relate when it comes to the determination of O, not on how that determination affects their interests (real or perceived).[16]

---

[15] We here take B's acts as meant to help cause or constitute some envisioned result. As John Searle notes, an agent can intend that their act F contributes to generating a certain result or goal G in two ways. They can see the relation as causal, intending G by means of F. Or they can see the relation as constitutive, intending G by way of F. This analysis applies also to collective cases in which an individual agent intends to do their part in what they see as a collective endeavour in which others are presupposed to be doing their respective part. Searle (2010: 50–5).

[16] My view of domination is here close to the one offered in Young (1990: ch.1). I also construe domination as a primarily procedural notion regarding the setting back of agents' self-determination, or their ability to shape the terms on which they live with others. Also, like Young, I do not take domination to exhaust the terrain of injustice. Young aptly distinguishes between domination and oppression. The latter is a distinctive harm regarding people's abilities of self-development (in my terminology, self-realization). My approach differs, however, in that it provides a unified account of the significance of, and relations between, problematic forms of domination and other forms of injustice, and does not take domination to range only over institutionalized contexts.

262 Human Dignity and Social Justice

Third, domination is seen as a specific form of power. It is a social rather than a self-regarding power. Furthermore, it is a specific form of social power, a case of power-over rather than a case of power-with others. A has *power over* B with respect to O in C to the extent that A can voluntarily determine the path of B's agency with respect to O in C. (A test for this phenomenon is to consider what would happen if the wills of A and B were to conflict. If A's will would likely prevail, and to the extent that it would, A has power over B. By contrast, B is free from A's power if, and to the extent that, it is B's will that would prevail.)[17] And finally, domination is a specific, heightened kind of power-over others in which the subject of power is deprived of the ability to set the terms of their practical engagement.

In our definition, domination is a highly asymmetrical form of power over others which is at or above a certain threshold of voluntary influence. There is some point at which A's power over B becomes domination. But above and below that point power-over is a scalar relationship. Above the threshold, the degree of power-over is also a degree of domination. How is the threshold identified? Intuitively, for B to be dominated by A it is not enough that A would likely win if there is a conflict. Something more dramatic is at work in the case of domination, so that B's agency is severely compromised rather than merely frustrated. This is marked by saying that when there is domination, the dominating agent determines the terms on which the dominated agent relates to certain outcomes. Beyond this general intuitive remark, I think that the question about thresholds is best answered with the context of description in view. For example, imagine a cooperative in which workers, after much deliberation, decide by vote that some decisions regarding production are to be made by certain appointed representatives, while reserving the right to remove them later on, or change the constitution of the system of representation, after a certain period of time. Day-to-day production in this cooperative would feature some agents making some unilateral decisions about what others do, but it does not seem to involve domination of the latter by the former. Things would be different if the managers were not at all accountable to the workers, as it happens in capitalist firms. What is key in the end is whether, with respect to the relevant object and in the relevant circumstances, the more powerful agent is the one ultimately setting the terms of engagement of the less powerful agent.

It is important to note that domination is hardly ever complete, in the sense of it being strictly impossible for the dominated to do otherwise than what

---

[17] I state how I understand power in Appendix I. The important point here is that domination is a very specific form of agential power. Succinctly: (Agential) Power $\supsetneq$ Social power $\supsetneq$ Power-over $\supsetneq$ Domination.

The Critique of Domination **263**

the dominator wants. Typically, domination occurs in a context of conflict between wills, and resistance is possible (even if costly or difficult).[18] The dominated will is still the will of an agent who has some freedom to push back.[19] Only at the limit of domination do we encounter the complete obliteration of the dominated agent so that the latter does not operate as an agent at all with respect to O but is turned into a mere object of causal manipulation by the dominator. So, the continuum of power-over is such that as this power increases it becomes domination, but at an even higher point power-over shifts away from domination to involve the sheer destruction of the agency of its subject.

Fourth, the definition of domination offered here is quite flexible. It allows for the identification of various specific analytic dimensions, such as the following:

- The *degree* of domination: the extent to which A has power over B (with respect to O in C). We discussed this dimension in the previous paragraphs.
- The *range* of domination: the set of objects, i.e. the specific issues or outcomes O1 ... On with respect to which A dominates B. Consider, for example, the varieties of domination of workers.[20] Slaves may be compelled to work through threats of violence, while wage labourers typically may not. In turn, wage workers may have more or less room for manoeuver to avoid working for an employer, or to stand up in negotiations with them, depending on whether they are permanent or temporary residents in the territory. Legal constraints may put limits on the number of days or hours a worker may be asked to work, or the kinds of danger they may be commanded to undergo as they perform their tasks.
- The *arenas, sites* of domination: the instances of social life in which domination might occur, such as intimate personal relations, markets in goods and services, or the formal political process. Particularly salient for our discussion are the three spheres of the relation between capitalists and wage-workers identified in Section 2—production, the labour market, and the wider political process.

---

[18] Domination can be seen as an aspect of a process rather than as a frozen state, so that conflict and opposing agential operations can exist and affect dynamically the course of the social relationship. See Boltanski (2009: 176).
[19] A significant metaphysical question, which will remain unexplored here, is whether, and to what extent, an account of domination must commit itself to the existence of freedom of the will.
[20] Piketty (2019: 250, 271). See also, Cohen (2001: ch.3).

264 Human Dignity and Social Justice

- The *scope* of domination: the set of agents (B1...Bn) who are dominated, and the set of agents (A1...An) who dominate, in a certain relationship.
- The *depth* of domination: the aspects of B's agency over which A has dominating power. They may concern, in particular, the junctures within the paths of agency mentioned above. A's domination of B is deeper the further 'inward' A can go to affect B's agency. The gradient goes from controlling whether someone achieves some intended results after they have acted, to how they act, to how they think and feel before acting.
- The *mechanisms* of domination: the mechanisms through which an agent can intentionally influence another agent's engagement with the relevant outcome. They include forms of power that are not objectionable as well as others that are—e.g. rational argument, force, coercion, or manipulation. These forms of power can also be forms of domination when they reach a threshold of asymmetry such that it is the will of the power-wielder, and not that of the subject of power, that ultimately determines how the relevant outcomes are generated.
- The *resources* of domination: what the dominator can use to exercise their power, such as their prestige, social status, authority, economic means, tools of violence, organization, knowledge, and rhetorical or argumentative skills.
- The *dynamic* dimension: the processes through which configurations of domination can be changed—either tempered or radically overhauled.

3.2 Structural domination

It is worth exploring in some detail the issue of the scope of domination. The agents involved can be of different kinds: single individuals, group agents (like business corporations), or individuals coordinating to act as a team (such as protesters).[21] These distinctions generate many logically possible cases. In a relation between A and B, either can be a single individual agent, a group agent, or a team. The power relations underpinning domination may also be polyadic and involve various criss-crossing alliances and

---

[21] Simpson (2017); Lovett and Pettit (2019). The list given above does not include another kind of collection of individuals, viz. multitudes, which have no common will. By contrast, group agents have organized mechanisms for generating and revising common judgements and decisions, and teams have at least an episodic will expressed in their joint intentions and strategizing (unlike the mere multitude, they feature common awareness of participants' desires, and some shared effort to fulfil them through their concatenated acts). See Lovett and Pettit (2019: 368–70, 377).

The Critique of Domination **265**

triangulations. Consider, for example, the Marxist view that economic domination holds between classes, that more than two classes might be involved (so that, for example, industrial capitalists may sometimes operate in alliance with self-employed owners of small businesses, or a landed aristocracy), and that the individuals within the classes may or may not succeed in associating or acting collectively.

The only restriction in this analysis is that domination holds between entities with a will, i.e. agents. But can non-agential entities such as social structures (i.e. certain patterns of economic, political, legal, or cultural relations within social practices) be dominators or are they, instead, to be seen as enablers of domination by agents? I favour the latter option. Large social structures, even when they are not directly controlled by any single agent, are relevant factors in describing domination. But, not being agents, they are not themselves dominators. The issue might be merely terminological if structures are seen as in principle explainable in terms of the states and activities of agents as they relate to each other in certain circumstances. Still, it is important to capture the phenomenon of structural domination, in which some agents are dominated by others thanks to the mediation of certain conventional rules and institutional setups. In structural domination, agents behave (at least in part) *as* bearers of certain roles or positions within social structures, so that the existence of these structures is significant for explaining how they act and what they can achieve.[22] If Felipe works under the direction of Gregory, their power relations would be different depending on whether Felipe and Gregory relate as slave and master or as wage labourer and capitalist employer. The same individuals inhabiting different structures regarding property in productive resources would be able to approach each other in different ways and achieve different results.[23]

---

[22] See the illuminating discussion in Haslanger (2016), which argues that structures are an aspect of social practices. Haslanger distinguishes the following factors conditioning one's engagement in a practice: (a) 'Personal *attitudes*, habits, dispositions; both mine and the personal attitudes of those I interact with'. (b) '*Resources*: the materials/tools available. (Note that materials/tools may also include skills, time?)'. (c) '*Schemas*: the collective concepts, narratives, expectations, of those in my cultural milieu' (Ibid: 127). In Haslanger's account, personal attitudes yield 'psychological constraints', resources yield 'physical constraints', and schemas yield 'social constraints'. Structures belong to the third component. Given certain resources, schemas generate choice architectures for agents, making certain types of action available. Haslanger seeks to distinguish this approach from methodological individualism by presenting schemas as independent of personal attitudes. I do not think, however, that rejection of methodological individualism is necessary. Schemas can be accounted for in a social psychology that does not reify structures but sees them instead as aspects of individuals' psychological life as they form, sustain, and change how they approach each other in their practical entanglements. They do not exist above and beyond those mental processes.

[23] In terms of the analytic grid of power offered in Appendix I, social structures would be relevant for identifying resources, enabling conditions, and unintended outcomes of power.

266   Human Dignity and Social Justice

If we combine the foregoing points that the scope of domination may feature multiple agents and that it may engage certain rules and institutional setups, we can propose the following definition of *structural domination*:

> *Structural domination*: In C, and with respect to O, certain members of the set of agents G are structurally dominated by certain members of the set of agents F if and only if, and to the extent that, their relative social positions enable these members of F to ultimately set the terms on which these members of G engage O.[24]

It is an important task of social theory to account for structural power and domination in a more detailed way. There are difficult questions here. For example, how can this be done within an agential framework—which would reject the reification of structures and avoid the idea of 'agentless domination' as a category mistake? Could it be that some situations sometimes referred to as cases of structural domination are instead predicaments involving not domination but agentless pressure or influence? I will not fully answer these questions, but I offer some remarks which bear on the goal of this chapter of illuminating the normative structure of domination and its application to the issue of the domination of workers.

Let us consider the alleged domination of workers in the sphere of exchange. To illuminate the phenomenon of domination in the labour market, consider the common *Dominating Deal* type of case. The following Table 7.2 identifies a setup with some possible outcomes and their associated pay-offs (stated in ordinal scores such that 3 is the best and 1 is the worst, and ranging over whatever considerations are subjectively significant for the agents involved).

In the case of the labour market, in which A is a capitalist and B a worker, the typical situation is as follows. The capitalist offers the worker employment under their direction. Taking the job is better for the worker than no job. Even better for the worker would be an alternative deal in which the worker has more freedom at the workplace (or more of other benefits, such as pay). But the situation for the capitalist is the opposite, preferring scenario (ii) to (iii).

---

[24] This is a revision of O'Shea's (2019: 18) illuminating definition of structural domination, which states: '*X* is structurally dominated by the set of agents *Y* to the extent that their relative social positions enable the members of *Y* to arbitrarily determine whether *X* has the material, social, or political capability to function as an equal citizen'. The main difference in my rendering is its wider and more neutral reference to O instead of the narrower, and what strikes me as implicitly moralized, reference to certain civic capabilities. We should not confuse discussion about what it is for someone to be dominated with discussion of what instances of domination are unjust, wrongful, or otherwise normatively problematic. My focus here is on the previous, conceptual and descriptive issue only. O'Shea's analysis could be defended by saying that it is not an implication of it that domination is always wrongful—even if it *is* part of the general rationale for indexing domination to civic capabilities that these are normatively important for citizenship and individuals' quality of life. I thank O'Shea for discussion on this point.

The Critique of Domination 267

Table 7.2 Dominating Deal.

	Agent A	Agent B
i. No deal (with outcome (a) merely allowed by or (b) created by A)	2 (or 1?)	1
ii. Deal proposed by A	3	2
iii. Alternative, less inegalitarian deal	1 (or 2?)	3

The bargaining between the capitalist and the worker depends on how bad scenarios (i) and (iii) are for each of them. If (i) is clearly preferable to (iii) for the capitalist (if, say, the capitalist can easily hire someone else who would accept the deal), then the capitalist is more likely to get the worker to accept (ii) than if the reverse were the case. The worker's bargaining power increases to the extent that the worker's scores in (i) are improved (for example, if there are other jobs available that are at least as good, if there is a strong safety net regarding unemployment insurance and health care, and so on) and the scores in (i) for the capitalist are worsened (if, for example, hiring another worker is harder), so that the worker can credibly hold out to push negotiation in the direction of (iii).

Consider now the sphere of production. Something important in this discussion is whether a worker can exit their relationship with a capitalist. If so, some argue, the worker is free in the sense of avoiding domination. In reply, socialists emphasize two important points. First, a legal right to exit voluntarily (which workers typically have in capitalism, as different from what they face in a system of slavery) is not enough to avoid domination. The transition costs from one job to another must be perceived as acceptable for the option to be real. Second, it is important that there be options that do not feature, yet again, the limitations on self-determination we are worrying about. If all firms feature these limitations, then the worker is bound to be under the thumb of *some* capitalist, even if not necessarily the thumb of *this* or *that* capitalist.[25] Being able to choose your tyrant doesn't make you free from tyranny (you cannot be counted to really choose it if all the real options open to you feature it). To be free from domination, the worker must not only be able to exit the firm in which they are currently subject to the diktats of a capitalist, but to be in some firm in which they are not. This may mean there being real options to join other firms that foster the self-determination they are not able to enjoy where they are, or changing the firm in which they are so

[25] According to Marx (1978g: 205), workers 'belong not to this or that capitalist but to *the capitalist class*' (they must sell their labour power to *some* member of the capitalist class).

268 Human Dignity and Social Justice

that self-determination is given traction. In the absence of these alternatives, workers face structural domination.[26]

But could it be that in capitalism workers lack self-determination without also being dominated? This is how the puzzle arises. Assume a capitalist structural setup including the institutional facts that there is private property of means of production by capitalists, ownership of their labour power by workers, and access to consumption goods mostly mediated by money. Given this setup, an individual who is not a capitalist, is not wealthy (a rentier), and cannot make a living as an independent self-employed producer will have to seek employment under the direction of some capitalist or other. Thus, this worker will lack self-determination regarding work. They will not be in charge of the issues of whether and how to work, and will not have a real choice whether to work for some capitalist or other—i.e. they will lack self-determination in the spheres of production and exchange. Now, put aside the case in which this worker faces a monopsonic employer, and assume that the cost of exiting a workplace are not sufficiently high as to make the option of switching jobs personally intolerable. These assumptions are sometimes false, but not always. Now, in these conditions, the worker will not be at the mercy of any particular capitalist, but of some capitalist or other. The worker lacks self-determination, but are they also dominated? By whom? Not by any particular capitalist. Although in virtue of the structural setup, each capitalist has more power than each worker they deal with, the degree of power does not seem to rise to the level of domination. Could it be that the worker is dominated by the set (or an important subset) of capitalists in the society? For this to be true, the set has to operate as an agent (for we are assuming that domination is an inter-agential relation). This could happen when the capitalist employers operate as a group agent or as a team. And this is indeed the case to some extent in many actual contexts. For example, capitalists associate and influence the property and labour law in their society. (Recall the significance of the third sphere regarding the wider political processes, and its impact on the others.) Another, weaker version of this arises when capitalists are capable of forming groups or teams to act in these ways even if they are not doing so at the moment. This may suffice to lead the worker to adapt to the wishes of the capitalist they deal with. The worker could associate with others too, but facing much more cost and difficulty, and with much lower prospects of influencing the contours of the social order.

If any of these stories is plausible, then there is a sense in which the worker is dominated by a set of capitalists even if they are not dominated by any single

---

[26] I clarify the notion of 'self-determination' used here later in the chapter (beginning in Section 3.4).

The Critique of Domination **269**

one of them in particular. When they work under the direction of a capitalist, the latter does dominate them in some respects, within the workplace. But they do so because they also dominate them, in a different sense, *as members of the set of capitalists* with the power of intervention described above. This, I think, is the point that Marxists want to make when they talk about structural class domination. It is not that structures themselves dominate (they are not agents), or that there is agentless domination[27] (a problematic notion). What happens, instead, is that individual capitalists personally dominate some workers who work for them by using the structural power they have in the capitalist economy, and that capitalists collectively (as members of an actual or potential collective agent) dominate workers in virtue of their structural position and the resulting collective abilities to further influence the social rules shaping economic life.

If the foregoing stories fail, then workers lack self-determination without being dominated by capitalists. It could be that the capitalists themselves have little power to operate differently. Marxists indeed also sometimes emphasize the impersonal nature of economic processes in which capitalists and workers are cogs in a machinery beyond their control.[28] Thus, capitalists themselves have little choice but to treat workers as they do if they are to survive in harsh competitive environments—they may go out of business if they do not maximize profit at the expense of their workers' self-determination (and self-realization). If this, perhaps hyperbolic, picture is correct, then there is not domination in the strict sense. (A process, or the structure of it, does not dominate, because, again, it is not an agent.[29]) But this does not mean that

---

[27] This notion is used in Vrousalis (2021a: 51).

[28] Recall some of the passages from Marx cited in note 2. Individuals' freedom is constrained by 'the silent compulsion of economic relations' (Marx 1990: 899). Although workers voluntarily enter the contract of exploitation, they are 'compelled [to do so] by social conditions' (Ibid: 382). 'The silent compulsion of economic relations sets the seal on the domination of the capitalist over the worker' (Ibid: 899). Although here Marx takes capitalists to dominate workers, he also argues elsewhere that both are under the sway of the mechanisms shaping the capitalist economy. There is also a sense in which capitalists are not in control, but are instead to be described as 'personifications of economic categories, the bearers of particular class-relations and interests' (Ibid: 92). Marx refrains from holding the individual capitalist 'responsible for relations whose creature he remains, socially speaking, however much he may subjectively raise himself above them' (Ibid: 92). Now, the kind of limitation of freedom at stake here is not a form of domination but an agentless limitation of people's abilities for self-determination that is generated by the capitalist system as a whole. Also relevant here is Marx's discussion of commodity fetishism, a phenomenon in which producers' 'own movement within society has for them the form of a movement made by things, and these things, far from being under their control, in fact control them' (Ibid: 171). Again, this is not domination, but an agentless depression of producers' self-determination. Marx thinks it can be overcome through a rearrangement of the economy in which the 'freely associated' workers gain understanding and mastery of the production process (Ibid: 173). But the condition of lack of freedom overcome through this collective self-determination need not be seen as one of domination. It could instead be an instance of alienation.

[29] So, if the notion of 'impersonal domination' is used to refer to domination by no agent, it is metaphysically mysterious. For use of this notion, see, e.g., Roberts (2017: 102). For discussion on agential vs. non-agential accounts of structural power, see Hayward (2018); Lukes (2018); Gilabert (2018a); Forst

270 Human Dignity and Social Justice

there is no normative issue regarding freedom. It is just that the issue is not one of domination. It is one of depressed self-determination. (I return to this important distinction in 3.4 below.) If, even though not as capitalists and as wage-workers, but as human individuals pondering whether to maintain the current social structure in place, the people involved in this process could act together to change the structural setup, then this deficit of self-determination might not only be a bad thing but can constitute an injustice. After all, social structures are created and sustained by agents, and can be changed by them. Those who benefit the most from the setup, and have the most potential influence to change it, the capitalists, are perhaps more blameworthy. But workers could act too. In general, the most important task here may be not to point fingers and blame, but to identify who can do what to help change a setup that avoidably and foreseeably depresses people's self-determination (as well as their self-realization).

3.3 Change

I want to insist that relationships of domination have a dynamic aspect. They can be changed. The changes could be more or less dramatic. They could, for example, amount to partial reform or involve instead radical transformation or revolution. Partial reforms feature changes in degree of an existing form of domination. More radical alterations feature a dissolution of the form of the relationship so that the domination it carries disappears. One way in which this may happen is that the personal, social, or material circumstances C are changed into new ones C*, so that the previous relationship R becomes a new one R*. The agents themselves may change in crucial ways (re-categorizing themselves from A to A* and from B to B*).[30] Using terminology from the account of feasibility offered in Chapter 4, we can say that these processes

(2018). For a helpful discussion of how we can make sense of structural domination of workers without assigning agency to structures, see Gourevitch (2013: 603–7).

[30] To mark the distinctions, we can express this more formally by identifying three scenarios: (a) The status quo: R (A, B) in C; (b) Partial reform: R'(A, B) in C'; and (c) Deep transformation: R* (A*, B*) in C*. Notice that when the change deepens from C' to C* and from R' to R*, the parties to the relationship themselves change so that they no longer stand in the structural setup that preceded the change.

Marx, for example, viewed social reality as involving historical change of social structures. That view can be summarized through a schema comprising the following statements (which account for the modification of some interactive structure S):

1. S is complex, including various internal aspects, components, or poles, e.g., s1 and s2;

2. s1 and s2 define the identity of S, and their own identity, though their relations;

3. s1 and s2 are in a situation of dialectical contradiction: they simultaneously support and are in conflict with each other (and this contradiction also operates as an internal tension within themselves);

4. If the contradiction between s1 and s2 is very acute, then the interactive structure S will be transformed rather than merely reformed;

5. In the transformation of S into another interactive structure S*, one of the poles has primacy over the other (e.g., s1 has primacy over s2);

The Critique of Domination   271

of structural change (or of dissolution of a certain form of structural domination) involve agents' use of their *dynamic power*, their ability to alter their circumstances so that new forms of life become feasible. This use of their dynamic power might even be the object of *dynamic duties* to expand the feasibility set in that way.[31]

At the end of Section 2, we considered examples of changes in the relation between wage workers and capitalists. Stronger constraints in labour law and unionization rights allow workers to bargain in bolder ways with their capitalist employers. The introduction of a universal basic income could further enable them to credibly threaten to refuse or exit jobs that do not meet certain basic standards.[32] Socialist transformations would go even further because they involve structural change. By socializing the control of the means of production, they would facilitate relations of production which no longer feature a class of property-less workers having to toil under the direction of a different class of property-owning capitalists but are instead arenas of cooperation in which workers who are structurally equal codetermine the use their own economic resources.

The dynamic dimension is crucially linked to the dimension of depth, as both the reproduction and the change of relations of domination must engage what the agents involved take to be their reasons to behave towards in each other in certain ways. It is important to note that when accounting for juncture (a) of the path of agency, we are focusing on how agents' operative rather than normative reasons are affected. Operative reasons are reasons in the descriptive sense—they state what in fact leads agents to act as they do, what they take as significant and shapes their motives and attitudes. Normative reasons are different: they are what agents ought to recognize as grounds for their actions. Thus, it is possible for an agent to have operative

---

6. Although the dissolution of S involves the dissolution of its components $s1$ and $s2$, the component with primacy (e.g., $s1$) will have led this self-destruction as simultaneously being a positive self-construction, of which the new interactive structure S^* is a crystallization.

This is a modified version of the schema proposed in Gilabert (1998: 132). Examples of uses of this schema in Marx's works include his dynamic accounts of the relations between wage-workers and capitalist employers, civil society and the state, productive forces and relations of production, and use value and exchange value.

[31] See also the related, historical dimension of power stated in Appendix I. Historical processes could increase the ability to counter domination. But, as Teresa Bejan pointed out to me, they could also hamper it, as when subjection and abuse in the past makes an agent less capable to resist similar treatment in the present. Indeed, domination can have a sedimentation effect.

[32] A guaranteed income can also enable people to experiment with economic activity that is not organized on capitalist terms. Furthermore, it can benefit people who do not even have the option to join the labour market (either formal or informal). This is a predicament faced by many, especially in the Global South. With an income support from the state, they can set up their own economic ventures. An example is the 'economía popular' ('popular economy') schemes that emerged in Argentina after the economic crisis of 2001. These included cooperative production and exchange that operated outside the formal labour market, and allowed its participants to secure their subsistence as well as increase their self-determination and self-realization. I thank Roberto Gargarella and Romina Rekers for discussion on this point.

272   Human Dignity and Social Justice

reasons to dominate, or accept their domination by another agent, and yet lack normative reasons to do so, and vice versa. Sociological descriptions of domination typically canvass configurations of operative reasons, while moral assessments track normative reasons. Sometimes these two operations are combined in the same intellectual endeavour. Consider, for example, what is sometimes called 'ideology critique'. A critic says that an existing societal outlook celebrating the existence of private property rights in means of production and an open labour market in which workers owning their labour force make contracts to work under the direction of owners of means of production is ideological. To explain this, the critic says that accepting the outlook shapes individuals' maintenance of the capitalist system, and that this system works in the end against their real interest to live in an alternative economic system in which they enjoy greater self-determination. The first point refers to operative reasons. The second point also makes descriptive (predictive) claims about how certain putative interests would be affected by alternative economic systems, but, in addition, draws on normative reasons regarding what interests are real. Talk about 'real interests' is often contrasted with talk about 'apparent' or 'perceived' interests. When talking about workers' real interests, the critic is typically making claims about what workers ought to care about, not about what they in fact care about (which may or may not be greater self-determination).

There are other issues to explore regarding the dynamics and depth of domination, such as long-term processes shaping non-conscious habits, dispositions, and physiological configurations. Desires, beliefs, and emotions can be construed in a broad sense to include processes or states that are intentional but unconscious or that are relatively diffuse. But even then, we may also have to consider these other factors. These additional, non-conscious factors certainly affect how an agent behaves, and also the beliefs, desires, and emotions they are likely to form. Importantly, they are the target of both efforts to dominate and to overcome domination. Think about struggles over the shaping of routines and rhythms of production and the spatial configuration on the shop floor, or over the extent to which workers have a say or can take the initiative in determining how production unfolds. Processes of training or habit formation are used to get agents to more or less automatically accommodate to the will of dominators, and are contested by subjects of domination who are engaged in a process of self-affirmation and emancipation. Such processes of contestation include the cultivation of alternative habits and practices that undermine the depth of domination.[33]

---

[33] For a survey of the sociological literature on the ideological and cultural shaping of agents' desires, beliefs, and dispositions, see Wright (2010: 283–6). Foucault's (2001) insight that power and domination involve 'constitution' of besides 'interference' with agents' subjectivity is also relevant. See further Lukes's

The Critique of Domination   **273**

3.4 Agential power, self-determination, and non-domination

Before turning to the task of developing a substantive normative account of domination, I introduce a final set of analytic points which will be important for that discussion. They concern the differences between agential power, self-determination, and non-domination.

We start with the general notion of *agential powers, abilities,* or *capabilities.* Consider the difference between the following items:

(i)   Basic capacities;
(ii) Circumstances (personal, material, social);
(iii) Agential powers, abilities, capabilities.

Agential powers, abilities, or capabilities (I use the terms as synonymous) concern an agent's level of voluntary control of certain outcomes, the extent to which whether they arise is up to them. Now, abilities are a function of the combination of the other items in the list: certain basic capacities and certain enabling or supporting circumstances, such as some personal, material, and social features of the context of action. These distinctions are analytic (the components are in fact typically intertwined) and the terminology is stipulative (the terms have been used in other ways as well).

For example, an agent has basic capacities for prudential and moral judgement. They can reason from a concern for what is good for them, and also from a concern for what is good for all. But to be able to make significant prudential and moral choices that affect political outcomes, the agent needs more than these capacities. The capacities must be developed, and this requires practical exercises of them in favourable circumstances in which they can be honed. If the agent is malnourished, or if they will be tortured or shot or discriminated against if they attempt to engage in political action, then their power with respect to political matters in these contexts is rather low. If they have resources and opportunities, and are allowed and helped when they try to act politically, then their power will be far greater. An agential power is a property held by an agent, expressed by the modal auxiliary 'can voluntarily', or with the phrase 'it is feasible', and has as its object certain outcomes (certain acts and their consequences). (Another relevant way to put this is to say that it is up to S whether O materializes.) 'S can voluntarily determine O', or 'it is feasible for S to determine O', in turn, can be illuminated by saying that S would determine O if S tried (and S can try). Thus, to say that

---

(2005) discussion of the 'third dimension' of power and Rainer Forst's (2017b: ch.2) account of 'noumenal power' as involving the ability to shape the operative reasons others draw on when they act.

274 Human Dignity and Social Justice

Sarah has political power would involve, for example, that if she went for it (as she can), she would speak publicly, vote, or run for office, and in these and other similar ways she would influence the policies enacted in her political environment.[34]

Let us turn now to the notion of *self-determination*. In general, agents are self-determining when (and to the extent that) they can or do voluntarily shape how they live their lives. The reference to both 'can' and 'do' in this definition is meant to mark the distinction between self-determination as a possibility and as its successful actualization (the term is often used in both senses, with the context clarifying which one is at play). More formally, an agent S's self-determination with respect to a certain outcome or issue O is their ability (or the exercise of this ability) to control the terms on which they relate to O. S determines themselves with respect to O to the extent that they can, or do, control their pursuit of O. It is enhanced, for example, when S can or does choose what to do, reflectively endorses the motives on which they base their choices, and obtains certain results as intended. There may indeed be different aspects of this relation: whether S intentionally targets O at all, whether S controls whether O occurs, whether the intentions of S regarding O are based on S's own desires and beliefs, and whether those desires and beliefs are rationally controlled by S (whether for example they are reflectively endorsed—or reflectively endorsable—by S rather than the result of internal compulsions or external manipulation).[35] The more S displays these features, the deeper their self-determination is. S's self-determination in their life activities is hampered or expanded depending on what happens with these relations. The extent of self-determination turns on how much S

---

[34] Like John Maier, I take abilities to be agential powers with action-related objects. See Maier (2021: sect. 1) However, I take the relevant objects to also include activities without an outward behavioural counterpart (such as formulating in inner thought a French sentence without uttering it in public), and to range over not only acts but also their intended results. I use the broad term 'outcome' to capture these various items in the object domain of an ability. An outcome can include a certain state of affairs that the agent is achieving intentionally in, or by means of, doing a certain act. We could use Maier's term 'general abilities' to refer to what I call 'basic capacities', but I think that a different label is helpful to refer to the basic capacities of an agent, and reserve the term 'ability' for the cases in which those capacities are developed and ready to deploy in action thanks to various personal, material, or social circumstances. Here I think that Martha Nussbaum's distinctions between basic, internal, and combined capabilities is helpful, and my account has similarities with it. (See Nussbaum 2011: ch.2.) Indeed, agential powers as I view them can also be characterized as combined capabilities.

[35] I do not assume that self-determination implies that the reasons S relies on to assess their desires, beliefs, and other attitudes must themselves be constructed by S. S's reflective endorsement may aim at recognizing external reasons—so that operative reasons are aligned with what the agent takes to be normative reasons. Metaethical realism about prudential and moral reasons is thus compatible with this account. I actually endorse that realism, and would invoke it to make sense of the significance of self-determination itself. We have reason to have self-determination whether we already value it or not. When we figure out whether to value it, we ask ourselves a normative question, not a descriptive, psychological one.

The Critique of Domination 275

is determinant in the junctures of their paths of their agency. Correspondingly, empowerment or disempowerment, in their instances as deficit of or gain in self-determination, can occur regarding those different junctures: choice of acts, the sub-intentional formation of choices, and the generation of effects of individual actions and of the aggregate acts by many individual agents.

Given the purposes of our current discussion, it is important to note that self-determination is not identical with *non-domination*. Domination involves a limitation of self-determination, but not every limitation of self-determination is a case of domination. When another agent dominates you, their ability to intervene in your life (or their use of that ability) deprives you of control over your choices, the consequences of your choices, or the deliberative formation of your intentions. But you may undergo deficits regarding these forms of control which are not the result of someone else's domination, or are only in part the result of it. Your lack of self-determination may also result from internal compulsions like obsessional desires, or insufficient skills to achieve what you want, which are not themselves, or at any rate not wholly, the result of actual or possible intervention by others. Your deficit in self-determination may also come from impersonal social processes or structures. An important example is a situation in which market competition imposes severe constraints on capitalists (a phenomenon, emphasized by Marxists, which we discussed in Section 3.2). Even if capitalists dominate workers, they themselves are pushed to behave in certain ways on pain of losing the competitive race with other capitalists and going out of business. Since markets and economic systems are not themselves agents, the reduction of self-determination they generate is not exactly domination (although, as we saw, they may be relevant for understanding the structural domination of some agents operating within them).[36] It may instead be a case of alienation. Domination is not simply lack of *self*-determination, but a lack of self-determination involving control by *another* over what the self does not control.

We arrived at the important point that deficits of self-determination may result from certain personal and social circumstances which are not, or are not entirely, accurately describable by reference to domination. What about

---

[36] A possible response is to talk about 'impersonal domination'. But I agree with O'Shea (2020) that this talk would sever the important link between domination and another agent's uncontrolled will. An important lesson from this point (which O'Shea does not consider), is that socialist freedom goes beyond republican non-domination. It requires workers' empowerment to shape the economic systems under which they toil so as to maximize their feasible prospects for self-determination and self-realization. This does not only involve limiting domination by other agents, but also countering non-agential constraints that do not involve domination (such as some impersonal market mechanisms).

276 Human Dignity and Social Justice

the relation between self-determination and agential power? Are they identical? I have construed self-determination quite broadly, as ranging over the three junctures of agency. But there could be a narrower interpretation that takes self-determination to focus on junctures (a) and (b) while excluding (c). Here self-determination would concern issues of choice and motivation, but not the issue whether the intended results of actions are in fact achieved. If this narrower construal is used, then there is a clear possibility that some deficits in agential power are not deficits in self-determination. You might be unable to determine O even if no other dominates you with respect to O, and even if you are capable of fully autonomous (competent and authentic) deliberation and choice regarding whether and how to pursue O, simply because you lack the material resources, or opportunities, to causally determine O as you intend. For example, you may be poised, as far as you are concerned, to develop and exercise your creative talents at work, but still lack the ability to do so because of the absence of jobs in which you can do it.

I have chosen to construe self-determination in the broader way because I think that the third juncture of agency is intuitively significant for capturing the idea of an individual shaping their own life. But I acknowledge that there is no extensional loss if we construe self-determination more narrowly and capture the issues regarding the third juncture with an additional notion within a wider discussion about agential power. There is, however, another reason to insist on a distinction between agential power and self-determination, which I think is more consequential.

We can distinguish between the issue whether your intended results materialize and the issue whether other results you have not intended to bring about could materialize. Your self-determination is set back when your autonomously formed intentions are frustrated. But there could be some possible intentions which you form non-autonomously, or could form autonomously but do not, which might or might not be fulfilled in the circumstances. The prospective success or failure regarding those additional, hypothetical intentions would affect your agential power. Sometimes this may not be normatively relevant, but sometimes it might. This depends at least on whether there is anything of independent value that would be tracked by the intentions not formed. If there is, then there could be cases in which you might, for example, have self-determination without also having self-realization. You may, after due reflection, decide to seek a certain job, and succeed at getting it and doing as you perform it precisely the kinds of tasks you chose. But perhaps your creative talents would have been developed more fully in a different kind of job. It might be important whether a job

The Critique of Domination   277

of that other kind is available to you. That availability could be significant independently of self-determination, as what is important is not simply that you have a wider set of options to choose from. It is not just the number of options that matters, but the content of them. And it is not just the issue whether the options you go for are ones you have chosen after reflection, but whether your reflection tracked the value of those options appropriately. The significance of certain expansions of agential power that give more valuable options cannot be fully understood by reference to increases in self-determination.

This also means that the moral significance of what other agents can and choose to do with respect to the determination of your options is not just the one captured by the idea of domination. That idea focuses on whether other agents can or do remove, change, or give you options to make you do what they want you to do. But, in addition, we need another idea of possible or actual interventions by others that give you, or fail to give you, options to do what is valuable. When others do not give you those options when they could, the problem, when there is one, would not be one of domination but of lack of aid. It is not that they are imposing their will to make you do what they want, but that they are not willing to help you by giving you an option to do something you would have reason to do if you could (and have reason to prefer to be able to do). Besides negative duties regarding non-domination, others could have positive duties of aid.

So, in general, agential power or ability properly includes self-determination and self-determination properly includes non-domination. There is more to agential power than self-determination, and there is more to self-determination than non-domination. Still, it is fruitful to understand domination as a specific kind of limitation of self-determination, and deficits of self-determination as a specific kind of deficit of power or ability.

The foregoing discussion has important consequences for substantive normative debate. If the overall moral goal is some form of *empowerment*, as the (positive) freedom of agents to shape their own lives effectively and on their own terms, then we should not only aim at securing non-domination. As we saw, self-determination involves more than the absence of domination. It requires that agents control the relevant outcomes, not only that others do not control them in their stead. Furthermore, self-determination itself is insufficient. The ability to effectively secure certain outcomes requires certain options to do so. And not all outcomes, or options to get them, may be worth generating. Not all forms of empowerment are worth pursuing. Hence, if social justice requires certain *worthy* forms of empowerment, its implementation includes instances of non-domination and self-determination but

278 Human Dignity and Social Justice

cannot be exhausted by them. The helpful generation of worthy options is also important. The development of these points is the subject of the next section.

4. The Dignitarian Approach and Domination

We now turn to the substantive normative exploration of domination. It is important to distinguish between sociological and moral claims about domination. In a sociological mode, we can, for example, note that A can impose their will on B in a way that complies with some norms which either A or B or both deem legitimate. In a moral mode, we can proceed to assess whether such norms are themselves correct.[37] Put in another way, we can distinguish, as is sometimes done in discussions within philosophy of law, between positive norms and critically justified norms.[38] The former are the ones mentioned by the observer (such as the sociologist) when they describe how people think and behave, while the latter are the ones affirmed by a practical reasoner (including moral or political philosophers) when they try to figure out how they, or other people, ought to think and behave. Our focus now is on the latter.

I will argue that domination is a very important factor that bears on determining wrongful behaviour and injustice, but strictly speaking is by itself neither always a sufficient nor a necessary condition for them. To identify the precise significance of domination, we need a normative approach which can help us illuminate when, how, and to what extent it really matters morally. The Dignitarian Approach gives us a compelling way do this. Or so I will also argue.

4.1 Domination as a limited but important normative factor

We sometimes want to claim something like the following:

(A) A certain relationship R between agents A and B in which A has highly asymmetric power over B with respect to some object—some issue or outcome—O in context or circumstances C, morally ought to be avoided—i.e. it is wrongful.

---

[37] McCammon (2018: sect. 4).
[38] See, e.g., Nickel (2007: 28–9.) Nickel distinguishes between 'positive legal rights' and 'moral rights' and, within the latter, between rights as part of actual moralities and as part of critical or justified moralities.

The Critique of Domination **279**

Why might we claim this? There could be various justifications.[39] I will consider the view according to which R is wrongful because:

(B) R involves domination (i.e. in C and with respect to O, A is able to impose their will on B).

On this account, domination is a wrong-making feature of power-over relationships.[40] Is the connection between domination and wrongful behaviour, or injustice, this straightforward? It is not.

Consider two intuitively plausible moral cases (a third is added in 4.2). The first is the restraining by a third party of the movements of a murderous aggressor who is bent on continuing to kill others. Temporarily locking them up against their will would involve dominating the aggressor with respect to their movements. But, at least in some cases, it may be justified. If this is so, then domination is not a sufficient condition for moral wrongfulness. The second case is the requirement to rescue people in dire straits when this can be done at no grievous cost, such as when someone has been left on the side of the road and needs immediate medical assistance and you can drive them to the nearest hospital. It would be wrong that you do not do it, but avoiding domination is not what is at issue here. Thus, domination is also not a necessary condition for wrongful action. Domination is, at most, a limited normative factor.

It might seem that these cases can be explained through indirect reference to non-domination. But this would not work in all cases, and it would not always give what strikes us as the right, or complete, explanation. For example, restraining the killer may be justified as a means to preventing their domination of their victims. But it is not clear that killing is a form of domination (as the target is the life, not the will, of the victim—although certainly the victim's will as to whether they live is overrun). And even if the aggressor's ability to kill also puts them in a position to impose their will on their victims,

---

[39] Here I focus on relations of determinative justification rather than of epistemic justification. The issue is what makes it the case that certain responses are normatively required, not what warrants beliefs that they are. On this difference see Cullity (2018: 12–4).

[40] I focus on domination as a wrong-making feature. It can also be seen as a bad-making feature (taking 'bad' to refer to a prudential or some other, perhaps impersonal value). Similarly, freedom from domination may be seen as a good besides as a moral right. (For example, Forst tends to emphasize deontic statements referring to rights, while Pettit, in a consequentialist vein, uses formulations about the good.) See Lovett and Pettit (2019: 365); Forst (2013: 154–68). Thus, a condition of non-domination can be seen as (a) a good to be promoted or as (b) a right to be respected or protected. Still, it is worth noting that (a) is consistent with seeing non-domination as a right (as such a right can be given a rule-consequentialist justification) and (b) is consistent with there being a prudential interest in avoiding domination.

280 Human Dignity and Social Justice

the saving of the life of the victims, as different from their freedom from domination, provides an independent, and at least in some cases the main reason for the restraining. In the rescue case, it is true that needing rescue makes an individual highly vulnerable to the caprices of other people (who could, for example, put a price tag on their help). This is indeed an important point. But, again, it may not always be true, and it may not be necessary for explaining why the rescue is owed. To explain why you ought to help the individual in dire straits, you do not always need to say that you would be removing them from a situation in which you or others dominate them. It may be enough to say that you would be saving their life. And the remaining worry about vulnerability to domination could be attended to by not only requiring rescue, but by also forbidding that it be performed in a way that involves taking advantage of the individual in need (for example by penalizing the demand of rewards in exchange for aid). When help under these constraining conditions is not given, the wrong is not one of domination.

These cases can be extended to discussions of social justice. The conditions of justified imprisonment constitute a central topic of criminal justice. And some duties of rescue can be seen as enforceable duties of justice (and they are recognized as such in some legal systems).[41] The worries about domination not being, at least in some cases, either a sufficient or a necessary condition for the relevant normative judgements arise in those contexts as well.

Still, although the importance of domination is limited, claims (A)–(B) do seem to track a genuine intuition that domination is a very important normative factor. Return to the case of imprisonment. Imagine it applies to an individual who has committed many murders and is manifestly determined to continue doing so. If this individual is imprisoned against their will (they do not wish to be imprisoned, and they even deplore the legal system and the rules that authorize their imprisonment), they are clearly dominated regarding their movements but, arguably, this domination is justified. The justification could be one that says that this imprisonment is not wrongful at all because with their crimes the individual has forfeited some of their liberties. Another justification could be that the imprisonment is pro tanto wrongful but all things considered justified in view of other, weightier considerations (such as the importance of protecting the life of innocent individuals in imminent danger)[42] At the very least, it seems that the bar for justifying

---

[41] Fabre (2002).
[42] The analytic threshold between power-over and domination and the moral threshold of wrongful domination (pro tanto or all things considered) need not coincide. Determining the latter is a matter of substantive moral argument. For use of the example of justified imprisonment to prompt the question

The Critique of Domination   **281**

imprisonment must be set high. There seems to be a pro tanto right, or at least a presumption, against the domination that imprisonment enacts.

In other words, by justifying the response mentioned in (A) by citing the fact in (B), we could be invoking the following norms:

(C) Agents have a pro tanto, or at least a presumptive moral duty to avoid dominating others.

And:

(D) Agents have a pro tanto, or at least a presumptive moral right to be free from domination by others.[43]

But are (C) and (D) always true? And why are they true, when they are? What makes it the case that the fact that a relationship involves domination justifies a duty to avoid it, and a correlative right to be free from it? Again, different justifications are possible.[44] I will consider two justifications targeting intrinsic and instrumental features of relationships that involve domination.

On the first, intrinsic line of consideration, domination is wrongful because:

(E) Domination constitutes a violation of agents' right to self-determination.

On the second, indirect line of consideration, domination is wrongful because:

(F) Domination jeopardizes the implementation of agents' right to access the conditions for their well-being (such as their self-realization).[45]

---

whether domination is always a wrong-making feature, see also List and Valentini (2016); Claassen and Herzog (2021). I thank Natalie Stoljar and Éliot Litalien for discussion.

[43] I construe norms regarding domination as stating correlative duties and rights concerning its avoidance. I take these rights and duties to hold pro tanto, or at least presumptively, to allow for the possibility that they might be outweighed or undercut by other considerations when all things considered requirements are identified for the relevant circumstances. For ease of expression, I will not repeat these qualifications in future formulations unless needed.

[44] For example, besides the argument from self-determination, there could be an argument against domination based on a relational concern against being ruled by others which is independent from a concern in favour of ruling oneself. Doing what some lottery determines could prevent being ruled by others without instancing self-rule. See Kolodny (forthcoming).

[45] (D), (E), and (F) have parallels in prudential terms: (D') Agents have an interest in being free from domination by others, (E') Domination sets back agents' interest in self-determination, and (F') Agents have an interest in accessing the conditions for their well-being. The relations between (D) and (D'), between (E) and (E'), and between (F) and (F') are important and worth exploring. Indeed, the dignitarian account I offer later in this chapter illuminates them.

282 Human Dignity and Social Justice

Notice that (E) targets procedure-based considerations, while (F) targets additional, results-based considerations. The former concerns how agents go about deciding how they live, while the latter concerns the contents, or the further consequences of their decisions and acts.[46]

As we saw, self-determination can be defined as people's ability to shape their own lives—to determine what they do, why they do it, and the results of their acts. It seems important that people live lives they themselves shape, or author, so that they are not helplessly pushed around by forces they cannot control. This intrinsic value of self-determining agency is directly affronted by domination. When I dominate you, I deprive you of your self-determination. I crush your agency, rendering you a puppet of my will. Domination also seems problematic in a less direct way. This is so because the self-determination curtailed by domination can be causally, epistemically, and even constitutively linked to the access to conditions fostering people's well-being. When you steer your own life, you typically (although of course not always) try to figure out what is good for you and try to get it. What you end up doing may partly be good for you precisely because it is an activity you yourself chose to engage in. When I dominate you, and deprive you of your self-determination, your access to what is good for you is rendered less secure. It now depends on what I know, what I care about, and what I choose. Since, typically, others are less reliable graspers and seekers of your own good than yourself, your pursuit of well-being is rendered insecure by domination.[47] For example, you are less likely to get a pay raise, or the respite from intense rhythms of production that you need, if you work in a capitalist firm operating under the unilateral will of a powerful boss than if you work in a capitalist firm that features a union and a works council through which you can influence managerial decisions, or, more dramatically, in a cooperative that is democratically run by you and other workers.

Domination seems problematic because of its tendency to conflict with self-determination's intrinsic and instrumental contributions. To develop

---

[46] I say 'further consequences' to mark the point that we are focusing here on the 'culmination' part of 'comprehensive outcomes' (see note 14 above).

[47] This line of argument is important to defend democratic systems featuring citizens' political self-determination as better than authoritarian systems ruled by guardians. See Dahl (1989: 101–4). Thus, e.g., women's and workers' interests were taken far more seriously after they became enfranchised. 'The fundamental interests of adults who are denied opportunities to participate in governing will *not* be adequately protected and advanced by those who govern. The historical evidence on this point is overwhelming' Dahl (1998: 77). For a dignitarian account of political empowerment, see Gilabert (2019a: chs. 7 and 10). Landemore (2020) argues convincingly for democratizing work on the basis of intrinsic reasons regarding the value of autonomy and instrumental reasons concerning an increase in collective intelligence leading to better decisions improving workers' living conditions (such as reduced inequality in income, less discrimination, more resilience in times of crisis, more responsiveness to environmental issues, and enhanced disposition to participate in the wider civic and public sphere).

The Critique of Domination   **283**

these points more fully, we need a normative framework to explain their force and limits.

4.2 The Dignitarian Approach

How are self-determination and secure access to the conditions for well-being normatively important? And how can we account for the problematic obstacles to them imposed by domination while considering also the limits of domination as a normative factor? There are three such limits, or explanatory gaps, regarding domination as a consideration determining injustice (and other moral wrongs): it is not always a sufficient condition for injustice, it is not always a necessary condition for injustice, and it may often need to work in tandem with considerations about the independent value of the paths of agency it affects. The first two gaps were revealed by the cases of restraining the murderer and the rescue of the person in dire straits. A revealing case for the third gap can be produced by comparing two factories in which workers are equally dominated by their bosses, but in one of which they have more chances to unfold their creative talents than in the other. The latter is more morally problematic than the former, but considerations about domination are incapable of explaining this. These three cases (*restraining the murderer, rescue of someone in dire straits*, and *two factories*), are intuitively compelling and they are not far-fetched. They, and similar plausible scenarios the reader can surely think of, strongly suggest that the three explanatory gaps are real and must be filled.

In the remainder of this chapter, I deploy the Dignitarian Approach to account for the normativity of the critique of domination in a way that also fills these gaps.

Let us first briefly recall the core aspects of this approach. The fundamental idea is this:

Dignitarian Approach
We have reason to organize social life in such a way that we respond appropriately to the valuable features of individuals that give rise to their dignity.

People have *status-dignity*, which is a non-conventional, normative standing calling for certain forms of respect and concern towards them. *Dignitarian norms* state the respectful and concernful treatment status-dignity calls for. When we treat people in the ways called for—when the dignitarian norms are implemented—they also enjoy *condition-dignity*. People have

284 Human Dignity and Social Justice

status-dignity in virtue of some basic capacities which are valuable, such as their capacities for prudential and moral judgements, theoretical knowledge, sentience, empathy, creativity, and so on. A disjunctive list of these capacities constitutes the *basis of dignity*. Whenever an individual has some of these features, they have status-dignity. The content of dignitarian norms tracks those features, asking that we engage them in appropriate ways when their maintenance, development, or exercise face problems that can be ameliorated through social action. These predicaments constitute the *circumstances of dignity*. Social ideals or projects attending to such problems in some context, at various institutional and personal sites, must be envisioned to articulate and fulfil dignitarian norms for that context. We display *dignitarian virtue* when, and to the extent that, we are disposed to orientate ourselves by such ideals and projects.

To articulate the normative requirements flowing from the Dignitarian Approach, I have suggested the following ideal:

Solidaristic Empowerment

We should support individuals in their pursuit of a flourishing life by implementing both negative duties not to destroy or block their valuable capacities and positive duties to protect and facilitate their development and exercise of these capacities.

As we saw in the chapter on alienation, we can construe this ideal as demanding that we overcome or reduce conditions in which people suffer from morally problematic forms of lack of freedom, or unfreedom, in which we can observe:

(PLF1) obstacles to positive freedom (*agential power, ability, or capability deficit condition*),

(PLF2) which are feasible to remove or reduce through human action and social institutions (*feasibility of change condition*),

(PLF3) and which some agents have reason to so remove or reduce (*desirability of change condition*).

Solidaristic Empowerment demands mutual support. We should organize our social life so that we do not unduly curtail and so that we also foster our positive freedom to maintain, develop, and exercise our valuable capacities.

We can envision an egalitarian development of this perspective, in which everyone has rights to equal, effective, and worthy opportunities fostering their positive freedom. The schedule of opportunities should maximize, in feasible and reasonable ways, the prospects of each to maintain, develop, and exercise their valuable capacities. We could also articulate, within this perspective, our concerns regarding self-determination and the access to

The Critique of Domination **285**

conditions for well-being. The object of the rights would include feasible and reasonable support for people's abilities so that self-determination and self-realization (among other dimensions of well-being) are effectively accessible.[48] This framework provides us with what we need to illuminate the normative contours of the critique of domination. Or so I will argue. In 4.3, I explain more fully the dignitarian account of rights regarding domination, and in 4.4 I show how the resulting approach to domination is explanatorily fruitful and fares well by comparison to other approaches. I will continue illustrating the theoretical points by reference to the predicament of workers in the three spheres of exchange, production, and the wider political process.

4.3 Human dignity and the justification of the critique of domination

Recall that, as per (E) and (F), domination conflicts with people's right to self-determination and to access the conditions for their well-being. But what, in turn, justifies these rights? I will propose a specific, dignitarian line of normative justification. As explained in Chapter 1, the justification of moral humanist rights can be guided by the following idea:

Schema of dignitarian justification
Rights are justified if, and to the extent that, their implementation (through some institutions, practices, or acts) is either necessary for, or strongly contributes to, the feasible and reasonable support for interests regarding the maintenance, development, and exercise of certain valuable capacities of the relevant individuals—the ones at the basis of their dignity.

What is key, then, in justifying a certain right, is to show, regarding the putative right-holders and duty-bearers in the relevant circumstances, that (i) the object of the right concerns the right-holders' maintenance, development, or exercise of capacities in the basis of dignity—and thus that they have an important interest in accessing it; and (ii) the requirements the right imposes on the duty-bearers are feasible and reasonable (given their own abilities and important interests). Notice that this schema tracks responses to the conditions regarding problematic limits to positive freedom mentioned in Section 4.2: that there are situations that set back important interests in their object, that they are feasibly ameliorable, and that there are reasonable responses on the part of some agents to contribute to such amelioration.

---

[48] I rely here on the account self-realization provided in Chapter 6.

286 Human Dignity and Social Justice

We can now take up the task of providing a dignitarian justification of the rights to self-determination and to access the conditions for well-being mentioned in (E) and (F), and in this way back the critique of domination as a problematic limitation of their enjoyment. The main points in this strategy of justification are the following:

(G) The capacities involved in self-determination are at least part of the basis of agents' dignity (as status-dignity).

(H) Enjoying feasible and reasonably unhindered (or less hindered) self-determination is at least part of agents' condition-dignity.

(I) Domination involves a direct affront, and supporting access to a feasible and reasonable condition of freedom from domination involves an appropriate response, to agents' status-dignity.

(G)–(I) constitute the intrinsic dignitarian case against domination. The instrumental dignitarian case, in turn, involves the following core points:

(J) The capacities involved in well-being, such as those relevant for self-realization, are also part of the basis of agents' dignity.

(K) Enjoying access to feasible and reasonable conditions for self-realization (as well as other important aspects of well-being) is also part of agents' condition-dignity.

(L) Domination involves an indirect threat, and supporting access to a feasible and reasonable condition of freedom from domination involves an appropriate response to, agents' status-dignity.

The justificatory links can be revealed by reflecting on the fact that the normative requirements of dignity implement the ideal of solidaristic empowerment of agents as they unfold their valuable capacities—an ideal centred on supporting agential abilities or powers, which are precisely what domination sets back. What is key here is to identify forms of empowerment regarding the maintenance, development, and exercise of important capacities in the basis of dignity which domination hinders and whose avoidance enhances in feasible and reasonable ways. The two sequences in this justificatory strategy have a similar form. The first proposition identifies capacities in the basis of dignity. The second, in turn, alleges that some feasible and reasonable responses to people with those capacities are dignitarian requirements, or the object of rights. Finally, the third statement identifies a moral problem with domination insofar as it clashes with the implementation of those requirements.

The Critique of Domination **287**

We already mentioned in Section 4.1 the direct link between non-domination and self-determination and the indirect link between self-determination and self-realization. The two sequences in the dignitarian strategy of justification address these links. What it adds is that the rights to self-determination and to the conditions for self-realization support interests in maintaining, exercising, and developing valuable capacities in the basis of dignity. If this is correct, then these rights, and the critique of domination as setting them back, are revealed to have a sharp moral rationale and strength. The interests invoked in the formulation of the content of the rights and in the articulation of the critique of domination are anchored in the valuable capacities pertaining to the basis of dignity, which ground the moral standing of people to claim those rights and reject the domination that clashes with them.

These claims are, indeed, intuitively plausible. (G) seems correct in holding that when people have capacities for prudential and moral judgement, and can thus orientate their own lives on the basis of reasons they themselves recognize, they have a standing that calls for our respectful response. At least presumptively, or barring powerful conflicting considerations, we should avoid imposing our will on these people, and refrain from ruling their lives for them. Domination is indeed a direct affront to people as self-rulers. This case against domination engages the direct importance of self-determination both for the agents in relation to themselves and as a matter of their social standing in their relations with others: it is important that agents are able to exercise self-direction and that they are regarded as so being by others (i.e. self-determination is both a self-regarding and an other-regarding expressive ideal).[49]

The first part of the dignitarian strategy condemns domination for setting back people's interest in self-determination quite independently of other, indirect results of domination. But, as we said in 4.1, typically domination also has problematic consequences regarding other concerns. It has a tendency to set back other important interests. For example, when people are dominated, and consequently lack self-determination, they are less secure in their access to conditions for the maintenance, development, and exercise of many valuable capacities, such as their capacities to engage in activities displaying creativity, cooperation, and contribution to the needs of others. Proposition (J) seems intuitively correct in holding these remarkable capacities as giving rise to status-dignity in the people who have them. In restricting

---

[49] Anderson (2017: 126–31).

288 Human Dignity and Social Justice

self-determination, domination also hampers people's ability to pursue interests linked to them. The prospect of such a pursuit is now hostage to the vagaries of the will of others, and is thus less secure than it is reasonable for people to want or expect.[50]

The foregoing statements are quite abstract. But they provide a framework to criticize domination which fills the three explanatory gaps stated in the first paragraph of 4.2 and account for the three intuitive cases revealing them. We can see that domination is an important normative factor because of its conflicts with self-determination and self-realization, which are significant for condition-dignity. But since Solidaristic Empowerment calls for responding to the dignity of all, some forms of domination might be all things considered justifiable. If some acts involve an initiative to prevent or destroy the condition-dignity of others (as in the case of the anti-dignitarian aims of the aggressor discussed in 4.1), then a putative right to engage in them is ruled out by the protection of the dignity of others. The presumption against interventions that limit self-determination does not hold for those acts. And even when there is a pro tanto right to perform certain acts, for example when they are not constitutively but only incidentally deleterious of the condition-dignity of others, this right may be outweighed by what is needed to fulfil other, more important rights that protect weightier interests of others in the circumstances. So we can account for the case of *restraining the murderer*. Second, it is not assumed that all rights deficits are a case of domination. Solidaristic Empowerment can include requirements to support the self-determination and self-realization of others which hold quite independently of the prevention of domination. If the dignity of people is as important as to generate negative duties to refrain from dominating them, it can also be important enough to generate positive duties to sustain and enhance their agential power to live flourishing lives. This should be done in extreme situations like the one of *rescuing someone in dire straits*, but also more generally by doing one's fair share in shaping wider social practices and institutions so that they foster other people's well-being. The third gap is also filled,

---

[50] I have focused on how domination often frustrates other people's self-determination and self-realization. But domination also frustrates important interests of the dominating agent. For example, it is one of the lessons of Hegel's dialectic of the lord and the bondsman that genuine and authoritative recognition from others, which you may need to form a positive sense of self, can only be obtained when they are not subject to your domination. See Hegel (1977: ch. IV). The free involvement of others is also important when you want to engage in activities which have value, at least in part, precisely because they enact a form of joint agency in which various individuals constitute a group agent with a collective identity and project. It is much clearer that the project is *ours* rather than only *yours* when I join in it of my own initiative. Here having dominating 'power-over' others frustrates the valuable prospect of having 'power-with' them. Finally, domination can also damage the self-respect of the dominating agents: in dominating others, you neglect and corrode your own capacities for moral judgement and empathy. I return to these points in Sections 4.4.4–5.

The Critique of Domination   **289**

finally, because not all instances of non-domination, self-determination, and agential power are seen as mattering equally. Their significance depends on how strongly they link to the maintenance, development, and exercise of valuable capacities at the basis of dignity. We can in this way capture the intuition encapsulated in the *two factories* case. Some forms of domination are morally worse than others precisely because of the greater extent to which they hamper people's ability to unfold those valuable capacities.

We can illustrate the strengths of this approach by returning to the issue of the domination of workers. Work is an enormously important social practice. It is very hard to avoid. Most people must work to escape great material penury and gain social recognition. Work also potentially offers intrinsic goods of great significance. At work we can actualize and express our capacities for self-directed activity, creativity, cooperation, and contribution to the well-being of others. For many (perhaps most) people, these goods are difficult to achieve to a sufficient extent outside of work. Finally, working activities are also a potential terrain of great limitations of freedom or empowerment. They can involve humiliation and the stunting of our valuable capacities, and this on a daily basis, for most of our adult lives. This crushing of self-determination and self-realization is all the more consequential when we have no real options to access them to a sufficient extent in other activities, as it is the case for many people. For these reasons, work is indeed a major domain for the dignitarian critique of domination.

We should critically examine practices of work to identify problematic forms of domination, and envision feasible and reasonable changes that expand the freedom of workers to realize their interests in developing and exercising their valuable capacities. Thus, for example:

- When considering the range and sites of domination, we should illuminate how workers' self-determination is set back in the three spheres of production, exchange, and the wider political process, and entertain changes empowering them through works councils, unions, protective labour law, and a more level playing field to influence electoral politics and government administration. These changes would deactivate some mechanisms of domination, and provide workers with resources to defend their interests. Since these spheres are causally linked in multiple ways, it is important to target change in all of them.
- We should question the common ideological narrative that blackmails people into working under conditions of domination as the price they must pay to gain self-respect as responsible contributors to society. To reduce the depth of domination, educational and other cultural

290 Human Dignity and Social Justice

interventions can affirm a link between the duty of social contribution and the rights of solidaristic empowerment, so that no one is pushed to contribute according to their abilities without also benefitting according to their needs (as the Abilities/Needs Principle would recommend).

- We should recognize the increased vulnerability to domination faced by people of disadvantaged groups, such as racialized individuals, immigrants, women, people of LGBTQ+ sexual orientations, people with disabilities, and workers feeding supply chains in countries of the Global South. To reduce the scope of domination, we can articulate its critique within the sharply universalist horizon of human dignity, and take the self-determination of each and every individual worker as morally significant.
- Finally, the dynamic aspect of domination should be taken seriously. Schemes of domination are social creations that can be changed through progressive activism by individuals who cultivate their dignitarian virtue. We can imagine and experiment with feasible and reasonable agendas of reform and even structural transformation. Besides enhancing the self-determination of workers in the three spheres mentioned above, we can bolster social security mechanisms granting workers generous unemployment benefits, retraining, and health care. This safety net allows them to stand up to bosses on stronger terms. Workers' bargaining power would be increased further if a high unconditional basic income is introduced to enable them to refuse work that is humiliating or stunting. Changes could be even deeper, with democratic socialist experiments that give workers control of the means of production they toil with.

The preceding points are illustrative suggestions. A full account of workers' non-domination would necessarily be more complex and is beyond the scope of this book. A source of complication is worth mentioning, however, because of its significance for our current theoretical purpose of illuminating the core normative structures of the dignitarian approach to domination. It concerns the interaction between pro tanto rights in the articulation of overall, all things considered judgements. Thus, for a first example, ponder that reducing the domination of workers in the sphere of production might have to be weighed against the empowerment of individuals more generally, taking into account access to objects other than self-determination at the workplace. It is conceivable that certain hierarchical dynamics at the level of production make for greater efficiency or productivity in the economy as a whole, which would benefit everyone (workers included). This point can be challenged.

The Critique of Domination **291**

Some argue that greater self-determination of workers in fact increases productivity.[51] And we could argue that its limitation is legitimate only if it emerges from democratic governmental regulation which the workers themselves have fair opportunities to shape—so that, at least to some extent, the limitations on their agency in economic life is self-imposed through the exercise of their agency in the broader political process. Clearly, much substantive normative and empirical inquiry would be needed for a lucid appraisal of the relations between workers' self-determination in the three spheres, and to assess the relations between workers' self-determination in those spheres and support for other interests that they and other people have.[52] Tensions and trade-offs may arise.

A second example of complexity is the relation between individual and collective self-determination. Self-determination may be enjoyed by single individuals or by individuals as members of groups (for example, by workers as members of a works council, a union, or a labour party). Against domination, Solidaristic Empowerment extolls efforts to support people's self-determination. But this self-determination may generate different requirements. Social power or self-determination—understood as the capacity of individuals to act together on reasons identified in common deliberative practices—is indeed valuable.[53] But individual self-determination is independently significant, and its weight vis-à-vis collective self-determination must be explicitly explored. It seems appropriate to grant individuals some

---

[51] Piketty (2019: 512, 578–98, 1118–22). Recall also the discussion of the influence of self-determination in production on self-determination in wider politics when addressing the 'two levels objection' in Chapter 6.

[52] It is not wrongful, for example, to require workers to support people who cannot work.

[53] See Wright's (2010: 113) account of 'social power' as the 'the capacity to mobilize people for voluntary collective actions'. Social power, thus defined, operates by convincing others through reasonable argumentation rather than by forcing or bribing them. Now, the danger I am concerned with is when the right to collective self-determination becomes the right of everyone to monitor the personal life of each. The sphere of genuine personal choice might shrink under the pressure of having to behave in ways that others would approve of. The risk is having a 'free society' that is not also a 'society of free people' (Van Parijs 1995: 15–7) but rather a society in which 'the "self-government" spoken of is not the government of each by himself, but of each by all the rest' (Mill 1991: 8). Socialists are, but should be more, alive to this risk. Thus, for example, when Wright (2010: 12) states his principle of 'political justice', which calls for '*all people* [... *to*] *have broadly equal access to the necessary means to participate meaningfully in decisions about things that would affect their lives*', he perspicuously includes reference to both '*the freedom of individuals to make choices that affect their own lives as separate persons*' and '*their capacity to participate in collective decisions which affect their lives as members of a broader community*'. However, his subsequent discussion of this principle does not address the possibility of tension between the implementation of its two components. The boundaries between the two spheres assumed in the principle is a subject of difficult negotiation. Further discussion is also needed to address the relations between this principle and the principle of 'social justice' calling for '*broadly equal access to the necessary material and social means to live flourishing lives*' (Ibid: 12). Although the implementation of each principle is typically likely to contribute to the implementation of the other, conflicts could arise here as well. Just as the democratic will of the people may sometimes fail to protect personal civil liberties, so it may fail to select optimal opportunity sets for flourishing lives. I acknowledge that similar tensions can arise regarding requirement (f) of the interpretation of the Abilities/Needs Principle I proposed in Chapter 3.

292 Human Dignity and Social Justice

(reasonably constrained) liberties to decide on issues that greatly affect their personal life without having to submit those decisions to the opinion and veto of others, even when those others might be affected. Thus, individuals should be able to choose whether and where they work, and, to some extent, how they do it, without having to recruit the agreement of others about every aspect of these decisions. By exploring these complexities, we could identify normative packages of social and individual freedom that track people's various political and civil liberties, with their independent significance, weight, and interactive roles. Again, the issues arising must be the subject of sustained normative and empirical inquiry.[54]

As we engage in these complex justificatory efforts, it is important to keep in mind the different dimensions of a conception of social justice. Thus, recall the difference, within dimension DI, between ideals (DIa) and prescriptive principles (DIb). It could be that at the evaluative level DIa, the Dignitarian Approach is close to an anarchistic view extolling forms of coordination that proceed through voluntary social cooperation and is devoid of any coercion. But once feasibility issues are factored in, together with the opportunity costs they impose on the designs of social schemes regarding various instances of self-determination and other values, it may be that all things considered prescriptions (at DIb), or at least their practical implementation (at dimension DII), should include some limitations on self-determination. A burden of proof can be placed on those proposing such limitations, and the acceptable limitations may have to be quite constrained or qualified. In other words, a presumption in favour of self-determination seems reasonable. But it is defeasible. There may be important tensions within the space of self-determination itself and between self-determination and other values, such that when specific rights and duties are articulated, certain trade-offs will have to be recognized.

Complications will also arise when dimension DIII is explored to identify specific duties or proposals implementing the general demands stated in (I) and (L). When a problematic domination only concerns a punctual interaction between two individuals, undoing it may often be a relatively simple task. The agents involved could reshape the terms of their interaction so that the extreme power asymmetry dissolves. Thus, an armed individual dominating an unarmed individual may disable their weapon. This may not always be feasible or desirable even in these contexts. Perhaps the domination holding between these individuals is a function of their different bodily or mental powers. But the feasibility challenges mount as soon as we consider large societal structural setups. Often when an individual abandons their position in a

---

[54] An example of this inquiry is the normative and empirical work in social choice theory.

The Critique of Domination   **293**

social structure, another will likely rush to take up the vacant role. A capitalist employer may decide to abandon the capitalist class and become a wage worker. But another capitalist will likely take hold of their assets and proceed much as the quitter did before. The individual could instead surrender their assets to their employees, allowing them to turn their firm into a worker-run cooperative. But isolated acts like this, although not insignificant, will not go very far in affecting the overall structure of the society, or in benefitting the bulk of those suffering wrongful domination in it. The elaboration of duties to counter problematic domination will have to illuminate how the acts of individuals can link up in collective efforts to reshape large societal processes and institutions.[55]

4.4 The advantages of the Dignitarian Approach to domination

The Dignitarian Approach illuminates the contours of domination as a normative factor. It helps us understand why it matters, how much it matters, and that it is not the only thing that matters. The Dignitarian Approach explains how non-domination is important for, but also why it does not exhaust, social justice. The justificatory connections explored in this chapter so far are mostly determinative. But we can also identify connections of epistemic justification. We can note that:

(M) The core ideas of the Dignitarian Approach are themselves intuitively plausible.

(N) The deployment of the Dignitarian Approach helps us articulate and explain intuitively plausible normative judgements about domination (such as about when it is wrongful, its relative weight, and its limits).

(O) The deployment of the Dignitarian Approach helps illuminate our discussion of salient and controversial cases of domination—such as the domination of workers in capitalism.

(P) The Dignitarian Approach to domination has greater explanatory power than other, competing accounts (such as some republican, neo-Kantian, or relational egalitarian accounts).

(Q) The Dignitarian Approach helps refine and perhaps even revise some of our previous considered judgements (such as those regarding the significance of independence and self-respect).

---

[55] I thank Will Roberts for discussion on these matters.

294 Human Dignity and Social Justice

I think that the dignitarian account of domination holds up well in reflective equilibrium. The discussion in the chapter so far supports (M), (N), and (O), for example. The remainder of the chapter will support these epistemic points further, as well as add reflections to develop the connections of determinative justification. In addition, I will address points (P) and (Q).

4.4.1 The Dignitarian Approach helps identify the wrongs of domination and their weight

Let us take stock of the discussion so far. Domination is pro tanto, or at least presumptively wrongful because it sets back people's self-determination. Self-determination has great normative significance. It matters intrinsically, as it is an ability that involves the unfolding of valuable basic capacities for prudential and moral reasoning and choice that are at the basis of people's dignity. Domination enacts a procedural harm, consisting in the frustration, circumvention, suppression, or colonization of the will of others. Where there is domination, some agents live on terms dictated by others rather than on terms they themselves have an active role in shaping.[56]

Self-determination also matters indirectly. This is because using it is often causally, or epistemically, linked to people's access to the conditions that would allow them to unfold other valuable capacities, such as those underpinning their self-realization. When they exercise their capacities for prudential reasoning and choice, people typically try to figure out what is good for them, and pursue it. The service of self-determination regarding well-being may even be partly constitutive. An otherwise equivalent path may be better for you than an alternative one if it has been autonomously chosen by you rather than imposed by others. Correspondingly, domination is also pro tanto or at least presumptively wrongful because it interrupts this indirect service of self-determination. Since the valuable capacities engaged in self-realization are also significant for dignity, this additional problem with domination is one that dignitarian reflection targets for critical assessment. It is an advantage of the Dignitarian Approach that it makes these points sharply.

What makes the power asymmetry that domination consists in wrongful is that it sets back the valuable capacities at the basis of the dignity of the agents involved. The primary concern, as we saw, is with the curtailment of the self-determination of the dominated. (I address self-directed harms below.) The more serious this procedural diminution of self-rule, the

---

[56] The experience of cooperatives illustrates the intrinsic importance of self-determination. Even though his salary is lower, a member of the cooperative Musicop in Spain declared that 'we're better off today, because we are empowered'. Another worker, member of the cooperative firm Viome in Greece, declared: 'We don't want to hide it: above and beyond our own jobs and our families' futures, this is about equality, democracy, the whole employer-employee relationship', 'We're working for each other. That's the difference'. Guardian Reporters (2015).

The Critique of Domination   **295**

worse, in one respect, is the domination. But there is more, because some such curtailments may be worse than others not only as a function of how much self-determination is depressed, but also as a function of how much this depression hampers the development and exercise of other capacities of the agents involved. The more the interests people have in the unfolding of these additional capacities are set back, the worse, in another respect, is the domination. Indeed, some trajectories of self-determination are more important than others not only because of the intrinsic significance of self-determination, but also because of its indirect significance regarding the development and exercise of other capacities which are also at the basis of dignity, such as those relative to self-realization.[57] (It is perhaps in part for this reason that self-determination is sometimes construed in idealized ways—as being a matter of rational and well-informed will formation. The idealizations track readiness to hook onto additional substantive considerations such as those mentioned here.)

Thus, the Dignitarian Approach also illuminates how considerations of self-determination and other considerations such as the importance of self-realization combine to appraise the *weight* (in addition to the existence) of the wrongs of domination. An interesting issue, which merits further reflection, is how these latter, substantive or results-based considerations might be not only contributory to the wrongness of some instances of domination all things considered (by making it more clearly momentous, or worse), but also provide (as we saw in 4.3) external considerations to be weighed against non-domination as pro tanto requirements which may compete with it. There are thus a number of potential issues of normative structure, about the relations between various kinds of self-determination and between self-determination and self-realization (as well as other considerations of well-being), which can work in synergy or in conflict.

4.4.2 The Dignitarian Approach helps to notice the limits of non-domination as a normative key to social justice

Because of the multiple normative considerations involved, the critique of domination turns out to be a rather complex task. But the fact that the

---

[57] In making this point, we consider how the Dignitarian Approach helps understand both the distinction and the relation between prudential and moral forms of normativity. We can explore how domination bears on people's pursuit of self-determination, self-realization, and self-identification as constituents of their appropriate flourishing. We consider how domination sets back people's potential or actual trajectories of personal unfolding. To do this, we explore the relations of various people to themselves and to each other. That is, we identify a vertical axis of reflexive, intrapersonal relations and a horizontal one of interpersonal and systemic (institutional) relations. For each, we explore how agents either support trajectories of flourishing or crush or bend them. The Dignitarian Approach helps illuminate the connections between the two axes (e.g. how solidarity fosters personal flourishing on both ends of the nexus) and criticize paternalistic tendencies (e.g. by noting that self-determination contributes to personal flourishing, again on both ends of the relation).

296   Human Dignity and Social Justice

dignitarian perspective clues us to this complexity is an advantage, not a defect of it. Narrower, or simpler approaches might be more elegant, but at the cost of missing normatively significant issues that bear on people's interests and rights.

To illustrate this point, I will discuss some important philosophical views about domination and social justice recently offered by Philip Pettit, Rainer Forst, and Elizabeth Anderson, to identify some deficiencies of such views which could be overcome by deploying the broader framework offered by the Dignitarian Approach.

(i) Pettit and republican distributive justice

We already considered some elements in Pettit's republican approach. I endorsed and built on its view of domination as a relationship between agents' wills, while recommending a broader understanding of its depth, range, and mechanisms. Here I would like to comment on Pettit's monistic view of social justice as only based on a principle of freedom as non-domination.

In his account of social justice, Pettit addresses the issue of *insuring* people's freedom of choice. Two types of support are considered. The first concerns *resourcing* choice (compensating for its vitiation). This involves improving people's abilities to act by increasing their personal, natural, and social resources. To avoid introducing dependence on others, the resourcing can proceed uniformly for all, and if special needs exist, through schemes of rights that target them. The second type of support concerns *protecting* choice (guarding against its invasion). This involves preventing or inhibiting interference by making the option to interfere disappear or be ineligible (too costly). The overall aim is to maximize expected non-domination. Success may come in degrees, with benchmarks of adequate protection to be determined contextually.

Now, in Pettit's monistic political philosophy, the single core ideal is freedom as non-domination. Requirements of economic support are justified as part of social justice only when and to the extent that they contribute to insuring people against domination. This is unsatisfactory.

The limitations of the republican approach are here twofold. To begin with, it fails to provide the normative grounds to make the point that resourcing is desirable because it allows people to lead flourishing lives in which they develop and exercise their various valuable capacities. This point is independent of non-domination. But if this is so, then a different normative platform is needed. We need a view that affirms positive duties of solidarity to support the positive freedom of others (their capabilities or abilities) to

The Critique of Domination   297

flourish. This is what the Dignitarian Approach, with its ideal of Solidaristic Empowerment, would indeed recommend.[58]

The second weakness of the republican approach concerns its implications for distributive justice. As I proceed to argue, the forms of support that republicanism justifies fall short of what egalitarian distribution would call for (except perhaps coincidentally, but then failing to illuminate it as an independently significant goal).

When it comes to its implications for distributive justice, republicanism is characterized by Pettit as either a form of sufficientarianism (requiring that everyone have enough resources to achieve the status of free, non-dominated citizen) or as a strategy of 'equalizing derived returns' (requiring that material inequalities not be so wide that equality of status of all as free, non-dominated citizens is jeopardized).[59] As Pettit realizes, this view is likely to be criticized as demanding too little. It indeed falls short of what luck-egalitarianism and Rawls's second principle of justice require.[60] Pettit responds that republicanism is nonetheless quite demanding, as constraining the spread of inequalities in private wealth and power are necessary to prevent domination.[61] However, this is not enough to respond to the objection. Pettit grants that inequalities of private wealth and power are compatible with republicanism (within limits securing non-domination). Distributive egalitarians will say that some of these inequalities are problematic from the point of view of justice. Even if

---

[58] It also seems to me that Pettit's approach lacks enough substance to explain what liberties should be supported. Thus, to identify the basic liberties a just society would safeguard, Pettit (2012: ch.2) offers two criteria. They must concern choices that are (a) coexercisable and (b) cosatisfying. He also says that to secure the possibility of a full and meaningful life for all citizens, we should entrench liberties that are also the most (i) distal and (ii) general with respect to people's specific life-projects. Pettit argues that these criteria are not value-laden but offer sufficiently determinate guidance. But his arguments are not convincing. First, Pettit's discussion of (b), and of (i)–(ii), does seem to be value-laden and perhaps—problematically—conservative in deferring to existing, conventional views about well-being (as when Pettit invokes the 'received social criteria' (Ibid: 98)). Second, the criteria are too formal. This is important, because there could be different conceivable packages of freedoms that fulfil them to the same extent. How do we choose between them? Pettit's account does not tell us. Rawls' approach, which Pettit disparages, is in fact better. Rawls proceeds by identifying morally important capacities to form and pursue conceptions of justice and the good. He thus provides substantive guidelines for identifying the basic liberties that social justice must support—they are the liberties that are important for developing and exercising these two morally important capacities—while still leaving plenty of room for diverse personal lifepaths. Rawls (2001: sects. 13 and 32).

The ideal of non-domination helps identify the content of some basic liberties to be safeguarded, and to figure out certain thresholds for resourcing them. But it does not illuminate the assessment of liberties beyond their significance for non-domination. The independent significance of various civil liberties is not captured. Furthermore, as I proceed to argue in the main text, the importance of distributive fairness regarding access to resources to exercise them beyond the threshold of non-domination is ignored.

[59] Pettit (2012: 88).

[60] Ibid: 126. Luck-egalitarianism says that no one should have less access to resources than others through no choice or fault of their own. Rawls's second principle says that economic inequalities are acceptable only if they work to the maximal benefit of the worst-off and arise against a background of fair equality of opportunity.

[61] Ibid: 90–1.

298 Human Dignity and Social Justice

they do not enable domination, they might constitute unfair social configurations in which some have lower levels of opportunity, or capability, to lead a flourishing life, or access welfare, than others, and this through no choice or fault of their own.

The complaint has intuitive force. Consider an example. Alberto and Bruno are musicians. They are equal in musical talent, and have worked equally hard to develop it. They are also equal in wealth. But then Alberto inherits a considerable sum of money from his parents. He buys sophisticated instruments with which he can make music he was unable to make before. Bruno would love to explore the new musical landscape now open to Alberto, but he can't because he cannot afford the instruments. Or imagine that Alberto buys a new home with a nice backyard for his children to play in, while Bruno's children have no such amenities (they can't joyfully jump around like Alberto's children; they are confined within the walls of an apartment, with neighbours complaining when they are noisy). Conceivably, Alberto and Bruno can still look each other in the eye without reason to fear each other (they meet republicanism's 'eyeball test'). There is no domination here. But there is a significant inequality in access to the conditions for well-being that seems unfair. This kind of unfairness could be limited through state policies targeting inheritance and bequest. But since domination is not at issue here, the policies are not justifiable on republican grounds. This shows that republicanism does not provide all we need to justify claims of distributive justice. Non-domination is an important value, but promoting expansive, and equal, chances to pursue well-being is important too.[62]

Pettit does little to respond to this kind of worry. He simply does not seem to think that material inequalities that do not generate domination matter politically. Thus, after acknowledging that the demand of republican justice regarding material distribution falls short of what luck-egalitarianism or Rawls's theory of justice demand, he says:

> But those theories often seem like moral fantasies: manuals for how God ought to have ordained the order of things—or manuals for how we ought to rectify God's failures—rather than real-world manifestos for what the state should do in regulating the affairs of its citizens.[63]

For further support he quotes Hegel: 'One cannot speak of the injustice of nature in the unequal distribution of possessions and resources, for nature is not free and is therefore neither just nor unjust'.[64]

---

[62] For similar worries applied to relational conceptions of egalitarianism, see Kymlicka (2006).
[63] Pettit (2012: 126).
[64] Ibid.

The Critique of Domination **299**

This response is weak. First, many inequalities such as those arising between Alberto and Bruno are either largely shaped by social institutions (there is no need to refer to God's design or to only refer to the effects of 'nature') or could be redressed through social action. Second, Pettit's response does nothing to actually assess the view that to the extent that they reasonably can, people should reduce unfair inequalities (including but going beyond those securing the threshold of non-domination). There is a lot that the state, and people individually, can do. The state can impose more stringent taxation and redistribution, or dispersal of control of economic assets, than republicanism requires. And individuals may adopt a less self-serving attitude when choosing what parties to vote for, or how hard to bargain for higher profits or salaries (as Cohen argues in his critique of the 'incentives argument' for inequality).[65] Third, notice that I formulated the distributive egalitarian ideal as something that people should implement 'to the extent that they reasonably can'. The view accepts feasibility limits and the importance of other normative ideals. Thus, some inequalities might be irreducible, or their reduction should be avoided if it involves violations of certain civil or political liberties. For these three reasons, it is false that the distributive egalitarian ideal can be dismissed as a 'moral fantasy'.

Pettit claims that 'if we look after the requirements of equal freedom as non-domination ... we will have looked after the requirements of many other values as well'.[66] But distributive equality might not be fully catered for in a republican society. A public moral and political culture only based on republican values would not affirm it as an intrinsically important goal. And standard republican policies may fail to produce what this value demands. Thus, the republican account of social justice is not sufficient. There is more to social justice than non-domination.

The economic support for others envisioned by republican theory is limited in that it focuses only on securing conditions of non-domination. It does not require that we foster, equally, everyone's chances to lead a flourishing life. This is a very serious shortcoming from the point of view of a conception of social justice that includes an ideal of distributive equality, as such an ideal is (at least in some, plausible versions of it) directly concerned with people's ability to pursue their well-being. The dignitarian perspective would embrace this ideal, and go beyond republicanism by recommending egalitarian support for people's access to the conditions for developing and exercising their valuable capacities.

---

[65] Cohen (2008).
[66] Pettit (2012: 127).

300 Human Dignity and Social Justice

We can identify a third difficulty with the republican ideal of independence from the will of others, this time regarding its feasibility. Even when we implement resourcing through a system of rights (as we indeed regularly should when we can), this does not mean that there will not be vulnerability or dependence with respect to the uncontrolled will of others. Other people have to help enshrine, specify, interpret, and conscientiously implement those rights. These other people—be they state officials or citizens more broadly—have to put their shoulder behind the scheme. Each beneficiary of the scheme is at their mercy for accessing the object of the rights. In the end, we are always at the mercy of others.

The worry about the feasibility of independence is also explored in Thomas Simpson's powerful critique of the republican ideal of freedom.[67] Understood in its strict, most demanding form, republican freedom does not seem feasible. According to republican political theory, an individual is fully secure from 'horizontal' domination by other individuals if there is a state that protects them from it. Now, to avoid the concomitant prospect of 'vertical' domination by the state, individuals must be able to team up to resist it. But then each individual is at the mercy of some potential team's invading power strong enough to resist the state, or if the latter does not exist, then that the individual is at the mercy of the invading power of the state. Either way, strict republican freedom is not on the cards. Republicanism runs against the conditions of human sociality, which imply that we are always, to some extent, at the mercy of others. Thus, as a feasible ideal for social life (rather than as a prospect for an isolated individual like Robinson Crusoe), non-domination would have to require not absolute security or strict independence from the will of others, but some morally appropriate form of interdependence between individuals' wills.

---

[67] See Simpson (2017; 2019). I raise similar worries regarding the infeasibility of ever being independent from the will of others in Gilabert (2015c). Pettit (2012: ch. 3) argues that the republican democratic state gives people access to a good they could not otherwise achieve: 'status freedom' (Ibid: 181) as independence from an alien will. This good could not be achieved in a stateless Kantian Kingdom of Ends which, although seemingly desirable, would not institutionally guarantee the basic freedoms of each individual—they would remain vulnerable to the weak, ill, or evil will of others (Ibid: 181–4). But there are problems with this line of argument. It assumes scenarios in which the ideal is not implemented (for when people's wills are ill, evil, or weak, they do not embody the Kantian ideal). So, if the discussion is about pure ideal theory, then it seems methodologically flawed. Pettit replies to this charge that his discussion is sound because it does not assume actual non-compliance with Kantian norms, but only its *possibility* (which is enough to show that citizens' freedom is insecure, or insufficiently robust). See Pettit (2015). Even if this response succeeds, two further challenges should be answered. First, the argument misses the benefits of respect and concern that is given in a thoroughly voluntary, non-coercive arrangement. A virtuous anarchist condition might well be ideally best in this regard. Second, people are not really independent from the will of others in the republican state either. As Pettit recognizes (e.g. in his discussion of the importance of a vigilant and resistant citizenry—Pettit 2012: 173–4), in the end citizens themselves have to choose to sustain the scheme. Pettit should say that the republican democratic state is best not as a matter of the purest form of ideal theory, but as a matter of finding the best feasible political configuration.

The Critique of Domination **301**

I suggest that the ideal of non-domination could then be restated to require both external and internal checks, calling for (a) external limitation (not elimination—which is infeasible) of others' ability for uncontrolled interference; and (b) internal limitation by each individual of their own intentions to interfere in problematic ways. The right to non-domination would have, as correlative duties, the adoption of (a) and (b) as goals by all relevant agents, and their implementation through legal institutions, social norms, and personal choices. This rendering of republicanism would be more realistic.

I note, in passing, that this restatement does not collapse the ideal of non-domination into the requirement of absence of actual interference (the liberal view of freedom as republican critics describe it). This is so because (a) still partly focuses on what others are able to do, not merely on what they do—it calls for reducing people's capabilities for uncontrolled interference, not merely the absence of acts of uncontrolled interference. Furthermore, (a) and (b) can also track the ideal of civic virtue that republicans often emphasize—the readiness of citizens to resist domination and to avoid collaborating with it. Still, my revision brings the account closer to the liberal view, because (a) and (b) must also, and perhaps predominantly, focus on what does or is likely to happen, assuming that the possibility of uncontrolled interference remains. If the abilities for this interference cannot be eliminated in a social context but only reduced, then the buck of non-domination stops, in the end, with individuals' wills.[68]

The ideal of non-domination cannot bear the full weight of justifying the requirements of social justice. It does not tell us enough to know what opportunities we should secure or foster, it does not cater for them equally, and it does not fully appreciate the inescapability of our dependency on other people's wills.

(ii) Forst and justificatory, discursive self-determination

I have been arguing that although the avoidance of domination, and the respect for self-determination, is important and, often, crucial for justice, it

---

[68] Lovett and Pettit (2019) reply to Simpson that the conditions making a team capable of controlling the government would not also make it capable of controlling individuals. Laws and social norms allowing harmful teams to gain common awareness of their aims and to develop strategies to fulfil them would not arise. But this seems naïve. Laws and social norms can either change or lose psychological hold on people rather quickly when new circumstances, such as a deep economic crisis, a war, or a pandemic, occur. Certain tendencies to embrace groupthink and scapegoating of minorities can gain traction rapidly, and in view of historical examples (such as that of Germany between the two world wars), it seems that individuals from minority groups have reason to fear that majorities might turn on them. What warrants this fear is not just considerations of logical and metaphysical possibility, but awareness of sociological and psychological possibilities and even the likelihood of their actualization.

302 Human Dignity and Social Justice

is not identical with it. Let us consider this thesis when self-determination, and non-domination, are construed in terms of people's involvement in practices of discursive deliberation, or justification, regarding what norms should shape their social life. The thesis now is that justificatory, discursive self-determination is insufficient for justice. This thesis would apply to Rainer Forst's important view of 'justice as non-domination', which precisely centres on justificatory self-determination.[69] On this view, each individual has a fundamental right to justification such that they may not be subjected to norms or institutional normative orders which they did not have a chance to shape as autonomous, codetermining reasoners in discursive exercises that include all affected individuals as free and equal partners. Domination is the subjection to arbitrary ruling, which is precisely ruling that does not respect the right to justification. It consists in being treated as a rule-taker who is not also a rule-maker. At the level of the state, the right to justification would require robust democratic processes. But it can be implemented in other arenas of social life as well, such as the workplace.

For an intuitive diagnosis supporting my critical thesis, consider the following points (each of which suggest the insufficiency of considerations of justificatory self-determination and the importance of other, independent normative considerations):

- *Current deliberation.* When a set of people are trying to figure out how to organize their social life, they have reason to include each individual in their deliberation as a free and equal participant, and to identify norms they could all reasonably accept. Thus, the self-determination of each is to be respected. But this cannot be all. As they try to identify the appropriate norms and the reasons backing them, they must track independent normative considerations as the basis for their specific moves in the game of justification. They cannot just say, 'Let's adopt the norms we all agree to adopt'. They are trying to figure out *which* norms *to* adopt, which ones *are* the best to adopt.[70] Thus, they also need to entertain considerations such as, 'This putative norm N1 is better than that other N2 when it comes to serving the further normative consideration C, and this is why we should adopt it'. Thus, if people are trying to determine whether to adopt norms of equality of opportunity in access to education and the job market that include not only restrictions on discrimination but also redistribution to offset relative disadvantages resulting from

---

[69] Forst (2017b: 153–62). The phrase 'justice as non-domination' occurs, e.g., at p.156.
[70] I thank Arash Abizadeh for discussion on this formulation.

The Critique of Domination   303

differentials in wealth, they will have to draw on considerations such as the importance of education and work for personal flourishing, and the unfairness of some people being able to access less of those goods than others due to circumstances that are beyond their control, like their family's wealth.

- *Retrospective judgements.* Sometimes the discursive deliberators will change the list of norms they recognize as valid. But how do they make sense of the change? Often, they will do it by telling themselves 'This new norm N1 is better than that other N2, the one we previously adopted, because it better caters for the further normative consideration C'. If we assume that the deliberation in the present includes just as much self-determination as that in the past, the change would often be seen to involve progress rather than involution, or mere drift, precisely because it better tracks what the deliberators have reason to accept (not only the fact that they accept it). They see themselves as having recognized and corrected a mistake. But the mistake was about substantive content, not procedure (such as excluding some people from the processes of justificatory self-determination altogether, or treating disrespectfully those who participate in it).

- *Comparing trajectories.* Sometimes deliberators will engage in hypothetical appraisals, and compare different trajectories in a society (their own or some other), which are equivalent regarding the presence of self-determination but different regarding the norms adopted in deliberation. If one trajectory featuring N1 is judged better than another featuring N2, and thus the society featuring N1 is seen as more just than the society featuring N2, then the judgement would again sometimes be tracking more than self-determination.

- *Judgement in non-ideal conditions.* Sometimes people will have to make choices that seriously affect others without being able to engage in discursive justification with them. Whatever they do (including deciding not to act) will have important consequences for others. The determination of what to do in these circumstances must sometimes track more than the value of self-determination. The chooser should surely think about how to act to make deliberative self-determination with others feasible in the future. But they also must choose what to do now, when (by hypothesis) this codetermination is not feasible. To determine whether to follow N1 or N2 this chooser will, again, have to consider what further considerations C might be correct. It is true that sometimes C will include some virtual tracking of self-determination—i.e. sometimes the chooser will ask themselves 'What would they prefer that I do

304 Human Dignity and Social Justice

to them? Or, if they could choose, what would they choose?' But further considerations may be relevant as well. The chooser would, as best they can, have to try to track them.

- *Euthyphro-style question.* The intuitive diagnosis suggested by these cases can also be driven home by entertaining a Euthyphro-style question about discursive, justificatory self-determination: 'Is a consideration C correct because we accept it in our deliberation, or do we (or should we) accept C in our deliberation because it is correct?' If, like me, you believe that it is the second disjunct that is intuitively compelling, then you also see deliberation (and with it the procedure of self-determination itself) as partly a matter of tracking independent reasons.

I do not want to exaggerate my disagreement with Forst. He advances two very important claims about the importance of justificatory self-determination.[71] He shows, first, that it plays a key *epistemic* role. Engaging others in deliberative practices helps figure out what considerations C are relevant, and what candidate norms N1, N2, etc. are worth taking into account or adopting. Second, discursive deliberation has a directly *practical (moral and political)* point. When we include each other in discursive deliberation about what norms should shape our social life, we respect each other's dignity as agents capable of self-determination. Social justice is to be seen as ideally a matter of autonomous achievement, not as a predicament to be delivered to passive recipients by paternalist authorities. As Forst argues, proper reasoning about justice is *reflexive*: the practice of justification is itself part of the content of justice.

My critical discussion is not meant to dismiss these compelling points. What I am trying to do, instead, is to show that proper reasoning about justice is not only *reflexive* but also *reflective*: It tracks independent considerations whose normativity cannot be reduced to the fact that they are accepted by the participants in discursive deliberation. Thus, for a final example, consider that the Abilities/Needs Principle can be violated without domination. The question this principle answers about how to organize economic cooperation cannot be settled by interpreting it as requiring something like 'To each according to what the relevant individuals or collective decides in deliberation'. The decision may be self-determined but fail to give each their fair share.[72]

---

[71] See, e.g., Forst (2014b: 211–2).

[72] I should also note that Forst usefully distinguishes between 'fundamental' and 'full justice': 'the task of fundamental justice is to construct a *basic structure of justification*, the task of full justice is to construct

The Critique of Domination **305**

I should also note that I have a different view of the basis of dignity. Forst focuses only on the capacity for autonomous reasoning as giving rise to status-dignity.[73] While I agree that this capacity is of great significance when present, I have a more inclusive view. For this reason, the Dignitarian Approach proposed in this book can capture more fully the dignitarian credentials of supporting self-realization and other forms of well-being that engage valuable capacities of people other than those underpinning their self-determination.

(iii) Anderson and the critique of 'private government'
Elizabeth Anderson provides a powerful examination of domination in the workplace. She coins the term 'private government' to illuminate a form of power that is arbitrary, unaccountable, and potentially abused.[74] Focusing on the contemporary situation in the United States, she argues that employers wield this power over workers regarding various issues at work and even outside the workplace:

> Walmart prohibits employees from exchanging casual remarks while on duty, calling this 'time theft.' Apple inspects the personal belongings of their retail workers, who lose up to a half-hour of unpaid time every day as they wait in line to be searched. Tyson prevents its poultry workers from using the bathroom. Some have been forced to urinate on themselves, while their supervisors mock them. About half of U.S. employees have been subject to suspicionless drug screening by their employers. Millions are pressured by their employers to support particular political causes or candidates.[75]

Anderson criticizes private government as a problematic form of social inequality. 'Private government at work embeds inequality in authority, standing, and esteem in the organizations upon which people depend for their livelihood.'[76] In these social hierarchies, respectively, some have little decision-making power, their interests are discounted, and they are seen as

---

a *fully justified basic structure*' (Forst 2017b: 157). Forst could recognize the points I am making as relevant to the discussion of full justice. His main point, then, would be to frontload the epistemic and practical significance of self-determination, urging the creation of practices and structures of autonomous, discursive deliberation as an urgent (and for him the first) requirement of justice. Forst also says that 'justice is a matter of *who determines who receives what* and not only or primarily of who should receive what' (Ibid: 155). This statement is ambiguous. Does justice *also*, even if secondarily, concern who receives what? If so, aren't there independent criteria for those distributions (which autonomous co-reasoners should do their best to track)? If so, then justice includes, but is not identical with, non-domination.

[73] See, e.g., Forst (2017b: 150, 115, 157). Although we both draw inspiration from Kant, my view of the basis of dignity is less Kantian. See my discussion on Section 2.2. of Chapter 2 of this book.

[74] Anderson (2017: 44–5, 133).

[75] Ibid: xix.

[76] Ibid: 130.

306 Human Dignity and Social Justice

of inferior social rank.[77] Being under private government is bad for those governed. Hierarchy of authority denies them the 'exercise of autonomy', which is a 'basic human need', and the hierarchies of esteem and standing involve 'expressive injury on workers', over and above material distributive disadvantages.[78] We should worry about the organization of a society in which workers 'cannot opt out of the wage labor system that structurally degrades and demeans them'.[79] At the very least, the constitution of the workplace, which depends on the state's regulations, should be reformed so that workers gain a voice within it.

Anderson does an excellent argumentative and rhetorical job in urging us to put issues about the constitution of the workplace at the centre of our political debate. She is especially effective in showing that besides distributive outcomes concerning wages, workers have reason to be worried about relational matters, such as their being treated as inferiors in their daily dealings with employers. Her account can help illuminate other important relational problems faced by workers, such as bullying and harassment.

There are, however, some difficulties and imprecisions in Anderson's analytical framework. Take first her account of the interests at stake. The notion of interests appears twice in her discussion, when tackling issues of standing within the workplace (such as workers' access to breaks) and when considering distributive outcomes (such as wages). Since Anderson's primary focus is relational issues within the workplace and not the distributive outcomes of wage labour, the latter do not feature much in her analysis. But arguably they should have a more central role, as the access to so many goods and services crucial for the well-being of workers and their families depends on what they can afford with their salaries. Furthermore, hierarchies of standing are construed in binary terms, but it is more intuitive to see them as sometimes being scalar (so that we can state our worry that some workers' interests are given less importance, even if they are given some). Finally, arguably interests appear a third time in the analysis, when considering the 'basic human need' for the exercise of autonomy. In sum, the interests at stake and their functions in the argument are not fully clear.

Second, the focus on expressive harms is important but should not obscure other harms. It is not clear it covers fully the harms involved in hierarchies of authority.[80] The distributive issues beyond expressive harms are, as

---

[77] Ibid: 3–4.
[78] Ibid: 127–8, 128–30.
[79] Ibid: 130.
[80] In fact, Anderson uses 'expressive injury' when addressing esteem and interests, and mainly she focuses on the former. See, e.g., Ibid: 128–30.

The Critique of Domination   **307**

mentioned above, very important. Trade-offs between these could arise, and the framework of private government does not tell us how to articulate them. Anderson rightly points out that in addition to republican freedom (non-domination), we have reason to care about negative freedom (the absence of interference by others with our choices) and positive freedom (the availability of an ample set of options that are effectively available to us, given our resources). She states that these kinds of freedom are independently valuable and can be traded against each other.[81] But her analysis concentrates only on republican worries and does not explore their relation and weight vis-à-vis worries regarding the other freedoms.

Third, Anderson rightly gives issues of authority and autonomy a separate treatment. But the deontological significance of autonomy (as a right rather than a good) is not fully explained, and its significance for prudential reasoning about personal flourishing independently of relational standing is not explored. We need a fuller understanding of these connections, which are very important when assessing working conditions.

Finally, although Anderson often uses the term 'dignity' when arguing that private government at the workplace involves mistreatment of workers, it is not clear what exactly its meaning and roles are. For example, 'dignity' is frequently used in conjunction with well-being, autonomy, freedom, needs, and standing.[82] But it is not clear whether these additional terms in the conjunctions are meant to elaborate on what dignity amounts to, or to be independent considerations.

The discussion of dignity in this book can be used to articulate Anderson's important points while also dealing with some of the difficulties just mentioned. The Dignitarian Approach provides a systematic account of the concept of dignity. It can be deployed to illuminate, in an integrated way, both expressive and outcome-based issues. The variety of the interests involved can be seen as normatively important because they concern the development and exercise of valuable capacities at the basis of dignity. Because of that, they can also be invoked not only to shape and assess the texture of intersubjective attitudes in social relationships, but also the distributive outcomes for people engaging in them.

The Dignitarian Approach is also more demanding in the rights it grounds. Their object includes more than the access to an appropriate

---

[81] Ibid: 45–8.
[82] Ibid. See, respectively, 139; xiii, 140, 143, 144; 71; 135; 140, 144.

308 Human Dignity and Social Justice

social-conventional status.[83] As an objective moral status based on a rich set of valuable capacities, status-dignity calls for a variety of responses. For example, condition-dignity includes, but goes beyond the enjoyment of a favourable reputation or the avoidance of insult or shaming. It also includes support for accessing the conditions of self-determined flourishing. As noted above, the Dignitarian Approach can combine worries about the expressive relational injury that often goes with domination—the treatment of people with less decision-making power or authority as being less worthy of esteem or standing—with distributive concerns about how well-off they end up being in respects other than their social rank. Dignitarian harms cannot be reduced to reputational and other expressive harms. Condition-dignity is not only a matter of how we shape our mutual regard and appearance in social interactions and institutional conventions, to make sure we are not disparaging, demeaning, or condescending. It is also a matter of making it the case, through appropriate changes in those interactions and the institutions underpinning them, that each has effective opportunities to thrive in their paths of freely chosen personal development.[84]

4.4.3 The Dignitarian Approach helps steer the ideal of non-domination away from an ideal of independence construed as self-sufficiency

Orientated by Solidaristic Empowerment, dignitarian justice targets a form of positive freedom. It urges us to support, in feasible and reasonable ways, each individual's maintenance, development, and exercise of their valuable capacities. On this view of social justice, non-domination is an important consideration, but it is only one amongst others.

It is also important, I think, to avoid an understanding of the ideal of non-domination as aiming for self-sufficiency, or self-reliance (as different from self-determination, which I have defended as an appropriate consideration).[85] Independence as self-reliance is infeasible and undesirable. It is infeasible because we are always, to some extent and so long as we remain in the social world, at the mercy of others, even when it comes to the processes that set protective limits on arbitrary interference. But it is also undesirable, because we cannot survive or flourish without the help of others. We are multiply vulnerable and in need of their support, and, because of this,

---

[83] My view contrasts with narrower accounts of dignity that tend to focus only on symbolic and expressive aspects of how we regard each other in social life. See Rosen (2012) and Anderson (2014). For discussion, see Gilabert (2019a: 114–5, 122–6).

[84] The republican focus on distributive issues only insofar as they bear on securing that domination is prevented also fails in this respect. For an argument that republicanism is narrowly, and problematically, fixated on how people appear in the eyes of others, see Goodin (2003: 61–6).

[85] Recall the ideologies of security or independence mentioned in the last section of Chapter 1.

The Critique of Domination **309**

we are also always to some extent potential targets of domination. We can, and should, structure these relationships of interdependence so that we can exercise self-determination to set their terms. But complete security from potentially harmful interference cannot be achieved, and sometimes seeking it would deprive us of many of the goods of social life.

In making these points, the Dignitarian Approach contrasts with some versions of liberalism and republicanism that recognize only negative rights and duties as the core requirements of social justice. The approach has important affinities with views emerging from human rights, feminism, and socialism. Recall the case of rescue mentioned in Section 4.1. Human rights doctrine typically recognizes various positive rights to health care and other forms of help for people who cannot fend for themselves.[86] Some feminists warn about the perils of construing non-domination as invulnerability,[87] and emphasize the importance of mutual aid and solidarity as an integral part of the ideal of human freedom.[88] Finally, socialists extoll community as a valuable readiness of each to serve others and be served by them,[89] and their Abilities/Needs Principle enjoins people to organize production and distribution so that the needs of each individual are met. These views are directly attuned to the inescapability of vulnerability, and affirm core positive duties and rights to shape social life so that it includes practices and institutions of appropriate interdependence rather than chimerical and ultimately undesirable schemes of self-reliance.

We should be critical of a moral culture that shames people when they make claims of need. Some hold the intuition that we may make claims of justice when our lack of the relevant goods is the result of others' depriving us of access to them through relations of domination, exploitation, and so on, but not otherwise. In these cases, help is a duty of justice, but in the other cases it is only a matter of generosity or beneficence, which carry no correlative rights. However, I think that the shame in asking for help is best seen as a remnant of the problematic ideal of independence as self-sufficiency. Solidaristic Empowerment does not endorse this script.

The critique of the script of self-reliance is also relevant for the discussion of the domination of workers in capitalist societies, especially when it comes to its depth. We should, I think, be critical of a moral culture that uses the script to blackmail people into choosing work under dominating conditions to avoid the shame and guilt of having to depend on the help of others if they

---

[86] Gilabert (2019a).
[87] Friedman (2008: 250–9).
[88] Gould (1988).
[89] Cohen (2009); Sypnowich (2020).

310 Human Dignity and Social Justice

do not. When a society pressures people to take certain options of productive activity, we should ask what is the baseline to appraise these options. What is the relevant range of choices? Is it, for example, working under domination, or not working at all and pleading for the help of others to subsist? This range is unduly narrow. Society should also provide people with options to work under conditions of self-determination. Or it should, perhaps, structure access to means of production so that workers are not deprived of control of them (as this circumstance slants the social playing field to their detriment from the start). This wider set of options would allow people to avoid the double-bind of having to choose between toil under domination and the guilt and shame of not contributing to the social product from which they must draw. Society should also recognize, in addition, that a floor of basic needs satisfaction should be put under people's feet, so that they can bargain for good employment conditions in which they are not used as mere tools, but also so that they are not discarded and ignored as tools are when they are no longer usable.

The Abilities/Needs Principle helps here because it affirms a conjunction of duties to contribute and rights to receive help. It is genuinely problematic (and perhaps an appropriate source of guilt) when I claim help from others but am not ready to do my fair share to generate the pool of resources I want to draw from. But if I cannot contribute because I cannot work, or if I contribute but my productive capabilities are lower than those of others, it is not a problem if I make a claim to net transfers from them. I am not instrumentalizing others in unconscionable ways. The Abilities/Needs Principle requires fair reciprocity among those who can contribute, not self-reliance of producers (or, relatedly, strict equivalence in the economic value of what they exchange). As I argued in Chapter 3, this principle also justifies unconditional support for basic needs.

4.4.4 The Dignitarian Approach helps illuminate the struggle against domination

I conclude this chapter with remarks (in this section and the next) about how the Dignitarian Approach helps us think about processes of social transformation. They engage the notion of dignitarian virtue and its significance for the dimensions of depth and dynamic change of configurations of domination.

When we consider some people (ourselves or others) in some context, we can make an analytical distinction between two aspects of them. We can see them, on the one hand, as bearers of status-dignity, and, on the other, as

The Critique of Domination   **311**

entangled in behaviour in which they adopt certain social roles (such as those of a capitalist or a wage worker). Using this distinction, we can critically assess instances of the second aspect by relying on the first. We can ask: Is what these people are doing, and the ways in which they approach each other as they act, such that the status-dignity of each is given its due? Sometimes we can notice that the practical entanglements under scrutiny are not a good fit for the valuable capacities of those involved, that these capacities are for example ignored, stunted, or misused. We can then pivot dynamically from this awareness of a lack of fit to the envisioning of projects of change. We can transform the relevant social practices so that we come to respond appropriately to the status-dignity of each participant, and in this way increase everyone's autonomy and well-being.

These changes may target power configurations that involve domination, and envision alternative configurations that enact solidaristic empowerment. Consider a team of workers in an enterprise. Imagine that some members are particularly talented when it comes to activity that features systematic understanding and execution of complex schedules, whereas others are instead gifted for tasks of creative formulation of new ideas for production. Now imagine that the former team members have much more decision-making power within the firm, and routinely disparage the latter as 'abnormal' (as being undisciplined, unfocused, suffering from ADHD, and so on) and push them to fall in line with the tasks they unilaterally establish. This setup could be criticized as being a poor fit for the valuable capacities of the more creative but less disciplined workers. The team could be refashioned so that the latter gain more say in the articulation of tasks, and their talents for invention are given opportunities to unfold. The mutual solidaristic support in the new configuration would work to the benefit of all. The more creative workers would find new ideas to solve problems, and the more structured workers would devise systematic implementations of those ideas. The more creative workers would no longer be disparaged as abnormal people who must simply adapt to 'what normal people do'. They would be recognized instead as equal contributors in a team boasting a pool of people with diverse but valuable capacities that deserve to be acknowledged and supported, and whose unfolding benefits all—as the Abilities/Needs Principle would indeed recommend.

Interestingly, these exercises of reconfiguration of social practices and institutions are also an endeavour of *self*-reconfiguration. This is where dignitarian virtue comes in. When we pivot dynamically in the ways envisaged, we reshape ourselves into agents who are more attuned to status-dignity. We

312 Human Dignity and Social Justice

become more ready to recognize and implement norms that really support the unfolding of the valuable capacities in the basis of the dignity of the people we affect.

Reflection on dignitarian virtue indeed helps us cast light on the responsibilities of social change to reduce or overcome instances of domination. Now, these responsibilities do not only include duties to others. They also arguably include duties to self.

As argued in this chapter, domination often involves failure to respond appropriately to people's status-dignity. But domination does not only involve a failure to appropriately respond to the status-dignity of others. It also includes failing to respond to *one's own* dignity. Domination can be harmful to the dominators because it involves neglect of their own valuable prudential and moral capacities. In crushing the will of others, dominators also misshape their own will in impoverished ways, downplaying their ability to flourish in mutually caring and supportive social relationships. Their own life becomes bleaker as a result. More controversially, we can also say that domination can feature self-harm on the part of the dominated. The dominators fail to unfold their own moral capacities when they disrespect the dominated, but the dominated who fail to approach their predicament critically and do not try to pursue feasible changes to it may also be failing to affirm their own dignitarian status and respect themselves.

There are difficult questions about how responsibilities for overcoming injustice should be construed and allocated, especially when the injustices are systemic and cannot be overcome by the isolated acts of any small number of people entangled in them. These questions deserve careful treatment.[90] My point here is simply that, as we tackle them, it is important to notice the role of dignitarian virtue and that dignitarian virtue encompasses requirements for both the dominators and the dominated. Both may fail to respond appropriately to their status-dignity when they do not envision ways to contest unjust social orders of domination.

In addition to power over others, we can have power over ourselves, which we can use to reshape our reactions to injustice. Exploring this fact may help in addressing criticism of accounts of power and domination over others which emphasize their depth—i.e. their shaping of the operative reasons on which others choose to act. Thus, a worry about such accounts is that 'when applied to situations of oppression, [they tend ...] toward the old cliché that "no one can oppress you without your permission", a view that puts too much responsibility on the victims of domination and not enough on those who are

---

[90] For seminal work, see Young (2011).

The Critique of Domination   **313**

doing the dominating.'[91] It can indeed be odious to insist on blaming some-one whose face is under the boot of a more powerful agent for being in that position, instead of charging the more powerful agent for the pressure they are applying with their foot. But a defender of the Dignitarian Approach need not do that when they explore the psychological processes that go on in the subject of power. What is key is to notice whatever power there is, wherever it lies (without inaccurate exaggerations or omissions), and to notice that, from their own perspective, the oppressed can also often ask themselves whether, how, and when they might resist their oppression. Even if they can reason-ably conclude that in a particular conjuncture the odds are not in their favour and should not (yet) rise up, they owe it to themselves to entertain ques-tions of this kind. It would be condescending to talk about them as if it were not appropriate for them to engage in self-critical examination as to whether they are capitulating when they should fight. Respect for the oppressed starts with recognizing their dynamic agency. Similarly, self-respect starts with recognizing one's own. Our status-dignity always affords us a ground for crit-ical reflection to pivot dynamically away from domination, and to envisage responses that shatter moulds of activity and self-perception which are not a good fit for it.[92]

4.4.5 Further remarks on dignity and self-respect

The discussion in 4.4.4 mentioned the idea of self-respect. We may add some thoughts about this important idea, considering how the Dignitarian Approach helps illuminate its role in struggles against injustice.

Self-respect is a form of self-appraisal in which agents see themselves in a positive light. It addresses the moral aspects of the self, and, because of this, it is more specific than the broader phenomenon of self-esteem. This self-appraisal can first be focused on how agents appear to themselves as a function of how they have acted. In this form of self-respect, agents see them-selves as upright actors who have complied with moral norms. This notion of self-respect may be used not only to characterize oneself in light of whether one's actions have given others their due. It can also be used to reflect on actions in which one affirms, protects, or otherwise responds appropriately

---

[91] See Allen's contribution in Allen et al (2014: 27). Allen discusses here Forst's account of 'noumenal power', which ploughs the dimension of depth of domination.

[92] It is true that it can be offensive for the members of a privileged group to tell members of an oppressed group that they ought to resist their oppression. The former could be ignoring the hardships that the latter experience, and the particular challenges they face when fighting to overcome it. But the main point in the text still stands, at least as one to be addressed by the members of the oppressed group themselves, as they (alone or in association with others acting in solidarity with them) develop attitudes and practices of self-empowerment.

314 Human Dignity and Social Justice

to one's own value. Self-directed duties to avoid acting in meek and humiliating ways in the face of arbitrary displays of power by others are of this sort.[93] A second, more basic and general use of the notion of self-respect is also important. Self-respect may be an attitude owed to oneself as an individual with morally important features independently of whether one has behaved rightly or not. One can have self-respect in this second form even if one does not have it in the first form.

It is fruitful to explore further this difference between self-respect that reflects what one is and self-respect that reflects what one does. For example, we can distinguish between more or less constant and more or less contingent features. So, you can have a positive relation to yourself simply as a human individual with capacities for moral and prudential reasoning, sentience, empathy, and so on, or, more specifically and contingently, as the carrier of a specific role, such as that of being a painter, a cook, a member of parliament, or a parent. Self-respect can link to actions in different ways as well. For example, you can appraise yourself in light of actions that are occasional acts or in light of more or less regular practices.

Self-respect can play a role in domination. The depth of domination can be increased by manipulating it. Thus, someone might get you to do something they want by convincing you that you would loathe yourself unless you do it, that even if you do not want to do it, your wants are not important enough to ground complaints against their demand that you do it, as self-respect is more important than the selfish satisfaction of your wants. Putative moral principles can thus be used as whips of domination. The dominator can invoke them to guilt-trip people into giving them what they want. For another example, a dominator can invoke principles that are infeasible to fulfil, and get you—especially if you care enough about morality to feel bad when you do not honour its requirements—to lose self-respect when you do not fulfil them and thereby make yourself available for tasks of atonement or reparation which are carefully scheduled by the dominator for their own benefit. The problem here is not with morality as such, however. The problem is with the use of putative moral principles that are remote from what is feasible for agents to achieve, or which do not track their own autonomous reasoning or give proper attention to their own good. What we find here is a manipulation

---

[93] See Kant's striking discussion of the vice of 'servility' as a failure to fulfil duties to oneself. Kant, *The Metaphysics of Morals,* in Kant (1996a: 353–603, at 6:434–7). See also Mills's (2018: 19–20) forceful exploration of the duty to respect oneself on the part of members of oppressed racialized groups. For example, affirmations of 'black pride' (as featured in the rallying cry that 'Black Lives Matter!') involve a 'repudiation of the status of sub-personhood', and a justified rejection of the inclination to defer to dominators and the conventional social norms cementing their rule.

The Critique of Domination **315**

of moral discourse. The critique of operations like these is itself a moral task, drawing on genuine moral principles that take the dignity of the dominated seriously.

Struggles against domination can also be linked to self-respect. One step in pushing back against arbitrary power is to come to see oneself as valuable and as meriting standing up for. Here the different forms of self-description discussed above are important. People may resist domination by affirming their value under a certain role description or by referring to certain practices. For example, they may affirm themselves as workers who make the economy run even if they are, unduly, cast away from decisions about how it is managed or deprived from enjoyment of the riches they produce. Or they may resist some forms of domination by affirming their worth quite generally as human individuals with valuable capacities. For example, when resisting slavery or despotism, people may simply say that these institutions affront their dignity as beings capable of self-determination. Some conventional roles, and the social structures generating them, may be rejected outright as debasing.

Arguably, in struggles against domination there are dynamic duties to reframe our relation to ourselves so that we gain the kind of self-respect that gives us the confidence we need to affirm our rights. Such a positive self-identification is also directly appropriate, as the self-recognition that is fitting given who we are.

The idea of status-dignity in the Dignitarian Approach is key here. As a normative status inherent in people in virtue of their valuable basic capacities, it constitutes a reason for a form of self-respect that is invariant across their behaviour and current social conditions. No negative self-appraisal based on specific acts or conventional social roles, even when it is justified, can extinguish this reason for self-respect.[94] This means that we always have a core in ourselves from which we can derive a sense of worth and which we can engage to pivot critically and dynamically to improve our lot—to change our behaviour and habits, or to challenge social structures and roles that do not reflect the value that inheres in us. Status-dignity is a resilient basis for self-affirmation, the cultivation of dignitarian virtue, and even some hope that our endeavours will reach fruition. Dominated people (and dominators too) can always draw on it to do better.

---

[94] Recall (from Chapter 1) the distinction between achievement-based and endowment-based dignity. The former arises when agents successfully act in the ways an appropriate response to the latter calls for. But agents retain endowment-based dignity even when they fail to gain achievement-based dignity.

316 Human Dignity and Social Justice

5. Appendix I: Analytical Grid of Power

Agential power is a kind of power that can be had and exercised only by entities with a will and which involves that will. It is different from non-agential power, the existence and exercise of which do not necessarily feature an agent or their will. Thus, a stone has the power to displace water as it falls into a pond. But it does not have the agential power to do so. I may also have a power to displace water as I fall into a pond. But this is not an agential power unless the displacement of water with my body is an object of my possible or actual intentional actions. We can understand agential power as follows:[95]

> *Agential power*: In certain circumstances C, an agent A has power with respect to some outcome O to the extent that A can voluntarily determine whether O occurs.

We can add some further detail when needed. For example, when thinking about relations of "power-over," we can say that, in certain circumstances C, an agent A has power over a subject S (where S is either a thing or an agent, be it agent A or some other) with respect to whether O occurs to the extent that A can voluntarily determine whether S exists or how S operates so as to generate O.[96]

To provide a handy framework to organize substantive explorations, I suggest that we can formulate and seek answers to the following questions about a certain power:

 i. Who has or exercises this power? (Agents of power—power-holders or power-wielders. This includes individual and group agents, and cases in which agents have "power-with" others.)
 ii. Over what or whom is this power held or exercised? (Subjects of power.)
 iii. What outcomes does this power help create or facilitate? (Outcomes of power. Range of power.)

---

[95] The formulations in this Appendix are based on, and revise, the statements in Gilabert (2019a: sect. 7.2.3), and (2018a: 88–9).

[96] We can also add time indices to make the account even more explicit. We can talk about A having power at time t1 with respect to an outcome at tn—where tn coincides with, or comes later than, t1. Furthermore, it is common to add a counterfactual clause saying that the outcome of power exercise would not have occurred without that exercise. One should phrase this point carefully, however, as it could be that, e.g., if A had not exercised power over B to get B to produce O, O would have still been produced by B because, say, C got B to do it, or because B decided to do it independently of anyone else's prompting. What is crucial for the counterfactual is that O would not have arisen in the exact same way (the one whose description makes reference to the agent of power).

The Critique of Domination   **317**

iv. To what extent would these outcomes be under the voluntary determination by the agent? (Degree of power.)

v. How far inwards into the paths of agency of the subject of power does the agent have influence (the consequences of their acts, their acts, their motives, etc.). (Depth of power.)

vi. What are the unintended effects (to be distinguished from the intended consequences) of power relationships and exercise? (This relates to historical issues—see below.) (Intended and unintended outcomes of power.)

vii. What are the means, or mechanisms, through which the agent can exercise this power, and help create or facilitate the relevant outcome? (Force, coercion, inducement, persuasion, etc.) (Mechanisms, forms of power.)

viii. What are the resources the use of which enable the agent to exercise this power? (Prestige, status, authority, economic resources, tools of violence, organization, knowledge, rhetorical and argumentative skills, etc.) (Resources of power.)

ix. Why, and in what circumstances, do the agents of this power want to have or use this power (if they do)? (Operative reasons for power.)

x. Why, and in what circumstances, do the agents of this power have reason to have or use this power (if they do)? (Normative reasons for power.)

xi. What are the enabling, and what might be some disabling, conditions for the agent to exercise their relevant power? (e.g. circumstances that might be necessary for the agent to use certain resources successfully, or that may prevent or reduce the likelihood that their intentions are fulfilled, etc.) (Enabling and disabling conditions or circumstances of power.)

xii. How did circumstances C arise? (History of circumstances of power.) (This includes the constitution of the agents and subjects of power; which may themselves be the effect of previous processes involving power.)

xiii. How might C change? What reforms or transformations are feasible and how feasible are they? What degree of power do agents have to introduce them? (Feasibility of change in circumstances of power; dynamic power.)

xiv. How should C be changed (if C should indeed be changed)? (Desirability of change in circumstances of power.)

318 Human Dignity and Social Justice

xv. If there is reason to reform or transform C, how does this change relate to the relations of power under discussion (both normatively and causally)?

xvi. If certain power relations are desirable but not sufficiently feasible or reasonably accessible in C, is there reason to change C (into different circumstances C*) so that the new relations emerge? If so, what could and should be done to change C in this way? (Dynamic duties to change circumstances of power.)

These dimensions are of course intertwined. We can talk about *power configurations* in which we identify various items of these dimensions in relation with items in others. Thus, a power relationship between A and B occurs in a certain context or in certain circumstances C, with respect to some outcomes O. What renders A powerful over B regarding O might not render A powerful over B regarding some other outcome O', or in different circumstances C'. The discrepancies involve different power configurations.

6. Appendix II: Domination, Alienation, and Exploitation

How should we think about the relations between the critiques of domination, alienation, and exploitation?[97] These phenomena overlap and relate in various ways, but since they are not identical the critique of social injustice should not be reduced to the discussion of any single one of them.

Consider first the relation between domination and exploitation. As indicated in Chapter 5 (Section 4.1), domination does not imply exploitation. An individual A might dominate another individual B without extracting any net resources from them. But does exploitation imply domination? There are many cases in which exploitation occurs in a context of domination. But there could be cases in which, intuitively, exploitation seems to occur without domination (although it does involve power asymmetries).

The typical case of exploitation involving domination is one in which A, the exploiter, offers B, the exploited, an option that B cannot refuse (in some sense of 'cannot' to be specified), because the alternatives to that option are simply unacceptable to B (in some sense of 'unacceptable' that also has to be

---

[97] In Marx's discussions of capitalism, the three critiques operated simultaneously. See, e.g., Marx (1990: 799).

The Critique of Domination **319**

specified).[98] So, for example, A, who is an entrepreneur in a very poor area, offers a sweatshop job to B, which would allow B to survive (B's alternative prospect to taking this job is starving).

But there can be cases in which the option offered by A is better than the alternatives available to B, but not in such a way that the option is unrefusable. So, A offers B a job that pays better than the job B has, and more than any other that is available to B. B's alternative options are not catastrophic. B can refuse the deal offered by A. But A could offer a much better deal to B, which A will not (there are people other than B competing with B for this job, and A does not need to sweeten the offer to get one of them). A's bargaining power is higher than B's, and A uses the asymmetry to offer B a deal that might seem unfair because of independent considerations about what workers deserve as remuneration for their contribution. Many working conditions in rich societies involve this kind of exploitation. If this is so, there are cases of exploitation without domination. They do display asymmetry of social power—an asymmetrical power-over relationship—but the asymmetry does not raise to the level of domination.

If the foregoing remarks are correct, then there are three possible theoretical upshots. First, we can hold that indeed exploitation does not imply domination. Second, we can say that exploitation does imply domination, but that the second case has to be re-examined to reveal that in fact there is domination in it, even if domination is still to be understood as involving unrefusability of the options offered by the exploiter. This could be done, perhaps, by digging into the depth of domination to find that the exploited is caught in a psychological whirlpool such that taking the deal offered by the exploiter is so hard to resist that they must count as dominated. Third, as in the second upshot, exploitation does imply domination, but the notion of domination should be revised so that it does not assume, for the cases of exploitation, that the exploitative option is unrefusable. The first upshot has the advantage of preserving the intuition that exploitation involves asymmetric power, and it accounts quite straightforwardly for the second kind of scenario described. But the other possibilities deserve more discussion. For example, if we explore the issue of degrees of domination further, we might find that when unrefusability holds in exploitation this happens in cases in which exploiters have a very high degree of dominating power over the exploited.

---

[98] In running this discussion, I am entertaining the view that the offer of a rewarding option (such as a job) involves domination only if that option is not refusable. I am inspired here by the discussion in Pettit (2012: 53–4). The phrases 'cannot refuse' and 'cannot accept' clearly need further exploration.

320 Human Dignity and Social Justice

Consider now the relation between domination and alienation. Domination and alienation clearly overlap. In my normative account of it in Chapter 6, alienation involves failure of successful and appropriate self-identification. Such a form of self-identification tracks the unfolding of capacities regarding self-determination and self-realization. Since self-determination is important in this account, domination, by setting it back, also carries alienation.

Still, domination and alienation remain different phenomena. Some forms of alienation do not necessarily carry domination. This is so, for example, when deficits in self-realization are not the result of the imposition of the will of others. Even some cases of deficit of self-determination which could be socially ameliorated might not be instances of domination. We have identified possible cases in this chapter (see Sections 3.2, 3.4, and 4.4.1). Furthermore, some forms of domination may be more alienating than others (see Section 4.2). They are all alienating insofar as they hamper self-determination. But some may be worse (alienation-wise) if, in addition, they set back interests of the parties involved which concern their self-realization.

The explanation of domination and alienation cannot be reduced to each other.[99] But the connections are important, and it is worth exploring further how the critiques of domination and alienation can be combined. For example, an important issue is how domination links to forms of categorization and identity-formation. One way in which alienation may arise is

---

[99] Discussions about alienation sometimes centre on a putative distinction between an agents' best, or real interests and their merely apparent, or false interests, and the concept of domination is used to explain the distinction. The alienated agent would be one who fails to be guided by their real interests and is instead swayed by false interests imposed by others. Figuring out what is the criterion to distinguish these two kinds of interests is difficult, but it is important to note that it is a matter of tracking normative reasons which are not exhausted by procedures of domination and their outcomes. A common strategy is explanatorily insufficient. It says that a putative interest of an agent is false just in case the agent either did not control its genesis or would not endorse it on reflection. The first variant of this suggestion (drawing on the idea of self-shaping) is implausible, as the etiology of an operative reason does not settle the normativity of its content. I consider have some interest because of my biological make-up, which I have not shaped, or even as a result of manipulation by other agents, but I may still have normative reason to fulfil it. It is a real, not a false interest. The second variant is plausible as an epistemic procedure, but is not fully satisfactory in the order of explanation. It could very well be that the interests that are reflectively endorsable are the real ones, in the sense that we can reliably find the latter by means of the former. But this does not suffice to understand why some interests are real rather than false. It is odd to say that interests are real *because* (as opposed to merely *if*, or *when*) they are, or would be, reflectively endorsed by the agent who has them. We still need to consider what are the *reasons* the reflective agents have for endorsing the putative interests. And this points us to other aspects of self-assessment besides self-determination, such as the importance of self-realization and other aspects of well-being. Thus, an agent might have reason to reflectively endorse an interest because its object would involve the maintenance, development, or exercise of some valuable capacity of theirs. Reflective endorsement may successfully signal a real interest, but to explain why this is so we have to illuminate the normative reasons the reflective endorsement tracks. Furthermore, self-determination is itself the object of a real interest (even if it does not exhaust the normative terrain of real interests): agents have normative reason to seek it even if they do not currently have operative reasons to do so.

The Critique of Domination **321**

when people develop their self-understanding by using categories imposed by others, but come to experience a tension between the picture of themselves that emerges when using these categories and aspects of themselves which the pictures do not capture or address in ways that are experienced as inadequate or oppressive. Now, it is a common feature of struggles against domination that they involve efforts by agents to re-describe themselves in new ways that seem to them more accurate and affirming. Here our explorations of the dynamic aspects of the active responses to domination and alienation converge. A clear case of the dynamic pattern is offered by the struggle of LGBTQ+ communities, in which certain forms of sexuality which were ignored or cast as deviant and shameful are depicted in a new and positive light, as valuable forms of sexual self-determination and expression.

8
Comparing Socialism and Capitalism

1. How should we think about the comparison between socialism and capitalism? In this chapter I offer some tentative remarks about how to approach this question. I start by providing a working definition of capitalism and socialism (envisaged within dimension DII of a conception of social justice). I then discuss recent proposals by G. A. Cohen and Jason Brennan as to how to compare these social systems, and deploy some of the theoretical resources offered in this book to further frame and advance our normative inquiry on this important topic. I conclude by highlighting how the idea of dignity might play a role in the exercise.

Socialism is best defined in contrast with capitalism, as socialism has historically arisen both as a critical challenge to capitalism, and as a proposal for overcoming and replacing it. In the classical, Marxist definition, capitalism involves certain *relations of production*.[1] These comprise certain forms of control over the *productive forces*—the *labour power* that workers deploy in production and the *means of production* such as natural resources, tools, and spaces they employ to yield goods and services—and certain social patterns of economic interaction that typically correlate with that control. Capitalism displays the following constitutive features:

(i) The bulk of the means of production is *privately owned and controlled.*

(ii) People legally own their labour power. (Here capitalism differs from slavery and feudalism, under which systems some individuals are entitled to control, whether completely or partially, the labour power of others).

(iii) *Markets* are the main mechanism allocating inputs and outputs of production and determining how societies' productive surplus is used, including whether and how it is consumed or invested.

---

[1] Cohen (2001: ch. 3); Fraser (2014). The definitional discussion in this section draws on Gilabert and O'Neill (2019: sect. 1).

Human Dignity and Social Justice. Pablo Gilabert, Oxford University Press. © Pablo Gilabert (2023).
DOI: 10.1093/oso/9780192871152.003.0008

324 Human Dignity and Social Justice

An additional feature that is typically present wherever (i)–(iii) hold, is that:

(iv) There is a *class division* between capitalists and workers, involving specific relations (e.g. of bargaining, conflict, or subordination) between those classes, and shaping the labour market, the firm, and the broader political process.

The existence of a labour market featuring wage labour is often seen by socialists as a necessary condition for a society to be counted as capitalist.[2] Typically, workers (unlike capitalists) must sell their labour power to make a living. They sell it to capitalists, who (unlike the workers) control the means of production. Capitalists typically subordinate workers in the production process, as capitalists have asymmetric decision-making power over what gets produced and how it gets produced. Capitalists also own the output of production and sell it in the market, and they control the predominant bulk of the flow of investment within the economy. The relation between capitalists and workers can involve cooperation, but also conflict (e.g. regarding wages and working conditions). As discussed in the previous chapter, this more or less antagonistic power relationship between capitalists and workers plays out in a number of areas, such as within production itself and in the broader political process, as in both economic and political domains decisions are made about who does what, and who gets what.

There are possible economic systems that would present exceptions, in which (iv) does not hold even if (i), (ii) and (iii) all obtain. Examples here are a society of independent commodity producers or a property-owning democracy (in which individuals or groups of workers own firms). There is debate, however, as to how feasible—accessible and stable—these are in a modern economic environment.[3]

Another feature that is also typically seen as arising where (i)–(iii) hold is this:

(v) Production is primarily orientated to *capital accumulation* (i.e. economic production is primarily orientated to profit rather than to the satisfaction of human needs).[4]

In contrast to capitalism, socialism can be defined as a type of society in which, at a minimum, (i) is turned into (i*):

---

[2] See, e.g., Schweickart (2011: 23); Van Parijs (1991: 95); Wright (2010: 34).
[3] O'Neill (2012).
[4] Cohen (2001); Roemer (2017).

Comparing Socialism and Capitalism 325

(i*) The bulk of the means of production is under social, democratic control.

Most socialists also tend to agree that (iv) is a key feature of realistic forms of capitalism and worry about it. They think that workers should have a real option to avoid the role of wage worker. On the other hand, changes with regard to features (ii), (iii), and (v) are hotly debated amongst socialists. Regarding (ii), socialists retain the view that workers should control their labour power, but many do not affirm the kind of absolute, libertarian property rights in labour power that would, for example, prevent taxation or other forms of mandatory contribution to cater for the basic needs of others.[5] Regarding (iii), there is a bourgeoning literature on 'market socialism', where proposals are advanced to create an economy that is socialist but nevertheless features extensive markets. Finally, regarding (v), although most socialists agree that, due to competitive pressures, capitalists are bound to seek profit maximization, some puzzle over whether, when they do this, it is 'greed and fear' and not the generation of resources to make others besides themselves better off that is the dominant, more basic drive and hence the degree to which profit-maximization should be seen as a normatively troubling phenomenon.[6] Furthermore, some socialists argue that the search for profits in a market socialist economy is not inherently suspicious.[7] Most socialists, however, tend to find the profit motive problematic.

An important point about this definition of socialism is that socialism is not equivalent to, and is arguably in conflict with, statism. On this interpretation, (i*) involves expansion of a kind of social power—the 'power-with' others implicated in the capacity to mobilize voluntary cooperation and collective action. This is in contrast with the two kinds of 'power-over' others implicated in state power—power based on the control of rule-making and rule-enforcing over a territory—and economic power—power based on the control of material resources.[8] If a state controls the economy but is not in turn democratically controlled by the individuals engaged in economic life, what we have is some form of statism, not socialism.[9] Alternatively, we could of course distinguish between democratic and non-democratic forms of socialism. The difference would be that the former construes social property as envisioned in (i*) and the latter understands it in centralized,

---

[5] Cohen (1995).
[6] See note 47 below on the case of capitalists amassing wealth to give it away through charity.
[7] Schweickart (2011: 51).
[8] Wright (2010).
[9] See also Arnold (2016, 2022); Dardot and Laval (2014).

326 Human Dignity and Social Justice

non-democratic terms (thus presenting an additional option (i**)). My focus here will be on democratic socialism.

The foregoing characterization, although somewhat nuanced, is still highly schematic and in need of further refinement. For example, democratic socialism itself can be construed in different ways. Democratic mechanisms of control of the means of production can be envisioned for the macro-level regarding the decisions made by the government, or they could be entertained for the more micro-level of the decisions made within firms (say in a form of workplace democracy), with several variants and combinations between both being possible. Furthermore (and as pointed out later in this chapter), hybrid combinations of elements of socialism and capitalism could be constructed and monitored by citizens through the general democratic process (provided it is indeed robust and sufficiently insulated from capture by elites). Thus, the institutional specifics of possible forms of democratic socialism turn out to be quite diverse.[10]

2. In his *Why Not Capitalism?* Jason Brennan provides a trenchant critique of socialism as defended by G. A. Cohen in *Why Not Socialism?*[11] In the latter book, Cohen argues that an ideal socialist society in which people honour radical principles of equality of opportunity and community is better than a capitalist society. Capitalism is morally flawed because in it some people have worse life prospects than others through no choice or fault of their own, and because economic practices are largely based on awful motivations of fear and greed rather than on more desirable ones such as mutual caring. Cohen distills his principles of equality and community by asking us to reflect on why we approve of the standard way of organizing social life in a camping trip. In a camping trip, there typically is collective control of most productive resources—such as pots and fish rods—and shared understandings about how to use them. People 'cooperate within a common concern that, so far as is possible, everybody has a roughly similar opportunity to flourish, and also to relax, on condition that she contributes, appropriately to her capacity, to the flourishing and relaxing of others'.[12] Most of us would want to scale up the socialist organization of the camping trip. If we could, we would be happy to organize society along camping trip lines. The trouble is that we do not really know how to do it. But since we also do not know for sure that it is impossible, we should try to imagine ways to achieve, or approximate, a socialist

---

[10] See O'Neill (2022), which warns against a narrow, exclusive focus on structures of ownership of means of production (public or private).

[11] Brennan (2014); Cohen (2009). I discuss Cohen's arguments in Gilabert (2011a) and (2012c). Cohen hesitates to see community as a principle of justice; in (2012c) I argue that justice includes aspects of it.

[12] Cohen (2009: 4–5). Notice the kinship between with the Abilities/Needs Principle.

societal organization. Such prospect, it seems, is a fitting target for dynamic intellectual and practical exploration.

In his response to Cohen, Brennan makes two main points. The first point is methodological. Brennan says that Cohen's argument is flawed because he fails to compare 'like with like'. Cohen argues in favour of socialism on the basis of a comparison of cases of ideal socialism with cases of real capitalism. What he should have done, instead, is compare ideal with ideal and real with real. If he engaged in these, more appropriate comparisons, things might have looked rather different. Brennan's second point is that, carefully assessed in these ways, capitalism turns out to be better than socialism. True, there has been exploitation and nasty handling of some people by others in real capitalism, but the murderous and economically inefficient record of real communist regimes in Russia, Cambodia, and China is far worse. Surprisingly, if we compare their ideal forms, capitalism is also better than socialism, as every form of association envisioned by the latter is permitted by the former, and then some. In Brennan's ideal capitalism, both private and collective property of resources can coexist. Thus, ideal capitalism actually lets 'a hundred flowers blossom'.[13] To develop and defend his view of ideal capitalism, Brennan contrasts Cohen's exemplary scenario of the camping trip with his own. He asks us to consider a TV cartoon for children, the 'Mickey Mouse Clubhouse Village' show, in which various characters manage to thrive and live in social harmony while holding capitalist property rights. Brennan also identifies a set of principles that are implemented in his exemplary scenario. These are principles of voluntary community, mutual respect, reciprocity, social justice, and beneficence.[14] In the cartoon, people 'live together happily, without envy, glad to trade value for value, glad to give and share, glad to help those in need, and never disposed to free ride, take advantage of, coerce, or subjugate one another'.[15]

3. Brennan's discussion is intelligent and illuminating. Two excellent points are the following. First, he rightly calls us to pay critical attention not only to the motivations of fear and greed (the ones Cohen focuses on), but also to lust for dominating power over others.[16] Obsession with this kind of power has sadly been strong in various real (capitalist and socialist) regimes.[17] And

---

[13] Brennan (2014: 98).

[14] These principles (Ibid., 29–36) call people to secure access to a decent life but do not require material equality—which would reflect socially destructive envy (33–4). There is no limit to acceptable inequality: some may be 'ten or ten thousand times richer' than others (34).

[15] Ibid: 25.

[16] Ibid: 44, 64.

[17] Brennan also says that, when describing a social regime, we should focus on its formal institutions (such as its property rights profile), not on the motivations of agents living and acting under it (see Ibid: 62ff.). He says that Cohen conflates these two levels. But it is hermeneutically fairer to say that for Cohen

328 Human Dignity and Social Justice

attention to it helps us illuminate problems about state power besides difficulties regarding the organization of economic institutions. Second, Brennan is correct that an appropriate comparative assessment of the merits of socialism and capitalism must compare like with like.[18] We should compare ideal socialism with ideal capitalism, not with real capitalism, and we should compare real capitalism with real socialism, not with ideal socialism. That said, Brennan's arguments have serious flaws.

The main methodological difficulty is that there are in fact at least three, not two key comparisons that should be distinguished, and engaged, when contrasting socialism and capitalism. Brennan mentions comparisons between ideal socialism and ideal capitalism and between real socialism and real capitalism. But notice that the opposite of an ideal approach, a realistic one, can take into account two quite different categories: the 'actual' and the 'feasible'. Sometimes Brennan refers to examples of really existing, actual socialist and capitalist societies to refer to advantages or disadvantages of those regimes. These references focus on actual cases. But sometimes Brennan seems to refer to how capitalism could realistically be reformed and be made to be. He does this less with socialism, unfortunately. A symptomatic sentence is this: 'Ideal capitalism is better than ideal socialism, and realistic capitalism (of some sort) is better than realistic socialism'.[19] I take it that when Brennan qualifies his reference to capitalism, he thinks that there are different kinds of realistic capitalism, some better than others, and that we should address the best of them. But the same should be done with socialism. In particular, we should consider cases of socialism that protect liberal civil liberties and affirm democratic political rights. It is true that Russian and Chinese communist regimes flouted these, but it is also true that from Marx to the present, very many figures and strands in the socialist movement affirmed them unequivocally. Cohen himself, as Brennan recognizes, did not recommend anti-democratic, centrally planned regimes, and embraced an 'anarchist' form of socialism.[20]

To capture the relevant cases, I suggest that we need to entertain (at least) the following *three* comparisons:

---

the moral and political culture or social ethos that is dominant in a society is partly constitutive of it, and is a bona fide topic when assessing how just it is. It is otherwise hard to understand why Cohen criticizes (what he takes to be) Rawls's view that the primary focus of a theory of justice is only the basic institutional structure of a society. See Cohen (2008: ch. 3).

[18] Brennan (2014: 58).

[19] Ibid: 98–9.

[20] Ibid: 19. On Cohen's 'socialist/anarchist' outlook see, e.g., Cohen (2008: 1). Interestingly, Brennan also labels his view 'anarchist'—Ibid: 42, 75. There is indeed a point of convergence regarding anarchist ideas. Marxists often say (after Engels) that in the best society the state would 'wither away'.

Comparing Socialism and Capitalism 329

C1: between ideal socialism and ideal capitalism
C2: between (various cases of) actual socialism and actual capitalism
C3: between the best feasible socialism and the best feasible capitalism.[21]

Brennan concentrates on C1 and C2, neglecting C3. However, C3 is important theoretically, and certainly crucial for political practice.[22]

As noted, I agree with Brennan that we should avoid the common mistake of thinking that the comparison between socialism and capitalism would be settled by showing that the best conceivable forms of socialism are better than all of the really existing forms of capitalism. To be fair to our opponent, we should compare like with like. But a key kind of comparison (which Brennan does not focus on) is the comparison between the best feasible incarnations of capitalism and socialism. This comparative exercise has the double merit of helping us be critical of the status quo when we should (as the best feasible form of socialism or capitalism may not already exist) while also keeping an eye on what we can actually bring about through lucid political action. I am not saying that the other comparisons are irrelevant or uninteresting. In fact, in the dynamic approach to justice and feasibility offered in Chapter 4, I have argued that evaluative comparisons regarding desirability independently of feasibility play a role in shaping projects for feasible transformations with a long-term horizon. But, all things considered, a central practical question must be 'What is the best feasible option?'

Using the framework regarding the three dimensions of a conception of social justice, I suggest that a fully satisfactory critical appraisal of a social system, such as capitalism, by comparison to another, such as socialism, would involve the following tasks:

Task 1: Identify the relevant and correct ideals and principles at DI and appraise, when possible, their structure (e.g. their relative weight).
Task 2: Addressing DII, show that the critically targeted social system is significantly deficient with respect to the fulfilment of those ideals or principles.

---

[21] Notice that unlike C1 and C3, C2 does not only refer to good cases of socialism and capitalism. When comparing the actual with the actual, we should look at all the cases. Furthermore, C3 could be made more precise by entertaining 'maximally good feasible' cases of each regime—thus allowing that there may be more than one case ranked at the top. (X is maximally good when it is no worse than any alternative, while x is best when it is superior to every alternative.)

[22] Brennan seems aware that there are different modalities that might be relevant when characterizing social regimes (besides the categories of the real and the ideal). In particular, he hints at the distinction between what is 'attainable' (or simply possible) and 'realistic' (feasible) (see Ibid: 71). The former seems relevant for C1, while the latter is relevant for C3. The specificity of C3 is not worked out, however. Cohen himself neglects C3 in his (2009), although elsewhere he offers relevant remarks on how various forms of socialism and capitalism might distribute freedom (Cohen 2011: 163–5).

330 Human Dignity and Social Justice

Task 3: Still at DII, show that some workable alternative to this system would do better at fulfilling these ideals or principles.

Task 4: Addressing DIII, show that the alternative system would be accessible at reasonable cost.

This schedule of tasks is especially fitting for comparative exercise C3.

4. Turning to specific matters about each of comparison, I will highlight four sets of problems with Brennan's discussion. This critical assessment will help identify points that are fruitful for framing the positive exploration of the comparison between socialism and capitalism.

(i) The first problem concerns the appeal to exemplary scenarios. Cohen's camping trip is strikingly different from Brennan's cartoon. The camping trip is not really stipulative[23] at all, but an actual example which I think most of us have little difficulty in grasping (and which many of us have actually experienced), while the Disney scenario is a wholly fictional concoction which doesn't even involve human beings. People in the camping trip are like us. They have the same psychology and physiognomy. It is thus not surprising that Cohen's exemplary scenario is much more consequential to the reader as a source of intuition pumps. The difference between C1, on the one hand, and C2 and C3, on the other, is not that they assume a different kind of human nature, or deep differences in motivational profiles. The key difference, for Cohen, is in how different social designs diverge in triggering, or fostering, the various components of the same set of psychological tendencies (which includes a mixture of self-centred and other-regarding mechanisms).[24]

(ii) A second problem concerns the principles used in the comparisons between socialism and capitalism. While Brennan uses five principles, Cohen uses two. These normative platforms overlap. For example, they both include requirements of community and of basic, sufficientarian, material support. But they also diverge. For example, Cohen affirms, and Brennan denies, the desirability of equality of opportunity. Furthermore, although it is intuitively obvious that socialism involves principles of community and equality, it is not at all apparent that capitalism is inherently linked to a principle of beneficence. Brennan's labeling of some of his principles as 'capitalist principles' is surprising and seems oddly stipulative. In any case, the comparisons should

---

[23] Pace Brennan (2014: 65).

[24] I add that when we explore differences between ideal, actual, and best feasible cases, we should not only consider possible changes regarding cultural and institutional schemes, but also regarding material resources (levels of material scarcity). This point is neglected by Brennan, but has significant implications that will become salient when I discuss his argument for the alleged superiority of ideal capitalism over ideal socialism.

Comparing Socialism and Capitalism **331**

be made under the same principles.[25] Alternatively, there should be a separate exercise comparing the principles themselves.[26] Task 1 and 2 can be run simultaneously, but the first can, to some extent, be run separately.

Let me say more on the last point. A very powerful way to argue for a political view is to show to your audience that it is better than the relevant alternatives on account of values or principles your audience already holds dear. But this strategy of argument is not always sufficient. The reason is that socialists and capitalists may disagree at the level of value or principle. This may happen in at least two ways. First, even if they agree about what are the ideals or principles to assess societal structures, they may disagree about their relative importance in a way that yields different conclusions as to what structure we have reason to favour all things considered. So, for example, capitalists and socialists might agree that socialism does better than capitalism regarding democracy and that capitalism does better than socialism regarding some negative liberties, but disagree about the relative weight of these values. Capitalists might prefer a non-democratic regime that protects certain negative economic liberties to a democratic regime that constrains them. A second possibility is that socialists or capitalists accept certain ideals or principles which their opponents do not embrace. An example is the view that certain positive duties of solidarity or community may be enforceable. Socialists are generally amenable to this idea, while capitalists of a libertarian bent are hostile to it. When this is so, the discussion has to move to more fundamental levels in moral reflection.[27] Relatedly, socialists and capitalists may agree on some ideals but specify them differently at the level of prescriptive principles. Thus, many socialists and capitalists embrace an ideal of self-determination, but when certain socialists also have strong commitments to solidarity or community which certain capitalists lack, the former reject and the latter affirm a prescriptive principle of self-ownership that bans any

---

[25] For a sharp discussion of this methodological point, see Claveau (2014).

[26] If this is done, however, a more careful articulation of each set is needed. Regarding socialism, for example, an explicit statement of principles of personal freedom and of democratic politics should be added. They are not fully articulated in Cohen's discussion, although they are hinted at various points in his text (see, e.g., the reference to a personal prerogative in Cohen 2009: 47–7, 76).

[27] As articulated in Chapter 3, the Abilities/Needs Principle encodes strong positive duties. Other examples of socialist views with potentially controversial values are these. Albert's (2016) 'participatory planning' economy relies on a strong commitment to 'solidarity'. Schweickart's (2016) 'economic democracy' model draws on a commitment to (collective) 'participatory autonomy'. When defending workers' cooperatives and other forms of non-capitalist economic activity, Wright (2015b) invokes 'emancipatory ideals' such as 'equality, democracy, and solidarity'. Solidarity could underwrite support for the needs of others even when (due to their different capacities) they are less productive, and participatory autonomy could license collective decisions at workplaces that are at odds with some individuals' interests in certain forms of negative liberty. Socialists typically have expansive views of the scope and range of democracy (extending it across national borders and reaching into the details of an economic system). And their views of equality are typically also quite strong (including effective besides formal opportunity, and incorporating some demands of equality of condition—e.g. regarding health care).

332 Human Dignity and Social Justice

imposition of non-voluntary assistance to others (such as taxation to fund health care).[28]

A puzzling issue when we compare socialism and capitalism within Task 1 is that although it is quite clear that socialists often see themselves as holding a 'socialist' view regarding DI besides DII, it is not clear that their opponents hold themselves to be 'capitalists' about DI besides being 'capitalists' about DII. Typically, people endorsing capitalism at DII characterize their views at DI by using other terms, like 'libertarian' or 'liberal'. (Of course, some people holding socialist views at DI may concede to capitalism at DII, although typically with some strong qualifications.) Is this a mere terminological point or is there something deeper going here? One possibility is that socialists embraced much of the modern liberal credo regarding DI (such as the affirmation of civil and political liberties, formal equality of opportunity, and moral universalism) and focused on adding novel ideas regarding solidarity, effective self-determination, and self-realization at work. Because of this, they might be more ready than liberal defenders of capitalism to insist in articulating DI in a distinctive way.

(iii) When arguing that capitalism is better than socialism, Brennan often refers to the virtues of markets. But this neglects the varieties of socialism that also feature markets. Brennan acknowledges in passing the possibility of a market socialist view,[29] but then proceeds as if markets were a distinctive feature of a capitalist society.[30] This is unsatisfactory, as there are important proposals for socialist design (relevant for comparison C3, and perhaps also for C1) that couple socialized control of the means of production with markets for the allocation of labour or for goods and services (as well as with traditional liberal civil rights and democratic freedoms). In Schweickart's (2011) 'economic democracy' model, a democratically steered state leases out firms to worker-run cooperatives, while incentivizing through public banks certain forms of economic activity. In Roemer's (1994) coupon socialism, every citizen is initially provided with equal coupons they can use to get shares in firms. They cannot cash them to get money for consumption purposes, but they can get dividends from investing them. When they die, their coupons revert to the common pool for distribution to new generations. In Carens's (2003) proposal, markets are used to signal optimal intersections between the demand and supply of labour and consumption goods, but incomes are taxed to equality.[31]

---

[28] Recall discussion of the Sleepwalking Anna case in Chapter 1, Section 2.2.2. See also Gilabert (2012c).
[29] Brennan (2014: 16).
[30] E.g. Ibid: 15, 66, 87.
[31] I presented an amended version of Carens's proposal in Chapter 3. See further the survey in Gilabert and O'Neill (2019: sect. 4.2). It is also worth considering less radical views of socialism, such as the one

Because of the oversight of market socialism, Brennan's approach is not well-equipped to tackle Task 3 in the comparative assessment of socialism and capitalism. Perhaps Brennan's neglect of market socialism is a result of the dialectical context of his debate with Cohen. At times Cohen proceeds as if there is a necessary conflict between socialism and markets, and a tight relation between the latter and contra-egalitarian or contra-communitarian principles and motives. (This is not always obvious, however, given that Cohen accepts that some version of Carens's proposal, which does include market devices, could implement socialist principles fully.[32]) Another source of worry with markets in the Marxist tradition is that they seem to be in tension with the ideal of self-determination, and in this way generate alienation. The complexity of a market economy is such that many outcomes emerging from the aggregate of market transactions are not rationally controlled by the agents entangled in them. A centrally planned economy would not, however, solve this problem, as workers would not control it either, and in it they would likely enjoy even less self-determination overall (while suffering other problems regarding efficiency). A strong hypothesis for further exploration in Task 3 is then that market mechanisms could be introduced without certain costs in alienation, and that when some such costs arise, they must all things considered be accepted because the alternatives are even worse (in terms of alienation and other problems).[33]

(iv) Fourth, and relatedly, Brennan's arguments for his claim that ideal capitalism is superior to ideal socialism are not convincing. He characterizes capitalism as including (a) private property in means of production, (b) use of markets, and (c) extensive economic liberties for individuals.[34] Since in his comparisons he ignores market socialist proposals, he fails to show that ideal capitalism is better with respect to (b). The virtues of markets he lists (such

---

recently presented by Piketty (2019: ch. 17). Piketty's 'participatory socialism' does not eliminate private property in the means of production entirely. Instead, it recommends significant reforms such that property becomes, in significant ways, 'social' and 'temporary'. Large firms feature schemes of codetermination giving workers a say on how production proceeds. Capital is dispersed through progressive taxation on property, inheritance, and income, which is used to fund a capital grant for young people, a secure basic income for all, and the public services of a social sate (such as education and health care). Changes to the democratic process to make citizens' influence in it more equal, and international arrangements to restrict capital flight, are also envisioned.

[32] Cohen (2009: 62–5).

[33] As pointed out to me by Andrew Williams, the fact that many leftists have come to terms with the need for markets may be a reason (to be added to the four explored in Section 4 of Chapter 5) for the decrease in their interest in the discourse of alienation. There are other possibilities, however. For example, Albert's (2003) proposal of 'Parecon' (participatory economy) envisions a scheme of nested deliberative forums of producers and consumers which would work together to consolidate schedules of economic activity that combine planning and democratic decision-making. But there are serious worries about its feasibility. See Wright (2010: 260–5).

[34] Brennan (2014: 75).

334 Human Dignity and Social Justice

as their fostering prosperity, self-authorship, mutual trust, and a tendency of economic agents to put themselves in the shoes of others) can also be displayed by market socialism.

So the most relevant arguments should be those concerning (a) and (c). The arguments regarding (a) are likely to be especially significant, however, because (c) is often also affirmed by socialists in some forms. For example, what exercises many socialists the most is not the permission of entering wage labour contracts, but the lack of real opportunities to make a living without having to do so. Wage labour, they think, is a feature of actual and feasible capitalist societies which is pervasive and extremely hard to avoid. So, in the controversy between socialism and capitalism, the most important question seems to be: Should we acknowledge private property in the means of production and contractual relations between capitalists who own means of production and wage workers who do not (i.e. features (i) and (iv) of capitalism as characterized in section 1) as structuring features of the economy which are pervasive and extremely hard to avoid? Socialists, and some liberal egalitarians, tend to answer negatively, saying that rights regarding (i) and (iv) should be either rejected or seen as non-basic and open to very severe qualifications.

Brennan acknowledges that in ideal scenarios people do not *need* capitalist property rights, that ideal socialist citizens would respect and tolerate others' pursuit of their economic projects, allowing them to use economic resources to advance them. But he says that people would be better off if they did have these rights.[35] I could not understand why. Brennan invokes the importance of being able to pursue our own projects without constantly asking for others' permission whenever we use the resources we need, and of 'feeling at home' in our economic activities.[36] But ideal socialism could give individual agents opportunities to achieve these goods. In a market socialist society, individuals or groups can gain significant control of means of production, which they can use in their own way without having to constantly ask for others' permission. Of course, there would be constraints (such as limits on selling or inheriting these resources). But Brennan's own view of property rights takes these rights to be only prima facie (or pro tanto) claims that have to be weighed against other normative considerations.[37] Socialists can also weigh social ownership against various concerns regarding the self-determination

---

[35] Ibid: 79. In ideal socialism people would tolerate individuals with capitalist preferences. But if it is still desirable (although not necessary) to establish conventional rights to the tolerated behaviour, then the socialist could make a similar move and ask for more than the kindness and charity of the wealthy in ideal capitalist societies to secure people's access to conditions of fair equality of opportunity.
[36] Ibid: 78–83.
[37] Ibid: 77.

of individuals and groups. Brennan presents his ideal capitalist society as a hybrid system including both private property in some means of production and collective property in others. Socialists can of course also do that (and in fact they do so).[38]

We should also consider whether there would be material scarcity in the ideal scenarios envisaged. If there were not, then both socialism and capitalism would allow completely unrestricted access to and control of any resource whatsoever. If there were scarcity, then both regimes would impose limits when there are competing desires regarding the control or use of resources. Either agents would have to share and ask for permission from others to access the resources, or some would face a greater risk of being completely deprived of them. (Socialists are more likely to choose the former, and capitalists the latter.) Various instances and combinations of these arrangements are possible in both regimes, through hybrid frameworks that for example allow some producers relative independence in the use of certain resources for some purposes and for some time, or give them private property but tax economic activity to subsidize access to important resources on the part of others. In both cases, the arrangements could be implemented through coercive institutional frameworks or via informal voluntary schemes.

So, pace Brennan, ideal socialism can allow a hundred flowers to blossom. If it imposes restrictions (given material scarcity), they would overall be fairly circumscribed, and not unlike the ones Brennan's ideal capitalism would (or should[39]) itself have to impose. There is conceptual and moral space, in both cases, for coercive or noncoercive ways of implementing the relevant norms, and for hybrid institutional structures.

Properly understood, the socialist ideal includes requirements of personal and political freedom besides community and equality. A desirable form of socialism would recognize negative and positive duties to respect and enable each individual to pursue their flourishing. What is the difference with ideal capitalism then? A key difference is that socialists have an explicit commitment to equal chances.[40] Brennan does not take ideal capitalism to require equality of opportunity. No help to the worse off is required beyond support

---

[38] On hybrid social systems, see Wright (2010) and O'Neill (2020: sect. 2).

[39] I add 'should' because a key issue here is whether we should secure robust equality of opportunity.

[40] Even if neither an ideal socialist nor an ideal capitalist regime had a state coercively enforcing its norms, a socialist would say that there is more justice when people use their liberty to pursue schemes of cooperation that foster equally the capabilities to flourish of all. Practices of liberty that, avoidably, do not aim at achieving this are morally deficient even if they should not be coercively restricted. Another difference concerns democracy, which is not affirmed by Brennan but is embraced by many socialists. In democratic socialism people choose through their democratic institutions the composition of their hybrid system. So democratic socialists would likely criticize, but would certainly accept as legitimate, democratically selected hybrids that give private property more sway than they think fair.

336 Human Dignity and Social Justice

for basic needs and the conditions for a decent life. The more demanding idea of material equality is summarily dismissed as reflecting the socially destructive sentiment of envy. This is a typical right-wing complaint against egalitarianism.[41] And it is not convincing. We can defend robust equality of opportunity as a matter of the socially constructive concern for fairness, and design economic systems so that they provide everyone ample and equal effective chances to pursue their life projects. Only a fetishistic obsession with property in material stuff would motivate complaints against a redistributive regime that grants each person plenty of room for developing and exercising their capacities but also gives them roughly equal prospects for effectively doing so.[42] Brennan's capitalism seems to find no difficulty with massive inequalities in access to material resources (including means of production) that result from inheritance, a paradigmatic case of unfair inequality of opportunity.[43] So of the hundred flowers blossoming in capitalism, some will likely shine a lot less brightly than others, unfairly and avoidably, through no choice or fault of their own.

The differences between the ideal capitalism of Brennan and the ideal socialism of liberal and democratic socialists are smaller than expected. Both accept hybrid institutional regimes that accommodate much of what the other calls for. The differences are likely to be much more significant when we turn to the comparison of feasible (but perhaps not ideally perfect) cases, i.e. C3. And this, arguably, is the politically most important comparison when it comes to choosing between socialism and capitalism as competing accounts of how ultimate control of means of production in a society should be allocated.[44] The denizens of Brennan's Disney cartoon might be too good-hearted to use their superior bargaining power to exploit and dominate the less wealthy or strong. But the rich and strong engage extensively in this kind of treatment in every actual capitalist society.[45] Importantly, they do it all the more the less their capitalist property rights are constrained by regulations geared to the protection of everyone's civil, political, and socioeconomic rights.[46] One really has to wonder how feasible it would be to have a capitalist

---

[41] For responses, see Rawls (1999: sect. 81) and Scanlon (2018: 2–8).

[42] Brennan (2014: 79) says that the denizens of his capitalist utopia are not fetishistic regarding their control of material resources. But the claims that capitalist property rights are necessary for 'feeling at home' in the world, and that redistribution to foster equality of opportunity would be an unacceptable violation of liberty seem to me to reflect exactly that fetishism.

[43] See Hall (2018).

[44] I say 'ultimate control' to allow for the possibility (common in proposals of market socialism) that democratic decisions are made to give sub-groups of society relative (potentially quite significant) control of means of production for certain periods of time and under certain conditions.

[45] Brennan seems to acknowledge this (Brennan 2014: 86, 94, 106n.18).

[46] It has been argued that deregulation in capitalist societies increases economic inequality (Piketty 2014), that economic inequality translates into political inequality (Gilens and Benjamin 2014), and that there is a deep tension between capitalism and democracy (Bowles and Gintis 1986; Wright 2010: 81–4).

Comparing Socialism and Capitalism 337

society that allows for extensive private property in means of production, and thus for the formation of classes and the division of economic agents into capital owners and wage workers, without also introducing exploitation and domination.[47] In actual and feasible capitalist societies, wage workers have much less real freedom than their employers to author their lives on their own terms, and they must indeed constantly ask for permission to engage in economic activities. Lacking control of means of production, they must (on pain of severe material hardship) sell their labour power to some capitalist who owns them. Then they must follow the orders of their employers' managers at every turn, every working day, as they toil under them. Besides exploitation and domination, they experience extensive alienation. They often do not feel at home in an economic environment they have little power to shape, and in which their talents are not unfolded. It is not clear that a hundred flowers do indeed blossom in the feasible world of capitalism. That picture seems like false advertising. Self-determination and self-realization turn out to be a dream which in the end only some can achieve, or that some achieve much more profoundly than others (and this partly as a result of their taking unfair advantage of the weaker bargaining power of the underachievers). It is surely worth exploring whether there are feasible forms of socialism that do better than the actual and feasibly best forms of capitalism when it comes to securing for all equal real chances to lead flourishing lives. We should try to do better than capitalism. Maybe we can. Due appreciation of our dignity calls for this exploration.

5. The main upshot of the foregoing discussion is that the project of envisioning socialist alternatives to capitalism is very much alive, both for ideal and best-feasible comparisons. Now, an important framing point to

---

Some defenders of capitalism might respond that they envision a form of capitalism featuring small property-owning producers who face each other in market relations that do not extensively include wage labour. But it is unlikely that a modern capitalist economy can proceed for long without generating wide inequalities and wage labour arrangements between highly unequal bargainers. See Cohen (2001: ch.7, sect. 2). Arnold (2013: 393–8) offers an effective response to the speculations that a minimally regulated market economy would maximize the income and wealth of the worst-off, or make it feasible for workers to develop their own, democratically run cooperative workplaces if they chose to avoid capitalist firms. Arnold (2020) in turn challenges Brennan's depiction of the ideal capitalist society. Overall, the odds are that an initial setup of small property holdings will unravel in the direction of concentrations of ownership and power. I add that inequalities of bargaining power will exist in the initial setup itself due to differences in natural endowments (talents, physical abilities, etc.). With more socialized forms of control of means of production, these tendencies could be more effectively confronted from the start.

[47] Fear and greed are systematically mobilized in current capitalism. And perhaps the best feasible versions of it would include more of them than the best feasible versions of socialism. In polemic with Cohen, Steiner (2014) notes that it is a mistake to assume that there cannot be market transactions without fear and greed. But I think that Cohen's considered view is that *capitalist* markets (unlike socialist ones of the Carens's type, for example) *typically* involve those motives. Of course, the rich (like Andrew Carnegie in Steiner's example) could use their wealth for charitable purposes. But even then, it would be better if people did not have to depend on their discretionary will (however beneficent) to get certain benefits. In a more egalitarian society, they could access them more robustly as a matter of right.

338 Human Dignity and Social Justice

keep in mind as we engage in comparative assessments is that a plausible, democratic socialism should be seen as a successor of capitalism that absorbs its progressive elements while taking the emancipatory agenda forward. Socialism is not a return to a collectivist past. It is an attempt to support individual freedom in a way that recognizes the significance of solidarity. This attempt might, to some extent and in some respects, involve restrictions of liberty, but it will also involve for the most part its deepening and expansion, and its equal accessibility to all.

This agenda could be advanced by deploying the idea of human dignity. We could, for example, develop an account of socialism as a dignitarian outlook, and consider how it would diverge from capitalism by developing a different view of the principles emerging at DI and of the institutions and practices at DII. Potentially different pictures regarding DIII could arise as well.

So, regarding DI, we might think that both socialists and capitalists embrace the dignity of each individual. But socialists might articulate the idea in distinctive ways, for example by linking it to (a) self-determined self-realization at work, (b) the affirmation of stronger (even enforceable) positive duties, (c) stronger equality of opportunity (for example fostering more equal initial capabilities and regular alterations of unequal outcomes to preserve some of the more egalitarian setup over time), and (d) a stronger commitment to democratic decision-making (and this in various arenas of social life, to include economic besides state or governmental affairs). As presented in this book, the development of the Dignitarian Approach through the ideal of Solidaristic Empowerment and the Abilities/Needs Principle would capture these points. With them in mind, socialists can also articulate a distinctive rendering of the traditional ideas of freedom, equality, community, and democracy.

These differences might have an impact on how we envision societal frameworks at DII. Thus, capitalist relations of production and the insufficiently solidaristic ethos tied to them might be shown to do worse than socialist relations of production and a more solidaristic ethos regarding (a)–(d). Even where hybrid forms of socialist and capitalist organization at DII are entertained, the divergence at DI could motivate different dynamic paths when these combinations are selected for the short and the long term.

Regarding DIII, there would be obvious differences in that the evaluation of the status quo and the goals of transition would be different. There might also be differences about the structure of normative judgement within DIII as a result of the emphasis on solidarity at DI. Socialists would ask currently privileged individuals to sacrifice their personal economic interests more than capitalists would. It is important to insist, however, that democratic

Comparing Socialism and Capitalism 339

socialists do not dismiss people's civil and political rights as some caricatures of socialism allege.[48]

Besides the question of what are the appropriate standards of comparison between socialism and capitalism, there is the question of who is to do the comparing. Who gets to say what social regime is better? I think that in metaphysical terms the right answer is that no one does. A social formation is better than another not because anyone says so, but because it *is* so. People should embrace a view of justice because it is correct, not the other way around. On the other hand (but compatibly), on epistemic and directly normative terms it makes sense to say that everyone should be able to join the discussion. Everyone makes mistakes and could help and be helped by others to correct them. And people's self-determination is a central value. This is why a primary task of social change should always be to increase the power of those affected by social injustice to formulate alternatives to it. A result is an additional, albeit partial test of justice for a social system: How much power does it allow people to assess whether it is the right one for them to live under? A system that suppresses political speech and blocks political action, generates deeply unequal distribution of information and education, and deprives people of the time they need to enlighten themselves and participate in politics is, in this respect, worse than another that generates fewer of these deficits in political autonomy. Correspondingly, an important way to defend an outlook on social justice is to show that its implementation affords people greater chances to figure out whether it or another outlook they might entertain is best. A properly democratic socialism would strongly affirm this second-order political autonomy. Such an affirmation would certainly flow naturally from the dignitarian perspective, due to its emphasis on self-determination.

6. In this book I have explored some elements of an articulation and defence of socialism at DII and DIII on the basis of a substantive normative conception of human dignity at DI. It could be objected that this enterprise is unnecessarily controversial. Why work out a new justification of socialism along these lines instead of proceeding on the basis of a set of ideas

---

[48] It is true that some actual experiments in socialist politics have unjustifiably flouted these rights. On democratic views of socialist transition, see Gilabert and O'Neill (2019: sect.5). The historical record of capitalism features important deprivations as well, for example in the early stages of transformation away from feudalism or authoritarian communism, in the processes of primitive accumulation involving imperialism and slavery, in cross-border interventions and wars, and in the repression of socialist and other forms of activism. For discussion on whether these issues are ongoing, see Fraser and Jaeggi (2018).

340 Human Dignity and Social Justice

already currently shared (such as some notion of freedom or democracy)? In response, I want to make four points.

The first is that it may not really be the case that there is a set of substantive grounds that is already shared which is sufficient to justify socialism. The set might be too thin to provide enough resources to defend socialism and further, controversial grounds might have to be added. Even if the set is sufficient, it might be that it would only prove to be so once it is interpreted in a specific way that turns out to be controversial. On the other hand, the idea of human dignity might not itself be so controversial. It is, after all, at the core of human rights practice, which advances one of the most broadly shared political projects of our time. True, we would be developing a certain interpretation of this idea, which will likely be controversial, but this would not land the approach into a worse situation than the one faced by the alternatives strategy discussed here (given the likely disagreements on the allegedly shared ideas it relies on).

Second, at least in some of its interventions, philosophy is primarily aimed at finding the truth rather than at winning disputes. The Dignitarian Approach I develop in this book strikes me as true. It is up to the reader to do what they may with it—although I do hope they will share it.

Third, there could be multiple grounds at DI for the same propositions at DII and DIII. Even if you do not accept the Dignitarian Approach, you could defend socialism on other grounds you find more appealing. It might even be a good thing that we articulate a multiplicity of justificatory sources of the social outlook we hold dear, as this may make its pursuit—the accessibility and the stability of its realization—more robust in a context of diversity in people's moral commitments.

Finally, engaging the dignitarian perspective does actually have practical significance, especially if we focus on the long term. I think that social and political philosophers with socialist leanings should confront the failure of some forms of liberalism and libertarianism to give solidarity its due. I have articulated the Dignitarian Approach so that positive duties and rights are explicitly embraced (although, of course, several negative ones are also recognized). Solidarity is at the heart of socialism, and socialists should aim to shape moral and political culture so that it is acknowledged as the crucial value that it is. Philosophers have a role to play in articulating this value in an upfront and uncluttered way. Narrowly focusing on quick dialectical victories would detract from this important task.

Bibliography

Albert, Michael. 2003. *Parecon: Life After Capitalism.* London: Verso.

Albert, Michael. 2016. 'What's Next? Parecon, or Participatory Economics'. https://thenextsystem.org/node/211

Allen, Amy, Forst, Rainer, and Haugaard, Mark. 2014. 'Power and Reason, Justice and Domination: A Conversation'. *Journal of Political Power* 7: 7–33.

Alston, Philip. 2005. 'Labor Rights as Human Rights: The Not So Happy State of the Art'. In P. Alston ed., *Labour Rights as Human Rights.* Oxford: Oxford University Press, 1–24.

Anderson, Elizabeth. 1999. 'What is the Point of Equality?' *Ethics* 109: 287–337.

Anderson, Elizabeth. 2014. 'Human Dignity as a Concept for the Economy'. In Marcus Düwell, Jens Braarvig, Roger Brownsword, and Dietmar Mieth, eds., *The Cambridge Handbook of Human Dignity.* Cambridge: Cambridge University Press, 492–97.

Anderson, Elizabeth. 2015. 'Equality and Freedom in the Workplace: Recovering Republican Insights'. *Social Philosophy & Policy* 31: 48–69.

Anderson, Elizabeth. 2017. *Private Government.* Princeton: Princeton University Press.

Arneson, Richard. 1987. 'Meaningful Work and Market Socialism'. *Ethics* 97: 517–45.

Arneson, Richard. 2016. 'Exploitation, Domination, Competitive Markets, and Unfair Division'. *Southern Journal of Philosophy* Suppl. 54, 9–30.

Arnold, Samuel. 2012. 'The Difference Principle at Work'. *Journal of Political Philosophy* 20: 94–118.

Arnold, Samuel. 2013. 'Right-wing Rawlsianism: A Critique'. *Journal of Political Philosophy* 21: 382–404.

Arnold, Samuel. 2016. 'Socialism'. *Internet Encyclopedia of Philosophy.*

Arnold, Samuel. 2017. 'Capitalism, Class Conflict, and Domination'. *Socialism and Democracy* 31:106–24.

Arnold, Samuel. 2020. 'No Community without Socialism: Why Liberal Egalitarianism Is Not Enough'. *Philosophical Topics* 48: 1–22.

Arnold, Samuel 2022. 'Socialisms'. In C. B. Melenovsky ed., *Routledge Handbook of Philosophy, Politics, and Economics.* New York: Routledge

Arnsperger, Christian and Van Parijs, Philippe. 2003. *Éthique Économique et Sociale.* Paris: La Découverte.

Arthurs, Henry. 2011. 'Labour Law After Labour'. In Davidov and Languille, *The Idea of Labour Law* (2011), 13–29.

Barry, Christian and Valentini, Laura. 2009. 'Egalitarian Challenges to Global Egalitarianism: A Critique'. *Review of International Studies* 35: 485–512.

Berlin, Isaiah. 2000. 'Realism in Politics'. In Berlin, *The Power of Ideas.* London: Pimlico, 134–42.

Blake, Michael. 2020. 'The Hermeneutics of Dignity: On Disability, Defiance, and Death'. *Journal of Global Ethics* 16: 316–25.

Bloodworth, James. 2018. 'I Worked in an Amazon Warehouse. Bernie Sanders is Right to Target Them'. *The Guardian*, 17 September.

Boltanski, Luc. 2009. *De la Critique.* Paris: Gallimard.

Boltanski, Luc and Chiapello, Eve. 1999. *Le Nouvel Esprit du Capitalisme.* Paris: Gallimard.

342 Bibliography

Bovens, Luc and Lutz, Adrien. 2019. '"From Each according to Ability; To Each according to Needs"' Origin, Meaning, and Development of Socialist Slogans'. *History of Political Economy* 51: 237–57.

Bowles, Samuel and Gintis, Herbert. 1986. *Democracy and Capitalism*. New York: Routledge.

Bowles, Samuel and Gintis, Herbert. 2011. *A Cooperative Species*. Princeton, Princeton University Press.

Bowles, Samuel and Gintis, Herbert. 1992. 'Power and Wealth in a Competitive Economy'. *Philosophy and Public Affairs* 21: 324–53.

Brennan, Geoff and Southwood, Nicholas. 2007. 'Feasibility in Action and Attitude'. R. Rasmussen, T. Petersson, P. Josefsson, and D. Egonsson, eds., *Hommage a Wlodek*. Available at www.fil.lu.se/hommageawlodek.

Brennan, Jason. 2014. *Why Not Capitalism?* New York: Routledge.

Brink, David. 2019. 'Normative Perfectionism and the Kantian Tradition'. *Philosophers' Imprint* 19.45.

Carens, Joseph. 1981. *Equality, Moral Incentives and the Market*. Chicago: The University of Chicago Press.

Carens, Joseph. 2003. 'An Interpretation and Defense of the Socialist Principle of Distribution'. *Social Philosophy and Policy* 20: 145–77.

Castoriadis, Cornelius. 1978. *Les Carrefours du Laberynthe 1*. Paris: Seuil.

Castoriadis, Cornelius. 1979. *Le Contenu du Socialisme*. Paris: Éditions 10/18.

Chen, Michelle. 2015. 'This is How Bad the Sharing Economy is for Workers'. *The Nation*, 14 September.

Chen, Patricia. 2015. 'One Company's New Minimum Wage: $70,000 a Year'. *New York Times*, 13 April.

Chiaburu, Dan, Thundiyil, Tomas, and Wang, Jiexing. 2014. 'Alienation and its Correlates: A Meta-Analysis'. *European Management Journal* 32: 24–36.

Christiano, Thomas. 2008. *The Constitution of Equality*. Oxford: Oxford University Press.

Claassen, Rutger and Herzog, Lisa. 2021. 'Why Economic Agency Matters: An Account of Structural Domination in the Economic Realm'. *European Journal of Political Theory* 20: 465–85.

Claveau, François 2014. 'Review of Jason Brennan *Why Not Capitalism?*' *Philosophiques* 42: 198–201.

Cohen, G. A. 1983. 'The Structure of Proletarian Unfreedom'. *Philosophy and Public Affairs* 12: 3–33.

Cohen, G. A. 1988. *History, Labour, and Freedom*. Oxford: Oxford University Press.

Cohen, G. A. 1995. *Self-ownership, Freedom, and Equality*. Cambridge: Cambridge University Press.

Cohen, G. A. 2001. *Karl Marx's Theory of History. A Defense*, rev. ed. Princeton: Princeton University Press.

Cohen, G. A. 2008. *Rescuing Justice and Equality*. Cambridge, MA: Harvard University Press.

Cohen, G. A. 2009. *Why Not Socialism?* Princeton, NJ: Princeton University Press.

Cohen, G. A. 2011. *On the Currency of Egalitarian Justice*. Princeton: Princeton University Press.

Collins, Hugh. 2011. 'Theories of Rights as Justification of Labour Law'. In Davidov and Langille, *The Idea of Labour Law* (2011), 137–55.

Corneo, Giacomo. 2017. *Is Capitalism Obsolete?* Cambridge, MA: Harvard University Press.

Coutrot, Thomas. 2018. *Libérer le Travail*. Paris: Seuil.

Cullity, Garrett. 2018. *Concern, Respect, and Cooperation*. Oxford: Oxford University Press.

Dahl, Robert. 1989. *Democracy and its Critics*. New Haven, Yale University Press.

Dahl, Robert. 1998. *On Democracy*. New Haven: Yale University Press.

Bibliography **343**

Daniels, Norman. 2011. 'Reflective Equilibrium'. *The Stanford Encyclopedia of Philosophy*, URL=<http://plato.stanford.edu/archives/spr2011/entries/reflective-equilibrium/>.

Dardot, Pierre and Laval, Christian. 2014. *Commun. Essai sur la Révolution au XXIe Siècle*. Paris: La Découverte.

Darwall, Stephen. 2006. *The Second-Person Standpoint*. Cambridge, MA: Harvard University Press.

Davidov, Guy and Langille, Brian, eds. 2011. *The Idea of Labour Law*. Oxford: Oxford University Press.

De Swaan, Abram. 1988. *In Care of the State*. Cambridge: Polity.

Deakin, Simon 2011. 'The Contribution of Labour Law to Economic and Human Development'. In Davidov and Langille, *The Idea of Labour Law* (2011), 156–75.

Duhigg, Charles and Barboza, David. 2012. 'In China, Human Costs are Built into an Ipad'. *New York Times*, 25 January.

Edgell, Stephen and Granter, Edward. 2020. *The Sociology of Work*, 3rd ed. London: Sage.

Ehrenreich, Barbara. 2005. *Bait and Switch*. New York: Metropolitan Books.

Einstein, Albert. 1949. 'Why Socialism?' *Monthly Review* 1.

Elster, Jon. 1983. *Sour Grapes*. Cambridge: Cambridge University Press.

Elster, Jon. 1985. *Making Sense of Marx*. Cambridge: Cambridge University Press.

Elster, Jon. 1986. *An Introduction to Karl Marx*. Cambridge: Cambridge University Press.

Elster, Jon. 1989. 'Self-realization in Work and Politics'. In Elster and Moene, *Alternatives to Capitalism* (1989), 127–58.

Elster, Jon and Moene, Karl, eds. 1989. *Alternatives to Capitalism*. Cambridge: Cambridge University Press.

Enoch, David. 2017. 'Hypothetical Consent and the Value(s) of Autonomy'. *Ethics* 128: 6–36.

Estlund, David. 2011. 'Human Nature and the Limits (if Any) of Political Philosophy'. *Philosophy and Public Affairs* 39: 207–37.

Evelyn, Kenya. 2020. 'Amazon Fires New York Worker Who Led Strike Over Coronavirus Concerns'. *The Guardian*, 31 March.

Fabre, Cecile. 2002. 'Good Samaritanism: A Matter of Justice'. *Critical Review of International Social and Political Philosophy* 5: 128–44.

Ferreras, Isabelle, Battilana, Julie, and Méda, Dominique. 2020. *Le Manifeste Travail. Démocratiser, Démarchandiser, Dépolluer*. Paris: Seuil.

Forst, Rainer, 2013. 'A Kantian Republican Conception of Justice as Nondomination'. In Andreas Niederberger and Philipp Schink, eds., *Republican Democracy: Liberty, Law, and Politics* Edinburgh: Edinburgh University Press, 154–68.

Forst, Rainer. 2014a. *Justification and Critique*. Cambridge: Polity.

Forst, Rainer. 2014b. 'Justifying Justification: Reply to My Critics'. In Forst, *Justice, Democracy, and the Right to Justification. Rainer Forst in Dialogue*. London: Bloomsbury, 169–216.

Forst, Rainer. 2017a. 'Noumenal Alienation: Rousseau, Kant, and Marx on the Dialectics of Self-Determination'. *Kantian Review* 22: 523–51.

Forst, Rainer. 2017b. *Normativity and Power*. Oxford: Oxford University Press.

Forst, Rainer. 2018. 'Noumenal Power Revisited: Reply to Critics'. *Journal of Political Power* 11: 294–321.

Foucault, Michel. 2001. 'The Subject of Power'. In James Faubion, ed., *Power*. New York: The New Press, 326–48.

Fraga, Robert, Herzog, Lisa, and Neuhauser, Christian. 2019. 'Workplace Democracy—The Recent Debate'. *Philosophy Compass* 14.

Fraser, Nancy. 2009. 'Feminism, Capitalism, and the Cunning of History'. *New Left Review* 56: 97–117.

Fraser, Nancy. 2014. 'Behind Marx's Hidden Abode'. *New Left Review* 86: 55–72.

344 Bibliography

Fraser, Nancy and Jaeggi, Rahel. 2018. *Capitalism*. Cambridge: Polity.

Freeman, Samuel. 2007. *Rawls*. New York: Routledge.

Friedman, Marylin. 2008. 'Pettit's Civic Republicanism and Male Domination'. In Cecile Laborde and John Maynor, eds., *Republicanism and Political Theory*. Malden: Blackwell, 246–67.

Fudge, Jody. 2011. 'Labour as a "Fictive Commodity": Radically Reconceptualizing Labour Law'. In Davidov and Langille, *The Idea of Labour Law* (2011), 120–36.

Furendal, Markus. 2019. 'Defending the Duty to Contribute: Against the Market Solution'. *European Journal of Political Theory* 18: 469–88.

Geras, Norman. 1989. 'The Controversy About Marx and Justice'. In Alex Callinicos, ed., *Marxist Theory*. Oxford: Oxford University Press, 211–67.

Geras, Norman. 1992. 'Bringing Marx to Justice. An Addendum and a Rejoinder'. *New Left Review* I/195: 37–69.

Gheaus, Anca. 2013. 'The Feasibility Constraint on the Concept of Justice'. *Philosophical Quarterly* 63: 445–64.

Gilabert, 2015b. 'Human Rights, Human Dignity, and Power'. In Rowan Cruft, Matthew Liao, and Massimo Renzo, eds., *Philosophical Foundations of Human Rights*. Oxford: Oxford University Press, 196–213.

Gilabert, 2015c. 'Solidarity, Equality, and Freedom in Pettit's Republicanism'. *Critical Review of International Social and Political Philosophy* 18: 644–51.

Gilabert, Pablo. 1998. 'Relaciones Sociales, Conflicto e Historia. Una Interpretación de "Dialéctica" en Marx'. In María Femenías, ed., *Cuatro Concepciones de la Dialéctica*. La Plata: Editorial Universitaria de La Plata, 117–46.

Gilabert, Pablo. 2008. 'Global Justice and Poverty Relief in Nonideal Circumstances'. *Social Theory and Practice* 34: 411–38.

Gilabert, Pablo. 2009. 'The Feasibility of Basic Socioeconomic Human Rights: A Conceptual Exploration'. *Philosophical Quarterly* 59: 559–81.

Gilabert, Pablo. 2010. 'Kant and the Claims of the Poor'. *Philosophy and Phenomenological Research* 81: 382–418.

Gilabert, Pablo. 2011a. 'Feasibility and Socialism'. *Journal of Political Philosophy* 19: 52–62.

Gilabert, Pablo. 2011b. 'Humanist and Political Perspectives on Human Rights'. *Political Theory* 39: 439–67.

Gilabert, Pablo. 2012a. *From Global Poverty to Global Equality: A Philosophical Exploration*. Oxford: Oxford University Press.

Gilabert, Pablo. 2012b. 'Comparative Assessments of Justice, Political Feasibility, and Ideal Theory'. *Ethical Theory and Moral Practice* 15: 29–56.

Gilabert, Pablo. 2012c. 'Cohen on Socialism, Equality and Community'. *Socialist Studies* 8: 101–21.

Gilabert, Pablo. 2013. 'The Capability Approach and the Debate Between Humanist and Political Perspectives on Human Rights. A Critical Survey'. *Human Rights Review* 14: 299–325.

Gilabert, Pablo. 2015a. 'The Socialist Principle "From Each According To Their Abilities, To Each According To Their Needs"'. *Journal of Social Philosophy* 46: 197–225.

Gilabert, Pablo. 2016. 'Justice and Beneficence'. *Critical Review of International Social and Political Philosophy* 19: 508–33.

Gilabert, Pablo. 2017a. 'Kantian Dignity and Marxian Socialism'. *Kantian Review* 22: 553–77.

Gilabert, Pablo. 2017b. 'Justice and Feasibility: A Dynamic Approach'. In Michael Weber and Kevin Vallier, eds., *Political Utopias: Contemporary Debates*, Oxford: Oxford University Press, 95–126.

Bibliography   345

Gilabert, Pablo. 2018a. 'A Broad Definition of Agential Power'. *Journal of Political Power* 11: 79–92.

Gilabert, Pablo. 2018b. 'Dignity at Work'. In G. Collins, H. Lester, and V. Mantouvalou, eds., *Philosophical Foundations of Labour Law*. Oxford: Oxford University Press, 68–86.

Gilabert, Pablo. 2019a. *Human Dignity and Human Rights*. Oxford: Oxford University Press.

Gilabert, Pablo. 2019b. 'Facts, Norms, and Dignity'. *Critical Review of International Social and Political Philosophy* 22: 34–54.

Gilabert, Pablo. 2020. 'Defending Human Dignity and Human Rights'. *Journal of Global Ethics* 16: 326–42.

Gilabert, Pablo. 2022. 'Perfectionism and Dignity'. *European Journal of Philosophy* 30: 259–78.

Gilabert, Pablo. 'Inclusive Dignity'. Unpublished ms.

Gilabert, Pablo and Lawford-Smith, Holly. 2012. 'Political Feasibility: A Conceptual Exploration'. *Political Studies* 60: 809–25.

Gilabert, Pablo and O'Neill, Martin. 2019. 'Socialism'. In Edward N. Zalta, ed., *The Stanford Encyclopedia of Philosophy* (Fall 2019 Edition), URL=<https://plato.stanford.edu/archives/fall2019/entries/socialism/>.

Gilens, Martin and Page, Benjamin. 2014. 'Testing Theories of American Politics: Elites, Interest Groups, and Average Citizens'. *Perspectives on Politics* 12: 564–81.

Goldman, Alvin. 1986. 'Toward a Theory of Social Power'. In S. Lukes ed., *Power*. New York: NYU Press, 156–202.

Goodin, Robert. 1987. 'Exploiting a Situation and Exploiting a Person'. In A. Reeve, ed., *Modern Theories of Exploitation*. London: Sage, 166–200.

Goodin, Robert. 1995. 'Political Ideals and Political Practice'. *British Journal of Political Science* 25: 37–56.

Goodin, Robert. 2003. 'Folie Republicaine'. *Annual Review of Political Science* 6: 55–76.

Goodin, Robert and Pettit, Philip. 1995. 'Introduction'. In Robert Goodin and Philip Pettit, eds., *A Companion to Contemporary Political Philosophy*. Oxford: Blackwell, 1–4.

Gould, Carol. 1988. *Rethinking Democracy*. Cambridge: Cambridge University Press.

Gourevitch, Alex. 2013. 'Labor Republicanism and the Transformation of Work'. *Political Theory* 41: 591–617.

Graham, Peter. 2011. '"Ought" and Ability'. *Philosophical Review* 120: 337–82.

Gramsci, Antonio. 2000. *The Antonio Gramsci Reader*. David Forgacs, ed. New York: NYU Press.

Griffin, James. 2008. *On Human Rights*. Oxford: Oxford University Press.

Guevara, Ernesto, 1977. *El Socialismo y El Hombre Nuevo*. Mexico DF: Siglo XXI.

Guyer, Paul. 2014. *Kant*, 2nd ed. New York: Routledge.

Habermas, Jürgen. 1975. *Legitimation Crisis*. Boston: Beacon Press.

Habermas, Jürgen. 1992. *Moral Consciousness and Communicative Action*. Cambridge, MA: MIT Press.

Habermas, Jürgen. 1996. *Between Facts and Norms*. Cambridge, MA: MIT Press.

Hall, Edward. 2018. 'Why Not'. *European Journal of Political Theory* 17: 109–17.

Hamlin, Alan and Stemplowska, Zofia. 2012. 'Theory, Ideal Theory and the Theory of Ideals'. *Political Studies Review* 10: 48–62.

Haslanger, Sally. 2016. 'What Is A (Social) Structural Explanation?' *Philosophical Studies* 173: 113–30.

Hayward, Clarissa. 2018. 'On Structural Power'. *Journal of Political Power* 11: 55–67.

Hegel, G. W. F. 1977. *The Phenomenology of Spirit*. Oxford: Oxford University Press.

Heller, Agnes. 2018. *The Theory of Needs in Marx*. London: Verso.

Herzog, Lisa. 2013. 'Ideal and Non-Ideal Theory and the Problem of Knowledge'. *Journal of Applied Philosophy* 29: 271–88.

346 Bibliography

Hill, Thomas. 2002. *Human Welfare and Moral Worth*. Oxford: Oxford University Press.

Holmstrom, Nancy. 1977. 'Exploitation'. *Canadian Journal of Philosophy* 7: 353–69.

Hsieh, Nien-he. 2008. 'Justice in Production'. *Journal of Political Philosophy* 16: 72–100.

Hsieh, Nien-he. 2012. 'Work'. In Gerald Gaus and Fred D'Agostino, eds., *Routledge Companion to Social and Political Philosophy*. New York: Routledge, 755–63.

Human Rights Watch. 2015. 'Bangladesh: 2 Years After Rana Plaza, Workers Denied Rights'. 22 April.

Jaeggi, Rahel. 2014. *Alienation*. New York: Columbia University Press.

Jensen, Mark. 2009. 'The Limits of Practical Possibility'. *Journal of Political Philosophy* 17: 168–84.

Kagan, Shelly. 1998. *Normative Ethics*. Boulder, CO: Westview.

Kagan, Shelly. 2019. *How to Count Animals, More or Less*. Oxford: Oxford University Press.

Kandiyali, Jan. 2020. 'The Importance of Others: Marx on Unalienated Production'. *Ethics* 130: 555–87.

Kant, Immanuel. 1996a. *Practical Philosophy*. Cambridge: Cambridge University Press.

Kant, Immanuel. 1996b. *Religion and Rational Theology*. Cambridge: Cambridge University Press.

Kanto, Jodi and Streitfeld, David. 2015. 'Inside Amazon: Wrestling Big Ideas in a Bruising Workplace'. *New York Times*, 15 August.

Keynes, John M. 1923. *A Tract on Monetary Reform*. London: Macmillan.

Kolodny, Niko. Forthcoming. *The Pecking Order*. Cambridge, Mass: Harvard University Press.

Kymlicka, Will. 2002. *Contemporary Political Philosophy*, 2nd ed. Oxford: Oxford University Press.

Kymlicka, Will. 2006. 'Left-Liberalism Revisited'. In Christine Sypnowich ed., *The Egalitarian Conscience: Essays in Honour of G.A. Cohen*. Oxford: Oxford University Press, 9–35.

Kymlicka, Will. 2018. 'Human Rights without Human Supremacism'. *Canadian Journal of Philosophy* 48: 763–92.

Landemore, Hélène. 2020. 'Démocratiser l'enterprise'. In Ferreras et al *Le Manifeste Travail. Démocratiser, Démarchandiser, Dépolluer* (2020), 67–76.

Langille, Brian. 2011. 'Labour Law's Theory of Justice'. In Davidov and Langille, *The Idea of Labour Law* (2011), 101–19.

Laurence, Ben. 2021. *Agents of Change: Political Philosophy in Practice*. Cambridge, MA: Harvard University Press.

Lawford-Smith, Holly. 2013a. 'Non-Ideal Accessibility'. *Ethical Theory and Moral Practice* 16: 653–69.

Lawford-Smith, Holly. 2013b. 'Understanding Political Feasibility'. *Journal of Political Philosophy* 21, 243–59.

Leopold, David. 2016. 'Alienation'. In Zalta, *The Stanford Encyclopedia of Philosophy* (Fall 2016 Edition).

Levi, Margaret. 2015. 'A New Agenda for the Social Sciences'. *The Crooked Timber* Blog, 8 December.

List, Christian, and Valentini, Laura. 2016. 'Freedom as Independence'. *Ethics* 126: 1043–74.

Locke, Richard. 2013. *The Promise and Limits of Private Power. Promoting Labor Standards in the Global Economy*. Cambridge: Cambridge University Press.

Love, Suzanne. 2017. 'Kant after Marx'. *Kantian Review* 22: 579–98.

Lovett, Frank and Pettit, Philip. 2019. 'Preserving Republican Freedom: A Reply to Simpson'. *Philosophy & Public Affairs* 46: 363–83.

Lu, Catherine. 'Worker Rights, Structured Vulnerabilities and Global Labor Justice' (unpublished ms.).

Lukes, Steven. 1985. *Marxism and Morality*. Oxford: Oxford University Press.

Bibliography **347**

Lukes, Steven. 2005. *Power. A Radical View*, 2nd ed. London: Palgrave.

Lukes, Steven. 2018. 'Noumenal Power: Concept and Explanation'. *Journal of Political Power* 11: 46–55.

Mackenzie, Catriona. 2014. 'Three Dimensions of Autonomy. A Relational Analysis'. In A. Veltman and M. Piper, eds., *Autonomy, Oppression, and Gender*. Oxford: Oxford University Press, 15–41.

Maier, John. 2021. 'Abilities'. In Zalta, *The Stanford Encyclopedia of Philosophy* (Fall 2021 Edition).

Mantouvalou, Virginia, ed. 2015. *The Right to Work*. Oxford: Hart.

Marx, Karl. 1978a [1843]. 'On the Jewish Question'. In Richard Tucker, ed., *The Marx-Engels Reader*, 2nd ed. New York: Norton, 26–52.

Marx, Karl. 1973 [1857–8]. *Grundrisse*. London: Penguin.

Marx, Karl. 1978g [1849]. 'Wage Labor and Capital'. In Tucker, *The Marx-Engels Reader*, 203–17.

Marx, Karl. 1978b [1843–4]. 'Contribution to the Critique of Hegel's *Philosophy of Right*: Introduction'. In Tucker, *The Marx-Engels Reader*, 53–65.

Marx, Karl. 1978c [1844]. 'Economic and Philosophical Manuscripts of 1844'. In Tucker, *The Marx-Engels Reader*, 66–125.

Marx, Karl. 1978d [1845]. 'Theses on Feuerbach'. In Tucker, *The Marx-Engels Reader*, 143–45.

Marx, Karl. 1978e [1845–6]. *The German Ideology*. In Tucker, *The Marx-Engels Reader*, 146–200.

Marx, Karl. 1978f [1848]. *Manifesto of the Communist Party*. In Tucker, *The Marx-Engels Reader*, 469–500.

Marx, Karl. 1978h [1871]. *The Civil War in France*. In Tucker, *The Marx-Engels Reader*, 618–52.

Marx, Karl. 1978i [1875]. 'Critique of Gotha Program'. In Tucker, *The Marx-Engels Reader*, 525–41.

Marx, Karl. 1978j [1879]. 'Letter to Bebel, Liebknecht, Bracke'. In Tucker, *The Marx-Engels Reader*, 549–55.

Marx, Karl. 1990 [1867]. *Capital I*. London: Penguin.

Marx, Karl. 1991. *Capital III*. London: Penguin.

Marx, Karl. 1992 [1844]. 'Excerpts from Mill's *Elements on Political Economy*'. In Marx, *Early Writings*. London: Penguin, 259–78.

Mastracci, Tara. 2016. 'Why I Left the US to Work in the NHS: Compassion is Part of the Job'. *The Guardian*, 10 February.

McCammon, Christopher. 2018. 'Domination'. In Zalta, *The Stanford Encyclopedia of Philosophy* (Winter 2018 Edition), URL=<https://plato.stanford.edu/archives/win2018/entries/domination/>.

Mele, Alfred. 2003. 'Agents' Abilities'. *Nous* 37: 447–70.

Mill, John Stuart. 1991. 'On Liberty'. In John Stuart Mill ed., *On Liberty and Other Essays*. Oxford: Oxford University Press.

Mills, Charles. 2018. 'Black Radical Kantianism'. *Res Philosophica* 95: 1–33.

Moyn, Samuel. 2010. *The Last Utopia*. Cambridge, MA: Harvard University Press.

Moyn, Samuel. 2019. *Not Enough: Human Rights in an Unequal World*. Cambridge, MA: Harvard University Press.

Mundlak, Guy. 2007. 'The Right to Work—The Value of Work'. In Daphne Barak-Erez and Aeyal M. Gross, eds., *Exploring Social Rights*. Oxford: Hart, 341–66.

Narveson, Jan. 1988. *The Libertarian Idea*. Philadelphia: Temple University Press.

Neate, Rupert. 2020a. 'Jeff Bezos Sold $3.4bn of Amazon Stock Just Before Covid-19 Collapse'. *The Guardian*, 27 March.

348 Bibliography

Neate, Rupert. 2020b. 'Jeff Bezos, the World's Richest Man, Added £10bn to His Fortune in Just One Day'. *The Guardian*, 21 July.

Nell, Edward and O'Neill, Onora. 2003. 'Justice Under Socialism'. In James Sterba, ed., *Justice*, 4th ed., ed. Toronto: Thomson-Wadsworth, 77–85.

Nickel, James. 2007. *Making Sense of Human Rights*. Malden, MA: Blackwell.

Nielsen, Kai. 1985. *Equality and Liberty*. Totowa, NJ: Rowman & Allanheld.

Nove, Alec. 1991. *The Economics of Feasible Socialism Revisited*. London: Harper Collins.

Nozick, Nozick. 1974. *Anarchy, State, and Utopia*. New York: Basic Books.

Nozick, Robert. 1981. *Philosophical Explanations*. Cambridge, MA: Harvard University Press.

Nussbaum, Martha. 2000. *Women and Human Development*. Cambridge: Cambridge University Press.

Nussbaum, Martha. 2006. *Frontiers of Justice*. Cambridge, MA: Harvard University Press.

Nussbaum, Martha. 2008. 'Human Dignity and Political Entitlements'. In *Human Dignity and Bioethics*, ed. The President's Council on Bioethics. Washington DC: President's Council of Bioethics, 351–78.

Nussbaum, Martha. 2011. *Creating Capabilities*. Cambridge, MA: Harvard University Press.

O'Neill, Martin. 2012. 'Free (and Fair) Markets without Capitalism. Political Values, Principles of Justice, and Property-Owning Democracy'. In O'Neill and Williamson, *Property-Owning Democracy* (2012), 75–100.

O'Neill, Martin. 2020. 'Social Justice and Economic Systems: On Rawls, Democratic Socialism, and Alternatives to Capitalism'. *Philosophical Topics* 48: 159–202.

O'Neill, Martin and Williamson, Tad, eds. 2012. *Property-Owning Democracy*. Oxford: Wiley-Blackwell.

O'Shea, Tom. 2019. 'Are Workers Dominated?' *Journal of Ethics and Social Philosophy* 16.

O'Shea, Tom. 2020. 'Socialist Republicanism'. *Political Theory* 48: 548–72.

Offe, Claus. 2009. 'Basic Income and the Labor Contract'. *Analyse & Kritik* 1: 49–79.

Ostrom, Elinor. 2009. 'Engaging with Possibilities and Impossibilities'. In K. Basu and R. Kanbur, eds., *Arguments for a Better World*. Oxford: Oxford University Press, vol. 2, 522–41.

Parfit, Derek. 2011. *On What Matters*. Oxford: Oxford University Press, 2 vols.

Peterson, Sarah and Mesley, Wendy. 2020. 'Former Amazon VP Opens up About Decision to Quit in Support of COVID-19 "Whistleblowers"'. *CBC News*, 16 May.

Pettit, Philip. 2012. *On the People Terms*. Cambridge: Cambridge University Press.

Pettit, Philip. 2015. 'On the People's Terms. A Reply to Five Critiques'. *Critical Review of International Social and Political Philosophy* 18: 687–96.

Piketty, Thomas. 2014. *Capital in the Twenty-First Century*. Cambridge, MA: Harvard University Press.

Piketty, Thomas. 2019. *Capital et Ideologie*. Paris: Seuil.

Pinker, Steven. 2008. 'The Stupidity of Dignity'. *The New Republic* (28 May).

Pollard, Chris. 2018. 'Amazon Workers Pee Into Bottles to Save Time: Investigator'. *New York Post*, 16 April.

Quiggin, John. 2016. 'Predistribution: Wages and Unions'. *Crooked Timber* Blog, 28 April.

Rawls, John. 1999. *A Theory of Justice*, rev. ed. Cambridge, MA: Harvard University Press.

Rawls, John. 2001. *Justice as Fairness. A Restatement*. Cambridge, MA: Harvard University Press.

Rawls, John. 2007. *Lectures on the History of Political Philosophy*. Cambridge, MA: Harvard University Press.

Raz, Joseph. 1986. *The Morality of Freedom*. Oxford: Oxford University Press.

Raz, Joseph. 1994. *Ethics in the Public Domain*. Oxford: Oxford University Press.

Reich, Robert. 2020. 'It's Morally Repulsive How Corporations Are Exploiting This Crisis. Workers Will Suffer'. *The Guardian*, 22 March.

Bibliography 349

Reiman, Jeffrey. 1987. 'Exploitation, Force, and the Moral Assessment of Capitalism: Thoughts on Roemer and Cohen'. *Philosophy and Public Affairs* 16: 3–41.

Reisner, Andrew. 2013. '*Prima Facie* and *Pro Tanto* Oughts'. In H. LaFollette ed., *The International Encyclopedia of Ethics*. Oxford: Blackwell, 4082–86.

Guardian Reporters. 2015. 'Workers Find Strength in Unity'. *The Guardian Weekly* 8–14 May 2015.

Ripstein, Arthur. 2009. *Force and Freedom*. Cambridge, MA: Harvard University Press.

Roberts, Will. 2017. *Marx's Inferno*. Princeton: Princeton University Press.

Roemer, John. 1994. *A Future for Socialism*. Harvard, MA: Harvard University Press.

Roemer, John. 1996. *Egalitarian Perspectives*. Cambridge: Cambridge University Press.

Roemer, John. 2017. 'Socialism Revised'. *Philosophy and Public Affairs* 45: 261–315.

Roessler, Beate. 2012. 'Meaningful Work: Arguments from Autonomy'. *Journal of Political Philosophy* 20: 71–93.

Rosa, Hartmut. 2019. *Resonance*. Cambridge: Polity.

Rosanvallon, Pierre. 2011. *La Société des Égaux*. Paris: Seuil.

Rose, Julie. 2016. *Free Time*. Princeton: Princeton University Press.

Rosen, Michael. 2012. *Dignity*. Cambridge, MA: Harvard University Press.

Sainato, Michael. 2020. '"I'm Not a Robot": Amazon Workers Condemn Unsafe, Grueling Conditions at Warehouse'. *The Guardian*, 5 February.

Saltzman, Aaron. 2018a. 'Tim Hortons Heirs Cut Paid Breaks and Worker Benefits After Minimum Wage Hike, Employees Say'. *CBC News* (3 January).

Saltzman, Aaron. 2018b. 'Multiple Tim Hortons Franchises, Other Businesses Cut Pay, Benefits, Citing Minimum Wage Hike'. *CBC News* (5 January).

Sangiovanni, Andrea. 2017. *Humanity without Dignity*. Cambridge, MA: Harvard University Press.

Scanlon, T. M. 1998. *What We Owe To Each Other*. Cambridge, MA: Harvard University Press.

Scanlon, T. M. 2003. 'Rawls and Justification'. S. Freeman ed., *The Cambridge Companion to Rawls*. Cambridge: Cambridge University Press, 139–67.

Scanlon, T. M. 2011. 'How I Am Not a Kantian'. In Parfit, *On What Matters* (2011), vol. 2, 116–39.

Scanlon, T. M. 2018. *Why Does Inequality Matter?* Oxford: Oxford University Press.

Schacht, Richard. 1970. *Alienation*. New York: Anchor Books.

Schmidt, Andreas. 2016. 'Abilities and the Sources of Unfreedom'. *Ethics* 127: 179–207.

Schweickart, David. 2011. *After Capitalism*, 2nd ed. Lantham, MD: Rowman & Littlefield.

Schweickart, David. 2016. 'Economic Democracy' (2016), at https://thenextsystem.org/node/204.

Searle, John. 2010. *Making the Social World*. Oxford: Oxford University Press.

Sebo, Jeff. Forthcoming. 'Moral Circle Explosion'. In D. Copp, C. Rosatti, and T. Ruli, eds., *The Oxford Handbook of Normative Ethics*. Oxford: Oxford University Press.

Sen, Amartya. 2009. *The Idea of Justice*. Cambridge, MA: Harvard University Press.

Simpson, Thomas. 2017. 'The Impossibility of Republican Freedom'. *Philosophy & Public Affairs* 45: 27–53.

Simpson, Thomas. 2019. 'Freedom and Trust: A Rejoinder to Lovett and Pettit'. *Philosophy & Public Affairs* 47: 412–24.

Southwood, Nicholas. 2016. '"The Thing To Do" Implies "Can"'. *Noûs* 50: 61–72.

Southwood, Nicholas. 2018. 'The Feasibility Issue'. *Philosophy Compass* 13: 1–13.

Spafford, Jesse. 2020. 'An Anarchist Interpretation of Marx's "Ability to Needs" Principle'. *Journal of Value Inquiry* 54: 325–43.

Stanczyk, Lucas. 2012. 'Productive Justice'. *Philosophy and Public Affairs* 40: 144–64.

Steiner, Hillel. 2014. 'Greed and Fear'. *Politics, Philosophy & Economics* 13: 140–50.

350 Bibliography

Supiot, Alain. 2011. *Le Droit du Travail*, 5th ed. Paris: Presses Universitaires de France.

Swift, Adam. 2008. 'The Value of Philosophy in Nonideal Circumstances'. *Social Theory and Practice* 34: 363–87.

Sypnowich, Christine. 2020. 'What's Wrong with Equality of Opportunity'. *Philosophical Topics* 48: 223–44.

Core Team. 2018. *The Economy*. Oxford: Oxford University Press.

Temkin, Larry. 2009. 'Illuminating Egalitarianism'. In T. Christiano and J. Christman, eds., *Contemporary Debates in Political Philosophy*. Oxford: Blackwell, 155–78.

The Economist. 2013. 'It's Complicated'. 23 November.

The Economist. 2015. 'Digital Taylorism'. 12 September.

The Economist. 2019. 'Engaged or Vacant?' 16 February.

The Economist. 2020. 'Lost in the Amazon Jungle'. 11 January.

Thompson, Gabriel. 2013. 'The Workers Who Bring You Black Friday'. *The Nation*, 26 November.

Valentini, Laura. 2012. 'Ideal vs. Nonideal Theory: A Conceptual Map'. *Philosophy Compass* 9: 654–64.

Van Parijs, Philippe. 1991. *Qu'est-ce qu'une Société Juste?* Paris: Seuil.

Van Parijs, Philippe. 1995. *Real Freedom for All*. Oxford: Oxford University Press.

Veneziani, Roberto. 2013. 'Exploitation, Inequality, and Power'. *Journal of Theoretical Politics* 25: 526–45.

Verbitsky, Horacio. 2019. *Vida de Perro*. Buenos Aires: Siglo XXI.

Vetter, Barbara. 2013. '"Can" Without Possible Worlds: Semantics for Anti-Humeans'. *Philosophers' Imprint* 13.16.

Vicks, Aki. 2022. 'Gig Companies are Disguising Exploitation as Social Justice'. *The Jacobin*, 19 February.

Vranas, Peter. 2007. 'I Ought, Therefore I Can'. *Philosophical Studies* 136: 167–216.

Vrousalis, Nicholas. 2013. 'Exploitation, Vulnerability, and Social Domination'. *Philosophy and Public Affairs* 41: 131–57.

Vrousalis, Nicholas. 2018. 'Exploitation: A Primer'. Philosophy Compass 13.

Vrousalis, Nicholas. 2021a. 'The Capitalist Cage: Structural Domination and Collective Agency in the Market'. *Journal of Applied Philosophy* 38: 40–54.

Vrousalis, Nicholas. 2021b. 'Socialism Revisited'. *Philosophy and Public Affairs* 49: 78–109.

Waldron, Jeremy. 2012. *Dignity, Rank, and Rights*. Oxford: Oxford University Press.

Waldron, Jeremy. 2017. *One Another's Equals*. Cambridge, MA: Harvard University Press.

Wall, Steven. 2015. 'Perfectionism'. In Jon Mandle and David Reidy eds., *The Cambridge Rawls Lexicon*. Cambridge: Cambridge University Press, 602–05

Wallace, R. Jay. 2019. *The Moral Nexus*. Princeton: Princeton University Press.

Wenar, Leif. 2021. 'Rights'. In Zalta, *The Stanford Encyclopedia of Philosophy* (Spring 2021 Edition), URL=<https://plato.stanford.edu/archives/spr2021/entries/rights/>.

White, Stuart. 2007. *Equality*. Cambridge: Polity.

White, Stuart, 2021. 'Social Minimum'. In Zalta, *The Stanford Encyclopedia of Philosophy* (Winter 2021 Edition).

Wiens, David. 2012. 'Prescribing Institutions without Ideal Theory'. *Journal of Political Philosophy* 20: 45–70.

Wiens, David. Forthcoming. 2015. 'Political Ideals and the Feasibility Frontier'. *Economics and Philosophy* 31: 447–77.

Wolff, Jonathan. 1998. 'Fairness, Respect, and the Egalitarian Ethos'. *Philosophy and Public Affairs* 27: 97–122.

Wolff, Jonathan. 2002. *Why Read Marx Today?* Oxford: Oxford University Press.

Wood, Allen. 1999. *Kant's Ethical Thought*. Cambridge: Cambridge University Press.

Wood, Allen. 2002. 'The Final Form of Kant's Practical Philosophy'. In Mark Timmons, ed., *Kant's Metaphysics of Morals*. Oxford: Oxford University Press, 1–21.

Wood, Allen. 2004. *Karl Marx*, 2nd ed. New York: Routledge.

Wood, Allen. 2005. *Kant*. Oxford: Blackwell.

Wood, Allen. 2008. *Kantian Ethics*. Cambridge: Cambridge University Press.

Wright, Erik. 2010. *Envisioning Real Utopias*. London: Verso.

Wright, Erik. 2015a. 'Working Class Power, Capitalist Class Interests, and Class Compromise'. In Wright, *Understanding Class*. London: Verso, 185–230.

Wright, Erik. 2015b. 'How to Be an Anticapitalist Today'. *Jacobin*, 12 February.

Wright, Erik. 2016. 'How to Think About (And Win) Socialism'. *Jacobin*, 27 April.

Wright, Erik. 2019. *How To Be an Anti-Capitalist in the 21-st Century*. London: Verso.

Young, Iris. 1990. *Justice and the Politics of Difference*. Princeton: Princeton University Press.

Young, Iris. 2011. *Responsibility for Justice*. Oxford: Oxford University Press.

Index

A

Abilities/Needs Principle
and alienation 112–115, 213, 229–230
difficulties 95
dignitarian justification 84, 97, 129–131
and domination 134–135
and exploitation 109–110, 176–177, 190
and ideological manipulation of duty to
contribute 133–135
initial appeal 90
implementation 115
liberal and democratic constraints 97
Marx's statement 83–84, 87n.1, 89
metric of needs 98
specific demands 105
and transition to socialism 122, 165–168
Albert, Michael 331–332n.27, 333n.33
alienation
and Abilities/Needs Principle 112–115,
213, 229–230
alienated work vs. work involving self-
determined self-realization 62–101,
210–211, 213, 219
concept 50, 209
and democracy 232
descriptive and normative
accounts 209n.5, 211, 216
dignitarian critique 81–83, 224
and domination 193n.23, 210–211,
216–217, 269–270, 275, 318
dynamic patterns 214, 219–220, 230, 237
and exploitation 193n.23, 318
and markets 333
Marx's account 209
moral account 212, 220
and objection regarding essentialism 225
and objection regarding gap between the
good and the right 229
and objection regarding paternalistic
imposition 230
prudential account 212, 217
in recent developments of capitalism 242

subjective and objective 81–82, 209, 214,
219–220
trade-offs between non-alienation at work
and other considerations 235–237
and the two-level justification
objection 232
Anderson, Elizabeth 45–46n.62, 252n.3,
287n.49, 305
Arnold, Samuel 51–52n.72, 93–94n.10,
220–221n.32, 235–236n.54, 254n.4,
325–326n.9, 336–337n.46

B

Brennan, Jason 326–337

C

capability approach 99–100, 102, 220–221
capitalism 76, 181–182, 222–223, 239–241,
323–324, 333–334
class division and struggle 250, 324,
336–337
different kinds 242–243, 250, 334–335
principles justifying capitalism 330–332
Carens, Joseph 24n.29, 115, 158–159,
165–166n.37, 193–194, 332, 333,
336–337n.47
cases (intuition pumps)
Alberto and Bruno the musicians 298
Ant and Grasshopper 199–200,
202–203n.41, 206
Camping trip (Cohen) 326–327
Construction site (Carens) 24
Dominating Deal 266–270
liquor cabinet (Pettit) 258–259
Mickey Mouse Clubhouse Village
(Brennan) 327
non-interfering master (Pettit) 258–259
Pit (Vrousalis) 197
Rescuing someone in dire straits 279,
283, 288–289
Restraining a murderer 279, 283, 288–289
Sleepwalking Anna 24–25, 331–332n.28
Two factories 283, 288–289

354 Index

Christiano, Thomas 99n.18
Cohen, G. A. 12–13, 57n.57, 81n.61,
    90n.4,n.7, 102n.25, 124–125n.57, 126–
    127n.62, 134–135n.72, 137–138n.1,
    141n.12, 152n.19, 178n.7,n.8, 181n.11,
    188–189n.18, 205n.45, 213n.20, 214–
    215n.23, 222–223n.35, 227–228n.45,
    235–236n.56, 263n.20, 299, 309n.89,
    335–337
comparative assessment of social
    systems 236–237, 327–330
contractualism 22
    Kantian contractualist standard 60, 62,
    85, 190, 202–203
critical theory 53, 156, 237, 271–272

D

democracy 30, 52, P72–85, 102–103, 168,
    170–171, 204, 232, 253–254, 282n.47,
    331–332, 335–336n.40
Dignitarian Approach
    core statement 4
    and deontology 71, 76, 99–100n.19,
    229–230n.48
    and feasibility 169–171
    fruitfulness of 14
    individual-centred focus 34–35, 98,
    99–100n.19, 128–129, 226–227
    justification of 14–15n.16, 71–74,
    293–294
    as a program 5–6
    Response or Reflection Model 74,
    145n.12, 304–305
    Schema of Dignitarian Justification 20,
    44–45, 103, 229–230, 285
    summary of the Dignitarian
    Approach 283–285
dignity
    basic and maximal dignity 11, 29–30
    basis of dignity 7–10, 56
    conceptual network of dignity 6, 187,
    283–284
    condition-dignity 6–7, 56, 187
    circumstances of dignity 10–11, 56
    dignitarian forum 11–12
    dignitarian norms 6–7, 56, 187
    dignitarian social ideals 11–12, 56, 187
    dignitarian virtue 13–14, 187, 206,
    311–312
    dignity and interests 18–23

dynamic dignity 14
endowment-based and achievement-
    based dignity 13–14,
    315
human dignity and dignity of non-human
    animals 16–17, 64
status-dignity 6–7, 56, 187
disabilities 9–10, 35–37, 64, 72–73,
    99–100n.19, 102n.26, 195–196,
    234–235n.53, 289
diversity 31, 99–100n.20, 105, 128–129, 311
domination
    and Abilities/Needs Principle 289, 304,
    311
    and alienation 193n.23, 216–217,
    269–270, 275, 318
    analytic dimensions of domina-
    tion (degree, range, site, scope,
    depth, mechanisms, resources,
    dynamism) 263
    concept 50, 249, 257
    contrast between the dignitarian and
    other approaches 295
    dignitarian critique 80–81, 249–250, 283,
    285, 294
    dynamic patterns 270, 310, 313, 320–321
    and exploitation 193n.23, 203, 318
    limited but important normative
    factor 278, 283
    in Marx's analyses 250–251n.2,
    269–270n.28
    non-domination, agential power, and
    self-determination 273
    and paths of agency 259–261
    and right against domination 281
    and right to access the conditions for
    well-being 281
    and self-respect 287–288n.50, 289,
    312–313
    as a specific form of power 262–263
    structural domination 203, 250
    three spheres of domination of workers in
    capitalism 80–81, 250, 266–270
    tradeoffs between non-
    domination and other normative
    considerations 290–291, 295
duties
    duties to contribute 48, 105, 107–108,
    133–135
    duties to self 310, 313

Index   355

dynamic duties 19, 163, 215–216, 315, 316

positive and negative duties 4, 18, 23, 53–54, 64–65, 188–190, 221–224, 277, 309, 331–332

E

efficiency 118–119n.45, 158–159, 203–204, 236, 246n.73, 290–291, 333

Elster, Jon 76n.53, 81–82n.63, 99n.17, 113n.41, 122–123n.56, 125–126, 160–161n.31165–166n.37, 181n.11, 184–185n.15, 194–195n.26, 205n.44, 212–213n.14, 217n.29,n.30, 219–220, 241n.64, 260n.13

environmental issues 203–204

equality 15, 47, 59, 73–75, 83, 90, 92, 99, 104–105, 109, 119–120, 126–129, 188, 234–235, 285, 297–299, 335–337

essentialism 224

exploitation

and Abilities/Needs Principle 109–110, 176–177, 190

and alienation 193n.23, 318

and class structures and class struggle 181–186

concept 50, 176–177

contra-solidaristic use of power account (CSP account) 179–180

contrast between the CSP, shaped by the Abilities/Needs Principles, and other accounts 194

and democracy 204

dignitarian critique 79, 190

and exploitation 193n.23, 203, 318

exploitation of labor in technical Marxian sense 78–79, 176–177

as a multidimensional process 200

normative sense 50, 78–79, 176–177

and relations between agents and social structures 203

three-levels picture 186–187, 202–203

wrongful use of power account (WP account) 78–79, 179

F

feasibility

and agential power 273–274

and agents' attitudes towards their undesirable situation 241–242

and articulation of three dimensions of a conception of justice 150

binary vs. scalar feasibility 141

and comparison between socialism and capitalism 160–161, 328–330

and the critique of alienation 214, 238–240, 333

and the critique of domination 270, 300–302

desideratum of ethical responsibility 142

and dignity 169–171, 315

and distinction between evaluative and prescriptive judgements 145–147

and distinction between pro tanto and all things considered judgements 147–148

and distinction between stability and accessibility 152–153

dynamic approach to the relation between justice and feasibility 150, 241–242

and dynamic duties 163, 270–271, 315, 316

in Kant 60–61

in Marx 75–76, 214, 238–240

and political imagination 158

role of concept and definition 138

soft and hard constraints 137–138, 141

and three explanatory gaps regarding injustice 283, 288–289

and transitional standpoint 157–158

twin intuitions regarding avoidance of naïve idealism and conservative realism and ethical responsibility 142

feminism 5, 156, 244–245, 305–306

flourishing 4, 70–71, 98–99, 188, 213, 217, 294–295n.57

Forst, Rainer 62–63n.20, 229–230n.48, 269–270.29, 272n.33, 279n.40, 301, 312–313n.91

Fraser, Nancy 242–243n.66, 244–245, 323n.1, 338–339n.48

freedom, see also self-determination

individual and collective 44, 118–119, 204, 291–292

Marx's analysis of unfreedom of workers in capitalism 250–251n.2

morally problematic lack of freedom (or unfreedom) 223–224

negative liberty 26–27, 44, 51–53, 80–81n.61, 97, 117, 222–223, 230306–307, 331–337

356 Index

freedom, *see also* (*Continued*)
  and paths of agency 259–261
  positive freedom 62–63, 80–81n.61,
    82–83, 213, 220, 230, 277–278, 306–307

G

Geras, Norman 75–76, 78–79n.57, 89n.3,
    95n.11, 102–103, 109–110n.34,
    212–213n.13
good (the) and right (the) 45–46, 51–53,
    93–94n.10, 98, 229–230
Goodin, Robert 78–79n.58, 150n.16,
    161–162n.33, 167n.39, 307–308n.84
Gould, Carol 102n.27, 120–121n.51,
    309n.88
Gramsci, Antonio 165–166n.37
Guyer, Paul 60n.12, 60–61n.13, 65n.27,
    65–66, 71–72n.46

H

Habermas, Jürgen 31n.35, 62–63n.20
Hegel, G. W. F. 209–210, 214, 227–228n.45,
    240, 287–288n.50, 298
Herzog, Lisa 119–120n.49, 137–
    138n.1, 147–148n.14, 155–156n.26,
    280–281n.42
Haslanger, Sally 265n.22
hope 14, 171, 315
human dignity, *see* dignity
human rights, *see* rights
humanism
  arc of humanist justice 28
  moral humanist rights 15

I

ideology 45–46, 85–86, 130–131, 159–160,
    203–204n.43, 214–215, 244–245,
    250–251n.2, 259–260, 271–272, 289
  and alienated self-realization and alienated
    self-determination 238, 244–246
  ideologies of contribution 48, 53–54,
    133–135, 289
  ideologies of independence or
    security 53–54, 84n.76
  and incitation of singularity and
    solidarity in production and con-
    sumption through the use of new
    technologies 246–247
incentives 115, 124, 126–127, 159–160
independence 26–27, 69–71, 90, 308

distinction between independence as self-
    determination and as self-reliance 69,
    105n.31, 308–309
interdependence 26–27, 69

J

Jaeggi, Rahel 225–226n.42, 228n.46,
    229–230n.48, 242–243n.66,
    338–339n.48

K

Kant, Immanuel 55, *see also* contractualism;
    feasibility; freedom; rights
Kymlicka, Will 16–17n.20, 92–93,
    109–110n.33, 112–113n.40, 298n.62

L

Leopold, David 209–211
LGBTQ+ people 15, 289, 320–321
liberalism 51–53, 92, 97, 230, 301, 328, 332,
    340
libertarianism 5, 105n.31, 109–110, 127,
    154, 325, 331–332, 340
Lukes, Steven 76n.53, 269–270n.29, 272n.33

M

Marx, Karl 55, *see also* Abilities/Needs
    Principle; alienation; domination;
    exploitation; feasibility; freedom
Mills, Charles 313–314n.93

N

needs 98
Nickel, James 278n.38
Nozick, Robert: Preface n.3, 5n.4,
    235–236n.54
Nussbaum, Martha 9n.9, 62–63n.20,
    99–100, 102n.26, 224–225n.32,
    273–274n.34

O

O'Neill, Martin 90n.8, 97n.16, 324n.3,
    326n.10, 334–335n.38
O'Shea, Tom 255–256n.7, 259n.10, 266n.24,
    275n.36

P

Parfit, Derek 22n.25, 57–58n.4, 64–65n.25,
    66n.30, 72–73n.48, 190n.21
paternalism 55, 61, 65, 72, 84–85, 103–105,
    230, 294–295n.57, 304

Index **357**

perfectionism 66–67, 93–94n.10, 112–113n.40
personal prerogative 107–108, 113–117, 134–135n.72, 234–235, 330–331n.26
Pettit, Philip 70–71n.44, 150n.16, 258–260, 264–265n.21, 279n.40, 296, 318–319n.18
power
  agential power 273, 316
  analytical grid of agential power 316
  dynamic power 164, 270–271, 316
  structural and associational power 254
  social power (power-with, power-over, domination) 262, 287–288n.50, 291–292, 316, 325–326
  see also Solidaristic Empowerment
procedural and substantive considerations 102–103, 200, 228–230n.48, 232–233, 261, 294–295, 301
productivism 107–108, 118–119n.45, 203–204

R
racism 12–CI.P21, 313–314n.93
Rawls, John preface page x, 4–5n.2, 51n.71, 51–52n.72, 62–63n.20, 68–69n.34, 90n.8, 92–94n.10, 97n.16, 99–100n.19, 107n.32, 125–128, 151–153, 154n.24, 296–297n.58, 297–298, 335–336n.41
Raz, Joseph 18n.21, 222n.34
real interests 99, 271–272, 320–321n.99
reciprocity 24, 90, 105, 108–112, 121, 126–127, 130, 194–195, 199–200, 234–235
reflective equilibrium 9–10, 14–15, 71–72, 87–88n.2, 154–157, 208–209, 252–293
  deliberative reflective equilibrium 154–156
republicanism 275n.36, 296
rights
  abstract and specific rights 39–40
  basic and maximal 48–49
  Bridge Principle 20, 44–45, 67–68, 99–100n.19, 229–230
  civil rights 30, 97, 104, 107, 291–292
  General Schema for justifying rights 18
  humanist moral rights 15
  human rights 16–17, 28, 41
  interests and rights 18–23, 44–46, 67–68, 229–230, 281n.45

Kant's conception of rights 58, 80–81n.61
  labour rights 16–17, 29–30, 37
  minimalist and expansive accounts 29–30
  property rights 60–61n.13, 70–71, 80–81n.61, 250–251n.2, 333–337
  right against domination 281
  right to access the conditions for well-being 281
  right to health care 19, 107
  rights to political participation 18, 22, 30, 45–46, 97, 104, 107, 291–292
  Schema of Dignitarian Justification 20, 44–45, 103, 229–230
Ripstein, Arthur 68–69n.34, 70–71n.44, 80–81n.61
Roberts, Will 269–270n.29, 292–293n.55
Roemer, John 124–125n.57, 158–159, 165–166n.37, 177–178, 181n.11, 181–182n.12, 188–190, 196n.29, 196–197n.30, 197–198n.32, 199, 324n.4, 332

S
Sangiovanni, Andrea 73–74
Scanlon, T. M. 22n.25, 31, 33–34n.38,n.40, 72–73n.48, 155–156n.25, 335–336n.41
Schweickart, David 158–159, 324n.2, 325n.7
self-determination 26–27, 50–51, 61, 105, 107, 170–171, 204, 212–213, 217, 231–232, 271–272, 274–278, 282, 339, *see also* freedom
self-esteem and self-respect 14n.15, 27, 42, 93–94n.10, 114–115, 134, 159–160, 170, 244, 287–288n.50, 289, 312–313
self-identification 36–37n.42, 217, 315
self-ownership 105n.31, 331–332
self-realization 50–51, 82–83, 98, 105, 112–115, 212–213, 217
Sen, Amartya 27, 90n.6, 99–100, 137–138n.1, 161–162, 163n.34, 164n.36, 167n.39, 220–221n.32
social justice
  basic and maximal 37, 48–49
  concept 5–6n.5
  and critique of injustice 53
  and human rights 29–30
  injustice 146, 223–224
  site 12–13

358 Index

social justice (*Continued*)
three dimensions of a conception of social justice 5–6, 87–88, 150, 178, 292–293, 329, 338–340
socialism
and Abilities/Needs Principle 87, 326–327n.12, 331–332n.27
actual, ideal, and best feasible versions 327–330
and central planning 115, 158, 333
comparison with capitalism 152, 222–223, 236–237, 239–241, 250–251n.2, C8
definition 76, 83–84, 87–88, 181–182, 323–326
democratic socialism 30, P72–85, 90, 97, 107, 152, 154, 255–256, 325–326, 328, 335–336n.40, 338–339
dignitarian defense 83, 103, 337–340
and human rights 30, 340
and hybrid social forms 181, 185, 255–256, 326, 334–337
and liberalism egalitarianism 30, 92, 152, 328, 332
market socialism 115, 124–125n.57, 159, 325, 332–333
and statism 158, 181–182, 325–326
transition 122, 255–256, 338–339
Solidaristic Empowerment 4, 57, 97–98, 187–188, 221–224
solidarity 23, 90, 105, 126–127, 130, 180, 188–190, 331–332, 340
Southwood, Nicholas 137–138n.1, 139–140n.5, 142n.9
structural and interpersonal justice and injustice 12–13, 78, 203
struggles against social injustice 27, 310, 313
sufficientarian requirements 104–105, 107, 119–120, 188, 234–235, 297–298, 330–331

T
tradeoffs between self-realization, consumption, and leisure 105, 112–113, 118–119, 235–237

V
Van Parijs, Philippe 195n.27, 220–221n.32, 291–292n.53, 324n.2

Vrousalis, Nicholas 110n.35, 189–190n.20, 195n.27, 197–200, 202–203n.42, 268–269n.27

W
Waldron, Jeremy 5–6n.20, 127–128n.65, 241n.63
Wallace, R. Jay 19n.23, 22–23n.27, 133n.70
well-being 64–69, 82–83, 93–94n.10, 98, 217
White, Stuart 49n.67, 105n.30, 247n.75
Wolff, Jonathan 81–82n.63, 122n.54, 147–148n.14
Wood, Allen 57–58n.4, 59n.10, 60n.12, 61n.14, 66n.30, 71, 75n.51, 81–82n.63, 82–83n.68, 211n.11
work
alienated work 101, 210–211, 219
and basic dignity 41
burdens of work 120–121, 194–195n.26
care work 47–48, 102n.26, 119–120n.49, 235–236, 255–256
changes in working conditions in neoliberal capitalism 242
definition 39–40n.54, 235–236
domination of workers in capitalism 250
exploitation of workers in capitalism 175
and maximal dignity 48
value of work 41–43, 93–94n.10, 101, 210–211, 289
work involving self-determination and self-realization 101, 105, 213, 289
work is hard to avoid 43, 52–53, 93–94n.10, 114, 233, 289, 334
Wright, Erik 83–84n.73, 121n.52, 122–123n.56, 165–166n.37, 167n.39, 185n.17, 241–242n.65, 254–256n.7, 272n.33, 291–292n.53, 324n.2, 325–326n.8, 331–332n.27, 333n.33, 334–335n.38, 336–337n.46

Y
Young, Iris 261n.16, 312n.90